Fromm

SO-AFA-648

Budapest & the Best of Hungary

6th Edition

by Andrew Princz
with Carolyn Bánfalvy, Anna Kutor, and Nóra Lakos

Here's what the critics say about Frommer's:

"Amazingly easy to use. Very portable, very complete."
—*Booklist*

"Detailed, accurate, and easy-to-read information for all price ranges."
—*Glamour Magazine*

"Hotel information is close to encyclopedic."
—*Des Moines Sunday Register*

"Frommer's Guides have a way of giving you a real feel for a place."
—*Knight Ridder Newspapers*

WILEY
Wiley Publishing, Inc.

Published by:

Wiley Publishing, Inc.
111 River St.
Hoboken, NJ 07030-5774

ISBN-13: 978-0-471-77819-6
ISBN-10: 0-471-77819-2

Editor: Stephen Bassman
Production Editor: Eric T. Schroeder
Cartographer: Elizabeth Puhl
Photo Editor: Richard Fox
Production by Wiley Indianapolis Composition Services

Front cover photo: Swimmer in Gellert Baths
Back cover photo: Detail of an archway at Fisherman's Bastion in Buda

For information on our other products and services or to obtain technical support, please contact our Customer Care Department within the U.S. at 800/762-2974, outside the U.S. at 317/572-3993 or fax 317/572-4002.

Wiley also publishes its books in a variety of electronic formats. Some content that appears in print may not be available in electronic formats.

Manufactured in the United States of America

5 4 3 2 1

Contents

6 Where to Dine in Budapest 93

7 Exploring Budapest 125

8 Strolling Around Budapest 155

9 Budapest Shopping 179

List of Maps

An Invitation to the Reader

In researching this book, we discovered many wonderful places—hotels, restaurants, shops, and more. We're sure you'll find others. Please tell us about them, so we can share the information with your fellow travelers in upcoming editions. If you were disappointed with a recommendation, we'd love to know that, too. Please write to:

Frommer's Budapest & the Best of Hungary, 6th Edition
Wiley Publishing, Inc. • 111 River St. • Hoboken, NJ 07030-5774

An Additional Note

Please be advised that travel information is subject to change at any time—and this is especially true of prices. We therefore suggest that you write or call ahead for confirmation when making your travel plans. The authors, editors, and publisher cannot be held responsible for the experiences of readers while traveling. Your safety is important to us, however, so we encourage you to stay alert and be aware of your surroundings. Keep a close eye on cameras, purses, and wallets, all favorite targets of thieves and pickpockets.

Author's Acknowledgments

We wish to thank our many friends and helpers: Réka Müller for her support, Tamás Galambos for his friendship and insight, Cherise Barsell for her fascinating appetite, Anna Bódi for her scoops on town happenings, and Stephen Bassman for editing. A very special thanks to Christina Shea, who literally taught me many moons ago while I was studying in Szeged. She and her team laid the solid foundations for this book in previous editions.

About the Authors

Andrew Princz is a freelance culture and travel journalist/consultant who has visited over forty countries. He has also worked for various governments, consulting on country tourism and awareness projects. Andrew was the founding editor of *DT – Diplomacy & Trade* magazine in Budapest, and he currently edits and publishes the travel and culture website OnTheGlobe.com. He is a regular contributor to *Wall Street Journal Europe* and various dance and film publications. **Carolyn Bánfalvy** is a Budapest-based freelance journalist who is currently writing a book about Budapest's food and wine. **Anna Kutor** is a freelance journalist based in Warsaw. **Nóra Lakos** is a travel and culture journalist currently completing film studies at the Hungarian Film Academy.

Other Great Guides for Your Trip:

Frommer's Vienna & the Danube Valley

Frommer's Austria

Frommer's Prague & Best of Czech Republic

Frommer's Europe

Pauline Frommer's Europe

Frommer's Europe from $85 a Day

Frommer's Star Ratings, Icons & Abbreviations

Every hotel, restaurant, and attraction listing in this guide has been ranked for quality, value, service, amenities, and special features using a **star-rating system.** In country, state, and regional guides, we also rate towns and regions to help you narrow down your choices and budget your time accordingly. Hotels and restaurants are rated on a scale of zero (recommended) to three stars (exceptional). Attractions, shopping, nightlife, towns, and regions are rated according to the following scale: zero stars (recommended), one star (highly recommended), two stars (very highly recommended), and three stars (must-see).

In addition to the star-rating system, we also use **seven feature icons** that point you to the great deals, in-the-know advice, and unique experiences that separate travelers from tourists. Throughout the book, look for:

Finds	Special finds—those places only insiders know about
Fun Fact	Fun facts—details that make travelers more informed and their trips more fun
Kids	Best bets for kids and advice for the whole family
Moments	Special moments—those experiences that memories are made of
Overrated	Places or experiences not worth your time or money
Tips	Insider tips—great ways to save time and money
Value	Great values—where to get the best deals

The following **abbreviations** are used for credit cards:

AE American Express	DISC Discover	V Visa
DC Diners Club	MC MasterCard	

Frommers.com

Now that you have the guidebook to a great trip, visit our website at **www.frommers.com** for travel information on more than 3,000 destinations. With features updated regularly, we give you instant access to the most current trip-planning information available. At Frommers.com, you'll also find the best prices on airfares, accommodations, and car rentals—and you can even book travel online through our travel booking partners. At Frommers.com, you'll also find the following:

- Online updates to our most popular guidebooks
- Vacation sweepstakes and contest giveaways
- Newsletter highlighting the hottest travel trends
- Online travel message boards with featured travel discussions

What's New in Budapest & Hungary

Budapest continues to attract many Europe-bound travelers, all while feeling the pinch in recent years from competition from the scenic coasts of Croatia and the price-friendly seaside of Bulgaria. Meanwhile, airlines are offering some incredibly low fares for European travelers.

The nightlife here continues to thrive, and we suggest that you talk to as many Hungarians as you can about the latest fashionable beer gardens (they're difficult to list, as they appear and disappear in the blink of an eye).

Since May 2004, Hungary has been a member of the European Union, although it is not expected to join the euro-zone until at least 2010. The new openness to the world that Hungary has experienced in recent years has benefited the young, who are now more mobile and have seen positive developments. The older generations, meanwhile, were the losers of the transition. Many pensioners lived better in Communist times, as they will not hesitate to tell you.

PLANNING YOUR TRIP Just how much of Hungary you can see will depend on how many days you plan to stay. Many cross-European travelers have typically spent 2 or 3 days in Budapest. As you will see in this book, the tourism infrastructure, sights, restaurants, and hotels have all expanded their services and now offer more variety. There are more and different spas that each offer different kinds of services. Basically, the traveler now has many more options than just a few years ago, leaving room for longer and more leisurely stays.

GETTING TO KNOW BUDAPEST The Palace of Art's **National Concert Hall** and **Festival Theater**—situated adjacent to the National Theater—are the latest performing arts venues in Budapest and are must-see venues for visitors to the capital. The theaters are situated in the Millennium City Center, which seems to grow every year. Plans for the arts complex include the development of a congress center, four- and five-star hotels, a spa, and even a casino. The main concert hall, however, is the finest modern classical music venue in Budapest and now hosts concerts from the most important orchestras from around the world. For more on the Palace of Art, see p. 205.

The *Budapest Visitors' Guide* contains extensive details on concerts, exhibitions, and other cultural events, and is available online at www.budapestsun.com, while the *Budapest Times,* also available online at www.budapesttimes.hu, is the newest entrant on the English-language printed weekly scene; www.ontheglobe.com, run by the author of these words, features a glimpse into the cultural life of Hungary and the world. Other useful Hungarian publications are listed on p. 36.

WHERE TO STAY Located at the base of Gellért Hill in Buda, on the bank of the Danube, the **Gellért** (p. 150) is the most famous of the several thermal bath hotels in Budapest, known for its beautiful tiles and Turkish inspiration. The

Danubius Grand Hotel Margitsziget (p. 88), on the other hand, offers another kind of spa experience. Pristine, clean, and equipped, it is a beautiful wellness hotel that offers all kinds of services including a fitness center, thermal baths, and massage.

After the Italian developer Boscolo Hotels began work on the historic but crumbling **New York Coffeehouse**, the building's renovation is nearly finished and much awaited. The historic coffeehouse, along with a new five-star hotel, VII. Erzsebet korut 9-11 (© **1/322-3849**), is set to open sometime in 2006. This newest hotel comes after the success of the renovation of the historic Gresham Palace, which is now the **Four Seasons Hotel Gresham Palace** (p. 73), the crown jewel among hotels in Hungary, probably in the whole central European region. The grand Art Nouveau structure at the head of the Chain Bridge in Pest has been beautifully restored by Canadian developers. The hotel also includes the Páva Restaurant with its six-course meals that are served in refined style and crowning elegance. The **Gresham Kávéház** (p. 102) is in fact not a coffeehouse at all, and we have even suggested that the management change its name. The contrast will certainly be evident when the historic New York will open.

Check out chapter 5, "Where to Stay in Budapest," for more on Budapest's accommodations.

WHERE TO DINE Although the law requires that all restaurants offer a nonsmoking section, most barely comply. You should expect restaurants, and especially cafes, to be as smoky as they've ever been.

Countless new and exciting restaurants, cafes, and bistros have recently opened along Pest's grand boulevard, **Andrássy út**, between Oktogon and Deák tér, turning this historic street into a concentrated hub of nightlife. (For a comprehensive list of all the attractions in

this area, old and new, visit **www.andrassy ut.lap.hu**.) With tables on the street, and a stylish young clientele, these places are bringing a bit of Paris to the Budapest landscape.

While Budapest has seen an expansion of its culinary palette, don't expect too much. We recommend that you try some of the many excellent traditional Hungarian restaurants that are now offering more variety than ever.

Some of the best dining these days can be had in tucked-away little restaurants that are nestled throughout the city. In the center of town, we suggest one with the simple name, **M** (p. 104), which is affordable, fun, and comfortable. The **Kacsa Vendéglő** (p. 112) and the **Ezüstponty** (p. 118) are the best if you're looking for traditional Hungarian fare.

EXPLORING BUDAPEST Nagymező utca (p. 181), between Andrássy and Bajcsy-Zsilinszky utca, the "Broadway of Budapest," is a pedestrian-only area. The floodlights in the pavement and the fountain have turned the once-ugly area into an attractive hub of the city's theater life, providing a pleasant atmosphere for nighttime strolling.

Another hot area with restaurants and bistros is the pedestrian-only **Ráday utca** (p. 181), which starts near Kálvin tér (metro: Blue line).

After a long period of lethargy, Budapest's public museums are showing signs of waking up. Armed with a new director, the **Szépművészeti Múzeum (Museum of Fine Arts)** has begun planning a series of ambitious exhibitions, and even an extension to the museum building itself. The new director wants to see the majestic museum regain the allure that it once had on the international stage, and to see the museum regain the role of an important European institution. The success or failure of his plans will depend as much on politics as his stewardship. See p. 129.

The **Ludwig Múzeum (Ludwig Museum of Contemporary Art),** now located in the recently opened Palace of Art and overlooking the Danube, houses a less-than-inspiring permanent exhibition of contemporary Hungarian and international art. The collection consists primarily of American pop art and central European contemporary works. It includes several late Picassos, Andy Warhol's *Single Elvis,* and a still functional Jean Tinguely. The design of the space is a feat in and of itself, since it is the first important Hungarian museum created for the display of contemporary art. See p. 136.

The private art gallery scene has also become lively, and numerous art galleries and auction houses are popping up, including the **Ernst Gallery** (p. 184), the **Kieselbach Gallery** (p. 184) and the **Mü-terem Gallery** (p. 184). The two later galleries also function as auction houses, while the Ernst Gallery presents modern Hungarian art as well as an exquisite selection of period furniture. For more, see chapter 7, "Exploring Budapest."

BUDAPEST SHOPPING The city of Budapest is awash in huge new Western-style malls. You can also patronize smaller local shops. You might want to check out the amazing **"Tropicarium"** at a mall in Southern Buda called **Campona** (p. 189). You can take the Red no. 3 bus that leaves from Móricz Zsigmond körtér in Buda, which is best reached by the no. 4 or 6 tram that circles the Outer Ring boulevard. The Tropicarium features both an aquarium—the largest in central Europe—and a miniature rainforest, with snakes, alligators, and the like (even rain!). You'll also find a bowling alley and an 11-screen multiplex cinema at the mall.

The grandest shopping mall in town, and in central Europe for that matter, is the **West End Center,** right behind Nyugati Railway Station. This is the first and allegedly the last mall to be built right in central Pest. This shopping center was built by local developers, backed by Canadian know-how and investment. The firm, Tri-Granit, has been busily transplanting its Budapest experience to dot the whole region with similar multipurpose malls.

For more, see chapter 9, "Budapest Shopping."

BUDAPEST AFTER DARK Prices for concerts, opera, and theater continue to rise more steeply than any other prices since the last edition of this book. Still, there are few if any events in Budapest beyond the means of the average Western budget traveler.

Jazz clubs have definitely taken hold in Budapest, with jazz even receiving state financing these days. Several new spots have opened that complement the more established clubs from the 1990s. We recommend several hot places, including **Fat Mo's Music Club** (great food, too; p. 209), **Old Man's** (catch the Hungarian blues legend Hobo; p. 210), and **Trafó** (located in a funky old converted electric power station; p. 211). Trafó has honed Hungarian audiences to the best that contemporary dance has to offer. Unfortunately, the Hungarian funding agencies and even audiences have a more narrow view of the world, and these performances tend to be appreciated more by foreign visitors and a small and enlightened group of Hungarian followers than local professional circles. The **A38** ship, which is anchored year-round at the Buda-side foot of the Petőfi Bridge, also continues to have a varied programming. See p. 208.

A complete rundown of Budapest's nightlife can be found in chapter 10, "Budapest After Dark."

THE DANUBE BEND The annual **Visegrád International Palace Tournament** has grown in scale in recent years and is now a must-see for medieval enthusiasts—it is an authentic medieval festival replete with dueling knights on horseback, and early music and dance. See p. 225.

In Esztergom you'll find a new sign of better days ahead for peaceful coexistence in central Europe. Though there is still deeply rooted tension between the Hungarians and the Slovaks, Esztergom is once again connected by **bridge** across the Danube to the Slovak town of Sturovo. The Germans blew up the old bridge connecting these towns in World War II. Until recently, all that remained was a curious stump on the river's edge, along with four unconnected pylons in the river—stark testimonials to the German rampage in Europe as well as to the continuing regional hostilities.

For more, see chapter 11, "The Danube Bend."

SOUTHERN HUNGARY: THE GREAT PLAIN & THE MECSEK HILLS The heart of **Szeged,** the proud capital of the Hungarian Great Plain (and the paprika capital of the world), is the main pedestrian-only "walking street," **Karász utca.** This street has just undergone a thorough and loving renovation, and is filled with a host of interesting little shops. There is no finer activity in Hungary than to stroll down the Karász utca on a lovely summer evening, winding your way from one pastry shop to the next; currently no fewer than six tempting shops compete with the traditional favorite, **Virág Cukrászda,** along the 400m (1,312-ft.) length of the street.

For other great things to do in the South of Hungary, see chapter 14, "Southern Hungary: The Great Plain & the Mecsek Hills."

1

The Best of Budapest

In 1994, I answered an advertisement in the local newspaper in my native Montréal that read, "Seeking a young, well-connected, Hungarian-speaking student for intriguing artistic project." The job was indeed intriguing and artistic: I traveled to Budapest for the summer to help prepare for Canada's participation in the 1996 Expo. The trip started my career as a journalist and, ironically, brought me back to the country my parents had escaped—as young journalists—some four decades earlier.

The country I saw that summer—and had occasionally seen as a child—was drastically different from the one my parents knew. They lived in a Hungary that had already lost two-thirds of its territory during World War I. By 1941, the country was plunged into World War II, after which followed the failed 1956 revolution against the Soviet occupation. To this day, bullet holes from the armed insurrection can still be seen on the facades of buildings.

While in Hungary, I searched the archives for the old articles that my father had published in the midst of that revolution. "I pick up my coat am back on the street again," read one of the coded articles, published just days after he had fled the country, "The rain no longer bothers me, nor does the autumn sadness. I do what needs to be done. I increase the pace, because there is much that lies ahead."

I walked the streets of Budapest that summer and saw a city that was blessedly starting to emerge from the shadows of its past. My Expo gig introduced me to many Hungarian personalities—artists, curators, government officials, and more—and while a few still held onto the mentality of communist Hungary, many were visionaries trying to break creative barriers and introduce change. Hungary was in the midst of a fierce, lively period of transformation after decades of communist rule.

My summer ended on a slightly disappointing note when I heard—over the radio in a taxi, no less—that the government had cancelled the Expo project. But while the Expo never happened, Hungary is still eager to move beyond a difficult century and reconnect with the world. After all, this country enjoyed a glorious early history. Budapest once rivaled its neighboring Vienna under the Austro-Hungarian monarchy and enjoyed a flourishing cultural life. In May 2004, Hungary became a member of the European Union and now has an opportunity to be an influential European nation.

Living and working in Budapest today, I see a buzzing culture that is becoming more and more dynamically European. A vibrant young generation is proof of this. While the political elite continue to argue about the past, the youth are concentrating on the future. They're becoming multi-lingual, they're creating new film festivals and fashion shows. The scene they're developing is vibrant and fun—if a bit secretive and clique-ish. While it might take some time to enter into their world, it's a fun journey in the end. They are playing catch-up, living off the seat of their pants.

Young and old alike, Hungarians love to live, and you'll find lots of friendly locals hanging out in bars and bistros. Travel the countryside, and take a dip in a relaxing spa. See nature and wildlife at the Tisza Lake, eat exquisite Hungarian fish soup, and venture off to Lake Balaton—their little sea. Get to know Hungary and Hungarians.

1 The Best Little Adventures in Budapest

- **Discovering the Courtyards of Budapest:** Budapest's residential streets are truly enchanting, but it is inside the courtyards of the buildings that the city's greatest secret is held: Budapesters are villagers at heart. Fruit trees and flower gardens flourish, cats lounge in the sun, and jars of pickled vegetables line the window ledges. Nearly every apartment building in this city has an open-air courtyard in its center, where pensioners sit on the common balconies smoking cigarettes, gossiping, and watching the children race around the yard, dodging flower pots and laundry racks. The main entrance doors to many apartment buildings are left unlocked during the daytime hours. See chapter 8, "Strolling Around Budapest," for further wanderings.

- **Exploring the Neighborhood Markets:** There is scarcely a neighborhood in Budapest without its own outdoor produce market. Professional vendors mix with elderly peasants who are in for the day with a wagon of fresh-picked fruits and veggies. Produce is fresh and inexpensive. Shop for a picnic lunch or simply wander around soaking up the vibrant workaday atmosphere. See p. 194 for details on market shopping.

- **Riding the Trams:** Armed with your daily transit pass, get the lay of the land and more from the windows of the city's many trams. Board a tram and ride it to the terminus and back, or disembark along the way for a closer look around—a great and economical way to spend a rainy day. See "Getting Around" in chapter 4, "Getting to Know Budapest," for details on public transportation.

- **Packing a Picnic for the City Park:** On a nice summer day, it seems that all of Budapest comes to City Park to enjoy the weather and one another's company. Children of all ages fill the playgrounds and linger by the entrances to the amusement park, the zoo, and the circus. Bathers flock to the historic Széchenyi Baths. Mostly, though, people come to stroll, a time-honored pastime in central Europe. See "Parks, Gardens & Playgrounds" in chapter 7, "Exploring Budapest."

- **Taking a Walk in the Buda Hills:** It's hard to believe that such a large expanse of hilly forest is right here within the capital city. There are hiking trails aplenty; every Budapest native has a favorite. Ask around. See chapter 7, "Exploring Budapest," for more about the Buda Hills.

- **Strolling Through the Jewish District:** Budapest has the largest Jewish population of any city on the European continent (outside Russia). Pest's historic Jewish neighborhood, run-down but relatively unchanged, resonates with the magic and tragedy of the past. See "Walking Tour 4: The Jewish District" in chapter 8, "Strolling Around Budapest."

Hungary

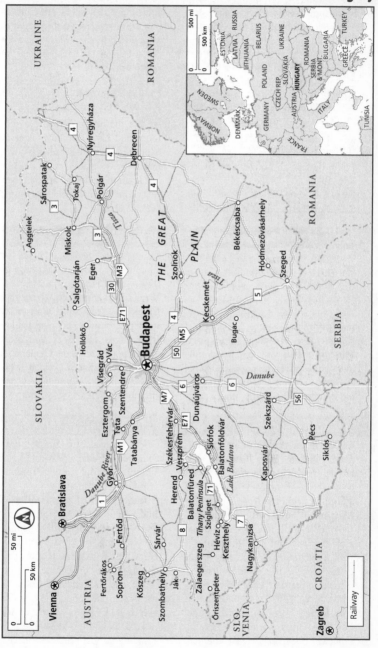

2 The Best Places to Enjoy a Sunset in Budapest

- **From the Riverside:** Locals and visitors alike stroll along the Danube bank (Pest side) in the early evening, taking in the changing light over the shimmering water. Find a free bench, or venture out onto one of the bridges that span the Danube to enjoy a different view of the glorious river that snakes its way through the soul of central Europe. See chapter 7, "Exploring Budapest," for more about Budapest's bridges and riverside walks.
- **From the Ferris Wheel:** The beautiful old yellow Ferris wheel in Budapest's amusement park will lift you gently up into the evening air. At the apex of the long, slow ride, you will have an astonishing view of the entire city and the falling sun. See p. 144.
- **From the Tower of Saint Stephen's Church:** This is the highest point in Pest; from here, the only barrier to a vista of the horizon is haze or smog (on a bad day). For those who can handle it, the long, arduous ascent makes the view all the more pleasurable. If climbing doesn't appeal to you, ride the newly installed lift to the top. See p. 131.

3 The Best Off-the-Beaten-Track Museums

- **Bélyegmúzeum (Postal Stamp Museum):** Generations of philatelists the world over have admired the artistic creations of Magyar Posta. Here you'll find rack after rack of Hungary's finest stamps. See p. 135.
- **Közlekedési Múzeum (Transport Museum):** This vast and wonderful museum features large-scale models of all sorts of vintage vehicles—trains, motorcycles, bikes, early-model cars, antique horse buggies, and more. Kids adore this fabulous trip through history. See p. 144.
- **Varga Imre Gyűjtemény (Imre Varga Collection):** This small museum features the sensitive, piercing work of Imre Varga, Hungary's best-known contemporary sculptor. Of particular note is the shaded garden where Varga's forlorn, broken figures stand and rest on benches. See p. 139.

4 The Best Places to Kill an Hour in Budapest

- **A Bench on the Danube Promenade:** Find an empty bench on this heavily trafficked pedestrian walkway on the bank of the Danube. Sit back and drink in Budapest.
- **Margaret Island:** This lovely park in the middle of the river between Buda and Pest is beautifully maintained, with fountains, floral gardens, green fields, and the like. Find yourself a piece of green and settle down for a while. See p. 140.
- **The Baths:** There is no place quite like the city's various baths to unwind. Budapest's fabled thermal waters invite you to loosen up, slow down, and relax. See "Spa Bathing & Swimming: Budapest's Most Popular Thermal Baths" in chapter 7, "Exploring Budapest."
- **A Traditional Coffeehouse:** Imperial Budapest is long, long gone, but a few of the trappings still remain and are creeping back into existence. None is quite so pleasant as the traditional, ornate coffeehouse, a symbol of *fin de siècle* Budapest. Coffee and sweets are sumptuous, and customers may linger for hours without drawing unkind looks from the waiters. See "Traditional Coffeehouses" in chapter 6, "Where to Dine in Budapest."

- **A Bench on Tóth Árpád sétány:** This is the perfect alternative to the Danube Promenade for those who prefer a quiet urban bench to one on a main thoroughfare. Tóth Árpád sétány is a surprisingly untraveled street that runs the entire length of the Castle District on the Buda side (that is, the non-Danube side). See "Walking Tour 2: The Castle District" in chapter 8, "Strolling Around Budapest."

5 The Best Experiences Outside Budapest

- **Cruising the Danube:** There's nothing like a boat ride on a fine sunny day. From Budapest, head up the river to the charming towns of Szentendre and Visegrád along the Danube Bend. See "Exploring the Danube Bend" in chapter 11, "The Danube Bend."

- **Visiting the Margit Kovács Museum (Szentendre):** The highly original works of Hungary's best-known ceramic artist are displayed in this expansive museum in a lovely village on the Danube Bend. Kovács's unique sculptures of elderly women and her folk-art-influenced friezes of village life are especially moving. See p. 222.

- **Hiking in the Hills Outside Szigliget:** You can hike up to the fantastic ruins of a 13th-century castle above this scenic little village in the Lake Balaton region, or go a few miles farther north and hike up into hills covered with vineyards. See p. 237.

- **Swimming in the Thermal Lake at Hévíz:** Even in the bitterest spells of winter, the temperature in Europe's largest thermal lake seldom dips below 85°F to 90°F (30°C–32°C). Hungarians swim here year-round, and you can, too! If you're here in winter, it'll be a particularly memorable experience. See p. 239.

- **Climbing the Eger Minaret:** Eger, a beautiful, small city in northern Hungary, is home to one of the country's most impressive Turkish ruins: a 14-sided, 33m-tall (110-ft.) minaret. Those who succeed in climbing the steep, cramped, spiral staircase are justly rewarded with a spectacular view. See p. 246.

- **Exploring Pécs:** This delightful city in southern Hungary is home to one of Hungary's most pleasing central squares and some great examples of Turkish architecture. See "The 2,000-year-old City of Pécs" in chapter 14, "Southern Hungary: The Great Plain & the Mecsek Hills."

- **Sampling Szeged's Fruit-and-Vegetable Market:** At the main open-air market behind the bus station, in this town near the Serbian and Romanian borders, local farmers sell their bounty of peaches, apricots, cherries, and pears in season, as well as fresh flowers, and, of course, dried paprika wreaths. See p. 262.

6 The Best Hotels in Budapest

- **Best Splurge Hotel:** The splendid, sprawling **Four Seasons Hotel Gresham Palace,** V. Roosevelt tér 5–6 (& **1/268-6000**), has, in a short time, gained the reputation as Hungary's foremost hotel. The Art Nouveau architecture is exquisite, and the customer care and attention to detail will leave you feeling pampered. See p. 73.

- **Best for Business Travelers:** The **Kempinski Hotel Corvinus,** 7–8 V. Erzsébet tér (& **800/426-3135** in North America, or 1/429-3777), is the hotel of choice for corporate visitors, with conference facilities, a state-of-the-art business center, and an efficient staff. See p. 74.

- **Best for a Romantic Getaway:** Any of the pensions in the Buda Hills are suitable, but the **Vadvirág Panzió,** II. Nagybányai út 18 (& 1/275-0200), is particularly fetching, surrounded as it is by sloping gardens and terraces. See p. 88.
- **Best for Families:** Parents will appreciate the location of the **Hotel Liget,** VI. Dózsa György út 106 (& 1/269-5300), which is across the street from City Park's zoo, amusement park, and circus. See p. 85.
- **Best Moderately Priced Hotel:** The homey **Hotel Astra Vendégház,** I. Vám u. 6 (& 1/214-1906), opened in 1997, is perfectly situated in Buda's quaint Watertown neighborhood, just a 10-minute walk from the Castle District, and minutes from the Danube embankment. See p. 81.
- **Best Budget Hotel:** The accommodations at **Charles Apartment House,** I. Hegyalja út 23 (& 1/212-9169), are comfortable and clean flats—complete with bathrooms and fully equipped kitchens—in Buda apartment buildings. See p. 83.
- **Best Pension:** The charming **Gizella Panzió,** XII. Arató u. 42/b (& 1/249-2281), built into the side of a hill, has a lovely view of the valley in a quiet neighborhood that's relatively easy to reach by bus. The rooms are quaint and sunny. See p. 87.
- **Best Location:** This one is a tie between the only two hotels in Buda's elegant and timeless Castle District: The **Hilton Budapest,** I. Hess András tér 1–3 (& 1/488-6600; see p. 83), is a luxurious lodging right next door to the Matthias Church and the Fisherman's Bastion, while **Hotel Kulturinnov,** I. Szentháromság tér 6 (& 1/355-0122), is a modest guesthouse just across the square.
- **Best View:** You'll either see the full Pest skyline or overlook the delightful streets of the Castle District at the **Hilton Budapest,** I. Hess András tér 1–3 (& 1/488-6600), widely considered the city's classiest hotel. See p. 83.

7 The Best Dining Bets in Budapest

- **Best for a Romantic Dinner:** At **Ezüstponty,** XII. Némethvölgy út 96 (& 1/319-1632), in the low Buda Hills, you can dine in the casual, elegant outdoor garden in summer, with live music at night. See p. 118.
- **Best Decor:** The huge branches of a wonderful old tree create a canopy under which guests dine by candlelight in the interior courtyard at **Kisbuda Gyöngye,** III. Kenyeres u. 34 (& 1/368-9246). See p. 119.
- **Best Wine List: Gundel,** XIV. Állatkerti út 2 (& 1/468-4040), the city's fanciest and most famous restaurant, complements its traditional dishes, which are prepared in innovative ways, with a fabulous and extensive wine list. See p. 109.
- **Best Wild Game:** At **Aranyszarvas,** I. Szarvas tér 1 (& 1/375-6451)—the restaurant's name means "the Golden Stag"—you can enjoy savory venison stew, pheasant, and wild boar. See p. 113.
- **Best Coffeehouse: Centrál Kávéház,** V. Károly Mihály u. 9 (& 1/266-2110), is the closest thing Budapest has to a certifiable classic coffeehouse. It is the central location for intellectuals, tourists, families, and more. Don't leave Budapest without stopping here. See p. 120.
- **Best Pastries:** Our favorite pastry shop is the century-old, utterly charming little **Ruszwurm Cukrászda,** I. Szentháromság u. 7 (& 1/375-5284), located in the heart of the Castle District. See p. 123.

2

Planning Your Trip to Budapest

Now that you've decided to travel to Budapest, you may have dozens of questions: Do I need a visa? What currency is used in Hungary, and can I get my hands on some at home? Will any festivals take place during my trip? What's the best route to get there? This chapter is devoted to providing answers to these and other questions.

1 Visitor Information

Tourism infrastructure has been developing at a furious pace in Hungary, be it through the development of high-quality hotels and restaurants, and even improvements to the service sector. In most cities you will find tourism-related information offices called **Tourinform** (© 1/438-8080; www.tourinform.hu), a branch of the Hungarian National Tourist Office, at Sütő u. 2, 1052 Budapest (© 1/438-8080 or 06/80-630800; www.tourinform.hu), open daily from 8am to 8pm. You'll also find a branch office in the heart of Budapest's Broadway, at Liszt Ferenc tér 11 (© 1/322-4098; fax 1/342-2541), open daily from 9am to 7pm. These offices will distribute pamphlets on events and attractions that can be found in the area that you are visiting, and help you with finding appropriate accommodations and restaurants. The tourism authority, **Magyar Turizmus Rt** (© 1/488-8701; www.hugarytourism.hu), also has offices throughout the world, and it is

their mandate to promote Hungary as a destination for tourism.

For general country information and a variety of pamphlets and maps before you leave, contact the government-sponsored **Hungarian National Tourist Office,** 150 E. 58th St., New York, NY 10155 (© 212/355-0240; www.gotohungary.com). In London the **Hungarian National Tourist Office** is at 46 Eaton Place, London SW1X 8AL (© 020/7823-1032). The Hungarian National Tourist Office's main website, a great source of information, is **www.gotohungary.com**.

Another site with lots of helpful information for visitors is **www.vista.hu**. Find general city information at **www.budapest.com**. To get news about Hungary, check out the Hungarian News Agency at **www.english.mti.hu**. It's updated daily. Current local news, entertainment listings, and the like can be found at either **www.budapestsun.com**, **www.budapesttimes.hu**, or **www.ontheglobe.com**.

2 Entry Requirements & Customs

ENTRY REQUIREMENTS
For information on how to get a passport, go to "Passports" in the "Fast Facts: Budapest" section in chapter 4—the websites listed provide downloadable passport

applications as well as the current fees for processing passport applications. For an up-to-date, country-by-country listing of passport requirements around the world, go to the "Foreign Entry Requirement"

Web page of the U.S. State Department at **http://travel.state.gov**.

CUSTOMS

WHAT YOU CAN BRING INTO HUNGARY

You're allowed to bring duty-free into Hungary 250 cigarettes, 2 liters of wine, and 1 liter of spirits. There is no limit to the amount of money you may bring into the country. However, you may not take out of the country more than 1,000,000 forints in Hungarian currency.

WHAT YOU CAN TAKE HOME FROM HUNGARY

Returning **U.S. citizens** who have been away for at least 48 hours are allowed to bring back, once every 30 days, $800 worth of merchandise duty-free. You'll pay a flat rate of duty on the next $1,000 worth of purchases. Any dollar amount beyond that is subject to duties at whatever rates apply. On mailed gifts, the duty-free limit is $200. Be sure to keep your receipts or purchases accessible to expedite the declaration process. *Note:* If you owe duty, you are required to pay on your arrival in the United States—by cash, personal check, government or traveler's check, or money order (and, in some locations, a Visa or MasterCard).

To avoid paying duty on foreign-made personal items you owned before your trip, bring along a bill of sale, insurance policy, jeweler's appraisal, or receipts of purchase. Or you can register items that can be readily identified by a permanently affixed serial number or marking—think laptop computers, cameras, and CD players—with Customs before you leave. Take the items to the nearest Customs office or register them with Customs at the airport from which you're departing. You'll receive, at no cost, a Certificate of Registration, which allows duty-free entry for the life of the item.

With some exceptions, you cannot bring fresh fruits and vegetables into the United States. For specifics on what you can bring back, download the invaluable free pamphlet *Know Before You Go* online at **www.cbp.gov**. (Click on "Travel," and then click on "Know Before You Go! Online Brochure.") Or contact the **U.S. Customs & Border Protection (CBP)**, 1300 Pennsylvania Ave., NW, Washington, DC 20229 (© **877/287-8667**) and request the pamphlet.

For a clear summary of **Canadian** rules, write for the booklet *I Declare,* issued by the **Canada Border Services Agency** (© **800/461-9999** in Canada, or 204/983-3500; www.cbsa-asfc.gc.ca). Canada allows its citizens a C$750 exemption, and you're allowed to bring back duty-free one carton of cigarettes, one can of tobacco, 40 imperial ounces of liquor, and 50 cigars. In addition, you're allowed to mail gifts to Canada valued at less than C$60 a day, provided they're unsolicited and don't contain alcohol or tobacco (write on the package "Unsolicited gift, under C$60 value"). All valuables should be declared on the Y-38 form before departure from Canada, including serial numbers of valuables you already own, such as expensive foreign cameras. *Note:* The C$750 exemption can be used only once a year and only after an absence of 7 days.

Citizens of the U.K. who are **returning from a European Union (E.U.) country** will go through a separate Customs Exit (called the "Blue Exit") especially for E.U. travelers. In essence, there is no limit on what you can bring back from an E.U. country, provided the items are for personal use (this includes gifts), and you have already paid the necessary duty and tax. Customs law, however, sets out guidance levels. If you bring in more than these levels, you may be asked to prove that the goods are for your own use. Guidance levels on goods bought in the E.U. for personal use are 3,200 cigarettes, 200 cigars, 400 cigarillos, 3 kilograms of smoking tobacco, 10 liters of spirits, 90 liters of wine, 20 liters of fortified wine (such as port or sherry), and 110 liters of beer.

The duty-free allowance in **Australia** is A$400 or, for those under 18, A$200. Citizens can bring in 250 cigarettes or 250 grams of loose tobacco, and 1,125 milliliters of alcohol. If you're returning with valuables you already own, such as foreign-made cameras, you should file form B263. A helpful brochure available from Australian consulates or Customs offices is *Know Before You Go.* For more information, call the **Australian Customs Service** at ℭ **1300/363-263,** or log on to www.customs.gov.au.

The duty-free allowance for **New Zealand** is NZ$700. Citizens over 17 can bring in 200 cigarettes, 50 cigars, or 250 grams of tobacco (or a mixture of all three if their combined weight doesn't exceed 250g), plus 4.5 liters of wine and beer, or 1.125 liters of liquor. New Zealand currency does not carry import or export restrictions. Fill out a certificate of export, listing the valuables you are taking out of the country; that way, you can bring them back without paying duty. Most questions are answered in a free pamphlet available at New Zealand consulates and Customs offices: *New Zealand Customs Guide for Travellers, Notice no. 4.* For more information, contact **New Zealand Customs,** The Customhouse, 17–21 Whitmore St., Box 2218, Wellington (ℭ **04/473-6099** or 0800/428-786; www.customs.govt.nz).

3 Money

The basic unit of currency in Hungary is the **forint (Ft).** Coins come in denominations of 1, 2, 5, 10, 20, 50, and 100 Ft. Banknotes come in denominations of 200, 500, 1,000, 5,000, 10,000, and 20,000 Ft.

The U.S. dollar has weakened over the past several years, but Hungary continues to be considerably less expensive for travelers than most Western countries. Labor-intensive services, such as picture framing, tailoring, shoe and watch repair, and the like, are particularly inexpensive.

As of this writing, the rate of exchange is US$1 = 200 Ft (or 100 Ft = US50¢), and this is the rate used to calculate all the U.S. dollar prices in this book. Of course, exchange rates fluctuate over time.

Note: Several hotels and pensions in Budapest list their prices in U.S. dollars, while most list prices in euros. This is done predominantly as a hedge against forint inflation; Hungary became a member of the European Union in May 2004, but is not planning to introduce the euro until, optimistically, 2010. All hotels in Budapest accept payment in Hungarian forints as well as in most foreign currencies.

CURRENCY

The best official rates for both cash and traveler's checks are obtained at banks.

The Hungarian Forint

For American Readers   At this writing US$1 = approximately 200 Ft (or 100 Ft = US50¢), and this was the rate of exchange used to calculate the dollar values given in this chapter.

For British Readers   At this writing £1 = approximately 370 Ft (or 100 Ft = 27p), and this was the rate of exchange used to calculate the pound values in the table below.

Note: The rates given here fluctuate and may not be the same when you travel to Hungary. Therefore, this table should be used only as a guide.

Ft	US$	UK £	Ft	US$	UK £
5	0.02	0.01	3,000	15.00	8.10
10	0.05	0.02	4,000	20.00	10.81
25	0.12	0.06	5,000	25.00	13.51
50	0.25	0.13	6,000	30.00	16.21
75	0.37	0.20	7,000	35.00	18.91
100	0.50	0.27	8,000	40.00	21.62
200	1.00	0.54	9,000	45.00	24.32
300	1.50	0.81	10,000	50.00	27.02
400	2.00	1.08	15,000	75.00	40.54
500	2.50	1.35	20,000	100.00	54.05
750	3.75	2.02	25,000	125.00	67.56
1,000	5.00	2.70	30,000	150.00	81.08
1,500	7.50	4.05	40,000	200.00	108.10
2,000	10.00	5.40	50,000	250.00	135.13

Exchange booths are also located throughout the city center, in train stations, and in most luxury hotels, but exchange booths almost uniformly offer less favorable rates than banks. ATMs are found in front of banks throughout the city or in major shopping malls. You may withdraw forints at the daily exchange rate from your home account through the Cirrus and PLUS networks (see "ATMs," below). At some banks and at all exchange booths, you will get a better rate when exchanging cash.

You should regard with extreme suspicion anyone who accosts you on the street wanting to change money, especially someone offering you a rate more than 2% to 3% better than the official one. Such a person is certainly out to cheat you. It is not recommended to exchange money in anything but a bank or a registered exchange booth.

Since 2001, with the full convertibility of the Hungarian forint, there are no longer any restrictions regarding re-exchange of forints back into your currency. Consequently, unlike in the past, you need not retain your currency exchange receipts as proof of exchange.

You'll avoid lines at airport ATMs (automated teller machines) by exchanging at least some money—just enough to cover airport incidentals and transportation to your hotel—before you leave home (though don't expect the exchange rate to be ideal). You can exchange money at your local American Express or Thomas Cook office or at your bank. American Express also dispenses traveler's checks and foreign currency via www. americanexpress.com or (C) **800/807-6233,** but they'll charge a $15 order fee and additional shipping costs. American Express cardholders should dial (C) **800/221-7282;** this number accepts collect calls, offers service in several foreign languages, and exempts Amex gold and platinum cardholders from the 1% fee.

ATMs

The easiest and best way to get cash away from home is from an ATM (automated teller machine). The **Cirrus** ((C) **800/424-7787;** www.mastercard.com) and **PLUS** ((C) **800/843-7587;** www.visa.com) networks span the globe; look at the back of your bank card to see which network you're on, then call or check online for ATM locations at your destination. Be sure you know your personal identification number (PIN) and daily withdrawal limit before you depart. *Note:* Remember that many banks impose a fee every time you use a card at another bank's ATM, and that fee can be higher for international transactions (up to $5 or more) than for domestic ones (where they're rarely more than $2). In addition, the bank from which you withdraw cash may charge its own fee. To compare banks' ATM fees within the U.S., use **www. bankrate.com**. For international withdrawal fees, ask your bank.

You can use your credit card to receive cash advances at ATMs. Keep in mind that credit card companies protect themselves from theft by limiting maximum withdrawals outside their home country, so call your credit card company before you leave home. And keep in mind that you'll pay interest from the moment of your withdrawal, even if you pay your monthly bills on time.

TRAVELER'S CHECKS

Traveler's checks are something of an anachronism from the days before the ATM made cash accessible at any time. Given the fees you'll pay for ATM use at banks other than your own, however, you might be better off with traveler's checks if you're withdrawing money often.

You can buy traveler's checks at most banks. **American Express** offers denominations of $20, $50, $100, $500, and (for cardholders only) $1,000. You'll pay a service charge ranging from 1% to 4%. By phone, you can buy traveler's checks by calling (C) **800/807-6233.** American Express cardholders should dial (C) **800/221-7282;** this number accepts collect calls, offers service in several foreign languages, and exempts Amex gold and platinum cardholders from the 1% fee.

Visa offers traveler's checks at Citibank locations nationwide, as well as at several other banks. The service charge ranges between 1.5% and 2%; checks come in denominations of $20, $50, $100, $500, and $1,000. Call (C) **800/732-1322** for information. AAA members can obtain Visa checks for a $9.95 fee (for checks up

---

(Tips Small Change

When you change money, ask for some small bills or loose change. Petty cash will come in handy for tipping and public transportation. Consider keeping the change separate from your larger bills, so that it's readily accessible and you'll be less of a target for theft.

Tips Dear Visa: I'm Off to Budapest!

Some credit card companies recommend that you notify them of any impending trip abroad so that they don't become suspicious of foreign transactions and block your charges. If you don't call your credit card company in advance, you can still call the card's toll-free emergency number (see "Fast Facts: Budapest," p. 60) if a charge is refused—provided you remember to carry the phone number with you. Perhaps the most important lesson here is to carry more than one card, so you have a backup.

---

to $1,500) at most AAA offices or by calling *©* **866/339-3378. MasterCard** also offers traveler's checks. Call *©* **800/223-9920** for a location near you.

Foreign currency traveler's checks are useful if you're traveling to one country, or to the euro zone; they're accepted at locations where dollar checks may not be, such as bed-and-breakfasts, and they minimize the currency conversions you'll have to perform while you're on the go. **American Express, Thomas Cook, Visa,** and **MasterCard** offer foreign currency traveler's checks. You'll pay the rate of exchange at the time of your purchase (so it's a good idea to monitor the rate before you buy), and most companies charge a transaction fee per order (and a shipping fee if you order online).

If you do choose to carry traveler's checks, keep a record of their serial numbers separate from your checks in the event that they are stolen or lost. You'll get a refund faster if you know the numbers.

CREDIT CARDS

Credit cards are another safe way to carry money. They also provide a convenient record of all your expenses, and they generally offer relatively good exchange rates. You can also withdraw cash advances from your credit cards at banks or ATMs, provided you know your PIN. If you don't know yours, call the number on the back of your credit card and ask the bank to send it to you. It usually takes 5 to 7 business days, though some banks will provide the number over the phone if you tell them your mother's maiden name or some other personal information. Keep in mind that many banks now assess a 1%-to-3% "transaction fee" on **all** charges you incur abroad (whether you're using the local currency or U.S. dollars). But credit cards still may be the smart way to go when you factor in things like exorbitant ATM fees and the higher exchange rates and service fees you'll pay with traveler's checks.

4 When to Go

Budapest has a relatively mild climate—the annual mean temperature in Hungary is 50°F (10°C). Nevertheless, summer temperatures often exceed 80° to 85°F (27°C–29°C), and sweltering hot, humid days are typical in July and August. January and February are the coldest months,

averaging 30°F (–1°C), though temperatures can dip well below that on any given day. Be prepared for damp and chilly weather in winter. Spring is usually mild and, especially in May, wet. Autumn is usually quite pleasant, with mild, cooler weather through October.

Budapest's Average Daily Temperatures & Rainfall

	Jan	Feb	Mar	Apr	May	June	July	Aug	Sept	Oct	Nov	Dec
Temp. (°F)	30	34	38	53	62	68	72	71	63	52	42	35
Temp. (°C)	–1	1	3	12	17	20	22	22	17	11	6	2
Rainfall (in.)	1.3	1.2	1.1	1.5	2.2	2.5	2	2	1.6	1.3	2	1.6

HOLIDAYS

Hungarian holidays are: January 1 (New Year's Day), March 15 (National Holiday), Easter Sunday and Easter Monday, May 1 (May Day), Whit Monday, August 20 (St. Stephen's Day), October 23 (Republic Day), November 1 (All Saints' Day), and December 25 and 26 (Christmas). Shops, museums, and banks are closed on all holidays.

HUNGARY CALENDAR OF EVENTS

With a little luck, your trip to Budapest will coincide with one or more of the city's cultural events. All inquiries about ticket availability and locations of events should be directed to Budapest's main tourist information office, **Tourinform** (see p. 11).

March

Budapest Spring Festival. For 2 weeks, performances of everything from opera to ballet, from classical music to drama, are held at all the major halls and theaters of Budapest. Simultaneously, temporary exhibitions open in many of Budapest's museums. Tickets are available at the **Festival Ticket Service,** V. 1053 Egyetem tér 5 (✆ 1/486-3300; www.fesztivalvaros.hu; Blue line: Ferenciek tere), and at the individual venues. Hotels book quickly for this time of year, so plan ahead. Mid- to late March.

Hollókő's Easter Festival. During Easter in this charming small town in northeastern Hungary, villagers wear traditional costumes and participate in a folk festival. Traditional song, dance, and foods are featured. For information, contact the **Hungarian Arts Festivals Federation** (✆ 1-202-1095; www.arts festivals.hu). Held on Easter Day.

May–June

Book Fair, Budapest. Publishers set up kiosks throughout central Pest to display the year's newly released titles. The main attractions, such as authors' signing sessions, are located in Vörösmarty tér. Most books are in Hungarian, of course, but there are always beautiful books on art, architecture, and other subjects. Last week of May or first week of June.

June–August

Open-Air Theater Programs, Budapest. A rich variety of open-air performances are given throughout Budapest during the summer. Highlights include opera and ballet at the Margaret Island Open-Air Theater, folklore and dance at the Buda Park Theater, musicals in Városmajor Theater, and classical music recitals in the Dominican Courtyard at the Hilton Hotel. For information, contact the Hungarian Arts Festivals Federation (✆ 1-202-1095). June through August.

Tips **Quick ID**

Tie a colorful ribbon or piece of yarn around your luggage handle, or slap a distinctive sticker on the side of your bag. This makes it less likely that someone will mistakenly appropriate it. And if your luggage gets lost, it will be easier to find.

Organ Concerts, Budapest. Concerts are given in the Matthias Church, in the lovely Castle District of Buda. See p. 133 for details. June through August. In addition, Budapest's largest church, St. Stephen's Basilica, also hosts organ concerts. See p. 131. July through August.

"Budafest" Summer Opera and Ballet Festival, Budapest. This 10-day festival is the only time to see a summer performance at the wonderful Hungarian State Opera House in Budapest. Tickets are available at the **Opera House** box office at VI. Andrássy út 20 (© 1/331-2550; www.opera.hu). August.

International Palace Tournament, Visegrád. Each summer, this ancient town on the Danube hosts an authentic medieval festival replete with dueling knights on horseback, and early music and dance. Contact **Visegrád Tours,** RÉV u. 15 in Visegrád (© 26/398-090; www.palotajatekok.hu). Second weekend in July.

International Guitar Festival, Esztergom. This stately little town on the Danube hosts a guitar festival that features performers from around the world. Classical concerts are performed in the Basilica. For information, contact **Gran Tours,** Esztergom at Széchenyi tér 25 (© 33/502-001; www.guitarfestival.hu). First week of August every other year; the next festival is scheduled for 2007.

Formula One Grand Prix, Budapest. One of the European racing circuit's most important annual events is held at Budapest's HungaroRing in Mogyoród. Hotels book quickly for this event, so plan ahead. Call © 28/444-444 or check out **www.hungaroring.hu**. Second weekend in August.

Island Festival (Sziget Fesztivál), Óbuda Island in the Danube. Established in 1994 as Hungary's very own

"Woodstock," the Sziget Festival (© 1/372-0650; www.sziget.hu) is a weeklong music festival that draws young people from all over Europe. The event features foreign and local rock, folk, and jazz groups on dozens of stages playing each day from early afternoon to the wee hours of the morning. Camping is available. You can get details and pick up a program schedule at **Tourinform** (p. 11) or check out their website. Usually begins the second week of August.

Traditional Handicraft Fair, Budapest. The Castle District is the site of a 3-day annual handicraft fair, which draws vendors from across Hungary and from Hungarian enclaves in neighboring countries, especially Romania. The wares are generally handmade and of high quality. This is a part of the St. Stephen's Day celebrations. August 20.

St. Stephen's Day, Budapest. This is Hungary's national day. The country's patron saint is celebrated with cultural events and a dramatic display of fireworks over the Danube at 9pm. Hungarians also celebrate their Constitution on this day and ceremoniously welcome the first new bread from the recent crop of July wheat. August 20.

National Jewish Festival, Budapest. In 1999 this annual festival arrived on the Hungarian cultural scene. The festival features a variety of Jewish culture–related events—from klezmer music to a book fair, from ballet to cabaret—held in "Gödör," a new cultural center that opened in Deák tér in 2004 (on the site of the former central bus station, which was at one time slated to be the location of a grandiose new national theater in Budapest). For information, contact the **Tourism and Cultural Center of the Budapest Jewish Community,** 1075 Budapest, Síp u. 12 (© 36/1-343-0420; www.jewishfestival.hu). Late August or early September; call for exact dates.

Szeged Summer Festival, Szeged. Szeged, the proud capital of the Great Plain, is home to a summer-long series of cultural events (ballet, opera, rock opera, open-air theater). For information, call ☎ **62/471-411;** www.szeged iszabadteri.hu. June through August.

September

Budapest International Wine Festival. This festival, in Budapest's Castle District, features wine tastings, displays, and auctions, as well as folk and classical music performances. The sponsor is the **Hungarian Viniculture Foundation,** XI. Bartók Béla út 152 (☎ **1/203-8507;** www.winefestival.hu). Early September.

Budapest International Fair. For 10 days, Budapest's HungExpo grounds are filled with displays of Europe's latest consumer goods. Contact ☎ **1/ 263-6000;** www.hungexpo.hu. Mid-September.

Budapest Art Weeks. In celebration of the opening of the fall season, special classical music and dance performances are held for 3 weeks in all the city's major halls. For information, contact the Hungarian Arts Festivals Federation (☎ **1-318-8165**). The festivals' traditional start is September 25, the day of Béla Bartók's death.

Contemporary Music Weeks, Budapest. Held in conjunction with the Budapest Art Weeks, this 3-week festival features contemporary music performances in all the capital's major halls. For information, contact the Hungarian Arts Festivals Federation (☎ 1-318-8165). Starts September 25.

5 Travel Insurance

Check your existing insurance policies and credit card coverage before you buy travel insurance. You may already be covered for lost luggage, canceled tickets, or medical expenses.

The cost of travel insurance varies widely, depending on the cost and length of your trip, your age and health, and the type of trip you're taking, but expect to pay between 5% and 8% of the vacation itself. You can get estimates from various providers through **InsureMyTrip.com.** Enter your trip cost and dates, your age, and other information, for prices from more than a dozen companies.

TRIP-CANCELLATION INSURANCE
Trip-cancellation insurance will help retrieve your money if you have to back out of a trip or depart early, or if your travel supplier goes bankrupt. Permissible reasons for trip cancellation can range from sickness to natural disasters to the State Department declaring a destination unsafe for travel. (Insurers usually won't cover vague fears, though, as many

travelers discovered when they tried to cancel their trips in Oct 2001.) In this unstable world, trip-cancellation insurance is a good buy if you're purchasing tickets well in advance—who knows what the state of the world, or of your airline, will be in 9 months? Insurance policy details vary, so read the fine print—and make sure that your airline or cruise line is on the list of carriers covered in case of bankruptcy. A good resource is **"Travel Guard Alerts,"** a list of companies considered high-risk by Travel Guard International (see website below). Protect yourself further by paying for the insurance with a credit card—by law, consumers can get their money back on goods and services not received if they report the loss within 60 days after the charge is listed on their credit card statement.

Note: Many tour operators, particularly those offering trips to remote or high-risk areas, include insurance in the total trip cost or can arrange insurance policies through a partnering provider, which is a convenient and often cost-effective way for the traveler to obtain insurance. Make sure the tour company is a reputable one, however, and be aware that some experts suggest you avoid buying insurance from the tour or cruise company you're traveling with. They contend it's more secure to buy from a third party than to put all your money in one place.

For more information, contact one of the following recommended insurers: **Access America** (© 866/807-3982; www.accessamerica.com); **Travel Guard International** (© 800/826-4919; www.travelguard.com); **Travel Insured International** (© 800/243-3174; www.travelinsured.com); and **Travelex Insurance Services** (© 888/457-4602; www.travelex-insurance.com).

MEDICAL INSURANCE For travel overseas, most health plans (including Medicare and Medicaid) do not provide coverage, and the ones that do often require you to pay for services upfront and reimburse you only after you return home. Even if your plan does cover overseas treatment, most out-of-country hospitals make you pay your bills upfront, and send you a refund only after you've returned home and filed the necessary paperwork with your insurance company. As a safety net, you may want to buy travel medical insurance, particularly if you're traveling to a remote or high-risk area where emergency evacuation is a possible scenario. If you require additional medical insurance, try **MEDEX Assistance** (© 410/453-6300; www.medexassist.com) or **Travel Assistance International** (© 800/821-2828; www.travelassistance.com; for general information on services, call the company's Worldwide Assistance Services, Inc., at © 800/777-8710).

LOST-LUGGAGE INSURANCE On domestic flights, checked baggage is covered up to $2,500 per ticketed passenger. On international flights (including U.S. portions of international trips), baggage coverage is limited to approximately $9.07 per pound, up to approximately $635 per checked bag. If you plan to check items more valuable than what's covered by the standard liability, see if your homeowner's policy covers your valuables, get baggage insurance as part of your comprehensive travel-insurance package, or buy Travel Guard's "BagTrak" product. Don't buy insurance at the airport, where it's usually overpriced. Be sure to take any valuables or irreplaceable items with you in your carry-on luggage, because many valuables (including books, money, and electronics) aren't covered by airline policies.

If your luggage is lost, immediately file a lost-luggage claim at the airport, detailing the luggage contents. Most airlines require that you report delayed, damaged, or lost baggage within 4 hours of arrival. The airlines are required to deliver luggage, once found, directly to your house or destination free of charge.

6 Health & Safety

STAYING HEALTHY

No shots or inoculations are required for entry to Hungary. To be on the safe side, bring enough of any prescription or other medication you may need. It is also good practice to take along a copy of all prescriptions—in their generic forms—in case you run out of any meds. Sunscreen and other toiletries are readily available.

GENERAL AVAILABILITY OF HEALTH CARE

Emergency medical treatment is provided free of charge in Hungary, but you'll have to pay for prescription medications and for non-emergency care. In most cases, your existing health plan will provide the coverage you need. But double-check; you may want to buy **travel medical** insurance instead. (See the section on insurance, above.) Bring your insurance ID card with you when you travel.

Contact the **International Association for Medical Assistance to Travelers (IAMAT)** (© 716/754-4883 or, in Canada, 416/652-0137; www.iamat.org) for tips on travel and health concerns in the countries you're visiting, and for lists of local, English-speaking doctors. The United States **Centers for Disease Control and Prevention** (© 800/311-3435; www.cdc.gov) provides up-to-date information on health hazards by region or country and offers tips on food safety. The website **www.tripprep.com**, sponsored by a consortium of travel medicine practitioners, may also offer helpful advice on traveling abroad. You can find listings of reliable clinics overseas at the **International Society of Travel Medicine** (www.istm.org).

WHAT TO DO IF YOU GET SICK AWAY FROM HOME

Any foreign consulate can provide a list of area doctors who speak English. If you get sick, consider asking your hotel concierge to recommend a local doctor—even his or her own. You can also try the emergency room at a local hospital. Many hospitals also have walk-in clinics for emergency cases that are not life-threatening; you may not get immediate attention, but you won't pay the high price of an emergency room visit. We list hospitals and emergency numbers under "Fast Facts: Budapest," p. 61.

If you suffer from a chronic illness, consult your doctor before your departure. For conditions like epilepsy, diabetes, or heart problems, wear a **MedicAlert identification tag** (© 888/633-4298; www.medicalert.org), which will immediately alert doctors to your condition and give them access to your records through MedicAlert's 24-hour hot line.

Pack **prescription medications** in your carry-on luggage, and carry prescription medications in their original containers, with pharmacy labels—otherwise they won't make it through airport security. Also carry copies of your prescriptions in case you lose your pills or run out. Don't forget an extra pair of contact lenses or prescription glasses. Carry the generic name of prescription medicines, in case a local pharmacist is unfamiliar with the brand name.

For domestic trips, most reliable health-care plans provide coverage if you get sick away from home. For travel abroad, you may have to pay all medical costs upfront and be reimbursed later. See "Medical Insurance," under "Travel Insurance," above.

STAYING SAFE

Budapest is a fairly safe city, and violent street crime is far less common than in similar sized U.S. cities. However, you should always be on the lookout for pickpockets, especially on crowded buses, trains, and trams. Pickpockets generally work in teams, with one or more creating a distraction (bumping into people, falling down, staging a fake argument, and so on), while a partner takes advantage of the fact that their victim is distracted. One way to protect yourself is to always carry valuables in an inside pocket or in a money belt. There is no shortage of rambunctious drunks at night in Budapest, but they don't seem to pose much danger to others. Budapest is a city filled with underpasses. Be careful at night; you can always choose to cross a street above ground if an underpass appears deserted.

ECO-TOURISM

The International Ecotourism Society (TIES) defines eco-tourism as "responsible travel to natural areas that conserves the environment and improves the well-being of local people." You can find eco-friendly travel tips, statistics, and touring companies and associations—listed by destination under "Travel Choice"—at the TIES website, www.ecotourism.org. Eco-travel.com is part online magazine and part eco-directory that lets you search for touring companies in several categories (water-based, land-based, spiritually oriented, and so on). Also check out **Conservation** **International** (www.conservation.org)—which, with *National Geographic Traveler,* annually presents World Legacy Awards (www.wlaward.org) to those travel tour operators, businesses, organizations, and places that have made a significant contribution to sustainable tourism.

7 Specialized Travel Resources

TRAVELERS WITH DISABILITIES

Most disabilities shouldn't stop anyone from traveling. There are more options and resources out there than ever before.

Many travel agencies offer customized tours and itineraries for travelers with disabilities. **Flying Wheels Travel** (© 507/451-5005; www.flyingwheelstravel.com) offers escorted tours and cruises that emphasize sports and private tours in minivans with lifts. **Access-Able Travel Source** (© 303/232-2979; www.access-able.com) offers extensive access information and advice for traveling around the world with disabilities. **Accessible Journeys** (© 800/846-4537 or 610/521-0339; www.disabilitytravel.com) caters specifically to slow walkers and wheelchair travelers and their families and friends.

Avis Rent a Car has an "Avis Access" program that offers such services as a dedicated 24-hour toll-free number (© 888/879-4273) for customers with special travel needs; special car features such as swivel seats, spinner knobs, and hand controls; and accessible bus service.

Organizations that offer assistance to travelers with disabilities include **Moss-Rehab** (www.mossresourcenet.org), which provides a library of accessible-travel resources online; the **American Foundation for the Blind (AFB)** (© 800/232-5463; www.afb.org), a referral resource for the blind or visually impaired that includes information on traveling with Seeing Eye dogs; and **SATH** (Society for Accessible Travel & Hospitality) (© 212/447-7284; www.sath.org; annual membership fees: $45 adults, $30 seniors and students), which offers a wealth of travel resources for all types of disabilities and informed recommendations on destinations, access guides, travel agents, tour operators, vehicle rentals, and companion services. **AirAmbulanceCard.com** is now partnered with SATH and allows you to preselect top-notch hospitals in case of an emergency for $195 a year ($295 per family), among other benefits.

For more information specifically targeted to travelers with disabilities, the community website **iCan** (www.icanonline.net/channels/travel) has destination guides and several regular columns on accessible travel. Also check out the quarterly magazine *Emerging Horizons* (www.emerginghorizons.com; $14.95 per year, $19.95 outside the U.S.); and *Open World* magazine, published by SATH (see above; subscription: $13 per year, $21 outside the U.S.).

GAY & LESBIAN TRAVELERS

The International Gay and Lesbian Travel Association (IGLTA) (© 800/448-8550 or 954/776-2626; www.iglta.org) is the trade association for the gay and lesbian travel industry, and offers an online directory of gay- and lesbian-friendly travel businesses; go to their website and click on "Members."

Many agencies offer tours and travel itineraries specifically for gay and lesbian travelers. **Above and Beyond Tours** (© 800/397-2681; www.abovebeyondtours.com) is the exclusive gay and lesbian tour operator for United Airlines. **Now, Voyager** (© 800/255-6951; www.nowvoyager.com) is a well-known San Francisco–based, gay-owned and operated travel service. **Olivia Cruises & Resorts** (ⓒ **800/631-6277;** www.olivia.com) charters entire resorts and ships for exclusive lesbian vacations and offers smaller group experiences for both gay and lesbian travelers. (In 2005, tennis great Martina Navratilova was named Olivia's official spokesperson.)

Gay.com Travel (ⓒ **800/929-2268** or 415/644-8044; www.gay.com/travel or www.outandabout.com) is an excellent online successor to the popular *Out & About* print magazine. It provides regularly updated information about gay-owned, gay-oriented, and gay-friendly lodging, dining, sightseeing, nightlife, and shopping establishments in every important destination worldwide. It also offers trip-planning information for gay and lesbian travelers for more than 50 destinations, along various themes, ranging from Sex and Travel to Vacations for Couples.

The following travel guides are available at many bookstores, or you can order them from any online bookseller: *Frommer's Gay & Lesbian Europe* (www.frommers.com), an excellent travel resource to the top European cities and resorts; *Spartacus International Gay Guide* (Bruno Gmünder Verlag; www.spartacusworld.com/gay guide) and *Odysseus: The International Gay Travel Planner* (Odysseus Enterprises Ltd.), both good, annual, English-language guidebooks focused on gay men; and the *Damron* guides (www.damron.com), with separate, annual books for gay men and lesbians.

SENIOR TRAVEL

Mention the fact that you're a senior when you make your travel reservations. Although all the major U.S. airlines except America West have canceled their senior discount and coupon book programs, many hotels still offer lower rates for seniors. In most cities, people over the age of 60 qualify for reduced admission to theaters, museums, and other attractions, and discounted fares on public transportation.

Members of **AARP** (formerly known as the American Association of Retired Persons), 601 E St. NW, Washington, DC 20049 (ⓒ **888/687-2277;** www.aarp.org), get discounts on hotels, airfares, and car rentals. AARP offers members a wide range of benefits, including *AARP: The Magazine* and a monthly newsletter. Anyone over 50 can join.

Many reliable agencies and organizations target the 50-plus market. **Elderhostel** (ⓒ **877/426-8056;** www.elderhostel.org) arranges study programs for those age 55 and over (and a spouse or companion of any age) in the U.S. and in more than 80 countries around the world. Most courses last 5 to 7 days in the U.S. (2–4 weeks abroad), and many include airfare, accommodations in university dormitories or modest inns, meals, and tuition. **ElderTreks** (ⓒ **800/741-7956;** www.eldertreks.com) offers small-group tours to off-the-beaten-path or adventure-travel locations, restricted to travelers 50 and older. **INTRAV** (ⓒ **800/456-8100;** www.intrav.com) is a high-end tour operator that caters to the mature, discerning traveler (not specifically seniors), with trips around the world that include guided safaris, polar expeditions, private-jet adventures, and small-boat cruises down jungle rivers.

Recommended publications offering travel resources and discounts for seniors include: the quarterly magazine *Travel 50 & Beyond* (www.travel50andbeyond.com); *Travel Unlimited: Uncommon Adventures for the Mature Traveler* (Avalon); *101 Tips for Mature Travelers,* available from Grand Circle Travel (ⓒ **800/221-2610** or 617/350-7500; www.gct.com); and *Unbelievably Good Deals and Great Adventures That You Absolutely Can't Get Unless You're Over*

50 (McGraw-Hill), by Joann Rattner Heilman.

FAMILY TRAVEL

Children are treated like royalty in Hungary, pampered not just by parents and extended family members, but also by shopkeepers, train conductors, and all sorts of other people. Budapest has numerous attractions geared toward children, from the zoo, circus, and amusement park in Pest's City Park to a range of museums, including ones dedicated to science, natural history, and transportation. There is even a miniature children's railway running through the hills of Buda, with children in official Hungarian railway dress serving as conductors. And in this land of sweet teeth, there are fresh pastries and ice-cream cones sold everywhere, seemingly from every open window along the commercial thoroughfares. This guide is full of recommendations for kids; in particular, see "Especially for Kids" in chapter 7, "Exploring Budapest."

Family travel can be immensely rewarding, giving you new ways of seeing the world through the eyes of children.

To locate accommodations, restaurants, and attractions that are particularly kid-friendly, refer to the "Kids" icon throughout this guide.

Familyhostel (© 800/733-9753; www.learn.unh.edu/familyhostel) takes the whole family, including kids ages 8 to 15, on moderately priced domestic and international learning vacations. Lectures, field trips, and sightseeing are guided by a team of academics.

Recommended family-travel Internet sites include **Family Travel Forum** (www.familytravelforum.com), a comprehensive site that offers customized trip planning; **Family Travel Network** (www.familytravelnetwork.com), an award-winning site that offers travel features, deals, and tips; **Traveling Internationally with Your Kids** (www.travelwithyourkids.com),

a comprehensive site offering sound advice for long-distance and international travel with children; and **Family Travel Files** (www.thefamilytravelfiles.com), which offers an online magazine and a directory of off-the-beaten-path tours and tour operators for families.

WOMEN TRAVELERS

More and more hotels are ratcheting up security measures for women traveling alone on business or for pleasure. Some are even offering secure "women only" floors, with the added perk of spa services.

Check out the award-winning website **Journeywoman** (www.journeywoman.com), a "real life" women's travel-information network where you can sign up for a free e-mail newsletter and get advice on everything from etiquette and dress to safety. The travel guide *Safety and Security for Women Who Travel* by Sheila Swan and Peter Laufer (Travelers' Tales, Inc.), offers common-sense tips on safe travel.

AFRICAN-AMERICAN TRAVELERS

The Internet offers a number of helpful travel sites for African-American travelers. **Black Travel Online** (www.blacktravelonline.com) posts news on upcoming events and includes links to articles and travel-booking sites. **Soul of America** (www.soulofamerica.com) is a comprehensive website, with travel tips, event and family-reunion postings, and sections on historically black beach resorts and active vacations.

Agencies and organizations that provide resources for black travelers include: **Rodgers Travel** (© 800/825-1775; www.rodgerstravel.com), a Philadelphia-based travel agency with an extensive menu of tours in destinations worldwide, including heritage and private-group tours; the **African American Association of Innkeepers International** (© 877/422-5777; www.africanamericaninns.com), which provides information on member B&Bs in the U.S., Canada, and the Caribbean; and **Henderson Travel & Tours** (© 800/327-2309 or 301/650-5700; www.hendersontravel.com), which has specialized in trips to Africa since 1957. For more information, check out the following collections and guides: *Go Girl: The Black Woman's Guide to Travel & Adventure* (Eighth Mountain Press), a compilation of travel essays by writers including Jill Nelson and Audre Lorde, with some practical information and trip-planning advice; *The African American Travel Guide* by Wayne Robinson (Hunter Publishing; www.hunterpublishing.com), with details on 19 North American cities; *Steppin' Out* by Carla Labat (Avalon), with details on 20 cities; *Travel and Enjoy Magazine* (© 866/266-6211; www.travelandenjoy.com; subscription: $38 per year), which focuses on discounts and destination reviews; and the more narrative *Pathfinders Magazine* (© 877/977-PATH; www.pathfinderstravel.com; subscription: $15 per year), which includes articles on everything from Rio de Janeiro to Ghana as well as information on upcoming ski, diving, golf, and tennis trips.

STUDENT TRAVEL

If you're planning to travel outside the U.S., you'd be wise to arm yourself with an **International Student Identity Card (ISIC),** which offers substantial savings on rail passes, plane tickets, and entrance fees. It also provides you with basic health and life insurance and a 24-hour help line. The card is available for $22 from **STA Travel** (© 800/781-4040 in North America; www.sta.com or www.statravel.com), the biggest student travel agency in the world. If you're no longer a student but are still under 26, you can get an **International Youth Travel Card (IYTC)** for the same price from the same people, which entitles you to some discounts (but not on museum admissions). (*Note:* In

2002, STA Travel bought competitors **Council Travel** and **USIT Campus** after they went bankrupt. It's still operating some offices under the Council name, but it's owned by STA.) **Travel CUTS** (© 800/667-2887 or 416/614-2887; www.travelcuts.com) offers similar services for both Canadians and U.S. residents. Irish students may prefer to turn to **USIT** (© 01/602-1600; www.usitnow.ie), an Ireland-based specialist in student, youth, and independent travel.

SINGLE TRAVELERS

On package vacations, single travelers are often hit with a "single supplement" to the base price. To avoid it, you can agree to room with other single travelers or find a compatible roommate before you go, from one of the many roommate-locator agencies.

Travel Buddies Singles Travel Club (© 800/998-9099; www.travelbuddiesworldwide.com), based in Canada, runs small, intimate, single-friendly group trips and will match you with a roommate free of charge. **TravelChums** (© 212/787-2621; www.travelchums.com) is an Internet-only travel-companion matching service with elements of an online personals-type site, hosted by the respected New York–based Shaw Guides travel service. **The Single Gourmet Club** (www.singlegourmet.com/chapters.php) is an international social, dining, and travel club for singles of all ages, with club chapters in 21 cities in the U.S. and Canada. Annual membership fees vary from city to city.

Many reputable tour companies offer singles-only trips. **Singles Travel International** (© 877/765-6874; www.singlestravelintl.com) offers singles-only trips to places like London, Fiji and the Greek Islands. **Backroads** (© 800/462-2848; www.backroads.com) offers more than 160 active-travel trips to 30 destinations worldwide, including Bali, Morocco, and Costa Rica.

For more information, check out Eleanor Berman's latest edition of *Traveling Solo: Advice and Ideas for More* *Than 250 Great Vacations* (Globe Pequot), a guide with advice on traveling alone, either solo or as part of a group tour.

8 Planning Your Trip Online

SURFING FOR AIRFARES

The "big three" online travel agencies, **Expedia.com, Travelocity.com,** and **Orbitz.com,** sell most of the air tickets bought on the Internet. (Canadian travelers should try expedia.ca and Travelocity. ca; U.K. residents can go for expedia. co.uk and opodo.co.uk.) **Kayak.com** is also gaining popularity and uses a sophisticated search engine (developed at MIT). Each has different business deals with the airlines and may offer different fares on the same flights, so it's wise to shop around. Expedia, Kayak, and Travelocity will also send you **e-mail notification** when a cheap fare becomes available to your favorite destination. Of the smaller travel-agency websites, **SideStep** (www. sidestep.com) has gotten the best reviews from Frommer's authors. The website (with optional browser add-on) purports to "search 140 sites at once," but in reality only beats competitors' fares as often as other sites do.

Also remember to check **airline websites,** especially those for low-fare carriers such as Southwest, JetBlue, AirTran, WestJet, or Ryanair, whose fares are often misreported or simply missing from travel agency websites. Even with major airlines, you can often shave a few bucks from a fare by booking directly through the airline and avoiding a travel agency's transaction fee. But you'll get these discounts only by **booking online:** Most airlines now offer online-only fares that even their phone agents know nothing about. For the websites of airlines that fly to and from your destination, go to "Getting There," p. 28.

Great **last-minute deals** are available through free weekly e-mail services provided directly by the airlines. Most of these are announced on Tuesday or Wednesday and must be purchased online. Most are only valid for travel that weekend, but some (such as Southwest's) can be booked weeks or months in advance. Sign up for weekly e-mail alerts at airline websites or check mega-sites that compile comprehensive lists of last-minute specials, such as **Smarter Travel** (smartertravel.com). For last-minute trips, **site59.com** and **lastminutetravel. com** in the U.S. and **lastminute.com** in Europe often have better air-and-hotel package deals than the major-label sites.

If you're willing to give up some control over your flight details, use what is called an **"opaque" fare service** like **Priceline** (www.priceline.com; www. priceline.co.uk for Europeans) or its smaller competitor, **Hotwire** (www. hotwire.com). Both offer rock-bottom prices in exchange for travel on a "mystery airline" at a mysterious time of day, often with a mysterious change of planes en route. The mystery airlines are all major, well-known carriers—and the possibility of being sent from Philadelphia to Chicago via Tampa is remote; the airlines' routing computers have gotten a lot better than they used to be. Your chances of getting a 6am or 11pm flight, however, are still pretty high. Hotwire tells you flight prices before you buy; Priceline usually has better deals than Hotwire, but you have to play their "name our price" game. If you're new at this, the helpful folks at **BiddingForTravel** (www.bidding fortravel.com) do a good job of demystifying Priceline's prices and strategies. Priceline and Hotwire are great for flights within North America and between the U.S. and Europe. But for flights to other parts of the world, consolidators will almost always beat their fares. *Note:* In 2004 Priceline added non-opaque service to its roster. You now have the option to pick exact flights, times, and airlines from a list of offers, or opt to bid on opaque fares as before.

SURFING FOR HOTELS

Shopping online for hotels is generally done one of two ways: by booking through the hotel's own website or through an independent booking agency (or a fare-service agency like Priceline; see below). These Internet hotel agencies have multiplied in mind-boggling numbers of late, competing for the business of millions of consumers surfing for accommodations around the world. This competitiveness can be a boon to consumers who have the patience and time to shop and compare the online sites for good deals—but shop they must, for prices can vary considerably from site to site. And keep in mind that hotels at the top of a site's listing may be there for no other reason than that they paid money to get the placement.

Of the "big three" sites, **Expedia** offers a long list of special deals and "virtual tours" or photos of available rooms so you can see what you're paying for (a feature that helps counter the claims that the best rooms are often held back from bargain-booking websites). **Travelocity** posts unvarnished customer reviews and ranks its properties according to the AAA rating system. (**Trip Advisor** [www.tripadvisor. com] is another excellent source of unbiased user reviews of hotels around the world. While even the finest hotels can inspire a misleadingly poor review from a picky or crabby traveler, the body of user opinions, when taken as a whole, is usually a reliable indicator.)

Other reliable online booking agencies include **Hotels.com** and **Quikbook.com**. An excellent free program, **TravelAxe** (www.travelaxe.net), can help you search

multiple hotel sites at once, even ones you may never have heard of—and conveniently lists the total price of the room, including the taxes and service charges. Another booking site, **Travelweb** (www. travelweb.com), is partly owned by the hotels it represents (including the Hilton, Hyatt, and Starwood chains) and is therefore plugged directly into the hotels' reservations systems—unlike independent online agencies, which have to fax or e-mail reservation requests to the hotel, a good portion of which get misplaced in the shuffle. More than once, travelers have arrived at the hotel, only to be told that they have no reservation. To be fair, many of the major sites are undergoing improvements in service and ease of use, and Expedia will soon be able to plug directly into the reservations systems of many hotel chains—none of which can be bad news for consumers. In the meantime, it's a good idea to **get a confirmation number** and **make a printout** of any online booking transaction.

In the opaque website category, **Priceline** and **Hotwire** are even better for hotels than for airfares; through both, you're allowed to pick the neighborhood and quality level of your hotel before paying. Priceline's hotel product even covers Europe and Asia, though it's much better at getting five-star lodging for three-star prices than at finding anything at the bottom of the scale. On the downside, many hotels stick Priceline guests in their least desirable rooms. Be sure to go to the BiddingForTravel website (see above) before bidding on a hotel room on Priceline; it features a fairly up-to-date list of hotels that Priceline uses in major cities. For both Priceline and Hotwire, you pay upfront, and the fee is nonrefundable. *Note:* Some hotels do not provide loyalty program credits or points or other frequent-stay amenities when you book a room through opaque online services.

SURFING FOR RENTAL CARS

For booking rental cars online, the best deals are usually found at rental-car company websites, although all the major online travel agencies also offer rental-car reservations services. Priceline and Hotwire work well for rental cars, too; the only "mystery" is which major rental company you get, and for most travelers the difference between Hertz, Avis, and Budget is negligible.

TRAVEL BLOGS & TRAVELOGUES

More and more travelers are using travel web logs, or **blogs,** to chronicle their journeys online. You can search for other blogs about Budapest at **Travelblog.com** or post your own travelogue at **Travelblog. org**. For blogs that cover general travel news and highlight various destinations, try **Writtenroad.com** or Gawker Media's snarky **Gridskipper.com**. For more literary travel essays, try Salon.com's travel section (**Salon.com/Wanderlust**), and **Worldhum.com,** which also has an extensive list of other travel-related journals, blogs, online communities, newspaper coverage, and bookstores.

9 Getting There

BY PLANE

Northwest Airlines (© 800/447-4747) and **Malév** (© 800/877-5429, 800/262-5380, or 800/223-6884), the former Hungarian state airline, offer nonstop service between North America and Budapest. Other leading carriers include **Lufthansa** (© 800/645-3880), **British Airways** (© 800/247-9297), **Delta Airlines** (© 800/241-4141), and **Austrian Air** (© 800/843-0002).

Budapest is served by two adjacent airports, **Ferihegy I** and **Ferihegy II,** located in the XVIII district in southeastern Pest. Generally, Ferihegy I serves low-cost carriers, while Ferihegy II (which has a **Terminal A** and a **Terminal B**) serves the flagship carrier and other traditional airlines. There are several main information numbers: For arrivals, try © 1/296-5052; for departures, call © 1/296-5883; and for general information, call © 1/296-7155. Make sure you pick up a copy of the free *LRI Airport Budapest Magazine* while at the airport, as it contains a wealth of valuable phone numbers and transportation-related information, as well as articles on Hungary.

All arriving flights are international since there is no domestic air service in Hungary. All arriving passengers pass through the same Customs gate and emerge into the bustling arrivals hall of the airport.

Though extended and modernized over the past few years, the airport remains quite small. In each terminal, you will find several accommodations offices, rental-car agencies, shops, and exchange booths. Note that exchange rates are generally less favorable here than in the city, so you may not want to change very much money at the airport.

Twenty-four-hour left-luggage service is available at Terminal B (© 1/296-8802).

GETTING THROUGH THE AIRPORT

With the federalization of airport security, screening procedures at U.S. airports are more stable and consistent than ever. Generally, you'll be fine if you arrive at the airport **1 hour** before a domestic flight and **2 hours** before an international flight; if you show up late, tell an airline employee and she'll probably whisk you to the front of the line.

Bring a **current, government-issued photo ID** such as a driver's license or passport. Keep your ID at the ready to present at check-in, the security checkpoint, and sometimes even the gate.

(Children under 18 do not need government-issued photo IDs for domestic flights, but they do for international flights to most countries.)

In 2003, the TSA phased out **gate check-in** at all U.S. airports. Passengers with e-tickets, which have made paper tickets nearly obsolete, can beat the ticket-counter lines by using airport **electronic kiosks** or even **online check-in** from their home computers. Online check-in involves logging on to your airline's website, accessing your reservation, and printing out your boarding pass—and the airline may even offer you bonus miles to do so! If you're using a kiosk at the airport, bring the credit card you used to book the ticket or your frequent-flier card. Print out your boarding pass from the kiosk and simply proceed to the security checkpoint with your pass and a photo ID. If you're checking bags or looking to snag an exit-row seat, you will be able to do so using most airline kiosks. Even the smaller airlines are employing the kiosk system, but always call your airline to make sure these alternatives are available. **Curbside check-in** is also a good way to avoid lines, although a few airlines still don't allow it; call for your airline's policy before you go.

Security checkpoint lines are getting shorter than they were during 2001 and 2002, but an orange alert, suspicious passenger, or high passenger volume can still make for a long wait. If you have trouble standing for long periods of time, tell an airline employee; the airline will provide a wheelchair. Speed up security by **not wearing metal objects** such as big belt buckles. If you've got metallic body parts, a note from your doctor can prevent a long chat with the security screeners. Keep in mind that only **ticketed passengers** are allowed past security, except for people escorting either passengers with disabilities or children.

Federalization has stabilized **what you can carry on** and **what you can't.** The general rule is that sharp things are out, nail clippers are okay, and food and beverages must pass through the X-ray machine—but security screeners can't make you drink from your coffee cup. Bring food in your carry-on rather than checking it, as explosive-detection machines used on checked luggage have been known to mistake food (especially chocolate, for some reason) for bombs. Travelers in the U.S. are allowed one carry-on bag, plus a "personal item" such as a purse, briefcase, or laptop bag. Carry-on hoarders can stuff all sorts of things into a laptop bag; as long as it has a laptop in it, it's still considered a personal item. The Transportation Security Administration (TSA) has issued a list of restricted items; check its website (www.tsa.gov/public/index.jsp) for details.

Airport screeners may decide that your checked luggage warrants a hand search. You can now purchase luggage locks that allow screeners to open and relock a checked bag if hand searching is necessary. Look for Travel Sentry certified locks at luggage or travel shops and Brookstone stores (you can buy them online at www.brookstone.com). Luggage inspectors can open these TSA-approved locks with a special code or key—rather than having to cut them off the suitcase, as they normally do to conduct a hand search. For more information on the locks, visit www.travelsentry.org.

FLYING FOR LESS: TIPS FOR GETTING THE BEST AIRFARE

Passengers sharing the same airplane cabin rarely pay the same fare. Travelers who need to purchase tickets at the last minute, change their itinerary at a moment's notice, or fly one-way often get stuck paying the premium rate. Here are some ways to keep your airfare costs down.

- Passengers who can book their ticket either **long in advance or at the last minute,** or who **fly midweek** or **at less-trafficked hours** may pay a fraction of the full fare. If your schedule is flexible, say so, and ask if you can secure a cheaper fare by changing your flight plans.
- Search **the Internet** for cheap fares (see "Planning Your Trip Online," earlier in this chapter).
- Keep an eye on local newspapers for **promotional specials** or **fare wars,** when airlines lower prices on their most popular routes. You rarely see fare wars offered for peak travel times, but if you can travel in the off-months, you may snag a bargain.
- Try to book a ticket **in its country of origin.** If you're planning a one-way flight from Johannesburg to Bombay, a South Africa–based travel agent will probably have the lowest fares. For multi-leg trips, book in the country of the first leg; for example, book New York–London–Amsterdam–Rome–New York in the U.S.
- **Consolidators,** also known as bucket shops, are great sources for international tickets, although they usually can't beat Internet fares within North America. Start by looking in Sunday newspaper travel sections; U.S. travelers should focus on the *New York Times, Los Angeles Times,* and *Miami Herald.* For less-developed destinations, small travel agents who cater to immigrant communities in large cities often have the best deals. *Beware:* Bucket shop tickets are usually nonrefundable or rigged with stiff cancellation penalties, often as high as 50% to 75% of the ticket price, and some put you on charter airlines, which may leave at inconvenient times and experience delays. Several reliable consolidators are worldwide and available online. **STA Travel** has been the world's lead consolidator for students since purchasing Council Travel, but their fares are competitive for travelers of all ages. **ELTExpress (Flights.com)** (℡ 800/TRAV-800; www.eltexpress.com) has excellent fares worldwide, particularly to Europe. They also have "local" websites in 12 countries. **FlyCheap** (℡ 800/FLY-CHEAP; www.1800flycheap.com) is owned by package-holiday megalith MyTravel and has especially good fares to sunny destinations. **Air Tickets Direct** (℡ 800/778-3447; www.airticketsdirect.com) is based in Montreal and leverages the currently weak Canadian dollar for low fares; they also book trips to places that U.S. travel agents won't touch, such as Cuba.
- Join **frequent-flier clubs.** Frequent-flier membership doesn't cost a cent, but it does entitle you to better seats, faster response to phone inquiries, and prompter service if your luggage is stolen or your flight is canceled or delayed, or if you want to change your seat. And you don't have to fly to earn points; **frequent-flier credit cards** can earn you thousands of miles for doing your everyday shopping. With more than 70 mileage awards programs on the market, consumers have never had more options, but the system has never been more complicated—what with major airlines folding, new budget carriers emerging, and alliances forming (allowing you to earn points on partner airlines). Investigate the program details of your favorite airlines before you sink points into any one. Consider which airlines have hubs in the airport nearest you, and, of those carriers, which have the most advantageous alliances, given your most common routes. To play the frequent-flier game to your best advantage,

consult Randy Petersen's **Inside Flyer** (www.insideflyer.com). Petersen and friends review all the programs in detail and post regular updates on changes in policies and trends. Petersen will also field direct questions (via e-mail) if a partner airline refuses to redeem points, for instance, or if you're still not sure after researching the various programs which one is right for you. It's well worth the $12 online subscription fee, good for one year.

LONG-HAUL FLIGHTS: HOW TO STAY COMFORTABLE

Long flights can be trying; stuffy air and cramped seats can make you feel as if you're being sent parcel post in a small box. But with a little advance planning, you can make an otherwise unpleasant experience almost bearable.

- Your choice of airline and airplane will definitely affect your leg room. Find more details at **www.seatguru. com**, which has extensive details about almost every seat on six major U.S. airlines. For international airlines, research firm Skytrax has posted a list of average seat pitches at **www.airlinequality.com**.

- Emergency exit seats and bulkhead seats typically have the most legroom. Emergency exit seats are usually left unassigned until the day of a flight (to ensure that someone able-bodied fills the seats); it's worth getting to the ticket counter early to snag one of these spots for a long flight. Many passengers find that bulkhead seating (the row facing the wall at the front of the cabin) offers more legroom, but keep in mind that bulkheads are where airlines often put baby bassinets, so you may be sitting next to an infant.

- To have two seats for yourself in a three-seat row, try for an aisle seat in a center section toward the back of coach. If you're traveling with a companion, book an aisle and a window seat. Middle seats are usually booked last, so chances are good you'll end up with three seats to yourselves. And in the event that a third passenger is assigned the middle seat, he or she will probably be more than happy to trade for a window or an aisle.

- Ask about entertainment options. Many airlines offer seatback video systems where you get to choose your movies or play video games—but only on some of their planes. (Boeing 777s are your best bet.)

- To sleep, avoid the last row of any section or the row in front of an emergency exit, as these seats are the least likely to recline. Avoid seats near highly trafficked toilet areas. Avoid seats in the back of many jets—these can be narrower than those in the rest of coach. You also may want to reserve a window seat so you can rest your head and avoid being bumped in the aisle.

- Get up, walk around, and stretch every 60 to 90 minutes to keep your blood flowing. This helps avoid **deep vein thrombosis,** or "economy-class syndrome," a potentially deadly condition caused by sitting in cramped conditions for too long. Other preventive measures include drinking lots of water and avoiding alcohol (see next bullet).

- Drink water before, during, and after your flight to combat the lack of humidity in airplane cabins—which can be drier than the Sahara. Bring a bottle of water on board. Avoid alcohol, which will dehydrate you.

- If you're flying with kids, don't forget to carry on toys, books, pacifiers, and chewing gum to help them relieve ear pressure buildup during ascent and descent. Let each child pack his or her own backpack with favorite toys.

BY TRAIN

Countless trains arrive in Budapest from most corners of Europe. Many connect through Vienna, where 11 daily trains depart for Budapest from either the Westbahnhof or Sudbahnhof station. Six daily trains connect Prague and Budapest, while one connects Berlin with Budapest and two connect Warsaw with Budapest.

The train trip between Vienna and Budapest takes about 3½ hours. Hungarian railway offers a great deal for short-term visitors coming from Vienna: a round-trip second-class ticket, valid up to 4 days, that includes a free pass for all public transport in Budapest. For more information on Vienna trains, contact the **Austrian National Tourist Board,** 500 Fifth Ave., Suite 800, New York, NY 10110 (© **212/ 944-6885**); 11601 Wilshire Blvd., Suite 2480, Los Angeles, CA 90025 (© **310/ 477-3332**); 30 St. George St., London W1R 0AL (© **020/7629-0461**); 2 Bloor St. E., Suite 3330, Toronto, ON M4W 1A8 (© **416/967-3381**); or 1010 Sherbrooke St. W., Suite 1410, Montreal, PQ H3A 2R7 (© **514/849-3708**).

Train travel within Hungary is generally very efficient; trains almost always depart right on time and usually arrive on time. You can access a full, user-friendly timetable on the Web, at **www.elvira.hu**.

Hungarian ticket agents speak little English, so you will need to know some basic terminology in Hungarian. *Indul* means "departure" and *érkezik* means "arrival." The timetables for arrivals are displayed in big white posters *(érkező vonatok),* while departures *(induló vonatok)* are on yellow posters. The relevant terms in the timetables are *honnan* (from where), *hova* (to where), *vágány* (platform), *munkanap* (weekdays), *hétvége*

Tips Coping with Jet Lag

Jet lag is a pitfall of traveling across time zones. If you're flying north-south and you feel sluggish when you touch down, your symptoms will be the result of dehydration and the general stress of air travel. When you travel east–west or vice versa, however, your body becomes thoroughly confused about what time it is, and everything from your digestion to your brain is knocked for a loop. Traveling east, say from Chicago to Paris, is more difficult on your internal clock than traveling west, say from Atlanta to Hawaii, because most peoples' bodies are more inclined to stay up late than fall asleep early.

Here are some tips for combating jet lag:

• **Reset your watch** to your destination time before you board the plane.
• **Drink lots of water** before, during, and after your flight. Avoid alcohol.
• **Exercise and sleep well** for a few days before your trip.
• If you have trouble sleeping on planes, **fly eastward on morning flights.**
• **Daylight** is the key to resetting your body clock. At the website for **Outside In** (www.bodyclock.com), you can get a customized plan of when to seek and avoid light. If you need help getting to sleep earlier than you usually would, some doctors recommend taking either the hormone **melatonin** or the sleeping pill **Ambien**—but not together. Some recommend that you take 2 to 5 milligrams of melatonin about 2 hours before your planned bedtime—but again, always check with your doctor on the best course of action for you.

(weekend), *munkaszüneti nap* (Sat), *ünnepnap* (holiday), *gyors* (fast train)— stops only at major cities, as posted, and *IC* (inter city)—stops only once or twice en route; you must reserve a seat for IC trains). Ticket terminology is as follows: *jegy* (ticket), *oda* (one-way), *oda-vissza* (round-trip), *helyjegy* (reservation), *első osztály* (first class), *másodosztály* (second class), *nem dohányzó* (nonsmoking), *ma* (today), and *holnap* (tomorrow).

A train posted as *személy* is a local train, which stops at every single village and town on its route. Always opt for a *gyors* (fast) or Intercity train to get to your destination in a timely manner. All Intercity trains (but no other domestic trains) require a *helyjegy* (seat reservation); ask for the reservation when purchasing your ticket. On Intercity trains, you must sit in your assigned seat. All Intercity trains now comply strictly with a new law imposing constraints on smoking in public spaces; they have a single car designated for smokers, while the rest of the train is nonsmoking. If you want a seat in the smoking car, you need to ask for *dohányzó* when buying your ticket. The gyors train is typically an old, gritty, rumbling train with the classic eight-seat compartments. The Intercity, a state-of-the-art, clean, modern train without compartments, is said to travel faster, but our experience has shown us that there's seldom more than 30 minutes difference between the two in terms of speed.

During the day, obtain **domestic train information** over the phone by dialing *©* **1/461-5400** and **international train information** at *©* **1/461-5500.** Purchase tickets at train station ticket windows or from the MÁV Service Office, VI. Andrássy út 35 (*©* **1/322-8405**, open Monday through Friday 9am to 6pm in summer, 9am to 5pm in winter. You need at least half an hour before departure time to make a reservation.

TRAIN PASSES

Regional passes, such as the **European East Pass,** are available. The pass covers Austria, Hungary, the Czech Republic, Poland, and Slovakia, and is good for 5 to 10 days of travel within a 1-month period. You must purchase the pass from a travel agent or Rail Europe (see contact information below) before you leave for Europe. You can also purchase a **Hungarian Flexipass** (www.eurorailways.com), which covers 5 days of travel within a 15-day period in Hungary. If you plan to visit only one European country or region, bear in mind that a country or regional pass will cost less than a Eurailpass.

EURAILPASS The **Eurailpass** entitles travelers to unlimited first-class travel over the 160,900km (100,000-mile) national railroad network in all western European countries, except Britain, and including Hungary in eastern Europe. It's also valid on some lake steamers and private railroads. A Eurailpass may be purchased for as short a period as 15 days or as long as 3 months. The passes are not available to residents of the countries where the pass is valid or to residents of the United Kingdom.

The Eurailpass, which is ideal for extensive trips, eliminates the hassles of buying tickets—just show your pass to the ticket collector. You should note, however, that some trains require seat reservations. Also, many of the trains have couchettes, or sleeping cars, for which an additional fee is charged.

The pass cannot be purchased in Europe, so you must secure one before leaving on your trip (see www.raileurope.com). Children under 4 travel free if they don't occupy a seat (otherwise they are charged half the fare); children under 12 are charged half the fare.

If you're under 26, you can obtain unlimited second-class travel, wherever Eurailpass is honored, on a **Eurail Youthpass.**

Groups of two or more people can save on train fairs with the **Eurailpass Saver Flexi,** and the company also offers a **Eurail Flexipass** and a **Youth Eurail Flexipass,** which allows more flexibility in travel times.

These passes are available from travel agents in North America, or you can contact **Rail Europe** by calling ✆ **800/848-7245** or surfing over to **www.raileurope. com**.

For British travelers, many different rail passes are available in the U.K. for travel in Europe. Stop in at the **International Rail Centre,** Victoria Station, London SW1V 1JY (✆ **171/834-2345**); or Wasteels, 121 Wilton Rd., London SW1V 1JZ (✆ **171/834-7066**).

BY BUS

Buses to and from western and eastern Europe and points in Hungary west of the Danube call at **Népliget.** You reach this station by getting off at the Népliget metro stop on the Red line. Buses to and from the Danube Bend and other points north of Budapest call at the **Árpád híd bus station** (✆ 1/320-9229 or 1/317-9886). Take the Blue line metro to Árpád híd. For domestic and international bus information, call ✆ **1/219-8080,** though you should be aware that it can be rather difficult to get through to the bus stations over the telephone and to reach an English speaker. Your best bet is perhaps to gather your information in person or ask for assistance at the Tourinform office (p. 11).

BY CAR

Several major highways link Hungary to nearby European capitals. The recently modernized **E60** (or M1) connects Budapest with Vienna and points west; it is a toll road from the Austrian border to the city of Györ. The **E65** connects Budapest with Prague and points north.

The **border crossings** from Austria and Slovakia (from which countries most Westerners enter Hungary) are hassle-free.

In addition to your passport, you may be requested to present your driver's license, vehicle registration, and proof of insurance (the number plate and symbol indicating country of origin are acceptable proof). A green card is required of vehicles bearing license plates of Bulgaria, France, the former USSR, Greece, Poland, Italy, Romania, and Israel. Hungary no longer requires the International Driver's License. Cars entering Hungary are required to have a decal indicating country of registration, a first-aid kit, and an emergency triangle. For traffic regulations, see "Getting Around," in chapter 4.

Driving distances are: from Vienna, 248km (154 miles); from Prague, 560km (347 miles); from Frankfurt, 952km (590 miles); and from Rome, 1,294km (802 miles).

BY HYDROFOIL

The Hungarian state shipping company **MAHART** operates hydrofoils on the Danube between Vienna and Budapest in the spring and summer months. It's an extremely popular route, so you should book your tickets well in advance. In North America or Britain, contact the Austrian National Tourist Board (see "By Train," above). In Vienna contact MAHART, Handelskai 265 (✆ **43/729-2161;** fax 43/729-2163). Or visit this website: www.besthotelz.com/hungary/hydrofoil/hydrofoil.htm.

From April 3 through July 2 the MAHART hydrofoil departs Vienna at 9am daily, arriving in Budapest at 2:30pm, with a stop in Bratislava when necessary (passengers getting on or off). From July 3 to August 29, two hydrofoils make the daily passage, departing Vienna at 8am and 1pm, arriving in Budapest at 1:30 and 6:30pm, respectively. From August 30 to November 1, the schedule returns to one hydrofoil daily, departing Vienna at 9am and arriving in Budapest at 2:30pm. Customs and passport control begin 1 hour prior to departure. Eurail-pass holders also receive a discount, as long as they buy the ticket before boarding. ISIC holders also receive a discount. The Budapest office of MAHART is at V. Belgrád rakpart (☎ 1/318-1880). Boats and hydrofoils from Vienna arrive at the international boat station next door to the MAHART office on the Belgrád rakpart, which is on the Pest side of the Danube, between the Szabadság and Erzsébet bridges.

10 Packages for the Independent Traveler

Before you start your search for the lowest airfare, you may want to consider booking your flight as part of a travel package. Package tours are not the same thing as escorted tours. Package tours are simply a way to buy the airfare, accommodations, and other elements of your trip (such as car rentals, airport transfers, and sometimes even activities) at the same time and often at discounted prices—kind of like one-stop shopping. Packages are sold in bulk to tour operators—who resell them to the public at a cost that usually undercuts standard rates.

One good source of package deals is the airlines themselves. Most major airlines offer air/land packages, including **American Airlines Vacations** (☎ 800/321-2121; www.aavacations.com), **Delta Vacations** (☎ 800/221-6666; www.delta vacations.com), **Continental Airlines Vacations** (☎ 800/301-3800; www.co vacations.com), and **United Vacations** (☎ 888/854-3899; www.unitedvacations. com). Several big **online travel agencies**—Expedia, Travelocity, Orbitz, Site59, and Lastminute.com—also do a brisk business in packages. If you're unsure about the pedigree of a smaller packager, check with the Better Business Bureau in the city where the company is based, or go online at www.bbb.org. If a packager won't tell you where they're based, don't fly with them.

Travel packages are also listed in the travel section of your local Sunday newspaper. Or check ads in the national travel magazines such as *Arthur Frommer's Budget Travel Magazine, Travel & Leisure, National Geographic Traveler,* and *Condé Nast Traveler.*

Package tours can vary by leaps and bounds. Some offer a better class of hotels than others. Some offer the same hotels for lower prices. Some offer flights on scheduled airlines, while others book charters. Some limit your choice of accommodations and travel days. You are often required to make a large payment upfront. On the plus side, packages can save you money, offering group prices but allowing for independent travel. Some even let you add on a few guided excursions or escorted day trips (also at prices lower than if you booked them yourself) without booking an entirely escorted tour.

Before you invest in a package tour, get some answers. Ask about the **accommodations choices** and prices for each. Then look up the hotels' reviews in a Frommer's guide and check their rates online for your specific dates of travel. You'll also want to find out what **type of room** you get. If you need a certain type of room, ask for it; don't take whatever is thrown your way. Request a nonsmoking room, a quiet room, a room with a view, or whatever you fancy.

Finally, look for hidden expenses. Ask whether airport departure fees and taxes, for example, are included in the total cost.

11 Recommended Books

A good number of the best books on Hungary are now out of print. If you can't find a given book in a bookstore or on the Internet, check in a university library. Many books published by Corvina, a Budapest-based English-language press, are recommended below. They can be purchased at English-language bookstores in Budapest, or you can write for a free catalog: **Corvina kiadó,** P.O. Box 108, Budapest H-1364, Hungary.

HISTORY & POLITICS   For an overview of Hungarian history, try László Kontler's *A History of Hungary* (Palgrave/Macmillan, 2002). If you can't obtain it before your journey, you can pick one up at the Central European University's bookshop (V. Nádor u. 9-11) in Budapest, where the author happens to be head of the history department. *A History of Hungary* (Indiana University Press, 1990), edited by Peter Sugar, is an anthology with a number of good essays. *The Habsburg Monarchy, 1809–1918* (London: Hamish Hamilton, 1948), by A. J. P. Taylor, is a lively and readable analysis of the final century of the Austro-Hungarian empire.

The Holocaust in Hungary: An Anthology of Jewish Response (University of Alabama Press, 1982), edited and translated by Andrew Handler, is notable for the editor's excellent introduction. Elenore Lister's *Wallenberg: The Man in the Iron Web* (Prentice Hall, 1982) recounts the heroic life of Raoul Wallenberg; the setting: Nazi-occupied Budapest.

Joseph Rothschild has written two excellent surveys of 20th-century eastern European history, both with large sections on Hungary. They are *East Central Europe Between the Two World Wars* (University of Washington Press, 1974) and *Return to Diversity: A Political History of East Central Europe Since World War II* (Oxford University Press, 1989).

MEMOIRS   Two memoirs of early-20th-century Budapest deserve mention: *Apprentice in Budapest: Memories of a World That Is No More* (University of Utah Press, 1988) by the anthropologist Raphael Patai; and *Budapest 1900* (Weidenfeld & Nicolson, 1989), by John Lukacs, which captures the feeling of a lively but doomed imperial city at the turn of the 20th century. Post-Communist Budapest is described in Marion Merrick's *Now You See It, Now You Don't; Seven Years in Hungary 1982–89* (Mágus, 1998). Another book of note is *In Search of the Mother Book,* a memoir by the American feminist literary figure Susan Rubin Suleiman, who fled Hungary after World War II and returned to the land of her birth in the late 1980s.

CULTURE & CUISINE   *Hungary* in the *Culinaria* series (2001) by Aniko Gergely provides an excellent and thorough cultural introduction to Hungarian cooking, in addition to a bunch of authentic recipes. The *Cuisine of Hungary* (Bonanza Books, 1971), by the famous Hungarian-born restaurateur George Lang, also contains a great deal of material on the subject.

Tekla Domotor's *Hungarian Folk Beliefs* (Corvina and Indiana University Press, 1981) covers witches, werewolves, giants, and gnomes. Zsuzsanna Ardó's *How to Be a European: Go Hungarian* (Biográf, 1994) is a witty little guidebook to Hungarian culture, etiquette, and social life.

Julia Szabó's *Painting in Nineteenth Century Hungary* (Corvina, 1985) contains a fine introductory essay and over 300 plates. In our opinion, the best traveler-oriented coffee-table book available in Budapest is *Budapest Art and History* (Flow East, 1992), by Delia Meth-Cohn.

FICTION   Not all the best examples of Hungarian literature are available in translation, but 2002 Nobel prize winner Imre Kertész's *Fateless* is a must. You should also look for any translations of the highly esteemed contemporary authors Péter Nádas and Péter Esterházy. Of particular interest is Esterházy's *Helping Verbs of the Heart* (Weidenfeld & Nicolson, 1991), a gripping story of grief following a parent's death, and Nádas's *A Book of Memories* (Penguin, 1998), which was assessed by Susan Sontag as the best European novel of the 20th century. You may also want to find and read the following: Gyula Illyés' *The People of the Puszta* (Corvina, 1979), an unabashedly honest look at peasant life in the early 20th century; György Konrád's *The Case Worker* (Penguin, 1987), a portrayal of a political system in disrepair; István Örkény's *The Toth Family and The Flower Show* (New Directions, 1966), a book with two stories: the first an allegorical story about fear and authority, and the second a fable about different types of reality in modern life; Zsolt Csalog's *Lajos M., Aged 45* (Budapest: Maecenas, 1989), an extraordinary memoir of life in a Soviet labor camp; Kálmán Mikszáth's *St. Peter's Umbrella* (Corvina, 1962); and Zsigmond Móricz's *Seven Pennies* (Corvina, 1988), a collection of short stories by one of Hungary's most celebrated authors.

3

Suggested Budapest & Hungary Itineraries

If you have only 1 or 2 days in Budapest, you will find that historic Budapest is surprisingly small, and many sights listed in the following pages can be reached by foot from the city center. Take the time to stroll from one place to the next—you'll find yourself passing magnificent, if often run-down, examples of the city's distinctive architecture. If your schedule allows for a few more days, we suggest adding 1- or 2-day side trips to small, quaint villages like Szentendre, Szeged, or Pécs, all within a few hours of the capital.

We encourage you to use these itineraries in conjunction with the walking tours listed in chapter 8, "Strolling Around Budapest."

1 The Best of Budapest in 1 Day

If you have only a day in Budapest, spend a few hours in the morning exploring the **Inner City** and **Central Pest**. Feel free to wander through the streets, and don't be afraid to get lost (our maps will get you back on track). Budapest is similar to Paris in that way; even if you stray from the itinerary, you can't go wrong. Walk the length of Váci utca, the city's most expensive shopping street, and don't miss the classy architecture at Vörösmarty tér. Stop for cappuccino and a slice of *almás rétes* (apple strudel) at the historic Gerbeaud coffeehouse. Then stroll along the Danube as far as the neo-Gothic **Parliament** building, noting along the way the **Chain Bridge** and the beautifully restored **Hotel Four Seasons Gresham Palace.** Save the whole afternoon for visiting the major sites of **Castle Hill** and the cobblestone streets of the **Castle District**, where you can visit the **Hungarian National Gallery.** *Start:* Deák tér, or anywhere in Inner City.

❶ Inner City and Central Pest ⊛

Budapest, a city whose wide boulevards were designed a little over a century ago, is a city that can be walked, so start off in the center city, wander the grand boulevards, and admire the architecture. For a fully-organized 3-hour tour of this area that hits all the attractions, see "Walking Tour 1: Pest's Inner City" in chapter 8, "Strolling Around Budapest."

Or take a more leisurely stroll around the area and visit a few museums and highlights of the area. You might duck into the **Hungarian National Museum** ⊛⊛ (see p. 125), the **Budapest Holocaust Memorial Center** ⊛⊛ (see p. 125), or the **Inner City Parish Church** ⊛ (see p. 131). As you tour the area, you'll begin to understand the incredible changes that the city has seen in recent years. Many buildings have been completely restored and renovated. Old decrepit spaces have become complexes, and many more projects are being developed.

Head over to **Váci utca**, which is the main shopping and walking street of Budapest. This booming shopping area developed in Hungary over the past decade and a half since the systemic changes of 1989. You might try the **Vali Folklór** folk craft shop (see p. 193), the **VAM Design Gallery** (see p. 192), and various clothing and bookstores (avoid the touristy cafes here).

Walk from Déak tér to the Danube Promenade. Then make your way toward the Kossuth tér metro for:

❷ Parliament ✺

You can't miss Budapest's grand, ecclectic Parliament building, which hugs the Danube. Designed by Imre Steindl and completed in 1902, the building mixes neo-Gothic style with a neo-Renaissance dome. It has been from the outset one of Budapest's symbols, though until 1989 a democratically elected government had convened here exactly once (just after World War II, before the Communist takeover). Since 2000, in addition to its government functions, it has also been home to the fabled Hungarian crown jewels. Unfortunately, you can enter only on guided tours (the half-hour tour is worthwhile for the chance to go inside). See p. 131 for tour times and information. See p. 138.

🍵 PARLAMENT KÁVÉHÁZ ✺

Per Hungarian tradition, sit down in a coffeehouse to read the newspaper, relax, ponder the past, and dream of the future! Situated adjacent to Hungary's parliament buildings, the Parlament Kávéház is decorated with an impressive rounded painting of the parliament buildings, and even a ceiling mural. V. Vértanúk tere 1. ✆ **1/269-4352** See p. 122.

Walk south about a ¼ of a mile toward the historic Chain Bridge, which you will see in the distance:

❹ Chain Bridge ✺

The Chain Bridge crosses the Danube and empties out into Roosevelt Square. The bridge holds the distinction of being the first permanent crossing to link Buda and Pest. It was initiated at the behest of 19th-century Hungarian reformer Count István Széchenyi after bad weather in 1820 had forced him to wait 8 days before being able to get to his father's funeral. Designed by William Tierney Clark, an Englishman, the bridge was one of the largest suspension bridges of its time when it opened in 1849. According to legend the omission of sculpted tongues on the lions which guard the bridge at either end caused the sculptor to drown himself in the river out of shame. See p. 134. (Note: You might duck into the **Four Seasons Hotel Gresham Palace** ✺✺✺ while you're here to view its breathtaking interiors; see p. 73).

Walk across the Chain Bridge, and take the funicular up to the:

❺ Castle District ✺✺

Castle Hill, a UNESCO World Cultural Heritage site, consists of two parts: the Royal Palace itself and the so-called Castle District, a mostly reconstructed medieval city. For a detailed, 3-hour itinerary of this area, see "Walking Tour 2: The Castle District" in chapter 8, "Strolling Around Budapest."

Otherwise, this is a great area for walking and wandering. You might stop into a few highlights, including the **Hungarian National Gallery** ✺ (see p. 132), the **Budapest History Museum** ✺ (see p. 132), and the **Ludwig Museum of Contemporary Art** ✺ (see p. 136).

6 RIVALDA CAFÉ & RESTAURANT

After a long day walking and sightseeing, you might want to have a meal at the Rivalda Café & Restaurant. This restaurant, the brainchild of the Canadian-Hungarian Agnes Weininger, retains the charm of the world of theater that Hungarians love so much. Here, a sole saxophonist plays his lonely tunes, dwarfed by the château yellow backdrop at the far end of the restaurant. Theater lights and riggings adorn the ceilings; the walls are painted with the backdrops of plays and are lined with caricatures of famous Hungarian actors. I. Színház u. 5-9. ✆ 1/489-0236. See p. 116.

After dinner, you might head back to your hotel to relax for a bit so you'll be ready to:

7 Socialize at a Bar, Club, or Bistro

Get a glimpse of Budapest's lively nightlife culture first hand at a bar, club, or bistro. You'll find all levels of partying available, whether you're looking for hardcore clubbing or just a pub for drinks with the locals. You also might try a hotel bar (see "Best Hotel Bars" on p. 212). Bistros such as **Café Incognito** (see p. 123) and **Paris, Texas** (see p. 124) are quite popular places for late night drinks and socializing, and you'll find locals of all ages mingling here. Hungarians can be a bit shy at first, but they open up the more you talk to them. Why not chat them up about your day in the city? See chapter 10, "Budapest After Dark," and, for a few talking points, see "How to Start a Conversation With a Local," on p. 45.

2 The Best of Budapest in 2 Days

After seeing Inner Pest and the Castle District on Day 1, now you can have a walk around the **Outer Ring Boulevard.** Note the **Nyugati Railway Station,** a grand example of turn-of-the-20th-century architecture, and right behind it is the **WestEnd City Center,** where you will find the largest selection of shops in Budapest. Stop for coffee and a slice of *dobos torta* (layer cake) at the **Lukács Cukrászda,** just a block away from Oktogon on grand Andrássy út, then visit the **House of Terror** (in that order, for your sake). Then you can stroll over to **Heroes' Square** and the **Museum of Fine Arts.** But save a few hours of your afternoon for a day at Buda's **Gellért Hotel** and unwind in the **medicinal spa** waters there. Then get ready for dinner and an evening at a concert hall. *Start:* Nyugati Station.

1 Nyugati Railway Station

The historic Nyugati Pályaudvar, or Western Railway Station, was built by Gustave Eiffel's firm, the same company that put up Paris' famous Eiffel Tower. Unfortunately, Budapest doesn't seem to appreciate this monument much. While massive and glorious in its grandeur, the impressive glass structure is notoriously dirty, and the building houses a flashy disco and a McDonald's. Needless to say, both would be well worth moving. Adjacent to the railway station is the **WestEnd City Center,** central Europe's largest shopping center (see p. 189), with over 400 stores.

Walk toward Oktogon, noting the grand turn-of-the-20th-century Pest architecture, then walk up to Andrássy u. 70:

2 LUKÁCS CUKRÁSZDA

A faithful reproduction of a vintage coffee-house, this large, airy establishment was created decades after a coffeehouse of the same name closed its doors. Never too crowded, it's a great spot for a quiet bite to eat and a cup of joe. Andrássy u. 70. ✆ 1/302-8747. See p. 121.

After lunch, walk a bit down the street to Andrássy u. 60:

❸ Terror Háza (House of Terror) ☆☆
The former headquarters of the AVH secret police, this building is witness to some of the darkest days of 20th-century Hungary. (You will be glad you already ate lunch.) This museum was set up as a memorial to the victims of both Communism and Fascism, and is an attempt to recapture life under successive oppressive regimes in Hungary. The tearing down of the ugly exterior facade has been the subject of much debate, however; for political reasons it has remained the sore thumb of the grand Andrássy Boulevard. The building was the headquarters of the Nazis in 1944, and many individuals were tortured and murdered in the eerie cellars of this building. The Communist secret police were next to use the venue as a place for their own torture and oppression.

Walk up the majestic Andrássy boulevard toward Heroes' Square and City Park:

❹ Andrássy Boulevard ☆
Lined with trees and a wealth of beautiful apartment buildings, this is *fin de siècle* Pest's greatest boulevard that is recognized as a World Heritage Site by UNESCO. Andrássy út is the home to a lively cafe-and-bar scene, as well as a number of small museums. There are colorful terraces, and delicious cakes and ice cream are sold under the shade of the huge trees all the way up to Oktogon.

Once you reach the end of Andrássy boulevard, adjacent to the Museum of Fine Arts, the Múcsarnok, and City Park, you'll find:

❺ Heroes' Square ☆☆
Heroes' Square, built as a project of the millennium over a century ago, celebrates the arrival of the Magyar tribes in the Carpathian Basin. The statues represent the chronology of some 1,000 years of Hungarian history. In 1896 during the famous world exhibition, this space was the apex of some 200 pavilions that made up the festivities.

To your left you will find the **Museum of Fine Arts** ☆ (see p. 129). The museum is the main repository of foreign art in Hungary and has one of central Europe's major collections.

Take the Yellow metro line, the oldest in continental Europe until Deák Tér, then take the 47 tram to the Gellért Baths:

❻ The Gellért Baths ☆☆
Prepare yourself for a relaxing afternoon, and allow yourself a few hours at Budapest's most spectacular bathhouse. The Gellért Baths are located in Buda's Hotel Gellért, the oldest Hungarian spa hotel and an Art Nouveau jewel. Enter the baths through the side entrance. The exterior of the building is in need of restoration, but once inside the lobby, you'll be delighted by the details. The unisex indoor pool is without question one of Europe's finest, with marble columns, majolica tiles, and stone lion heads spouting water. The two single-sex Turkish-style thermal baths, off to either side of the pool through badly marked doors, are also glorious, though in need of restoration. See a listing on p. 150, and see a "Thermal Bathing 101" box on p. 151.

After your afternoon of thermal bathing, you may want to head back to your hotel to rest and freshen up for your evening, and then head out to dinner. You'll be going to dinner from your hotel, so it's difficult to recommend a restaurant based on itinerary location. You should choose a dining spot from chapter 6, "Where to Dine in Budapest" and make a pre-theater reservation.

❼ Attend a Nighttime Concert ☆☆
Spend an evening attending a concert at the **Ferenc Liszt Academy of Music** (p. 206), or the recently opened **National Concert Hall at the Palace of Art** ☆☆, both Budapest's finest concert halls: The first is a more classical hall, while the National Concert Hall is the most modern hall in Budapest. The fine arts are alive and well in Budapest, and a nighttime concert is the perfect cap for your short stint in the city. Note that performances usually start at 7:30 or 8pm.

3 The Best of Hungary's Side Trip Options

You've seen Budapest; now its time to get outside of the capital and explore the land of the Magyars. Since the average visitor to Hungary spends less than a week in the country, we've opted to give you a few side trip options from Budapest, rather than a 1-week or 10-day tour of the entire country. The train system is Budapest-centric, so a full Hungarian tour would be difficult anyway; you'd need several weeks, traveling by bus (time-consuming) or by car (dangerous if you're not used to European driving). But trains, though not quite luxurious, are easy and safe, and they usually cost less than 4,000 Ft ($20) round-trip.

This section lists four options for your Hungarian side trip: **Szentendre** is a charming village and artist colony only 20km from the smog of the capital; **Keszthely** is at the far end of Lake Balaton and away from the throngs of tourists; **Keszthely** is a small scenic town, not far from the beaches, and nearby **Héviz** has lots of recently opened spa-hotels; **Pécs** is a burgeoning cultural center which has lately been attracting many young travelers; and the Southern Hungarian city of **Szeged** is another cultural center and Hungary's "spice capital."

Option ❶: A Day in Szentendre ✿✿

After 2 days in Budapest, you might visit Szentendre (pronounced *Sen*-ten-dreh), an artists' colony just north of Budapest and one of the most visited spots in all of Hungary. Take the HÉV (regional train) from Budapest's Batthyány tér metro for a 45-minute ride.

Visit the **Margit Kovács Museum** ✿✿✿ and see a wonderful collection of the late Margit Kovács. Her depictions of peasant life in Hungary are heartwarming. Have a late lunch at the **Aranysárkány Vendéglő** ✿, and take a walk along the river. Then spend your afternoon exploring the many shops, museums and galleries in town. Fő tér, the main drag, is enticing, but explore all the side streets of this small, manageable town. Try **Régimódi** ✿ for dinner, and stay at the **Róz Panzió**, which overlooks the Danube. (Reserve both several weeks ahead.)

See the "Szentendre" section in chapter 11.

Option ❷: Two Days in Keszthely ✿ & Héviz ✿✿

Keszthely and Héviz are tucked away in a quiet corner of Hungary's very own little "sea," Lake Balaton, almost 200 km (125 miles) from Budapest. The towns sit right in a micro-climate area, with warm summers, clear skies, and beautiful vistas and hills.

From Budapest, take a 3-hour express (*gyors*) train from Déli Station to Keszthely. Then explore its **Festetics Mansion** ✿, **Carriage Museum**, or try the puppet museum, the **Babamúzeum**. After roaming around Keszthely, have a traditional Hungarian meal, with a traditional Unicum, at the **Margaréta Étterem**. At night, check out a show at the **Balaton Congress Center and Theater**, and stay either in a "private room" or at the **Danubius Hotel Helikon.**

The next day take a bus to Héviz, 8km (5 miles) northeast of Keszthely, and head straight to the **Rogner Hotel and Spa Therme** ✿✿. Take a dip in Europe's largest thermal lake, nearby, for a dip, or spend your whole day unwinding at the hotel. Spa treatments include a selection of health cures, sports, wellness or even medical treatment programs.

You might shorten this side trip by heading straight to Héviz, then tour Keszthely a bit and relax in the spa hotel at night. See the "Keszthely" section in chapter 12.

Option ❸: Two Days in Pécs 🏛🏛🏛

The popular Pécs is the most culturally vibrant Hungarian city outside of the capital—warm and arid, with lots of museums, galleries, and a large student population.

Take an early morning Inter City train from Budapest's Déli Station to Pécs, a 2½-hour ride. Visit the **Tivadar Csontváry Museum** 🏛 and the **Victor Vasarely Museum** 🏛, institutions that celebrate two of Hungary's most notable artists. The **Zsolnay Museum** 🏛🏛🏛 houses a vast collection of vases, plates, cups, figurines, and even ceramic paintings. Then check out the hustle and bustle of the **Pécsi Vásár** 🏛🏛 flea market, where you can find traditional Hungarian wares. Head up on the hill for dinner at the **Bagolyvár Étterem** 🏛, where you can enjoy a fine Hungarian wine before checking in at the fun, centrally located **Hotel Fönix** 🏛🏛.

The next morning, have a coffee and cake at the **Mecsek Cukrászda** before checking out Pécs' houses of worship, the **Pécs Cathedral**, the **Pécs Synagogue** 🏛, and the largest standing Turkish structure, the **Mosque of Pasha Gazi Kassim**.

See the section "The 2000-Year-Old City of Pecs" in chapter 14.

Option ❹: Two Days in Szeged 🏛

The Southern Hungarian town of Szeged gets a lot of traffic from Romanian and Serbian visitors so it's a diverse city, with lots of students. If you're in Hungary in the summer, come here for the **Szeged Summer Festival** 🏛, which offers rock operas, classical music, ballet and contemporary dance. In July, **Thealter** is a sort of European "fringe festival" of alternative theater.

From Budapest, take the train from Nyugati Station. Start off with a coffee and pastry at the famous **Virág Cukrászda**. Then learn about some local history at the **Móra Ferenc Museum**. Take a walk on the river's edge, then head back to **Kárász utca** 🏛🏛, the main walking street which is usually bustling with students. Have an upscale dinner at **Zodiákus** or a more casual, boisterous meal at **HBH Bajor Söröző** 🏛. Try to get a room at the reasonably priced and clean **Hotel Matrix**, not far from the center of town.

On your second day here, check out the **Polish Market (Lengyel Piac)** 🏛 on the Southern edge of town and visit the beautiful and historic **Synagogue** 🏛. Then head for some hearty fish stew at **Kiskőrösi Halászcsárda** 🏛.

See the "Szeged: Hungary's Spice Capital" section in chapter 14.

4

Getting to Know Budapest

In this chapter, you'll find a host of practical information that should be useful during your stay in Budapest—from neighborhood orientation to listings of the cheapest rental-car agencies, from how to use a pay phone to how to avoid taxi hustlers. Glance through this chapter before your arrival, and consult it during your stay.

1 Orientation

ARRIVING

BY PLANE The easiest way into the city is probably the **Airport Minibus** (☎ 1/ 296-8555; www.bud.hu), a public service of the LRI (Budapest Airport Authority). The minibus, which leaves every 10 or 15 minutes throughout the day, takes you directly to any address in the city. From either terminal, it costs 2,300 Ft ($12); the price includes luggage transport. The trip takes from 30 minutes to an hour, depending on how many stops are made. The Airport Minibus desk is easily found in the main hall of both terminals. Minibuses also provide the same efficient service returning to the airport; arrange for your pickup from your hotel *1 full day in advance* by calling the number above. The minibus will pick up passengers virtually anywhere in the Budapest area.

We strongly discourage the use of cabs from the **Airport Taxi** fleet (☎ 1/296-6534), which are generally overpriced. A ride downtown from one of these cabs might cost significantly more than a recommended fleet (see "Getting Around," later in this chapter, for names and contact information). Unfortunately, for reasons no one has been able to explain to us with a straight face, cabs from the Airport Taxi fleet are the only cabs permitted to wait for fares on the airport grounds. However, dozens of cabs from the cheaper fleets that we recommend are stationed at all times at roadside pull-outs just off the airport property, a stone's throw from the terminal, waiting for radio calls from their dispatchers. All it takes is a phone call from the terminal and a cab will be there for you in a matter of minutes (see "Getting Around" and "By Taxi" later in this chapter). For three or more people traveling together (and maybe even two people), a taxi from a recommended fleet to the city, at approximately 4,500 Ft ($23), will be substantially cheaper than the combined minibus fares. A taxi from the airport to downtown takes about 20 to 30 minutes.

It's also possible to get to the city by public transportation; the trip takes about 1 hour total. Take the red-lettered **bus no. 93** to the last stop, Kőbánya-Kispest. From there, the Blue metro line runs to the Inner City of Pest. The cost is two transit tickets, which is 290 Ft ($1.45) all together; tickets can be bought from the automated vending machine at the bus stop (coins only) or from any newsstand in the airport.

Tips How to Start a Conversation With a Local

1. *"What's the city's best new open-air bar? I've heard about courtyard par-ties."* Most open air bars are not advertised, so you'll need to ask locals about them. See "Budapest's Underground Courtyard Parties," on p. 214.

2. *"Should Budapest be a 'cosmopolitan' city?"* This question divides Hun-garians. One camp wants a more urban, diversified city; another camp clings to old-world Budapest.

3. *"Why are they always repairing the Parliament?"* They have been chang-ing the stones of the parliament one by one, and everyone has a joke or two.

4. *"There sure is a lot of dog dung on the streets here."* Locals love to com-plain about dog owners who don't pick up after their pets.

5. *"What's the deal with all these Hungarian spy scandals?"* A lot of Soviet-era spies have been outed recently—from an ex Prime Minister to the Oscar-winning filmaker István Szabo.

Note: Tread carefully when talking about Hungarian politics. Hungary is politically divided between the conservative and right wing nationalists, lib-erals, and the socialists—and opinions can divide families. We advise you start with something light before moving into heated political debates.

BY TRAIN   Budapest has three major train stations: Keleti pályaudvar (Eastern Sta-tion), Nyugati pályaudvar (Western Station), and Déli pályaudvar (Southern Station). The stations' names, curiously, correspond neither to their geographical location in the city nor to the origins or destinations of trains serving them. Each has a metro sta-tion beneath it and an array of accommodations offices, currency-exchange booths, and other services.

Most international trains pull into bustling **Keleti Station** (✆ 1/314-5010), a clas-sic steel-girdered European train station located in Pest's seedy Baross tér, beyond the Outer Ring on the border of the VII and VIII districts. Various hustlers offering rooms and taxis woo travelers here. The Red line of the metro is below the station; numerous bus, tram, and trolleybus lines serve Baross tér as well.

Some international trains arrive at **Nyugati Station** (✆ 1/349-0115), another clas-sic designed by the Eiffel company and built in the 1870s. It's located on the Outer Ring, at the border of the V, VI, and XIII districts. A station for the Blue line of the metro is beneath Nyugati, and numerous tram and bus lines serve busy Nyugati tér.

Few international trains arrive at **Déli Station** (✆ 1/375-6293), an ugly run-down modern building in central Buda; the terminus of the Red metro line is beneath this train station.

MÁV operates a minibus that will take you from any of the three stations to the air-port for 2,000 Ft ($10) per person (minimum two persons), or between stations for 1,000 Ft ($5) per person (minimum two persons), with further discounts available for larger groups. To order the minibus, call ✆ 1/353-2722. Often, however, a taxi fare will be cheaper, especially for groups of two or more travelers (see "Getting Around," later in this chapter).

BY BUS   The Népliget Bus Station is the city's recently opened modern main bus terminal on the Red metro line at the **Stadionok** stop. The Blue line goes to the much smaller **Árpád híd bus station** that caters to domestic bus service only.

VISITOR INFORMATION

Since Budapest continues to undergo rapid changes, published tourist information is often out-of-date. The best information source in the city is **Tourinform** (© **1/317-8992;** www.hungarytourism.hu), the office of the Hungarian Tourist Board. Centrally located at V. Sütő u. 2, just off Deák tér (reached by all three metro lines) in Pest, the main office is open daily from 8am to 8pm. There is now another Tourinform office in the bustling entertainment district of Liszt Ferenc tér, open daily from 9am to 7pm in the high season (Liszt Ferenc tér is just down the street from Oktogon, reached by the Yellow line of the metro or tram no. 4 or 6). The staffs in both offices speak English and dispense advice on all tourist-related subjects, from concert tickets to pension rooms, from train schedules to horseback riding.

You can also access city information through the **"Touch Info"** user-friendly computer terminals located at the airport, at Déli Railway Station, at several of the larger metro stations, and in the market hall at Fővám tér.

Of the various free information pamphlets that you will find at tourist offices, pubs, and elsewhere in the city, the most useful is probably *Visitors' Guide,* a free English-language monthly publication with extensive entertainment listings for events in and around Budapest. The listings in *Pesti Est* and *Exit,* free mainly Hungarian-language weeklies that are widely available at clubs, bookstores, and other such places, are more extensive but harder, obviously, for the nonnative to understand. Three other useful free monthly publications are *Programme in Hungary, Budapest Panorama,* and *Where Budapest,* which are available at tourist offices and hotels. These contain information on scheduled cultural events.

The *Budapest Sun* (www.budapestsun.com) and *Budapest Times* (www.budapest times.hu), both English-language weekly newspapers, also have listings for concerts, theater, dance, film, and other events, along with restaurant reviews and the occasional interesting article; they are available at most hotels and many newsstands. *Budapest Week,* once a weekly magazine, is now strictly a website, **www.budapestweek.com,** which has a handy restaurant reservation network that lets you book your table online for free. **Ontheglobe.com** is another web-based resource that provides articles about Hungary and previews of cultural events. (Full disclosure: We write and edit ontheglobe.com, so we're a bit biased.) **Xpatloop.com** and **pestiside.hu** also attempt to map out Budapest's cultural and social scene.

CITY LAYOUT

You'll follow this section much better with a map in hand. The city of Budapest came into being in 1873, the result of a union of three separate cities: **Buda, Pest,** and **Óbuda.** Budapest, like Hungary itself, is defined by the **River Danube (Duna).** The stretch of the Danube flowing through the capital is fairly wide (the average width is 400m/1,325 ft.), and most of the city's historic sites are on or near the river. Eight bridges connect the two banks, including five in the city center. The Széchenyi Chain Bridge (Lánchíd), built in 1849, was the first permanent bridge across the Danube. Although it was blown up by the Nazis, it was rebuilt after the war.

MAIN STREETS & SQUARES

PEST   On the right bank of the Danube lies Pest, flat as a *palacsinta* (pancake), spreading far into the distance. Pest is the commercial and administrative center not just of the capital, but of all Hungary. Central Pest, the term used in this guide, is that part of the city between the Danube and the semicircular **Outer Ring boulevard (Nagykörút)**, stretches of which are named after former Austro-Hungarian monarchs: Ferenc körút, József körút, Erzsébet körút, Teréz körút, and Szent István körút. The Outer Ring begins at the Pest side of the Petőfi Bridge in the south and wraps itself around the center, ending at the Margit Bridge in the north. Several of Pest's busiest squares are found along the Outer Ring, and Pest's major east-west avenues bisect the Ring at these squares.

Central Pest is further defined by the **Inner Ring (Kiskörút)**, which lies within the Outer Ring. It starts at Szabadság híd (Freedom Bridge) in the south and is alternately named Vámház körút, Múzeum körút, Károly körút, Bajcsy-Zsilinszky út, and József Attila utca before ending at the Chain Bridge. Inside this ring is the **Belváros**, the historic Inner City of Pest.

Váci utca (distinct from Váci út) is a popular pedestrian-only shopping street between the Inner Ring and the Danube. It spills into **Vörösmarty tér**, one of the area's best-known squares. The **Dunakorzó (Danube Promenade)**, a popular evening strolling spot, runs along the river in Pest between the Chain Bridge and the Erzsébet Bridge. The historic Jewish district of Pest is in the **Erzsébetváros (Elizabeth Town)**, between the two ring boulevards.

Margaret Island (Margit-sziget) is in the middle of the Danube. Accessible via the Margaret Bridge or the Árpád Bridge, it's an enormously popular recreation park with restricted vehicular traffic.

BUDA & ÓBUDA   On the left bank of the Danube is Buda; to its north, beyond the city center, lies Óbuda. Buda is as hilly as Pest is flat. Streets in Buda, particularly in the hills, are not as logically arranged as those in Pest.

The two most dramatic points in central Buda are Castle Hill and Gellért Hill. **Castle Hill** is widely considered the most beautiful part of Budapest. A number of steep paths, staircases, and small streets go up to Castle Hill, although no major roads do. The easiest access is from Clark Ádám tér (at the head of the Chain Bridge) by funicular or from Várfok utca (near Moszkva tér) by foot or bus. Castle Hill consists of the royal palace itself, home to numerous museums, and the so-called **Castle District,** a lovely medieval neighborhood of small, winding streets, centered around Holy Trinity Square (Szentháromság tér), site of the Gothic Matthias Church. There's little traffic on Castle Hill, and the only industry is tourism.

Gellért Hill, to the south of Castle Hill, is named after the martyred Italian bishop who aided King István I (Stephen I) in his conversion of the Hungarian nation to Christianity in the 10th and 11th centuries. A giant statue of Gellért sits on the side of the hill, and on top is the Citadella, a fortress built by the Austrians.

An area of parks lies between Castle Hill and Gellért Hill, in the historic **Tabán** neighborhood, an impoverished quarter razed for hygienic reasons in the early 20th century. A few Tabán buildings still stand on the eastern edge of the quarter.

Below Castle Hill, along the Danube, is a long, narrow neighborhood known as **Watertown (Víziváros).** The main street of Watertown is Fő utca (Main St.).

Central Buda, the term used in this guide, is a collection of mostly low-lying neighborhoods below Castle Hill. The main square of central Buda is **Moszkva tér,** just north of Castle Hill. Beyond Central Buda, mainly to the east, are the Buda Hills.

Hungarian Address Terms

Navigating in Budapest will be easier if you are familiar with the following words (none of which are capitalized in Hungarian):

utca (abbreviated as *u.*)	street
út	road
útja	road of
körút (abbreviated as *krt.*)	boulevard
tér	square
tere	square of
köz	alley or lane
liget	park
sziget	island
híd	bridge
sor	row
part	riverbank
pályaudvar (abbreviated as *pu.*)	railway station
állomás	station

Óbuda is on the left bank of the Danube, north of Buda. Although the greater part of Óbuda is modern and drab, the area boasts both a beautiful old city center and the impressive Roman ruins of **Aquincum.** Unfortunately, the road coming off the Árpád Bridge slices the old city center in half, destroying its integrity. The historic center of the old city is **Fő tér (Main Sq.),** a square as lovely as any in Hungary. **Óbuda Island (Óbudai-sziget)** is home to a huge park and is the site each August of Hungary's own annual "Woodstock" music festival, called the Sziget (Island) Festival. For more on this event, see p. 18.

FINDING AN ADDRESS   Locating addresses in Budapest can be daunting at first, largely because of the strangeness of the Hungarian language. However, with a little practice and a good map, you should meet with success.

Budapest is divided into 22 districts, called *kerülets* (abbreviated as *ker.*). A Roman numeral followed by a period should precede every written address in Budapest, signifying the kerület; for example, XII. Csörsz utca 9 is in the 12th kerület. Because many street names are repeated in different parts of the city, it's very important to know which kerület a certain address is in. If the address you seek doesn't have a Roman numeral preceding it, you can also tell the kerület from the four-digit postal code. The middle two digits represent the kerület; thus, Csörsz utca 9, 1123 Budapest will be in district XII. The most popular neighborhoods for travelers are the V. kerület (the Inner City of Pest) and the I. Kerület (Buda's Castle District).

A common mistake made by visitors is to confuse **Váci út,** the heavily trafficked main road that goes from Nyugati Station toward the city of Vác, with **Váci utca,** the pedestrian-only street in the Inner City. Similarly, visitors sometimes mistake Vörösmarty utca, a station on the Yellow metro line, with Vörösmarty tér, the terminus of that same Yellow metro line. Read signs carefully—Hungarian is a language with a fine sense of detail. Refer to the "Hungarian Address Terms" box above.

Street signs are posted on buildings and give the name of the street or square, the kerület, and the building numbers found on that block. Even- and odd-numbered buildings are on opposite sides of the street. Numbers are seldom skipped; often you'll end up walking longer than you expected to reach a given number.

Many street names were changed following the systemic changes of 1989, reverting for the most part back to their pre–World War II names, aside from a handful of central streets with politically evocative former names, like Lenin körút (now Teréz körút) and Népköztársaság útja ("Road of the People's Republic," now Andrássy út).

Floors in buildings are numbered European style, meaning that the first floor is one flight up from the ground floor *(földszint)*, and so on. Addresses are usually written with the floor number in Roman numerals and the apartment number in Arabic numerals. For example, XII. Csörsz utca 9, IV/3 is on the fourth floor, Apartment 3.

STREET MAPS   A good map can save you lots of frustration in Budapest. Maps are sold throughout Budapest, but Cartografia, a Hungarian company, makes two maps that are substantially cheaper and cover Budapest in great detail. The Cartografia fold-out map is fine, but if you find its size awkward, you should pick up Cartografia's *Budapest Atlas.* Both maps are available throughout central Pest at kiosks and bookstores. Public transportation lines are shown on the maps, but, in places, the map is too crowded to make the lines out clearly. The BKV térkép (Budapest Transportation Authority map), available from metro ticket windows, is therefore recommended as a complement (see "Getting Around," below). If you plan on any hiking excursions in the Buda Hills, you should pick up the *A Budai Hegység map, no. 6* of the *Cartografia Turistatérképe* (Touring Map) series.

Our favorite **map stores** in Pest, where you can pick up the maps listed above (except the transit map), maps of other cities in Hungary, the Budapest-by-bike map, and international maps, are **Globe Map Shop,** at VI. Bajcsy-Zsilinszky út 37 (© **1/ 312-6001**), open Monday through Friday from 10am to 6pm (Metro: Arany János utca on the Blue line); and **Térképkirály (Map King),** at VI. Bajcsy-Zsilinszky 23 (© **1/472-0505;** www.mapking.hu), open Monday through Friday from 9am to 6pm, and Saturday 9am to 1pm (Metro: Arany János). You can also find maps in most of the bookstores recommended in chapter 9, "Budapest Shopping."

You'll also find an excellent online Budapest map with great search capabilities at **www.terkep.hu.** Enter the street name, and you'll get a detailed map.

NEIGHBORHOODS IN BRIEF
Pest

Inner City (Belváros) The historic center of Pest, the Belváros is the area inside the Inner Ring, bound by the Danube to the west. Many of Pest's historic buildings are found in the Belváros, as are the city's showcase luxury hotels and most of its best-known shopping streets.

Leopold Town (Lipótváros) Just to the north of the Belváros, Lipótváros is considered a part of central Pest.

Development began here at the end of the 18th century, and the neighborhood soon emerged as a center of Pest business and government. Parliament, plus a number of government ministries, courthouses, banks, and the former stock exchange, are all found here. Before the war, this was considered a neighborhood of the "high bourgeoisie."

Theresa Town (Terézváros) The character of Terézváros is defined by

Budapest at a Glance

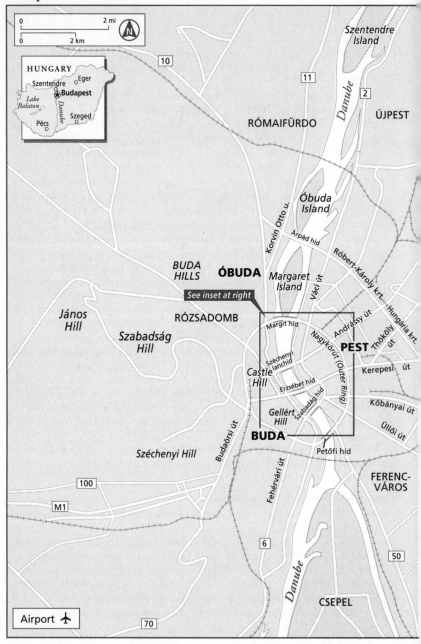

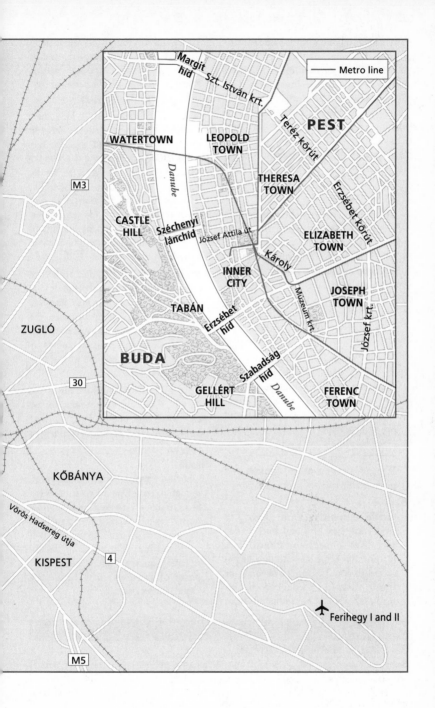

Metro line

BUDA

PEST

Margit híd

Szt. István krt.

Teréz körút

WATERTOWN

LEOPOLD TOWN

THERESA TOWN

M3

Danube

CASTLE HILL

Széchenyi lánchíd

Erzsébet körút

József Attila út

ELIZABETH TOWN

Károly

INNER CITY

TABÁN

Múzeum krt.

JOSEPH TOWN

ZUGLÓ

Erzsébet híd

József krt.

30

BUDA

Szabadság híd

Danube

GELLÉRT HILL

FERENC TOWN

KŐBÁNYA

Vörös Hadsereg útja

KISPEST

4

✈ Ferihegy I and II

M5

51

Andrássy út, the great boulevard running the length of the neighborhood from Hero's Square through Oktogon and down into the Inner City. This grand street has been regaining its reputation of elegance: Andrássy út is once again the "best address" in town. The Teréz körút section of the Outer Ring cuts through Terézváros; Oktogon is its major square. The area around Nagymező utca is the city's theater district.

Elizabeth Town (Erzsébetváros) Directly to the southeast of Terézváros, Erzsébetváros is the historic Jewish neighborhood of Pest. During the German occupation of 1944–45, a ghetto was constructed here. This district is still the center of Budapest Jewish life, though it is exceedingly run-down and is by no means as vibrant a place as it once was.

Joseph Town (Józsefváros) One of the largest central Pest neighborhoods, Józsefváros is to the southeast of Erzsébetváros. It has long had a reputation of being the seediest part of Pest, and for all appearances this reputation is a deserved one. József körút, the neighborhood's segment of the Outer Ring, is a center of prostitution and pornography.

Buda

Castle District (Várnegyed) The city's most beautiful and historic district dates to the 13th century. On a plateau above the surrounding neighborhoods and the Danube beyond, the Castle District is defined by its medieval walls. The immense Buda

Palace and its grounds fill the district's southern end. The northern end is home to small winding streets, Matthias Church, the Fisherman's Bastion, and the Hilton Hotel.

Watertown (Víziváros) A long, narrow neighborhood wedged between the Castle District and the Danube, the Víziváros is historically a quarter where fishermen and artisans reside. Built on the steep slope of Castle Hill, it has narrow alleys and stairs instead of roads in many places. Its main street, Fő utca, runs the north-south length of the Víziváros, parallel to and a block away from the river.

Buda Hills The Buda Hills are numerous remote neighborhoods that feel as if they're nowhere near, let alone within, a capital city. By and large, the hills are considered a classy place to live. Neighborhoods are generally known by the name of the hill on which they stand.

Rose Hill (Rózsadomb) This is the part of the Buda Hills closest to the city center and one of the city's most fashionable and luxurious residential neighborhoods.

Óbuda

Óbuda is a mostly residential area now, though its long Danube coastline was a favorite spot for workers' resorts under the old regime. Most facilities have been privatized, so a large number of hotels are found here. The extensive Roman ruins of **Aquincum** and the beautifully preserved old-town main square are Óbuda's chief claims to fame.

2 Getting Around

BY PUBLIC TRANSPORTATION

Budapest has an extensive, efficient, and inexpensive public transportation system. If you have some patience and enjoy reading maps, you can easily learn the system well enough to use it wisely. Public transportation, however, is not without its drawbacks. The biggest disadvantage is that except for 17 well-traveled bus and tram routes, all forms of transport shut down for the night at around 11:30pm (see "Night Service," below). Certain areas of the city, most notably the Buda Hills, are beyond the reach of this night service, and taxis are thus required for late-night journeys. Another problem with the system is that travel can be quite slow, especially during rush hour. A third disadvantage, pertinent mostly to travelers, is that Castle Hill can be reached in only three ways by public transportation and all of these modes of transportation are quite crowded in the high seasons. Finally, and perhaps most importantly, crowded public transport is the place where you are most likely to be targeted by Budapest's professional pickpockets (see "Staying Safe" in chapter 2, on p. 21).

FARES   **All forms of public transportation** (metro, bus, tram, trolleybus, some HÉV railway lines, and cogwheel railway) in Budapest require the self-validation of prepurchased tickets *(vonaljegy),* which cost 170 Ft (85¢) apiece (children under 6 travel free); single tickets can be bought at metro ticket windows, newspaper kiosks, and the occasional tobacco shop. There are also automated machines in most metro stations and at major transportation hubs, most of which have been recently modernized or installed and provide reliable service. We recommend that you buy a handful of tickets in advance so that you can avoid the trouble of constantly having to replenish your stock with the appropriate coins for the vending machines. For 1,450 Ft ($7.25) you can get a 10-pack *(tizes csomag),* and for 2,800 Ft ($14), you can get a 20-pack *(huszas csomag).*

While this standard ticket is valid on the metro, three types of optional single-ride metro tickets were introduced several years ago, making ticket buying a bit more complicated for those who are inclined to try to buy the most appropriate ticket for their journey. A "metro section ticket" *(metrószakaszjegy),* at 120 Ft (60¢), is valid for a single metro trip stopping at three stations or less. A "metro transfer ticket" *(metróátszállójegy),* at 270 Ft ($1.35), allows you to transfer from one metro line to another on the same ticket, without any limit to the number of stations that the train stops at during your journey. And a "metro section transfer ticket" *(metró-szakaszátszállójegy),* at 185 Ft (90¢), allows you to transfer from one metro line to another, but only for a trip totaling five or fewer stops.

For convenience, we recommend that you purchase a day pass or multiday pass while in Budapest. Passes need only be validated once, saving you the hassle of having to validate a ticket every time you board the metro. A pass will probably save you some money, too, as you are likely to be getting on and off public transportation all day long. Day passes *(napijegy)* cost 1,350 Ft ($6.75) and are valid until midnight of the day of purchase. Buy them from metro ticket windows; the clerk validates the pass at the time of purchase. A 3-day pass *(turistajegy)* costs 2,700 Ft ($14) and a 7-day travelcard *(hetijegy)* costs 3,100 Ft ($16); these have the same validation procedure as the day pass.

For longer stays in Budapest, consider a 2-week pass *(kéthétibérlet)* at 4,050 Ft ($20), or a monthly pass *(havibérlet)* or 30-day pass *(30 napos bérlet),* both at 6,250 Ft ($31). These two passes are available only at major metro stations, and you need to bring a regulation passport photo.

Dark-blue-uniformed inspectors (who even now flip out a hidden red armband when approaching you—a remnant of the not-too-distant past when they traveled the metro in plain clothes) frequently come around checking for valid tickets, particularly at the top or bottom of the escalators to metro platforms. On-the-spot fines of 2,000 Ft ($10) are assessed to fare dodgers; pleading ignorance generally doesn't work. Given how inexpensive public transport is, risking a time-consuming altercation with metro inspectors is probably not worth it. Metro tickets are good for 1 hour for any distance along the line you're riding, except for metro section tickets *(metrószakaszjegy),* which are valid only for 30 minutes. You may get off and reboard with the same ticket within the valid time period.

The **Budapest Card,** a tourist card that we do not particularly recommend (it does not pack any value), combines a 3-day *turistajegy* (transportation pass) with free entry to certain museums and other discounts.

SCHEDULES & MAPS   All public transport operates on rough schedules, posted at bus and tram shelters and in metro stations. The schedules are a little confusing at first, but you'll get used to them. The most important thing to note, perhaps, is when the last ride of the night departs: Many a luckless traveler has waited late at night for a bus that won't be calling until 6am!

The transportation map produced by the Budapest Transport Authority *(BKV térkép)* is available at most metro ticket windows for a small fee. Since transportation routes are extremely difficult to read on most city maps, we suggest that you buy one of these handy maps if you plan to spend more than a few days in the city. In addition, on the map's reverse side is a full listing of routes, including the all-important night-bus routes.

NIGHT SERVICE   Most of the Budapest transportation system closes down between 11:30pm or midnight and 5am. There are, however, 17 night routes (13 bus and 4 tram), and they're generally quite safe. A map of night routes is posted at many central tram and bus stops, and a full listing appears on the BKV transportation map. The no. 78É night bus follows the route of the Red metro line, while the no. 14É night bus follows the route of the Blue metro line. Though night buses often share the same numbers as buses on daytime routes (though with an É suffix, meaning *éjszaka,* or night), they may actually run different routes. Night buses require the standard, self-validated ticket. Many night buses skip stops, so pay attention.

UNDERPASSES   Underpasses are found beneath most major boulevards in Budapest. Underpasses are often crowded with vendors, shops, and the like; and many of them have as many as five or six different exits, each letting you out onto a different part of the square or street. Signs direct you to bus, tram, trolleybus, and metro stops, often using the word *fele,* meaning "toward." *Note:* Although Budapest is a very safe city, especially when compared to American cities of comparable size, underpasses tend to be among the more menacing places late at night, as various lowlifes enjoy hanging out in these subterranean confines.

Directions given throughout this book use a metro station as a starting point whenever possible. In cases where that's simply impossible, other major transportation hubs, such as Móricz Zsigmond körtér in Southern Buda, are used as starting points.

BY METRO

You'll no doubt spend a lot of time in the Budapest metro. The system is clean and efficient, with trains running every 3 to 5 minutes from about 4:30am until about 11:30pm. The main shortcoming is that there are just three lines, only one of which crosses under the Danube to Buda. (A fourth line has long been planned, but it will be several years before it becomes a reality.) The three lines are universally known by color—Yellow, Red, and Blue. Officially, they have numbers as well (1, 2, and 3, respectively), but all Hungarians refer to them by color, and all signs are color coded. All three lines converge at **Deák tér**, the only point where any lines meet.

The **Yellow (1) line** is the oldest metro on the European continent. Built in 1894 as part of the Hungarian millennial celebration, it has been refurbished and restored to its original splendor. Signs for the Yellow line, lacking the distinctive colored M, are harder to spot than signs for the Blue and Red lines. Look for signs saying *földalatti* (underground). Each station has two separate entrances, one for each direction. The Yellow line runs from Vörösmarty tér, site of Gerbeaud's Cukrászda in the heart of central Pest, out the length of Andrássy út, past the Városliget (City Park), ending at Mexikói út, in a trendy residential part of Pest known as Zugló. So, depending on the direction you're heading, enter either the side marked IRÁNY MEXIKÓI ÚT or IRÁNY VÖRÖSMARTY TÉR. Incidentally, somewhere in the middle of the line is a stop called Vörösmarty utca; this is a small street running off Andrássy út and should not be confused with the terminus, Vörösmarty tér. (However, at each of these stops you will find a splendid traditional coffeehouse, Gerbaud and Lukács, respectively.) It's worth taking a ride on this line, with its distinct 19th-century atmosphere.

The **Red (2)** and **Blue (3) lines** are modern metros and to reach them you descend long, steep escalators. The Red line runs from Örs vezér tere in eastern Pest, through the center, and across the Danube to Batthyány tér, Moszkva tér, and finally Déli Station. Keleti Station is also along the Red line. The Blue line runs from Kőbánya-Kispest, in southeastern Pest, through the center, and out to Újpest-Központ in northern Pest. Nyugati Station is along the Blue line.

On the street above stations of both the Red and Blue lines are distinctive colored **M** signs. Tickets should be validated at automated boxes before you descend the escalator. When changing lines at Deák tér, you're required to validate another ticket (unless you have a special "metro transfer ticket"). The orange validating machines are in the hallways between lines but are easy to miss, particularly if there are big crowds.

BY BUS

There are about 200 different bus *(busz)* lines in greater Budapest. Many parts of the city, most notably the Buda Hills, are best accessed by bus. Although buses are the most difficult to use of Budapest's transportation choices, with patience (and a BKV map) you'll be able to get around in no time. With the exception of night buses, most lines are in service from about 4:30am to about 11:30pm. Some bus lines run far less frequently (or not at all) on weekends, while others run far more frequently (or only) on weekends. This information is both on the reverse of the BKV transportation map and on the schedules posted at every bus stop.

Black-numbered local buses constitute the majority of the city's lines. Red-numbered buses are express; generally, but not always, the express buses follow the same routes as local buses with the same number, simply skipping certain stops along the way. If the red number on the bus is followed by an *E*, the bus runs nonstop between terminals (whereas an *É*—with an accent mark—signifies *éjszaka*, meaning night). Depending on your destination, an express bus may be a much faster way of traveling. A few buses are labeled by something other than a number; one you'll probably use is the *Várbusz* (Palace Bus), a minibus that runs between Várfok utca, up the steep hillside from Buda's Moszkva tér, and the Castle District. The buses themselves have always been blue, though now some express buses are beginning to appear in red.

Tickets are self-validated onboard the bus by the mechanical red box found by each door. You can board the bus by any door. Unlike metro tickets, bus tickets are valid not for the line, but for the individual bus; you're not allowed to get off and reboard another bus going in the same direction without a new ticket. Tickets cannot be purchased from the driver; see "Fares" on p. 53 for information on where to purchase public transportation tickets.

The biggest problem for bus-riding travelers is the drivers' practice of skipping stops when no one is waiting to get on and no one has signaled to get off. To signal your intention to get off at the next stop, press the button above the door (beware—some drivers open only the doors that have been signaled). Most stops don't have their names posted; a list of stops is posted inside all buses, but if stops are skipped, you may lose track. Chances are, though, that the locals riding a given bus will know exactly where your stop is, and will kindly help you to reach your stop. You can also ask the driver to let you know when he has reached your stop.

Avoid buses in central areas during rush hours, since traffic tends to be quite bad. It pays to go a bit out of your way to use a metro or tram at these times instead, or simply to walk.

BY TRAM

You'll find Budapest's 34 bright-yellow tram lines (known as *villamos* in Hungarian) very useful, particularly nos. 4 and 6, which travel along the Outer Ring (Nagykörút), and nos. 47 and 49, which run along the Inner Ring. Tram no. 2, which travels along the Danube on the Pest side between Margit híd and Boráros tér, provides an incredible view of the Buda Hills, including the Castle District, and is far better than any sightseeing tour on a bus.

Tickets are self-validated onboard. As with buses, tickets are valid for one ride, not for the line itself. Trams stop at every station, and all doors open, regardless of whether anyone is waiting to get on. *Important:* The buttons near the tram doors are for emergency stops, not stop requests.

When a tram line is closed for maintenance, replacement buses ply the tram route. They go by the same number as the tram, with a V (for *villamos*) preceding the number. See "Fares" on p. 53 for information on where to purchase public transportation tickets.

BY TROLLEYBUS

Red trolleybuses are electric buses that receive power from a cable above the street. There are only 14 trolleybus lines in Budapest, all in Pest. Of particular interest to train travelers is no. 73, the fastest route between Keleti Station and Nyugati Station. All the information in the "By Bus" section above regarding boarding, ticket validation, and stop-skipping applies to trolleybuses as well. See "Fares" on p. 53 for information on where to purchase public transportation tickets.

BY HÉV

The **HÉV** is a suburban railway network that connects Budapest to various points along the city's outskirts. There are four HÉV lines; only one, the Szentendre line, is of serious interest to visitors (see chapter 11, "The Danube Bend").

The terminus for the Szentendre HÉV line is Buda's Batthyány tér, also a station on the Red metro line. The train makes 10 stops in northern Buda and Óbuda en route to Szentendre. Most hotels, restaurants, and sights in northern Buda and Óbuda are best reached by the HÉV (so indicated in the directions given throughout this book). To reach Óbuda's Fő tér (Main Sq.), get off at the Árpád híd (Árpád Bridge) stop.

The HÉV runs regularly between 4am and 11:30pm. For trips within the city limits, the cost is one transit ticket, self-validated as on a bus or tram. Tickets to Szentendre cost 452 Ft ($2.25) (minus 170 Ft/85¢ for the portion of the trip within city limits if you have a valid day pass). HÉV tickets to destinations beyond the city limits are available at HÉV ticket windows at the Batthyány tér station, at the Margit híd station, or from the conductor onboard (no penalty assessed for such purchase).

BY COGWHEEL RAILWAY & FUNICULAR

Budapest's **cogwheel railway** *(fogaskerekű)* runs from Városmajor, across the street from the Hotel Budapest on Szilágyi Erzsébet fasor in Buda, to Széchenyi-hegy, one terminus of the Children's Railway (Gyermek Vasút) and site of Hotel Panoráma. The cogwheel railway runs from 5am to 11pm, and normal transportation tickets (see "Fares," above; self-validated onboard) are used. The pleasant route twists high into the Buda Hills; at 170 Ft (55¢), it is well worth taking just for the ride.

The **funicular** *(sikló)* connects Buda's Clark Ádám tér, at the head of the Széchenyi Chain Bridge, with Dísz tér, just outside the Buda Castle. The funicular is one of only two forms of public transportation serving the Castle District (the **Várbusz** and bus no. 16 are the other possibilities; see "By Bus," above). An extremely steep and short ride (and greenhouse-hot on sunny days), the funicular runs at frequent intervals from 7:30am to 10pm (closed on alternate Mon). Tickets cost 650 Ft ($3.25) to go up, and 550 Ft ($3) on the way down for adults and 350 Ft ($1.75) for children regardless of direction.

BY TAXI

We divide Budapest taxis into two general categories: large organized fleets and private fleets or privately owned taxis. If you only follow one piece of advice in this book, it's this: Do business with the former and avoid the latter. Because taxi regulations permit fleets (or private drivers) to establish their own rates (within certain parameters), fares vary greatly between the different fleets and among the private unaffiliated drivers.

The best rates are invariably those of the larger fleet companies. We particularly recommended **City Taxi** (© 1/211-1111). Other reliable fleets include **Volántaxi** (© 1/466-6666), **Rádió Taxi** (© 1/377-7777), **Fő Taxi** (© 1/222-2222), **Tele5** (© 1/355-5555), **6×6** (© 1/266-6666), and **Budataxi** (© 1/233-3333). You can call one of these companies from your hotel or from a restaurant—or ask whomever is in charge to call for you—even if there are other private taxis waiting around outside. You will seldom, if ever, wait more than 5 minutes for a fleet taxi unless you're in an extremely remote neighborhood (or in bad weather).

Finally, you are most likely dealing with a dishonest driver if he asks you to pay for his return trip, asks to be paid in anything but forints, or quotes you a "flat rate" in lieu of running the meter. If you desire a station wagon, ask for a *"kombi"* when calling for your taxi, and in the summer you can also request an air-conditioned vehicle.

Tipping is usually not more than 10%. Hungarians usually round the bill up. If you think the driver has cheated you, then you certainly should not tip. In fact, it is recommended that you call the company and complain, as most will punish their members for untoward behavior.

Though most people call for a taxi or pick one up at a taxi stand (a stand is basically any piece of sidewalk or street where one or more drivers congregate), it is possible to hail one on the street, though the base rate will be substantially higher. At taxi stands in Budapest, the customer chooses with whom to do business; as we said before, go with a cab from one of the recommended fleets, even if it's not the first in line.

Additional pointers are found in the brochure *Taking a Taxi in Budapest,* available at Tourinform and elsewhere.

BY CAR

There's no reason to use a car for sightseeing in Budapest. You may, however, wish to rent a car for trips out of the city (see chapters 11–14). Although Hertz, Avis, National, and Budget offices can be found in town and at the airport, marginally better deals can be had from some of the smaller companies. You are urged to reserve a rental car as early as possible. If you reserve from abroad, ask for written confirmation by fax or e-mail. If you don't receive a confirmation, it's wise to assume that the reservation has not been properly made.

We have quoted rates for the least expensive car type currently listed by each of the following recommended agencies:

We recommend **Fox Auto Rent,** XXII. Nagytétényi út 48–50, 1222 Budapest (ⓒ **1/382-9000;** fax 1/382-9003; www.fox-autorent.com), which rents the Fiat Panda for 44€ ($55) per day for a rental of 1 to 3 days, and 223€ ($279) for a week, insurance and mileage included. They also require a deposit of 400€ ($500) on a credit card. Though located far from the city center, Fox will deliver the car to you at your hotel without charge between 8am to 6pm.

The more expensive **Denzel Europcar InterRent,** VIII. Üllöi út 60–62, 1082 Budapest (ⓒ **1/477-1080;** fax 1/477-1099; www.nationalcar.hu), offers the Opel Corza or Fiat Punto for 55€ ($69) per day plus 9€ ($11) for insurance, or 46€ ($58) per day for 3 to 4 days. They also have a rental counter at the airport (ⓒ **1/296-6610**), but here you pay an additional 12% airport tax.

DRIVING TIPS

DRIVING REGULATIONS   The speed limit in Hungary is 50kmph (30 mph) in built-up areas, 90kmph (50 mph) on main roads, and 130kmph (75 mph) on motorways. Safety belts must be worn in the front seat and, when available, in the back seat; children under 6 may not sit in the front seat and may not travel without a safety belt. Horns may not be used in built-up areas, except in emergencies. Headlights must be on at all times on all intercity roads and highways. Drunk-driving laws are strictly enforced; any alcohol content in the driver's blood is illegal.

Cars are required to have in them at all times a first-aid kit and a reflective warning triangle. A decal indicating the country of registration is also required. These items should be included in all rental cars, so check or ask when you pick up your car. If you're driving a rental car rented from another country, make sure you have the so-called green card (proof of international insurance), not automatically given by all rental agencies. Rental agencies usually provide authorized permissions to cross international borders, so we recommend that you check your itinerary with the firm before departure. Hungarian police set up random checkpoints where cars are pulled over and drivers are made to present their papers. If all your papers are in order, you'll have no trouble. Still, foreigners residing in Budapest and driving cars with foreign plates report being routinely stopped by police and fined for rather ridiculous infractions. Hungarian police are no longer allowed to impose on-the-spot fines for driving violations, a favorite and much-abused practice of years gone by; they now must issue written tickets for infractions.

There are plenty of gas stations along major routes. Newly built sections of the major highways outside Budapest require payment of a toll. *Warning:* Some neighborhoods—notably Buda's Castle District—allow vehicular access only to cars with special resident permits.

BREAKDOWN SERVICES   The **Hungarian Auto Club (Magyar Autóklub)** operates a 24-hour free emergency breakdown service: Call ⓒ **188** (note, however, that not all operators speak English).

The Autóklub also has an **International Aid Service Center,** at II. Rómer Flóris u. 4/a (ⓒ **1/345-1744**), established specifically for international motorists. Stay on the line; you will be connected. Services provided include emergency aid, towing, and technical advice.

PARKING   Parking is very difficult in central Pest and parts of central Buda, but is relatively easy elsewhere in the city. People have always parked virtually anywhere that a car would fit—on the sidewalk, in crosswalks, and so on, but the introduction of awkward posts lined up along the curb in inner Pest has made this practice much more difficult in this part of the city. Cars are regularly fined for parking in illegal spots, so don't risk parking illegally. Parking fines are left on the windshield in a small plastic pouch. On practically all central streets, a *fizető* sign indicates that there's a fee for parking in that area. Purchase a ticket from the machine and leave the ticket on the dashboard (visible through the window). In some cases, a parking fee will be collected by an agent who will approach you as you park. Fees vary with the centrality of the location. There are several parking garages in the Inner City, including those at V. Aránykéz u. 4–6, V. Szervita tér 8, and VII. Nyár u. 20. The newest and biggest parking lot is located in the heart of the city, underground next to the cultural center called "The Ditch" (Gödör), in Erzsébet tér. Many vacant lots on Pest's Inner City side streets now house makeshift parking lots; prices are lower than they are at garages, but the lots are not always as secure.

BY BIKE

Budapest is not a bicycle-friendly city by any stretch of the imagination, though an effort to incorporate bike lanes into the city streets is underway. There are many bikers in Budapest, and they're always lobbying for better conditions and more bike paths (and yet most of them still refuse to wear helmets; go figure). As it stands, for safety reasons, *we do not recommend biking in the city, even with a helmet.*

That said, the brave and undaunted can rent bikes from **Charles Apartment House,** I. Hegyalja út 23 (ⓒ **1/201-1796**), for 2,000 Ft ($10) per day. A 20,000 Ft ($100) security deposit is required. Centrally located **Yellow Zebra Bikes,** V. Sütő u. 2 (ⓒ **1/329-2746;** www.yellowzebrabikes.com), open daily 9am to 7:30pm in high season, offers budget-minded guided bike tours, with optional helmets. Bike rentals cost 3,000 Ft ($15) per day, with a guided tour setting you back 5,500 Ft ($28) for an adult, 5,000 Ft ($25) for students. In contrast to the rest of Budapest, Margaret Island is closed to cars and, thus, is ideal for casual bike riding. **Bringóhintó,** XIII. Hajós A. sétány (ⓒ **1/329-2746**), on Margaret Island, rents bikes. Look for the map titled *Kerékpárral Budapeste* ("Budapest on Bike"), which shows biking trails and streets with bike lanes around the city. Inquire about organized bike tours at the tourism offices, where you can also pick up a Hungary bike tour map. A welcome development for cyclists is the bike paths along Lake Balaton (see chapter 12, "The Lake Balaton Region").

FAST FACTS: Budapest

American Express Budapest's only American Express office is between Vörös-marty tér and Deák tér in central Pest, at V. Deák Ferenc u. 10, 1052 Budapest (℗ **1/235-4330** or 1/235-4300; fax 1/267-2028). It's open Monday through Friday from 9am to 5pm. There's an American Express cash ATM on the street in front of the office.

For lost traveler's checks, come to the office as soon as you can and they will assist you. If you do not want to wait that long, use a 20 Ft coin to initiate a call to England; the call ((℗ **06/800-11128**) is otherwise toll-free. For a lost credit card, make a local call to ℗ **1/484-2639.** If this is unsuccessful, try calling England at ℗ **00-44-181-551-1111** (or dial ℗ **00/800-04411** for the U.K. direct operator, and ask to call collect).

Area Code The country code for Hungary is **36;** the city code for Budapest is **1.**

ATM Networks See p. 15.

Babysitters The former top babysitting companies in the city recently went out of business, so be sure to ask your hotel about its services before you book. Better hotels, including the Four Seasons Hotel Gresham Palace (p. 73), can offer reliable babysitters for guests within 6 hours of a request.

Business Hours Most **stores** are open Monday through Friday from 10am to 6pm and Saturday from 9 or 10am to 1 or 2pm. Some shops close for an hour at lunchtime, and most stores are closed Sunday, except those in the central tourist areas. Some shop owners and restaurateurs also close for 2 weeks in August. On weekdays, food stores open early, at around 6 or 7am, and close at around 6 or 7pm. Certain grocery stores, called "nonstops," are open 24 hours (however, a growing number of shops call themselves "nonstop" even if they close for the night at 10 or 11pm). **Banks** are usually open Monday through Thursday from 8am to 3pm and Friday from 8am to 2pm. **Museums** in Budapest are usually open Tuesday through Sunday from 10am to 6pm.

Car Rentals See "Getting Around," earlier in this chapter.

Climate See "When to Go" in chapter 2, "Planning Your Trip to Budapest."

Currency See "Money," in chapter 2, "Planning Your Trip to Budapest."

Doctors & Dentists We recommend the **American Clinic,** I. Hattyu u. 14 (℗ **1/224-9090;** www.firstmedcenters.com), a private outpatient clinic with two U.S. board–certified physicians and several English-speaking Hungarian doctors. There is an OB-GYN on staff, and an ultrasound machine on the premises; referrals are available for specialists. Payment is expected at the time of service (credit cards accepted), but the office will provide coded invoices in English in a form acceptable to most insurance carriers. The clinic is located in a modern building across the street from the Mammut shopping center, just a few minutes by foot from Moszkva tér (Red metro). Another suitable facility is **IMS,** a private outpatient clinic at XIII. Váci út 184 (℗ **1/329-8423**), with English-speaking doctors; it's reached via the Blue metro line (Gyöngyös utca). The same drill applies with respect to payment and insurance claims. IMS also operates an emergency service after-hours and on weekends, III. Vihar u. 29 (℗ **1/388-8257**).

For dental work, we recommend **Dr. Susan Linder,** who has an office at II. Vihorlat u. 23 (ⓒ 1/335-5245) (by foot from Pasaréti tér, which is reached by bus no. 5 or 29). Dr. Linder is the dentist for the U.S. and British embassies. Her hours are Monday, Tuesday, and Thursday from 8am to 6pm by appointment; she is also available for emergencies, except on weekends. In a pinch, you can also try **S.O.S. Dent Kft,** a 24-hour emergency dental clinic at VII. Király u. 14 (ⓒ 1/269-6010), just a few minutes by foot from Deák tér (all three metro lines); look for the red cross on the building. The dentists on staff do not all speak English. One more useful medical emergency number is the **Anonymous AIDS Advisory Service** (ⓒ 1/466-9283).

Driving Rules See "Getting Around," earlier in this chapter.

Drugstores See "Pharmacies," below.

Electricity Hungarian electricity is 220 volts, AC. If you plan to bring any North American electrical appliances, you'll need a 110–220 volt transformer/converter. Transformers are available at electrical supply stores throughout the city. We recommend **Trakis-Hetra Ltd.,** at VII. Nefelejcs u. 45 (ⓒ 1/342-5338 or 1/322-1459; metro: Keleti pu. [Red line]). If there is a transformer built into the adapter of the appliance that you are bringing, as there are in many laptop computers, you will need only a small adapter to fit the North American flat plugs into the round holes in the wall. This adapter may be hard to find in Budapest, so buy one before you depart.

Embassies The embassy of **Australia** is at XII. Királyhágó tér 8–9 (ⓒ 1/457-9777); the embassy of **Canada** is at II. Ganz u. 12-14 (ⓒ 1/392-3360); the embassy of the **Republic of Ireland** is at V. Szabadság tér 7 (ⓒ 1/302-9600); the embassy of the **United Kingdom** is at V. Harmincad u. 6 (ⓒ 1/266-2888); and the embassy of the **United States** is at V. Szabadság tér 12 (ⓒ 1/475-4400). New Zealand does not have an embassy in Budapest, but the U.K. embassy can handle matters for New Zealand citizens.

Emergencies Dial ⓒ **104** for an ambulance, ⓒ **105** for the fire department, or ⓒ **107** for the police. ⓒ **1/438-8080** is a 24-hour hot line in English for reporting crime.

Etiquette & Customs Old-world etiquette is still very much alive in Hungary. People speak very politely, hold doors open for women, readily give up seats on the bus for those who need them, and so on.

Eyeglasses Optika or ofotért is the Hungarian name for an optometrist's shop. The word for eyeglasses is *szemüveg.*

Internet Access The best place in town is **Kávészünet,** V. Tátra u. 12/b (ⓒ 1/236-0853). This is a comfortable and friendly place located in between Nyugati Pályaudvar and Jászai Mari tér, and is open Monday to Friday 8am to 10pm and 10am to 8pm on weekends. They serve coffee, sandwiches, and cakes and have rotating exhibitions of young artists, illustrators, or photographers. Minimum time is 15 minutes for just 100 Ft (50¢).

Another convenient spot is the 24-hour **Internet Café,** VI. Andrássy út 46 (ⓒ 1/474-0929). They provide full service, including Internet access (minimum 15 min. for 200 Ft/$1), CD burning for 500 Ft ($2.50) apiece, and scanning for

200 Ft ($1) per page. **Ami Internet Coffee,** V. Váci u. 40 ((C) **1/267-1644;** www.amicoffee.hu), near Ferenciek tére (Blue line), is open daily from 9am to 2am. This drab space has more than 20 terminals, and the cost is 200 Ft ($1) for up to 15 minutes, with pricing by 15-minute intervals. **Yellow Zebra,** V. Sütő utca 2 ((C) **1/266-8777;** www.yellowzebrabikes.com), a friendly hangout for backpackers, is open daily 8:30am to 8pm.

Language Hungarian *(Magyar),* a member of the Finno-Ugric family of languages, is unrelated to any of the languages of Hungary's neighboring countries. By and large, Hungarians accept the obscurity of their language and welcome and encourage any attempts at communication made by international travelers. Many Hungarians speak German and/or English. You shouldn't have much of a problem making yourself understood, particularly in Budapest. Everyone involved in tourism speaks at least a little English.

Colloquial Hungarian (published by Routledge, Chapman, Hall) is a good phrase book and comes with a cassette. Also, see "Appendix A: Help with a Tough Tongue," in the back of this book.

Laundry & Dry Cleaning Self-service launderettes *(patyolat)* are scarce in Budapest. The Mister Minit chain, a locksmith and shoe-repair service located in all large shopping centers throughout the inner city area, now offers a laundry service as well. Many hotels and pensions also provide laundry services. Private room hosts usually are happy to make a little extra money doing laundry.

Libraries The **United States Information Service (USIS)** has a public reference center in the Central Bank building, at V. Szabadság tér 7–9 ((C) **1/302-6200** or 1/302-0426). The USIS reference center holdings include a large CD-ROM database of recent newspapers and magazines, as well as a variety of reference texts. The former USIS book collection is now a part of the library of the **Faculty of the Arts at ELTE University,** XIV. Ajtósi Dürer sor 19–20 ((C) **1/343-0148,** ext. 4435). Known as the "American Library," it is open to the public. Hours reflect the university's calendar, so call ahead. It's open Monday through Friday from 9am to 5pm (except opening at noon on Wed).

The **British Council Information Centre** is at VII. Benczúr u. 26 ((C) **1/478-4751;** www.britishcouncil.hu). It's open weekdays from 11am to 5pm, with extended hours until 7pm on Monday and Thursday. Open Saturday 9am to 1pm.

Liquor Laws Alcohol is sold all over the place, and is available for purchase at all times. The legal drinking age in Hungary is 18.

Lost & Found Be sure to tell all of your credit card companies the minute you discover your wallet has been lost or stolen, and file a report at the nearest police precinct. Your credit card company or insurer may require a police report number or record of the loss. Most credit card companies have an emergency toll-free number to call if your card is lost or stolen; they may be able to wire you a cash advance immediately or deliver an emergency credit card in a day or two. Visa's U.S. emergency number is (C) **800/847-2911** or 410/581-9994. American Express cardholders and traveler's check holders should call (C) **800/221-7282.** MasterCard holders should call (C) **800/307-7309** or 636/722-7111. For other credit cards, call the toll-free number directory at (C) **800/555-1212.**

If you need emergency cash over the weekend when all banks and American Express offices are closed, you can have money wired to you via **Western Union** (© **800/325-6000;** www.westernunion.com).

Identity theft and fraud are potential complications of losing your wallet, especially if you've lost your driver's license along with your cash and credit cards. Notify the major credit-reporting bureaus immediately; placing a fraud alert on your records may protect you against liability for criminal activity. The three major U.S. credit-reporting agencies are **Equifax** (© **800/766-0008;** www. equifax.com), **Experian** (© **888/397-3742;** www.experian.com), and **TransUnion** (© **800/680-7289;** www.transunion.com). Finally, if you've lost all forms of photo ID, call your airline and explain the situation; they might allow you to board the plane if you have a copy of your passport or birth certificate and a copy of the police report you've filed.

The **BKV** (Budapest Transportation Authority) lost-and-found office is at VII. Akácfa u. 18 (© **1/267-5299**). For items lost on a train or in a train station, call © **1/312-0213.** For items lost on an intercity bus (not on a local BKV bus), call © **1/318-2122.** Good luck.

Luggage Storage There are left-luggage offices (*csomagmegőrző* or *poggyász*) and lockers at all three major railroad stations. At Keleti, the office is in the main waiting room alongside Track 6. It's open 4am to midnight. At Nyugati, the office is in the waiting room behind the international ticket office and is open 24 hours. The lockers are nearby, and the cost is also the same as at Keleti. Déli Station has a new automated locker system in operation in the main ticket-purchasing area; the lockers are very large, and directions for use are provided by a multilingual computer.

Mail & Post Office Mail can be received by clients at American Express (see "American Express," above); a single Amex traveler's check is sufficient to prove that you're a client. Others can receive mail by asking friends and family to address letters to "c/o Poste Restante, Magyar Posta, Petőfi Sándor u. 17–19, 1052 Budapest, Hungary," and can pick mail up at this same building, Petőfi Sándor u. 17–19 (© **1/318-3947** or 36/1-487-1100). This confusing office (Mon–Sat 7am–9pm), not far from Deák tér (all metro lines), is the city's main post office. There are also post offices near Keleti and Nyugati stations. The post office near Keleti is at VIII. Baross tér 11/c (© **1/322-9013**), and is open Monday to Saturday 7am to 9pm. The post office near Nyugati is at VI. Teréz krt. 51 (© **1/312-1480**), and is open Monday to Saturday 7am to 9pm and Sunday 8am to 8pm.

Maps See "City Layout" under "Orientation," earlier in this chapter.

Names Hungarians write their names with the family name first, followed by the given name. When mentioning Hungarian names in this book, we have employed the international form of given name followed by family name. The only exception is with street names, where we have used the Hungarian style: hence Ferenc Deák (the man) but Deák Ferenc utca (the street).

Newspapers & Magazines The *International Herald Tribune, USA Today, Guardian, Guardian Weekly, The Economist, Financial Times, Times of London,*

European, Newsweek, the *Wall Street Journal Europe,* and *Time* are all commonly found in luxury hotels and at kiosks and bookstores in the central Pest neighborhood around Váci utca. At larger newsstands you can also find *People, Vogue, Harper's,* and, once in a blue moon, the *New York Times.* On any given day at **Sajtó Térkép,** with locations at V. Kálvin tér 3 (Blue line) and V. Városház u. 3–5 (Ferenciek tere, Blue line), you might also find such periodicals as *Barron's,* the *Nation,* the *GQ, Architectural Digest,* and *House & Garden.*

For English-language articles on current events and politics in Hungary, pick up the *Budapest Sun* or the *Budapest Times,* both weeklies. The free monthly *Visitors' Guide* provides listings of cultural events, as does the trilingual *Pesti Est, Where Magazine,* and the Web-based *Ontheglobe.com* (which your humble author writes and edits). All of these publications are widely available.

Passports **For Residents of the United States:** Whether you're applying in person or by mail, you can download passport applications from the U.S. State Department website at **http://travel.state.gov.** For general information, call the **National Passport Agency** (✆ **202/647-0518**). To find your regional passport office, either check the U.S. State Department website or call the **National Passport Information Center** (✆ **900/225-5674**); the fee is 55¢ per minute for automated information and $1.50 per minute for operator-assisted calls.

For Residents of Canada: Passport applications are available at travel agencies throughout Canada or from the central **Passport Office,** Department of Foreign Affairs and International Trade, Ottawa, ON K1A 0G3 (✆ **800/567-6868;** www.ppt.gc.ca).

For Residents of the United Kingdom: To pick up an application for a standard 10-year passport (5-year passport for children under 16), visit your nearest passport office, major post office, or travel agency or contact the **United Kingdom Passport Service** at ✆ **0870/521-0410** or search its website at www.ukpa.gov.uk.

For Residents of Ireland: You can apply for a 10-year passport at the **Passport Office,** Setanta Centre, Molesworth Street, Dublin 2 (✆ **01/671-1633;** www.irl gov.ie/iveagh). Those under age 18 and over 65 must apply for a €12 3-year passport. You can also apply at 1A South Mall, Cork (✆ **021/272-525**) or at most main post offices.

For Residents of Australia: You can pick up an application from your local post office or any branch of Passports Australia, but you must schedule an interview at the passport office to present your application materials. Call the **Australian Passport Information Service** at ✆ **131-232,** or visit the government website at www.passports.gov.au.

For Residents of New Zealand: You can pick up a passport application at any New Zealand Passports Office or download it from their website. Contact the **Passports Office** at ✆ **0800/225-050** in New Zealand or 04/474-8100, or log on to www.passports.govt.nz.

Pharmacies The Hungarian word for pharmacy is *gyógyszertár,* or occasionally, *patika.* Generally, pharmacies carry only prescription drugs. Some hotels advertise "drugstores," but these are just shops with soap, perfume, aspirin, and other nonprescription items. There are a number of 24-hour pharmacies in the city—every pharmacy posts the address of the nearest one in its window. If necessary, ask for a specific address at Tourinform. Your best bet for 24-hour service year-round is Oktogon Patika on Teréz körút, next to Hotel Radisson (off Oktogon square, tram nos. 4 and 6). If you are looking for basics like pantyhose, chapstick, and so on, you'll want to find a drugstore rather than a pharmacy. A number of European drugstore chains have set up shop in Budapest; look for the Drogerie Mart, know as DM.

Police   Dial ℂ **107** for the police.

Religious Services in English   Roman Catholic Masses are held at 5pm on Saturday in the **Jesuit Church of the Sacred Heart,** VII. Mária u. 25 (ℂ **1/318-3479**). Nondenominational services are given on Sunday at 10:30am at the **Óbuda Community Center,** III. Kiskorona u. 7 (ℂ **1/250-0288**). Presbyterian and Anglican services are held on Sunday at 11am at VI. Vörösmarty u. 51 (ℂ **1/246-2258**). The **Christian Science Society** is located at II. Kútvölgyi út 20–22. Jewish Hungarian-language services are held at the **main synagogue,** VII. Dohány u. 2–8 (ℂ **1/342-8949**), on Friday at 6pm and Saturday at 9am.

Restrooms   The word for toilet in Hungarian is *WC* (pronounced vay-tsay). *Női* means "women's"; *férfi* means "men's."

Safety   See p. 21 in chapter 2.

Shoe Repair   The Hungarian word for cobbler is *cipész* or *cipő javitás,* and scarcely a neighborhood in the city is without one. You can try a Mister Minit shop (a chain of minishops found in many major shopping areas) if all you need is something quick and professionally less demanding. Ask your hotel reception for the nearest cobbler.

Smoking   Smoking is forbidden in all public places (including all public transportation), except in most restaurants and pubs, where smoking is considered to be an indispensable part of the ambience. Although a 1999 law requires all restaurants to have a nonsmoking section, the fact is that most barely comply. Expect most restaurants to be smoky places. *Tilos a dohányzás* or *Dohányozni tilos* means "No Smoking."

Taxes   Taxes are included in restaurant and hotel rates, and in shop purchases. International travelers are entitled, upon leaving the country, to a refund of the 25% VAT on certain purchases. See chapter 9, "Budapest Shopping," for details.

Taxis   See "Getting Around," earlier in this chapter.

Telephone   **To make local phone calls:** The Hungarian phone company MATÁV provides much better service than in the past, but it still falls significantly short of Western standards. For best results, dial slowly and don't be too quick to trust a busy signal; rather, try again.

The **area code** for Budapest is 1, and all phone numbers in Budapest (except mobile phones) have seven digits. Phone numbers in this book are printed with the area code. Most other towns in Hungary have a two-digit area code and six-digit telephone numbers. To make a call from one Hungary area code to another, first dial 06; when you hear a tone, dial the area code and number. Numbers that begin with 06-20, 06-30, or 06-70 followed by a seven-digit number are **mobile**

phone numbers. Mobile phones are extremely popular and some of the listings in this book are mobile phone numbers. Be aware that all phone calls made to a mobile phone are charged as long-distance calls, regardless of the location of the caller or the receiver. Budapest telephone numbers are constantly changing as MATÁV continues to upgrade its system. (You should note, for instance, that any Budapest number beginning with a "1" has been changed; try replacing the 1 with a 3 or a 4.) Usually, if the number you are dialing has recently changed, you will get a recording first in Hungarian and then in English, indicating the new number. If further information is needed, dial (C) **198** for **local directory assistance.**

Public **pay phones** charge varying amounts for local calls depending on the time of day that you place your call. It's cheapest to call late in the evenings and on weekends. Public phones operate with 20, 50, and 100 Ft coins or with phone cards (in 50 or 120 units), which can be purchased from post offices, tobacco shops, supermarkets, travel agencies, and any MATÁV customer service office (MATÁV Pont).

Hotels typically add a surcharge to all calls (although some allow unlimited free local calls).

To call to Hungary from abroad: Dial the appropriate numbers to get an international dial tone (011 from the U.S.), then dial 36 (Hungary country code), followed by the appropriate city code (for Budapest, 1), followed by the six- or seven-digit telephone number.

To make international calls: To make international calls from Hungary, first dial 00 and then the country code (U.S. or Canada 1, U.K. 44, Ireland 353, Australia 61, New Zealand 64). Next you dial the area code and number. For example, if you wanted to call the British Embassy in Washington, D.C., you would dial 00-1-202/588-7800.

For international calls to the U.S., there are several options. Our preferred method these days is to make all international calls from abroad through a U.S.-based "callback" service. These services allow you to gain access to a U.S. dial tone from abroad, typically by dialing in to a computer in the U.S. that then automatically calls you back with the dial tone. International calls made in this manner are billed at competitive U.S. calling rates, which are still significantly cheaper than Hungarian international rates. These services generally charge an activation fee and a monthly maintenance fee, as well as other fees, so you should decide whether you are likely to be making enough calls for this service to be worthwhile. A company called **Kallback** seems to offer the best package; call (C) **800/959-5255** or 800/516-9992, or visit www.kallback.com.

Alternatively, you can use a phone card and access the international operator through a public phone, though older phones are less reliable; again, a 20 Ft coin is required to start the call. You can also place an international call at the post office at VI. Teréz krt. 51 (near Nyugati railway station), as well as from the following MATÁV offices: MATÁV Pont in West End City Center near Nyugati Station, MATÁV Pont in Mammut at I. Széna tér, and MATÁV Pont Budai Skála at XI. Október 23 u. The main telecommunications office, at Petőfi Sándor u. 17 (near Deák tér), also provides telephone service.

Hungarian telephone books list the numbers of all countries that can be directly dialed. MATÁV also publishes a useful English-language pamphlet on international calling that includes country codes. Failing either of these resources, dial ℂ **199** for international directory assistance.

Those calling the U.S. can reach the **AT&T** operator at ℂ **06/800-01111**, the **MCI** operator at ℂ **00/800-01411**, and the **Sprint operator** at ℂ **00/800-01877**. **Australia Direct** (ℂ **06/800-06111**), **Canada Direct** (ℂ **00/800-01211**), **New Zealand Direct** (ℂ **06/800-06411**), and **U.K. Direct** (ℂ **06/800-04411** [BT], or **06/800-04412** [Mercury]) are direct-access numbers that connect you to operators in the country you're calling, with whom you can arrange your preferred billing.

For directory assistance: Dial ℂ **198** if you're looking for a number inside Hungary, and dial ℂ **199** for numbers to all other countries.

For operator assistance: If you need operator assistance in making a call, dial ℂ **199** if you're trying to make an international call and ℂ **198** if you want to call a number in Hungary.

Time Zone Hungary is on Central European time, 2 hours ahead of Greenwich Mean Time and 6 hours ahead of Eastern Standard Time from March 26 to October 26; from October 27 to March 25 (during the equivalent of daylight saving time), the difference is 1 hour and 5 hours, respectively.

Tipping The tipping rate is generally 10–20%. Among those who welcome tips are waiters, taxi drivers, hotel employees, barbers, cloakroom attendants, toilet attendants, masseuses, and tour guides. If a restaurant bill includes a service fee, as some restaurants do (be sure to ask), there is no need to tip; if not, add 15–20% to the bill. See "Check, Please: Paying Your Bill & Tips on Tipping," on p. 96, for more information.

Useful Phone Numbers U.S. Dept. of State Travel Advisory ℂ **202/647-5225** (manned 24 hr.); U.S. Passport Agency ℂ **202/647-0518**; U.S. Centers for Disease Control International Traveler's Hotline ℂ **404/332-4559**.

Water Tap water in Budapest is generally considered safe for drinking. Mineral water, which many Hungarians prefer to tap water, is called *ásványvíz*. Purified bottled water *(szénsav mentes)* is sold in delicatessens and groceries in the tourist areas; all brands have a pink label for identification.

5

Where to Stay in Budapest

Budapest's accommodations range from beautiful, historic gems that were built in the early 20th century, to drab, utilitarian establishments that are products of the city's Warsaw Pact days. A slew of four- and five-star hotels have opened recently, the most notable among them being the stunning Hotel Four Seasons Gresham Palace. Other distinctive Budapest hotels include the historic Art Nouveau Hotel Gellért, the Hotel Béke Radisson, and Castle Hill's Hilton Hotel—and they are among the city's priciest lodgings. Accommodations rates in Budapest, however, remain relatively palatable compared to the rates of other European capitals. Competition, also, has resulted in the prices for hotel rooms remaining stable in recent years.

With the addition of many new hotels and pensions (small innlike hotels) that have opened in recent years, Budapest has been playing catch-up, and as a result is not a city lacking in guest beds, as it once was. This said, in high season—or, say, during the Formula 1 weekend in August—it can still be quite difficult to secure a hotel or pension room or a hostel bed, so make reservations and get written confirmation well in advance of your stay.

When booking, keep in mind that if you want a room with a double bed, you should specifically request it; otherwise, you are likely to get a room with twin beds. Single rooms are generally available, as are extra beds or cots. Hungarian hotels often use the word "apartment" to describe connected rooms without a kitchen. In these listings, we have referred to such rooms as "suites," reserving the term "apartment" for accommodations with kitchen facilities.

BUDGET LODGINGS Although there is an unfortunate dearth of recommendable budget hotels in Budapest, travelers can take advantage of the wealth of good alternative accommodations. Small pensions, rooms in private homes, and a number of good youth hostels make the city inviting to travelers on any budget. Remember that location plays a significant role in cost: The norm is inflated prices for centrally located accommodations. Budapest's efficient public transportation means that reaching downtown from points outside the center of the city will not be as difficult as you might expect; if you're on a budget, consider staying outside of downtown in a room removed from the din and smog (and prices) of inner Pest. Pensions in the Buda Hills are far cheaper than downtown hotel rooms, and what's more, these pensions are generally located in quiet residential neighborhoods and often have lovely gardens. We have selected what we consider to be the nicest of the many pensions in the Buda Hills. We also urge you to consider booking a room in Buda's sleepy, but centrally located, Watertown neighborhood, home to a number of recommended hotels.

ACCOMMODATIONS AGENCIES Most accommodations agencies can secure private room rentals in private homes, help reserve hotel and pension rooms, and book you into a youth hostel.

The most established agencies are the former state-owned travel agents **Ibusz** (see below), **MÁV Tours** (© 1/182-9011), and **Budapest Tourist** (© 1/117-3555). Although newer private agencies continue to bloom, the older agencies tend to have the greatest number of rooms listed. There are agencies at the airport, in all three major train stations, throughout central Pest, and along the main roads into Budapest for travelers arriving by car. You can also reserve online through many of the agencies listed below.

The main **Ibusz reservations office** is at Ferenciek tere 10 (© 36/1-485-2700; fax 1/318-2805; www.ibusz.hu), accessible by the Blue metro line. This office is open year-round Monday through Friday 9am to 6pm.

SEASONS Most hotels and pensions in Budapest divide the year into three seasons. **High season** is roughly from March or April through September or October. (The weekend of the Grand Prix, which is the second weekend in Aug, is especially tight.) The week between Christmas and New Year's, Easter week, and the period of the Budapest Spring Festival (mid- to late Mar) are also considered high season. The months of March (excepting the Budapest Spring Festival in mid- to late Mar) and October and/or November are usually considered **midseason. Low season** is roughly November through February, except Christmas week. Some hotels discount as much as 30% in low season, while others offer no winter discounts—be sure to inquire.

PRICE CATEGORIES Most hotels and pensions in Budapest list their prices in euros. Listing rates in euros is not just intended as a means of transition to the E.U. currency (Hungary is expected to adopt the euro sometime after 2010), it is also a hedge against forint inflation (though the forint has been surprisingly strong over the past few years). All hotels in Budapest accept payment in Hungarian forints as well as in foreign currencies. Where prices are quoted in euros, we provide a dollar conversion. The exchange rate as this book goes to press is 1€ equals US$1.20. Exchange rates fluctuate over time, of course, so the price of a room in dollars will change as the euro-to-dollar exchange rate changes.

All hotels are required to charge a 12% value-added tax (VAT). Most build the tax into their rates, while a few tack it on top of their rates. When booking a room, ask whether the VAT is included in the quoted price. Unless otherwise indicated, prices in this book include the VAT.

Hotels in Hungary are rated by the international five-star system. In our view, however, the ratings are somewhat arbitrary and are not included in our entries for that reason. However, we have included our own star ratings throughout the guide. You can find an explanation of the Frommer's star ratings on the page preceding the "What's New" chapter.

Note: We have found that the websites of hotels are frequently inaccurate with respect to rates, so make sure to call the hotel to confirm.

1 The Inner City & Central Pest

VERY EXPENSIVE

Art'Otel Budapest by Park Plaza ★★   Opened in 2000 by a German chain, this is the first Art'Otel outside of Germany. The premise behind the concept is that each hotel spotlights the work of a single artist. In this case, the artist is Donald Sultan. There are more than 600 of his works in the hotel and he designed everything from the furniture and the carpets to the silverware. The modern side of the hotel is a seven-story building facing the Danube, while the rear comprises of four two-story baroque town houses, which now serve as rooms, suites, and the Chelsea Restaurant. There are

Where to Stay in Budapest

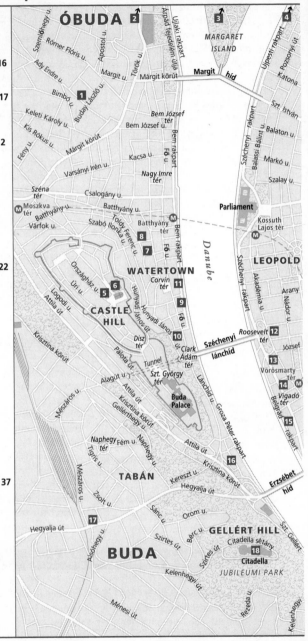

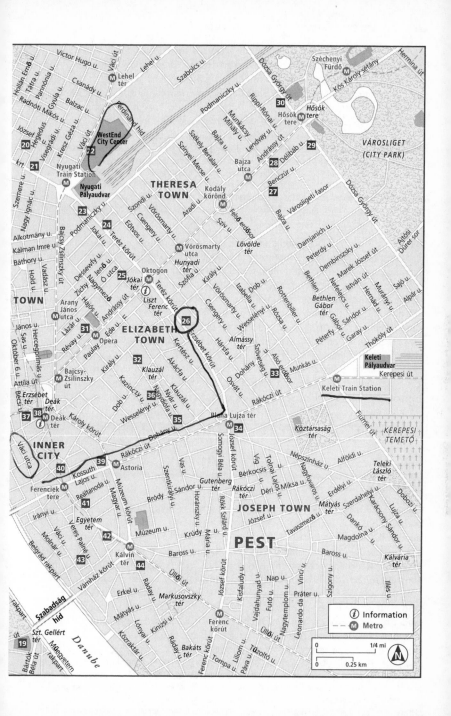

71

conference facilities more stylish than the average, a small fitness room with a sauna, and a lobby bar and cafe with a courtyard garden that is one of the highlights of the hotel. Rooms are minimalist and comfortable, all with original Sultan works—even in the bathrooms. Rooms on the top three floors of the new building facing the Danube command the best views, while rooms in the old houses have higher ceilings, some original fittings and features, but no view. Three floors are smoke-free.

I. bem rakpart 16–19, 1011 Budapest. ⓒ **800/814-7000** in North America, 0800/169-6128 in Britain, or 1/487-9487-5500. Fax 1/487-9488. www.artotels.com. 164 units. 198€–228€ ($237–$273) single and double; 100€ ($120) extra for suite; 20€ ($24) Danube view supplement. Lower weekend and Internet rates. VAT included. Children 12 and under stay free in parent's room. Breakfast included. AE, MC, V. Parking 3,000 Ft ($15) per day. Metro: Batthyány tér (Red line). **Amenities:** Restaurant; bar; sauna; exercise room; concierge; valet parking; business center; art shop; salon; limited room service; wireless Internet in public areas; rooms for those w/limited mobility. *In room:* A/C, TV w/pay movies, dataport w/ISDN, wireless Internet, minibar, coffeemaker (in suites and executive rooms), hair dryer, iron/ironing board on request, safe, voice mail, robe.

Astoria Hotel ⓖ   The Astoria was once one of the city's finest classic hotels, but became a tired, dusty remnant of its former self a few decades ago. Much of the hotel has undergone serious refurbishment since 2004, and the remainder will be completed by 2006. Located centrally downtown, the Astoria is now worth a second look. You may even already have seen it, as the hotel is a popular site for filming movies set in the turn of the 20th century. The Astoria Café Mirror is one of the few remaining traditional coffeehouses in the city, and attracts just as many locals as hotel guests. With its parquet floors, big crystal chandeliers, marble columns, and gold gilted molding, the cafe is one of the highlights of the hotel. The nightly piano music can be heard in both the cafe and the restaurant. One-third of the rooms are in the 1960s annex, but the better choices are in the original section of the building. Guests will have to head to one of the city's bathhouses, however, as the hotel lacks fitness and spa facilities. About a quarter of the rooms are nonsmoking.

V. Kossuth Lajos utca 19–21, 1053 Budapest. ⓒ **1/484-3200.** Fax 1/889-5801. www.danubiusgroup.com/astoria. 135 units. 155€–194€ double ($186–$233); 225€ ($306) suite. VAT included. Children 12 and under stay free in parent's room. Breakfast 14€ ($17) extra. AE, MC, V. Limited street parking available. Metro: Astoria (Red line). **Amenities:** Restaurant; cafe; concierge; travel services; car-rental desk; business center; gift shop; limited room service; laundry service; Internet corner; rooms for those w/limited mobility. *In room:* A/C, TV w/pay movies, wireless Internet, minibar, iron on request, safe.

Budapest Marriott ⓖ   This place has a massive cement exterior, but the interior measures up to international standards of luxury, and refurbishment of all of the rooms was completed in early 2005. The Marriott is a clean and efficient option with few surprises. Located near Pest's main shopping and business areas, the hotel hugs the Danube promenade between the Erzsébet and Chain bridges. Rooms, all of which look out to the river (most have balconies), are comfortable, with all of the amenities that you would expect from a Marriott. The tenth floor holds the executive lounge and commands the best view, and the "World Class" fitness center has a squash court and a top-notch fitness room, with classes available. Conference facilities dominate the mezzanine level, and rooms hold between 10 and 600.

V. Apáczai Csere János u. 4, 1052 Budapest. ⓒ **800/228-9290** in North America, 0800/221-222 in Britain, or 1/266-7000. Fax 1/266-5000. www.marriott.com. 362 units. 150€–265€ ($180–$318) double; 355€–1,050€ ($426–$1,260) suite. Lower weekend rates. VAT included. Breakfast 22€ ($26). AE, DC, MC, V. Parking 28€ ($34) per day. Metro: Vörösmarty tér (Yellow line). **Amenities:** 3 restaurants; indoor heated swimming pool; squash court; fitness center; sauna; concierge; car rental; business center; meeting facilities; souvenir shop; salon; 24-hr. room service; massage; babysitting; laundry service; wireless Internet in public areas; dry cleaning; rooms for those w/limited mobility nonsmoking rooms. *In room:* A/C, satellite TV, dataport, minibar, hair dryer, iron, safe, 2 phone lines.

Corinthia Grand Hotel Royal ⟨★★⟩   This impeccably decorated hotel opened at the end of 2002 after an astoundingly expensive renovation. Although it's located on one of Budapest's most heavily trafficked streets, once you ascend the grand staircase to the lobby, it's easy to forget about the outside world. With inner courtyards and glass and wrought-iron ceilings, natural light floods this hotel. The interior has been re-created in the original 19th-century style, and the facade is also original. Top-of-the-line conference rooms—some of the best in the city—can accommodate up to 2,200 guests and include a grand historically protected ballroom lined with paintings of famous Hungarian poets and heroes. Guest rooms come in two styles: Executive or Superior. The major difference is that the executive rooms come with access to the Executive Lounge. All rooms are quiet, either facing the street or the inner courtyards, and there are stunning architectural details throughout the whole hotel, which is one of Budapest's most beautiful. The swimming pool and spa were being renovated at the time of this writing, and will be open in early 2006. There are excellent dining options here: buffet breakfast is served in the Brasserie Royale; The Far Eastern Rickshaw Restaurant has a sushi bar and serves Japanese, Thai, and Chinese food for dinner; the lobby bar serves drinks in the evening with live piano music nightly; and the Bock Bisztró has a Mediterranean-influenced menu. Smoke-free.

VII. Erzsébet krt. 43–49, 1073 Budapest. ⟨☎⟩ 212/489-6086 in North America, 208/943-4194 in Britain, or 1/479-4000. Fax 1/479-4333. www.corinthiahotels.com. 414 units. 180€–300€ ($216–$360) single; 220€–340€ ($264–$408) double; 300€–3,000€ ($360–$3,600) suite. Lower weekend rates. VAT included. Children 12 and under stay free in parent's room. Breakfast 20€ ($24) extra. AE, DC, MC, V. Parking 100 Ft (50¢) per 12 min. Metro: Oktogon (Yellow line). Tram: 4 or 6 to Király utca. **Amenities:** 3 restaurants; cafe; bar; exercise room; baggage storage; concierge; car rental; business center; 24-hr. room service; massage; babysitting; laundry service; dry cleaning; wireless Internet on ground floor and conference areas; rooms for those w/limited mobility. *In room:* A/C, TV w/pay movies, dataport w/ISDN, minibar, hair dryer, safe, robe, CD player (executive rooms), voice mail, trouser press (superior rooms).

Four Seasons Hotel Gresham Palace ⟨★★★⟩   Prepare to have your breath taken away as you step into the Art Nouveau entrance of this elegant, palatial property, on par with the finest in the world. Directly opposite the Chain Bridge and a postcardlike view of the Buda Castle, the Four Seasons has the most picturesque location of any hotel in town, and rooms overlooking the Danube can rightfully claim to have the best views in the city. Opened in June 2004, the hotel was originally completed in 1906, and was nearly destroyed in World War II. It has now been painstakingly restored—in a 5-year $110-million renovation—down to the last detail. Like all Four Seasons' properties, this hotel strives to pamper guests in every way. From the lobby topped with a glass cupola and the chandelier made from clear glass leaves hanging in front of the reception desk to the fitness center and spa spanning the entire top "attic" floor of the hotel and bathrooms fitted with Spanish marble and deep-soak bathtubs, attention to detail here is strong. While all rooms are beautiful, the most expensive suites are equipped with bedroom sets made of mother of pearl. The restaurant Pava serves Italian cuisine and is one of the best in town, and the Gresham Kávéház is located on the site of a popular 1930s cafe and is a bit less formal. The Bar and Lobby Lounge is located below another glass cupola. Serving light snacks, a large selection of wine, and an extensive martini list (rare in Hungary), along with live nightly piano music.

V. Roosevelt tér 5–6, 1051 Budapest. ⟨☎⟩ 800/819-5053 in North America, or 1/268-6000. Fax 1/268-5000. www.fourseasons.com/budapest. 179 units. 280€–830€ ($336–$996) double; 950€–4,500€ ($1,140–$5,400) suite. VAT not included. Children stay free in parent's room. Breakfast 6,200 Ft ($31) extra. AE, DC, MC, V. Parking 9,000 Ft ($45) per day. Metro: Vörösmarty tér (all lines). **Amenities:** 2 restaurants; bar; indoor swimming pool; sauna; exercise room;

concierge; business center; salon; airport transfer; 24-hr. room service; massage; laundry service; dry cleaning. *In room:* A/C, satellite TV w/pay movies, fax machine available, high-speed Internet access, minibar, hair dryer, safe, robe, newspapers, voice mail.

Hilton Budapest WestEnd ✿
Located in WestEnd City Center (one of Budapest's largest shopping malls, next to Nyugati palyaudvar), this Hilton is clearly for the business set. Opened in 2000, this hotel is part of the "new" Budapest and its new group of five-star hotels. The airy, stylish, glass, chrome, and marble lobby is staffed with efficient receptionists, and the adjoining cafe is just as chic. A fitness center with top-notch equipment, substantial business services, and top-of-the-line meeting rooms are a few of the hotels' strengths. The fourth floor executive lounge (and its panoramic views) will make check-in quick and easy, and serves snacks and drinks throughout the day. Rooms are standardized, understated, and comfortable (even ergonomically correct). The stylish Arrabona Restaurant and adjoining Bar Kando on the upper level serve international food.

VI. Váci út 1–3, 1069 Budapest. ✆ **800/445-8667** in North America, 08705/909-090 in Britain, or 1/288-5500. Fax 1/288-5588. www.hilton.com. 230 units. 170€–260€ ($204–$312) single and double; 205€–385€ ($246–$462) suite. Lower weekend rates. VAT included. Breakfast 22€ ($26) extra. AE, MC, V. Parking 4,000 Ft ($20) per day. Metro: Nyugati pu. (Blue line). **Amenities:** Restaurant; bar; cafe; indoor swimming pool; sauna; exercise room; ice skating; baggage storage; concierge; car-rental desk; business center; secretary services; 24-hr. room service; massage; babysitting; laundry service; wireless Internet in public areas. *In room:* A/C, TV w/pay movies, dataport w/ISDN, minibar, coffeemaker, hair dryer, iron/ironing board, safe, robe, voice mail.

Inter-Continental Budapest ✿
Guests will want for little here as the place offers a host of personal and business services. Built in 1989, the interior is more elegant than the block-style exterior suggests. The spacious lobby lounge—tastefully outfitted with plush, comfortable love seats in green-and-black stripes, marble-topped coffee tables, and cream-colored walls brightened with elegant white moldings—is also a popular meeting spot for local business people. The Corso Restaurant & Bar in the rear on the ground floor has an outdoor terrace (weather permitting) on the pedestrian street overlooking the Danube. Meeting facilities are top-of-the-line here, one of the hotel's main attractions. The accommodations have a rich, elegant look. Executive rooms on the Club (top two) floors have better views, plus access to the club lounge, which offers more great views and loads of services. A small fitness center with sauna faces the Chain Bridge. More than half of the rooms overlook the Danube.

V. Apáczai Csere J. u. 12–14, 1051 Budapest. ✆ **1/327-6333**. Fax 1/327-6357. www.interconti.com. 398 units. 149€–239€ ($178–$286) double; 460€–1,510€ ($552–$1,812) suite. VAT not included. Children 12 and under stay free in parent's room. Breakfast 23€ ($27) extra. Rooms with Danube view are 40€ ($48) extra. Rates 8% lower in low season. AE, MC, V. Parking 28€ ($33) per day. Metro: Vörösmarthy tér (Yellow line). **Amenities:** Restaurant; bar; indoor swimming pool; sauna; exercise room; concierge; business center; salon; babysitting; 24-hr. room service; massage; laundry service; dry cleaning; rooms for those w/limited mobility; nonsmoking rooms. *In room:* A/C, TV w/pay movies, dataport, minibar, coffeemaker, hair dryer, safe, robe, pull-out sofa, scale.

Kempinski Hotel Corvinus ✿✿
Located in the heart of Pest, just off Deák tér, this slick German-run hotel, opened in 1992, has quickly earned a reputation as the hotel of choice for corporate visitors to Budapest (and also big-act musicians— Madonna, Michael Jackson, the Rolling Stones, and Bob Dylan have all stayed here). The building itself is, at least from the outside, a cement behemoth, one of a number of ugly new buildings marring this neighborhood (though the recent reconstruction of nearby Erzsébet tér has made the immediate neighborhood a lot nicer). On the inside, however, the decor is modern sleek German and everything is quietly and

unmistakably luxurious. The rooms are as well appointed as one might expect from such a hotel, and soundproof windows shield guests from the noise of the busy traffic below. Temporary art exhibitions line the walls, and the hotel has an impressive art and antiques collection. The impressive spa was renovated in early 2005, and transports guests to Asia with its authentic Tjai masseuses and Asian-accented rooms. It includes a fitness room, massage rooms, a solarium, steam baths, a sauna, a pool, and a number of other features. Rooms are equipped with up-to-date technology, including mobile Internet connections. The hotel has a number of excellent restaurants and its American-style buffet breakfast (not included in the rate) is exceptional. Almost half the rooms are smoke-free.

V. Erzsébet tér 7–8, 1051 Budapest. ✆ 800/426-3135 in North America, 00800/426-313-55 in Britain, or 1/429-3777. Fax 1/429-4777. www.kempinski-budapest.com. 365 units. 260€–450€ ($312–$540) double; 570€–2,600€ ($684–$3,120) suite. VAT not included. Children 12 and under stay free in parent's room. Breakfast 27€ ($32) extra. AE, MC, V. Parking 7,000 Ft ($35) per day. Metro: Deák tér (all lines). **Amenities:** 3 restaurants; 2 bars; indoor swimming pool; sauna; exercise room; concierge; car-rental desk; business center; conference facilities; shops; salon; 24-hr. room service; massage; laundry service; dry cleaning; rooms for those w/limited mobility. *In room:* A/C, satellite TV w/pay movies, high-speed Internet access, minibar, hair dryer, safe, separate shower, robe, 2 phones.

Le Meridien Budapest ✦✦

Centrally located next to Deák tér and the Kempinski, Le Meridien is part of Budapest's new group of five-star hotels. From the outside, the classical smooth white stone building that was the Communist-era police headquarters looks rather austere. Beautifully renovated before it opened at the end of 2002, the interior is luxurious with fine architectural details throughout, including hallways surrounded by wrought-iron railings overlooking the stained-glass dome topping the breakfast area below, a lobby full of Corinthian pillars and plush leather and corduroy sofas. Guest rooms are equally elegant with thick plush carpeting, gorgeous fabrics, mahogany furniture, and bathrooms fitted with marble floors and sink tops, and separate tubs and showers. Le Bourbon restaurant and its French chef serve excellent French cuisine, and Friday night is "Hungarian Night" with Hungarian food and a folk music show. The 8th-floor spa and fitness room—topped with a glass ceiling, full of natural light, and lined with elegant mosaic ceramic tile—is quite big for a hotel of this size.

V. Erzsébet tér 9–10, 1051 Budapest. ✆ 800/253-0861 in North America, 0845/6000-778 in Britain, or 1/429-5500. Fax 1/429-5555. www.lemeridien.com. 218 units. 399€–429€ ($478–$515) double; 359€–1,600€ ($430–$1,920) suite. VAT not included. Children 12 and under stay free in parent's room. Breakfast 25€ ($30) extra. AE, MC, V. Parking 7,000 Ft ($35) per day or 750 Ft ($3.75) per hour. Metro: Deák tér (all lines). **Amenities:** 2 restaurants; bar; indoor swimming pool; sauna; steam bath; massage; exercise room; concierge; tour desk; business center; conference facilities; salon; 24-hr. room service; babysitting; laundry service; wireless Internet on conference floor; currency exchange. *In room:* A/C, TV w/pay movies, satellite TV, dataport, minibar, coffee/tea, hair dryer, safe, PlayStations upon request.

NH Budapest ✦✦

As the Spanish hotel chain's first property in Hungary—and the region—NH Budapest is a pleasantly sleek, stylish hotel with luxurious guest rooms. The place opened in December 2003, and admits that it is still getting settled and working out the kinks that come along with a brand-new hotel (a few public areas looked unfinished and lacked artwork when we visited, for example). The kinks are few, however, as most details have been thoughtfully implemented—from the fresh orchids on every table in the still-unnamed bar to the male and female toiletry kits placed in every bathroom. All guest rooms are similarly decorated, with dark wood furniture, desks, bright red armchairs, and thick duvets. Rooms facing the front face the Vígszínház and are preferable to the back-facing rooms, which look over the neighboring courtyards. The small fitness room is accessible round-the-clock with room cards. Five meeting rooms occupy the first floor, and the chic ground floor restaurant serves tapas and has a Mediterranean-influenced menu. Wireless Internet access will be installed sometime in 2006. More than half of the rooms are smoke-free.

XIII. Vígszínház utca 3, 1137 Budapest. ℂ **0800/0115-0116** in Britain, or 1/814-0000. Fax 1/814-0100. www.nh-hotels.com. 160 units. 119€–202€ ($143–$242) single and double. VAT included. Children 12 and under stay free in parent's room. Breakfast 16€ ($19) extra. AE, MC, V. Parking 16€ ($19) per day. Metro: Nyugati pu. (Blue line). Tram: 4 or 6 to Jászai Mari tér. **Amenities:** Restaurant; bar; sauna; exercise room; solarium; bike rental; baggage storage; meeting facilities; concierge; car rental; travel services; limited room service; babysitting; massage; laundry service; Internet corner; rooms for those w/limited mobility. *In room:* A/C, TV w/pay movies, dataport with ISDN, minibar, coffeemaker, hair dryer, safe, voice mail.

Sofitel Budapest ✸   After a severe makeover completed in late 2005, the Sofitel Budapest (formerly the Hyatt) is unrecognizably chic and more business-friendly. Although from the outside the place still looks like a big box with windows, the brand-new lobby feels like a Parisian fashion boutique, with lush pink and purple accents—it's a welcome change from the drab old foyer filled with hanging plants. The lobby's former Italian restaurant is now the swank Paris-Budapest Café and serves French food from an open kitchen (still a rarity in Budapest). While rooms and hallways look a bit tired compared to the snazzy rest of the hotel—they'll be renovated by the end of 2006—they have been fitted with luxurious new bedspreads (actually layers and layers of them) and huge pillows. Bathrooms are a good size and have marble countertops. Rooms on the eighth-floor executive level have separate showers and bathtubsand access to the executive lounge. Executive guests also get complimentary massages daily in the fitness center, which has one of the largest indoor pools of any Budapest hotel, and access to some of the most high-tech conference rooms in the city. One floor is smoke-free.

V. Roosevelt tér 2, 1051 Budapest. ℂ **1/266-1234.** Fax 1/266-9101. www.sofitel.com. 351 units. 250€–320€ ($300–$384) double; 295€–1,150€ ($354–$1,380) suite. VAT not included. Breakfast 19€ ($23) extra. AE, MC, V. Parking 6,500 Ft ($33) per day. Metro: Vörösmarty tér (Yellow line). **Amenities:** 2 restaurants; bar; cafe; indoor swimming pool; sauna; exercise room; casino; baggage storage; concierge; car rental; business center; conference facilities; secretary services; 24-hr. room service; massage; wireless Internet throughout hotel; laundry service; executive lounge; rooms for those w/limited mobility. *In room:* A/C, TV w/pay movies, dataport, minibar, coffeemaker, hair dryer, iron/ironing board, safe, voice mail, robe, 3 phones with 2 separate lines.

EXPENSIVE

Best Western Hotel Art   This hotel, opened in a fully restored and renovated turn-of-the-20th-century building in 1994, is located on a quiet side street in the southern end of Pest's Inner City. The reception is a bit stuffy and overly formal for a hotel of this size and quality, but the rooms are clean and comfortable and come with air-conditioning, a rare amenity in the dry heat of the summer. The interior is nondescript but modern.

V. Királyi Pál u. 12, 1053 Budapest. ℂ **1/266-2166.** Fax 1/266-2170. www.hotelart.hu. 32 units. 110€ ($132) double in high season and 90€ ($108) in low season. Rates include buffet breakfast. AE, DC, MC, V. Parking available for 17€ ($20) per day at the nearby Hotel Corona. Metro: Kálvin tér (Blue line). **Amenities:** Restaurant; exercise room; sauna; laundry service. *In room:* A/C, TV, dataport, minibar.

Hotel Andrássy ✸✸ *(Finds)*   Formerly known as Hotel Centrál (which mainly housed visiting politicians from Communist-block countries), the Hotel Andrássy has since been expanded and renovated several times, most recently in mid-2004 and is now a luxurious boutique hotel worthy of the exclusive "Small Luxury Hotels of the

World" (www.slh.com). This little gem of a hotel is located in an exclusive embassy neighborhood just off Pest's Andrássy út, a minute's walk from Heroes' Square and the City Park, and a 25-minute walk from the center of Pest. The lobby is sleek, spacious, and tasteful, with everything done in shades of orange, and a glass wall with a flowing waterfall overlooks the bar of the stylish Zebrano restaurant below. The enormous suites are marvelous, featuring luxuriously large four-poster wrought-iron double beds, spacious bathrooms with massage showers, Jacuzzi bathtubs, vintage Hungarian furniture, carpets, and prints. (Standard rooms are also comfortable, but the spacious suites are worth the splurge.) Most rooms come with terraces. No fitness facilities here, but guests can use those at a partner hotel located nearby. About a quarter of the rooms are smoke-free.

VI. Andrássy út 111, 1063 Budapest. ✆ 1/462-2100. Fax 1/322-9445. www.andrassyhotel.com. 70 units (including 8 luxury suites). 203€–271€ ($244–$325) double; 298€–366€ ($357–$439) suite. AE, DC, MC, V. Parking 16€ ($19) per day. Metro: Bajza utca (Yellow line). **Amenities:** Restaurant; concierge; car rental; laundry service; 24-hr. room service; wireless Internet throughout hotel; rooms for those w/limited mobility. *In room:* A/C, satellite TV/VCR, dataport, minibar, hair dryer, safe, 2 phone lines, snacks, voice mail.

Hotel Béke Radisson ✰   The Béke Radisson, situated not far from the Nyugati Railway Station on Pest's Outer Ring (Nagykörút), carries on a tradition of fine hotels in this location. In 1914 the Art Nouveau Hotel Brittania opened on the same spot as one of the most modern Budapest hotels of its time. Unfortunately, the hotel was badly damaged in World War II, and it was not until 1955 that it was reopened under the hopeful name Béke (meaning "peace"). (The hotel was restored again in 1985.) Rooms are smartly furnished in dark wood, with plush carpeting and curtains; the style is self-consciously luxurious. Unfortunately, the soundproof windows don't quite muffle all the noise from the busy boulevard below. The hotel has a few restaurants, which charmingly retain their old-style atmosphere. The elegant Szondi Restaurant (named after a Hungarian hero who fought the Turks) serves Hungarian/International dinners accompanied by Gypsy music. The bright, friendly Shakespeare Restaurant serves breakfast and lunch when the Szondi is full. The intimate Kupola Bar serves drinks under a gorgeous stained glass cupola (from the original hotel), while the Zsolnay Cafe's delicious pastries are served on hand-painted Zsolnay porcelain. Pets are welcome throughout the hotel.

VI. Teréz krt. 43, 1067 Budapest. ✆ 1/889-3900. Fax 1/889-3915. www.radissonsas.com. 247 units. 145€–170€ ($174–$204) double; 340€ ($408) suite. VAT not included. In low season the rates are 10% less. Breakfast 17€ ($20) extra. AE, MC, V. Parking 5,400 Ft ($27) per day. Metro: Nyugati pu. (Blue line) or Oktogon (Yellow line). Pets welcome. **Amenities:** 2 restaurants; 2 bars; indoor swimming pool; fitness center; sauna; shops; tour desk; car-rental desk; business center; conference facilities; salon; 24-hr. room service; massage; babysitting; laundry service; dry cleaning; nonsmoking rooms; 1 room equipped for guests w/disabilities. *In room:* A/C, TV, high-speed Internet connection, minibar, hair dryer, safe.

Hotel Erzsébet ✰   If you want a modern, centrally located hotel at slightly lower prices than you'll find in other similar hotels, this could be your place. The Erzsébet, named after the queen of Austria-Hungary, was built in 1872 and last renovated in 2000, though it still looks a bit dated. But its central Pest location is unbeatable: The hotel is situated just a few minutes' walk from the southern end of Váci utca. Rooms are smartly furnished, with many features of a luxury hotel. But the rest of the hotel is pretty much no-frills, lacking in a business center and fitness/spa facilities. Be prepared for a less knowledgeable staff at the reception desk. Three levels are nonsmoking.

V. Károlyi Mihály u. 11–15, 1053 Budapest. ✆ 1/889-3700. Fax 1/889-3763. www.danubiusgroup.com/erzsebet. 130 units. 85€–95€ ($102–$114) single; 95€–105€ ($114–$126) double. Rates include breakfast. VAT included.

Discounts for groups of 15 or more. AE, MC, V. Free parking available for 12 cars. Metro: Ferenciek tere (Blue line). Pets permitted. **Amenities:** Restaurant; bar; car-rental desk; laundry service; dry cleaning can be arranged; rooms for those w/limited mobility. *In room:* A/C, TV w/pay movies, dataport, minibar, hair dryer.

K & K Hotel Opera 🅚 🆅🅰🅻🆄🅴   Operated by the Austrian K & K hotel chain, this tasteful, elegant establishment opened in 1994 and expanded in 1998. A complete renovation was completed in September 2005, and the hotel is a few steps above most of the city's other four-star hotels. Directly across the street from the Opera House in central Pest, the hotel building blends nicely with the surrounding architecture. The interior design is now even pleasing, with an understated elegance. The hotel is on a quiet residential street, and the soundproof windows in the guest rooms keep out street noise. A tastefully decorated bar/cafe/restaurant echoes the Asian touches found throughout the hotel. The staff is uniformly friendly and helpful, even when inundated with groups. This hotel is not only within close proximity of the Opera House, but is also right near Budapest's theater district. Half of the rooms are now nonsmoking, but there are no wheelchair-accessible rooms.

VI. Révay u. 24, 1065 Budapest. ✆ 1/269-0222. Fax 1/269-0230. www.kkhotels.com. 205 units. 168€ ($201) single; 209€ ($250) double; 336€ ($403) suite. Rates include breakfast. VAT included. AE, DC, MC, V. Parking 15€ ($12). Metro: Opera (Yellow line). **Amenities:** Exercise room; sauna; tour desk; car rental; business center; massage; babysitting; laundry service; currency exchange; Internet corner. *In room:* A/C, TV, high-speed Internet connection, minibar, coffeemaker, hair dryer, safe.

Mercure Hotel Budapest Nemzeti 🅵🅸🅽🅳🆂   Turn-of-the-20th-century Hotel Nemzeti, just off Blaha Lujza Square, underwent a 1987 restoration that reinstated much of the hotel's Art Nouveau splendor. This is one of Pest's most handsome historic hotels in its category, although rooms are a bit dated and commercial feeling. Its biggest drawback is its location; though very centrally located, the hotel directly overlooks what is perhaps the busiest square on the Outer Ring. Half the rooms face the heavily trafficked street (and the soundproofing does not mask the noise), while the other half face a lovely interior courtyard (request one of these!). The rooms, which were recently renovated a few years ago, have high ceilings and spacious bathrooms. Take the elevator to the top (fifth) floor for the largest and most interesting rooms, with slanted ceilings and funky windows. There are two nonsmoking floors, but no rooms equipped for guests with disabilities. The hotel's restaurant is topped with a stained-glass ceiling and retains that turn-of-the-20th-century ambience found throughout the hotel. In 2006 the restaurant will be renovated and turned into a less formal, more modern bistro-style eatery. There's also a small lobby bar, and guests can use fitness facilities at a sister hotel.

VIII. József krt. 4, 1088 Budapest. ✆ 1/477-2000. Fax 1/477-2001. www.mercure-nemzeti.hu. 76 units. 85€–110€ ($102–$132) double. VAT included. Breakfast 13€ ($16) extra. Lower weekend rates available. Children 12 and under stay free in parent's room. AE, DC, MC, V. Parking available in neighborhood garage for 3,400 Ft ($17) per day. Metro: Blaha Lujza tér (Red line). **Amenities:** Restaurant; bar; car-rental desk; limited meeting facilities; limited room service; laundry service; wireless Internet in public areas. *In room:* A/C, TV w/pay movies, dataport (modem or wireless), minibar, hair dryer, safe, phone.

MODERATE
City Panzió Pilvax 🅚   Opened in 1997, this is one of three Inner City pensions owned by the Taverna Hotel group, which also owns the large Hotel Taverna on Váci utca. The staff is friendly and the rooms are clean and functional, but this place lacks the charm found in many of the pensions in the Buda Hills. It costs a bit more than the Buda Hills pensions, too, but the location is obviously what you are paying for.

The pension is on a narrow, quiet street just a few minutes by foot from the hubbub of central Pest.

V. Pilvax köz 1–3, 1052 Budapest. ✆ **1/266-7660.** Fax 1/317-6396. www.taverna.hu. 32 units. 79€ ($94) single; 99€ ($118) double. Rates 20% lower in low season. Rates include breakfast. AE, DC, MC, V. Metro: Ferenciek tere (Blue line). **Amenities:** 2 restaurants; bar; bike rental; business center; laundry service. *In room:* A/C, TV w/pay movies, minibar, hair dryer, safe.

City Panzió Ring   Another of three central Pest pensions owned by the Taverna Hotel group, City Panzió Ring opened in 1997. This pension is located on Pest's bustling Outer Ring (Panzió Ring) boulevard (hence the name), on the fringes of the fashionable Újlipótváros neighborhood. It's just a block away from Nyugati Railway Station and a 10-minute walk from the Danube embankment and Margaret Island, the city's loveliest park. The small rooms are clean but lack character. This is a perfectly adequate place, but if you are looking for a pension with old-world charm, you'll have to stray farther from the center of the city.

XIII. Szent István krt. 22, 1137 Budapest. ✆ **1/340-5450.** Fax 1/340-4884. www.taverna.hu. 39 units. 98€ ($117) double; 72€ ($86) single in high season. Nov 1–Mar 31 72€ ($86) double, 53€ ($63) single. Rates include breakfast. AE, DC, MC, V. No parking. Metro: Nyugati pu. (Blue line). **Amenities:** Restaurant; bar; bike rental; business center; laundry service. *In room:* A/C, TV w/pay movies, minibar.

Club Hotel Ambra   The Hungarian-owned and -operated Club Hotel Ambra opened in 1998 and attracts a business clientele for the most part. The hotel houses 16 fully equipped apartments (with a bedroom, bathroom, kitchen, and living room) and five standard double rooms. Several of the apartments have terraces that look out over an interior courtyard. The sky-lit breakfast room and bar area are particularly inviting. This is a good place for those who want to stay close to central Pest but want some relative peace and quiet.

VII. Kisdiófa u. 13, 1077 Budapest. ✆/fax **1/321-1533.** www.hotelambra.hu. 5 units, 16 apts. Units (with no kitchen) 105€ ($126); apts 115€ ($138). Rates include breakfast. Rates 20% lower in low season. AE, MC, V. Parking in hotel garage 10€ ($12) per day. Metro: Oktogon (Yellow line). **Amenities:** Restaurant for breakfast; bar; Jacuzzi; sauna. *In room:* A/C, TV, minibar, full kitchen (apts only), safe.

Hotel Ibis Centrum ✮   Located just a few steps from bustling Kálvin tér, right smack in the new center of Budapest nightlife—Ráday utca—the conveniently located Hotel Ibis Centrum (opened in 1998) is a good downtown option. Comfortable, modern, neat as a pin, and reasonably priced, the hotel has three nonsmoking floors (a feature otherwise unheard of in this price category). There are also a roof garden and lobby bar.

IX. Ráday u. 6, 1092 Budapest. ✆ **1/215-8585.** Fax 1/215-8787. 126 units. 85€ ($102) double. Rate does not include breakfast, and add a 3% tax on the whole. Rates 15% lower in low season. MC, V. Parking available for 20€ ($24) per day. Metro: Kálvin tér (Blue line). **Amenities:** Bar; rooms for those w/limited mobility; nonsmoking rooms. *In room:* A/C, TV, dataport.

King's Hotel ✮ *Finds*   The King's Hotel opened for business in 1995 in a beautifully renovated and restored *fin de siècle* building in the heart of Pest's Jewish district. Despite the somewhat drab modern furnishings, the rooms retain a 19th-century atmosphere. Many rooms have small balconies overlooking the quiet residential street and most of the rooms have a private bathroom. The reception is uniformly friendly and helpful. The hotel restaurant is strictly kosher, the only one of its kind in Budapest. It is open for breakfast, lunch, and dinner; food is prepared under the observation of Rabbi Hoffman. Meals are served on weekends and Jewish holidays in the hotel's restaurant by prior arrangement only. *Note:* This hotel will be undergoing renovations shortly.

VII. Nagydiófa u. 25–27 Budapest. ℭ/fax **1/352-7675**. kingsbudapest.4t.com. 80 units. 60€ ($72) double; 50€ ($60) single. Rates include breakfast. AE, DC, MC, V. Metro: Astoria (Red line). **Amenities:** Restaurant (kosher). *In room:* A/C, TV, safe.

Peregrinus ELTE Hotel (Value)   Peregrinus ELTE Hotel is ideally situated in the heart of the Inner City of Pest, across the street from a historic Serbian Church on a small side street half a block from Váci utca, the popular pedestrian-only street. This is the guesthouse of Pest's ELTE University. While many guests are affiliated with the university, the hotel is open to the public as well. The building dates from the turn of the 20th century and was renovated before the hotel was opened in 1994. The rooms are simple but comfortable. You should reserve well in advance. Payment must be in cash in Hungarian forints.

V. Szerb u. 3, 1056 Budapest. ℭ **1/266-4911**. Fax 1/266-4913. 26 units. 24,000 Ft ($120) double; 18,000 Ft ($90) in high season. Rates include breakfast. No credit cards. No parking. Metro: Kálvin tér (Blue line). *In room:* A/C in the attic units, TV, minibar.

INEXPENSIVE

Hotel MEDOSZ (★ (Value)   The MEDOSZ was formerly a trade-union hotel for agricultural workers. It is located on Jókai tér, in the heart of Pest's theater district, just across the street from the bustling Liszt Ferenc tér. The neighborhood surrounding the hotels is also one of Pest's centers of nightlife. A couple of blocks from the Opera House, this is as good as it gets off the river in central Pest. The rooms are simple but clean. The hotel remains a great value given its location. Unfortunately, this hotel maintains discriminative pricing, with a separate pricing structure for Hungarians than for international guests. Next door to Hotel MEDOSZ is one of Budapest's special treats for children: a puppet theater *(bábszínház)*.

VI. Jókai tér 9, 1061 Budapest. ℭ **1/374-3000**. Fax 1/332-4316. www.medoszhotel.hu. 67 units. 65€ ($78) single; 55€ ($66) double. Rates are 20% lower in low season. Rates include breakfast. DC, MC, V. Metered on-street parking difficult in neighborhood; there is an indoor garage in nearby Aradi utca. Metro: Oktogon (Yellow line). **Amenities:** Restaurant; bar; laundry service. *In room:* TV.

2 Central Buda

VERY EXPENSIVE

Danubius Hotel Gellért (★ (Kids)   This splendid, sprawling Art Nouveau hotel first opened in 1918. Much of it is run-down now, but 38 rooms were refurbished in 2000, and there are tentative plans for more renovations. It's still one of the most charming hotels in Budapest, and the spa is among Budapest's most famous. Located at the base of Gellért Hill in Buda, on the bank of the Danube, the Gellért is one of several thermal bath hotels in Budapest that are managed or owned by Danubius Hotels. The circular hotel lobby has marble columns and a mezzanine level. The quality and size of the rooms vary greatly—it seems to be hit-or-miss. Only 29 rooms have air-conditioning and 38 rooms don't have tubs. Some rooms with balconies offer great views over the Danube, but these can be noisy since the hotel fronts loud and busy Gellért Square. Many of the back-facing rooms afford nice views of the baths and the neighboring gardens and buildings. For the best rooms, ask for a Danube-facing king-size refurbished room.

While the majority of guests don't come for the official spa treatment, there are a number of spa-related facilities that all guests can use free of charge: two pools (one indoor, and one outdoor with child-pleasing artificial waves), a steam room, and the Art Nouveau Gellért Baths, perhaps the most popular of Budapest's thermal baths (most travelers visit them at least once during their stay). If you come in the summer, a nighttime plunge under the stars is a must.

XI. Gellért tér 1, 1111 Budapest. ℂ 1/889-5500. Fax 1/889-5505. www.danubiusgroup.com/gellert. 234 units. 65€–160€ ($78–$192) single; 130€–210€ ($156–$252) double; 270€ ($324) suite. Rates include breakfast and use of the spa. AE, DC, MC, V. Parking 8€ ($9.60) per night. Tram: 47 or 49 from Deák tér. **Amenities:** 3 restaurants; bar; 2 swimming pools (1 indoor, 1 outdoor) and thermal pools; sauna; tour desk; car rental; business center; shops; limited room service; massage; babysitting; laundry service. *In room:* A/C (some rooms), TV, minibar, hair dryers (in refurbished rooms), robe, safe.

Hotel Budapest ☆   Though the Hotel Budapest is still a metallic-looking 1960s Socialist-style cylinder on the outside, the hotel's refurbished interiors sport newly upholstered furniture, new carpeting, and bright white paint. The result is a clean modern look, in as much as this kind of place can be. The hotel soars above the neighborhood and offers numerous views; each room boasts a full wall of windows. Your room may overlook the Danube or face up into the hills of Buda. Request a room on a high floor. The vista over the city from the roof garden is simply breathtaking at night. The hotel is within walking distance of Moszkva tér, Buda's central transportation hub, and just across the street from the base of the cogwheel railway, which takes you straight up into the Buda Hills. Locals love to hate the Hotel Budapest, and while it's somewhat of a blight on the landscape, it's also an intriguing place.

II. Szilágyi Erzsébet fasor 47, 1026 Budapest. ℂ 1/889-4200. Fax 1/889-4203. www.danubiusgroup.com. 289 units. 56€–77€ ($70–$96) single; 62€–85€ ($78–$106) double; 120€ ($144) suite. Rates include breakfast. Rates 20% lower in low season. AE, DC, DISC, MC, V. Parking 2,000 Ft ($10) per day. Tram: 56 from Moszkva tér to Fogaskerekú Vasút. Pets permitted. **Amenities:** 2 restaurants; bar; exercise room; sauna; car-rental desk; small business center; salon; 24-hr. room service; babysitting; laundry service. *In room:* A/C, TV, minibar.

EXPENSIVE

Carlton Budapest ☆ *Finds*   Formerly the Alba Hotel (built in 1990), this hotel was fully renovated in 1999–2000 and reopened under the name Carlton Budapest. The hotel belongs to a Swiss chain, and the Swiss influence is pervasive—from the buffet breakfast that features half a dozen kinds of muesli to the antiseptically clean rooms. The canary yellow no-frills hotel is nestled in a tiny cobblestone alley in Buda's Watertown, directly beneath Buda Castle. It has seven floors, but only the rooms on the top floor have views; the two best rooms are no. 706, which has a view of the castle, and no. 707, which overlooks Matthias Church. Other seventh-floor rooms offer a pleasing vista of the red-tiled Buda rooftops. Rooms have tiny bathrooms, and many have showers instead of tubs. Five floors are smoke–free, but there are no rooms equipped for guests with disabilities.

I. Apor Péter u. 3, 1011 Budapest. ℂ 1/224-0999. Fax 1/224-0990. www.carltonhotel.hu. 95 units. 90€ ($108) single. 105€ ($126) double. Rates include breakfast and VAT. Rates 15% lower in low season. AE, DC, MC, V. Parking 12€ ($14) per day. Many buses run to Clark Ádám tér, including no. 16 from Deák tér. **Amenities:** Bar; small conference room; limited business facilities; babysitting; laundry service. *In room:* A/C, TV, dial-up Internet connection, minibar, coffeemaker, hair dryer, safe.

Hotel Astra Vendégház ☆ *Finds*   This little gem of a hotel opened in 1996 in a renovated 300-year-old building on a quiet side street in Buda's lovely Watertown neighborhood. The rooms are large, with wood floors and classic Hungarian-style furniture;

the overall effect is a far more homey and pleasant space than is found in most Budapest hotel rooms. Indeed, the hotel is tasteful through and through, and the staff is friendly. Some rooms overlook the inner courtyard, while others face the street. There is a dark cellar bar with a pool table, and a simple, unadorned breakfast room.

I. Vám u. 6, 1011 Budapest. ℂ 1/214-1906. Fax 1/214-1907. www.hotelastra.hu. 12 units. All units are doubles and cost 150€ ($180) for 2 people and 90€ ($108) for 1. No credit cards. Rates include breakfast. Rates 10% lower in low season. Only meter parking is available on street. Metro: Batthyány tér (Red line). **Amenities:** Restaurant; bar; car-rental desk; babysitting (upon request). *In room:* A/C, TV, minibar.

Hotel Victoria 🐕 The Hotel Victoria, located in Buda's lovely Watertown district, is separated from the Danube bank only by the busy road that runs alongside the river. The lodging is situated in a narrow building, with only three rooms on each of its nine floors. Because of this design, two-thirds of the accommodations are corner rooms with large double windows providing great views over the river to Pest's skyline beyond. The rooms are quite large, with spacious bathrooms but outdated furniture. The middle rooms, though smaller than the corner rooms, also have windows facing the river. About one-third of the rooms have bathrooms with showers only, and the rest have tubs. Unfortunately, noise from the street beneath your window may disturb your rest. There is a sauna and a breakfast room that also functions as a bar, but no lunch or dinner options. The hotel is just minutes by foot from both Batthyány tér and Clark Ádám tér, with dozens of metro, tram, and bus connections.

I. Bem rakpart 11, 1011 Budapest. ℂ 1/457-8080. Fax 1/457-8088. www.victoria.hu. 27 units. 87€–112€ ($104-$134) single; 92€–118€ ($110-$141) double. Rates include breakfast and VAT. AE, DC, MC, V. 3 parking spaces 10€ ($12). Tram: 19 from Batthyány tér to the 1st stop. **Amenities:** Bar; sauna. *In room:* A/C, TV, dataport, wireless Internet, minibar, hair dryer, safe.

International Apartment House 🐕 *Value* This unique establishment, which opened in 1994, is located in a lovely apartment building in Buda's Watertown district. The owner, a German art collector, purchased 12 apartments in the building, renovated them, and installed an elevator for his guests. There is no sign on the street, just a bell with the name "International Apartment House." Reception is on the fourth floor. The building is a 5-minute walk from the metro station, on a quiet street in the upper part of Watertown. The apartments are all quite different from one another, both in terms of size and in terms of facilities and decor (hence the huge disparity in prices). Each apartment is decorated with original artwork and outfitted with a different design and modern furniture. Some apartments have balconies, while others have decks, and some have glorious views. Each apartment enjoys a fully equipped kitchen with microwave, toaster, and so on. In addition, each apartment has a CD player (each with an eclectic CD collection), a VCR (free videos available for borrowing), an answering machine, and a fax machine. Two apartments have air-conditioning, and several have built-in Jacuzzis. This is a place to come home to—the perfect choice for business travelers who are spending more than a few days in Budapest. Meal and shopping services are available for a fee.

I. Donáti u. 53, 1015 Budapest. ℂ 1/356-7198. Fax 1/214-3660. www.inapho.com. 12 units. 80€–160€ ($96–$192) apts (reduced rates for long-term stays). Continental breakfast is 10€ ($12) extra. No credit cards. Parking available on street. Metro: Batthyány tér (Red line). **Amenities:** Fully staffed business center; laundry service. *In room:* A/C in 2 apts, TV/VCR, fax, dataport, kitchen, minibar, coffeemaker.

MODERATE
Best Western Hotel Orion 🐕 Conveniently located in Buda's Watertown neighborhood, between Castle Hill and the Danube, this small five-story hotel is tucked

away on a relatively quiet street near many of the city's best sights. Though the rooms are bright and cheerful enough, and five have balconies, they unfortunately lack castle and river views. Döbrentei tér, a messy but convenient transportation hub, is a few minutes away by foot. Pets are welcome.

I. Döbrentei u. 13, 1013 Budapest. ℂ 1/356-8933 or 1/356-8583. Fax 1/375-5418. www.hotels.hu/orion. 30 units. 88€ ($105) single; 112€ ($134) double. Rates include breakfast. Rates lower in low season. AE, DC, MC, V. Free parking on street. Tram: 19 from Batthyány tér to Döbrentei tér. Pets welcome. **Amenities:** Restaurant; sauna; tour desk; car-rental desk; limited room service; nonsmoking floors. *In room:* A/C, TV, dataport, minibar.

INEXPENSIVE

Charles Apartment House ⭐ *Value*   This is one of the better housing deals in Budapest. Owner Károly Szombati has gradually amassed 70 apartments in a group of apartment buildings in a dull but convenient Buda neighborhood (near the Hotel Novotel). The apartments are a 30-minute walk or a 5-minute bus ride from downtown Pest. All accommodations are ordinary Budapest apartments in ordinary residential buildings. The furnishings are comfortable and clean, and all apartments have full bathrooms and kitchens. Hegyalja út is a very busy street, but only two apartments face out onto it; the rest are in the interior or on the side of the building. A nearby park has tennis courts and a track. There is a new restaurant in the apartment complex, and a pub and grocery store nearby. The friendly, English-speaking reception is open 24 hours.

I. Hegyalja út 23, 1016 Budapest. ℂ 1/212-9169. Fax 1/202-2984. www.charleshotel.hu. 70 units. 48€–136€ ($57–$163) apt for 1–4. Rates include breakfast. Rates approximately 5% lower in low season. AE, DC, MC, V. Parking 2,000 Ft ($10) per day. Bus: 78 from Keleti pu. to Mészáros utca. **Amenities:** Restaurant; bar; bike rental; tour desk; business center; babysitting; laundry service. *In room:* A/C, TV, kitchen, minibar, hair dryer, safe.

Hotel Papillon ⭐   The Hotel Papillon, opened in 1992 as a joint Hungarian-German venture, is a pleasing Mediterranean-style white building on a quiet Buda side street. It is located in the area where central Buda begins to give way to the greenery of the Buda Hills, but it is still an easy bus ride to the center of the city. A Mediterranean atmosphere pervades the interior and the spare pink guest rooms. Seven rooms have terraces; all have refrigerators. In summer the hotel's restaurant serves meals on a pleasant outdoor terrace.

II. Rózsahegy u. 3/b, 1024 Budapest. ℂ/fax 1/212-4003 or 1/212-4750. 20 units. 49€ ($58) double. Rates include breakfast. Rates 20%–25% lower in low season. Children under 6 stay free in parent's room. AE, MC, V. Parking: Just 4 free spaces in secure hotel lot. Bus: 91 from Nyugati pu. to Zivatar utca. Pets welcome. **Amenities:** Restaurant; bar; small outdoor pool; car-rental desk; limited room service; babysitting; laundry service; nonsmoking rooms. *In room:* TV, minibar, fridge.

3 The Castle District

VERY EXPENSIVE

Hilton Budapest   One of only two hotels in Buda's charming Castle District (the other is Hotel Kulturinnov), the Hilton, built in 1977, was widely considered to be the city's classiest hotel at the time. Its location, on Hess András tér, next door to Matthias Church and the Fisherman's Bastion, is no less than spectacular, but these days the Hilton lags behind many of its competitors in terms of service and facilities. The hotel's award-winning design incorporates both the ruins of a 13th-century Dominican church (the church tower rises above the hotel) and the baroque facade of a 17th-century Jesuit college, which makes up the hotel's main entrance. The ruins were carefully restored during the hotel's construction, and the results are uniformly magnificent. The building is clearly modern, and its exterior tends to stand out from the old surrounding Castle District architecture. The hotel has been undergoing renovations since 2000, and nearly everything but the restaurant has been refurbished. More expensive rooms have views over the Danube, with a full vista of the Pest skyline; rooms on the other side of the hotel overlook the delightful streets of the Castle District. Rooms are handsomely furnished and are equipped with such amenities as two-line telephones, webTV, and bathrobes. The luxurious Dominican Restaurant has an international menu; dinner is accompanied by piano music. The more traditional Corvina Restaurant has a Hungarian menu and nightly Gypsy music. Drinks are served in the tiny Faust Wine Cellar in the abbey and the Lobby Bar, which has outdoor tables behind the hotel by the Fisherman's Bastion. The lovely Dominican Courtyard is the site of summer concerts. 122 smoke-free rooms are available.

I. Hess András tér 1–3, 1014 Budapest. ℂ 1/488-6600. Fax 1/488-6644. www.hilton.com. 322 units. 140€–260€ ($168–$312) double; 450€–2,000€ ($540–$2,400) suite. VAT not included. Children stay free in parent's room. Breakfast 25€ ($30) extra. AE, DC, MC, V. Parking for 26€ ($31) per day in garage. Bus: Várbusz from Moszkva tér or no. 16 from Deák tér. **Amenities:** 2 restaurants; 2 bars; exercise room; sauna; concierge; tour desk; free airport minibus; shops; business center; meeting facilities; salon; 24-hr. room service; babysitting; laundry service; rooms for those w/limited mobility. *In room:* A/C, TV w/pay movies, WebTV, dataport, minibar, coffeemaker, hair dryer, iron/ironing board (on request), safe.

4 Outer Pest

VERY EXPENSIVE

Danubius Thermal & Conference Hotel Helia ★★ *(Kids)*   The Thermal Hotel Helia is one of several so-called "thermal" hotels in Budapest now managed and owned by Danubius Hotels. The hotel originally opened in 1990 as a Hungarian-Finnish joint venture. Despite the change in ownership, it continues to provide all the spa- and sauna-related amenities of the two cultures. While the majority of guests do not come for the official spa treatment, there are a number of spa-related facilities that all guests can use free of charge: thermal baths, a swimming pool, a sauna, a Jacuzzi, steam baths, more than a dozen types of massages and a fitness room. The bright, sunny guest rooms sport tall windows. Some rooms have balconies, and four suites have private saunas. Four of the six floors have been refurbished and offer high-speed Internet access, while the others only offer dial-up. The Jupiter Restaurant offers international cuisine with live music at dinner and serves both buffet and a la carte lunches and dinners.

XIII. Kárpát u. 62–64, 1133 Budapest. ℂ 1/889-5800. Fax 1/889-5801. www.danubiushotels.com/helia. 262 units (5 with wheelchair access). 135€–145€ ($162–$174) single; 154€–164€ ($185–$197) double; 266€–388€ ($319–$465) suite. VAT included. Danube view 10€ ($12) extra. Rates include breakfast and use of spa facilities. AE, MC, V. Trolleybus: 79 from Keleti Station. **Amenities:** 2 restaurants; indoor pool; thermal baths; health club; spa; business center; conference facilities; various shops; salon/barber; room service (6am–10pm); massage; babysitting; same-day laundry service; dry cleaning; nonsmoking rooms; dentist; rooms for those w/limited mobility. *In room:* A/C, TV, dataport, minibar, iron/ironing board.

EXPENSIVE

Hotel Andrássy ★★ *(Finds)*   The Hotel Andrássy is a little gem of a hotel, located in an exclusive embassy neighborhood just off Pest's Andrássy út, a minute's journey on foot from Heroes' Square and the City Park, and a 25-minute walk from the center of Pest. The lobby is spacious and tasteful, with marble columns. The enormous suites are marvelous, featuring luxuriously large double beds, spacious bathrooms with massage showers, and vintage Hungarian furniture, carpets, and prints. There's a safe in each suite and at the reception desk. The standard rooms, although quite nice and also furnished with vintage Hungarian furniture, carpets, and prints, can't compare to the suites in spaciousness, so a splurge is recommended here. Half of the guest rooms come with a terrace.

VI. Munkácsy Mihály u. 5–7, 1063 Budapest. ℂ 1/321-2000. Fax 1/322-9445. www.andrassyhotel.com. 70 units (including 8 luxury suites). 271€ ($325) double; 407€ ($488) suite. AE, MC, V. Parking 4,000 Ft ($20) per day. Metro: Bajza utca (Yellow line). **Amenities:** Restaurant; indoor heated swimming pool; exercise room; sauna; concierge; business center; 24-hr. room service. *In room:* TV/VCR, dataport, minibar, safe.

Hotel Liget ☆ (Kids)   Although this unabashedly modern hotel is somewhat out of sync with the surrounding architecture, it is well located just off Pest's Heroes' Square, across the street from the Fine Arts Museum and the City Zoo (a boon for families with young kids). It is a 30-minute walk to the center of Pest, and the Yellow metro line whisks you into the hub of the city in no time at all. The rooms are comfortable and modern, if unimaginatively furnished.

VI. Dózsa György út 106, 1068 Budapest. ℂ 1/269-5300. Fax 1/269-5329. www.taverna.hu. 139 units. 120€ ($144) double. Rates include breakfast. Rates 20% lower in low season. AE, MC, V. Parking 13€ ($15) per day in garage. Metro: Hősök tere (Yellow line). **Amenities:** Restaurant; bar; exercise room; sauna; bike rentals; tour desk; business services; limited room service; massage; laundry service; dry cleaning; nonsmoking rooms. *In room:* A/C, TV, dataport, minibar, hair dryer.

MODERATE
Hotel Délibáb   The ancient Hotel Délibáb enjoys a wonderful location across the street from Heroes' Square and City Park, in an exclusive Pest neighborhood that's home to most of the city's embassies. It's a 30-minute walk to the center of Pest, or a 5-minute ride on the old Yellow metro line. Rooms here are surprisingly spacious and have nice old wooden floors; the fixtures are also old, but everything works and is clean.

VI. Délibáb u. 35, 1062 Budapest. ℂ 1/342-9301 or 1/322-8763. Fax 1/342-8153. www.hoteldelibab.hu. 34 units. 68€ ($81) single; 79€ ($94) double. Rates 20% lower in low season. Rates include breakfast. AE, DC, MC, V. Parking in neighborhood difficult. Parking in the hotel's yard is 2,600 Ft ($13) per day. Metro: Hősök tere (Yellow line). **Amenities:** Restaurant; bar; business center; laundry service; nonsmoking rooms. *In room:* TV, Internet access, fridge (in some rooms).

Radio Inn ☆ (Value)   As the official guesthouse of Hungarian National Radio, the Radio Inn houses many visiting dignitaries, though it is also open to the public. The inn is in an exclusive embassy neighborhood (it's located next door to the embassy of the People's Republic of China), a stone's throw from City Park, and a block from Pest's grand Andrássy út. The metro's Yellow line takes you into the center of Pest in 5 minutes; alternatively, it's a 30-minute walk. Behind the building, there's an enormous private courtyard full of flowers. The huge apartments (all with fully equipped, spacious kitchens) are comfortably furnished and painstakingly clean. Note that the toilets and bathrooms are separate, European style. The management is somewhat old-system (read: begrudging with information, slightly suspicious of foreigners), yet cordial enough. Make sure you reserve well ahead of arrival. The restaurant housed in the same building is a superb place for dinner.

VI. Benczúr u. 19, 1068 Budapest. ℂ 1/342-8347 or 1/322-8284. Fax 1/322-8284. www.radioinn.hu. 36 units. 52€ ($62), 75€ ($90), and 92€ ($110) for 1-, 2-, and 3-person apts, respectively. Rates about 10%–20% lower in low season. Breakfast 7€ ($8.40) extra. AE, MC, V. Limited parking available on street. Metro: Bajza utca (Yellow line). **Amenities:** Restaurant; bar; 24-hr. room service; laundry service; nonsmoking rooms. *In room:* TV, kitchen (apts only), minibar, fridge.

Richter Panzió ⭐ *Finds*   Across the street from the towering Honvéd Hotel, the Richter Panzió sits in a busy part of Pest's Zugló neighborhood, just 5 minutes by bus from Keleti Station (on a night-bus route). A friendly staff manages the pension, which was opened in 1991 by the famous Hungarian circus family of the same name. The guest rooms are delightful, with light-wood floors and huge windows. Most rooms have double beds; the six rear rooms have terraces. There's a small bar in the cozy lobby and there's also an outdoor deck, a Jacuzzi, a sauna, and a pool table.

XIV. Thököly út 111, 1145 Budapest. ⓒ **1/363-5735** or 1/363-5761. Fax 1/363-3956. 29 units. 60€ ($72) double; 50€ ($60) single. Rates include breakfast. Rates 10% lower in low season. MC, V. Free parking. Bus: 7 (Black) from Keleti pu. to Kolumbusz (or Columbus) utca. **Amenities:** Bar; Jacuzzi; sauna; laundry service. *In room:* A/C in some units, TV.

5 Óbuda

VERY EXPENSIVE

Corinthia Aquincum Hotel ⭐ *Kids*   Located on the banks of the Danube, just minutes from Óbuda's lovely Old City center, the Corinthia Aquincum Hotel was opened in 1991. This is a "thermal" hotel, though not all guests come for the spa facilities. Spa-related facilities that all guests can use free of charge include a swimming pool, a sauna, thermal baths, a Jacuzzi, a kneipp pool, a steam bath, a hydromassage shower (in which you control the directions and strengths of the many jets), and a fitness room. This delightful, modern hotel is built on the site of a Roman spa, hence its Roman theme. The rooms are cheerful, with soundproof windows and complimentary bathrobes. Although the hotel is pleasant, it is nowhere near as luxurious, elegant, and architecturally interesting as the Corinthia Grand Hotel Royal in Pest (see earlier in this chapter). The spa facilities are really the main attraction here, and water is pumped in from Margit Island. The Restaurant Apicius serves both lunch and dinner, with a salad bar and buffet lunch. The chef has been named the best young chef by the Hungarian Society of Restaurateurs, and the Sunday wellness brunch is popular with locals. There's live piano or Gypsy music nightly. The Iris Night Club has live music and shows nightly, and the Calix Bar on the ground level is a more relaxed place for drinks and light snacks.

III. Árpád fejedelem útja 94, 1036 Budapest. ⓒ **1/436-4100.** Fax 1/436-4156. www.corinthia.hu. 310 units. 220€ ($264) single; 230€ ($276) double; 410€ ($492) suite. 25€ ($30) executive room supplement. Rates include breakfast, spa facilities usage, and VAT. Children 12 and under stay free in parent's room. DC, MC, V. Parking available for 12€ ($14) in garage. Train: HÉV suburban railway from Batthyány tér to Árpád híd. Small pets allowed. **Amenities:** Restaurant; 2 bars; indoor heated pool; health club; spa; Jacuzzi; sauna; bike rental; concierge; car-rental desk; currency exchange; meeting facilities; shops; business center; salon; 24-hr. room service; babysitting; laundry service; dry cleaning (weekdays only); executive rooms. *In room:* A/C, TV, dataport, minibar, hair dryer, robe, safe (executive rooms), trouser press (executive rooms).

MODERATE

Hotel Római ⭐ *Finds*   A former resort for minor Communist Party officials, this hotel is a bit off the beaten track, but its location in the Római Fürdő section of Óbuda, on the banks of the Danube, is refreshingly peaceful. The lobby is spacious and comfortable, equipped with pool tables and a bar. The rooms were recently renovated and refurbished, though they are pretty generic in design. Each room has a balcony. There's an outdoor swimming pool and a large garden. It takes a while to get here from the center of Budapest (especially if you do not have a car), but you will feel as if you are staying in the countryside.

III. Szent János u. 16, 1039 Budapest. ℂ/fax **1/388-6167.** 24 units; 12 apts. 56€ ($67) double; 82€ ($98) apt (sleeps 4). Breakfast included. V. Ample free parking. Train: Suburban HÉV line from Batthyány tér to Római Fürdő; then bus no. 34 to Szent János utca. **Amenities:** Restaurant; bar; outdoor pool; car-rental desk. *In room:* TV, fridge.

6 The Buda Hills
MODERATE

Beatrix Panzió   The Beatrix Panzió, situated in the Buda Hills and opened in 1991, is an agreeable, modern place with smart, comfortable rooms. The suites have private balconies and full kitchens. A sun deck is available for guests' use and the landscaped garden has a goldfish pond; in good weather, breakfast is served in the garden. Management, if requested, will cook up a traditional Hungarian barbecue (hearty goulash over an open fire) at a negotiable price. The staff will assist you with making touring plans. Though the pension is located on a small but heavily traveled road instead of a back street (on which most pensions are found), the guest rooms are not noisy. A well-stocked grocery store is conveniently located down the street.

II. Széher út 3, 1021 Budapest. ℂ/fax **1/275-0550.** www.beatrixhotel.hu. 15 units. 65€ ($78) double; 90€ ($108) suite. Rates include breakfast. Rates 20% lower in low season. No credit cards. Free parking in secured lot. Tram: 56 from Moszkva tér to the 7th stop. **Amenities:** Sauna; tour desk; 24-hr. room service; laundry service (limited). *In room:* TV, kitchen (suites only), minibar, safe.

Budai Hotel   A 15-minute winding walk from the tram station, the Budai sits high in a quiet section of the Wolf Meadow (Farkasrét) district of the Buda Hills. The rooms are simply furnished in a nondescript, ordinary eastern European style. All rooms have private bathrooms and some have terraces. The rooms on the top floor have the best views of the surrounding hills. The view from the hotel's terrace restaurant is also grand. *Note:* The receptionist speaks little English.

XII. Rácz Aladár u. 45–47, 1121 Budapest. ℂ/**1/249-0208.** www.hotels.hu/budaihotel. 23 units. 64€ ($76) double; 77€ ($92) suite; plus 3% tourist tax. Rates include breakfast. Rates 20% lower in low season. AE, MC, V. Free parking in street opposite the hotel, or in secure garage for 6€ ($7.50). Tram: 59 from Moszkva tér to the last stop. Pets welcome. **Amenities:** Restaurant; bar; 24-hr. room service; massage; laundry service; dry cleaning; nonsmoking rooms. *In room:* TV, dataport, minibar.

G.G. Panoráma Panzió ✿ *Finds*   G. G. are the initials of Mrs. Gábor Gubacsi, the friendly English-speaking owner of this small guesthouse. All guest rooms are on the top floor of the Gubacsi home, which is located on a steep, quiet street in the elegant Rose Hill (Rózsadomb) section of the Buda Hills. Several bus lines from different parts of the center city converge on the neighborhood, making it a fairly convenient place to stay. The rooms are small but tastefully furnished with wood IKEA-style furnishings; they share a common balcony, which has a great view of the hills. There's a common kitchen with full facilities and a dining area, as well as garden space for picnics, barbeque, reading, and relaxing. It's a casual but classy place, and the Gubacsis take good care of their guests.

II. Fullánk u. 7, 1026 Budapest. ℂ/fax **1/394-4718** or 1/394-6034. www.ggpanorama.hu. 4 units. 50€ ($60) double. Breakfast 4€ ($4.80) extra. No credit cards. Parking available on street. Bus: 11 from Batthyány tér to Majális utca or no. 91 from Nyugati pu. *In room:* TV, shared kitchen, shared telephone.

Gizella Panzió ✿   This fine pension is located in the Buda Hills, a 10-minute walk from the tram station. Built on the side of a hill, it has a lovely view and a series of terraced gardens leading down to a swimming pool. The pension also features a solarium. Owner Gizella Varga has good taste. Guest rooms are all unique but uniformly quaint and sunny. A sightseeing car and driver can be arranged for guests upon request. Gizella Panzió also rents fully furnished flats in the center of town for 61€ to 96€ ($76–$120), depending on the number of people.

XII. Arató u. 42/b, 1121 Budapest. ℰ/fax **1/249-2281**. www.gizellapanzio.hu. 9 units. 60€ ($72) double; 75€ ($90) suite. Rates include breakfast. Rates lower in low season. DC, MC, V. Free parking. Tram: 59 from Moszkva tér to the last stop. Pets welcome. **Amenities:** Bar; outdoor pool; exercise room; sauna; limited room service; massage; babysitting; laundry service; dry cleaning. In room: TV, minibar.

Hotel Bobbio ⍟   Formerly known as the Hotel Queen Mary, this fine little establishment is situated high up in the hills in a tranquil, affluent neighborhood. The rooms are modern and functional, the windows filled with greenery. Each room has a terrace, though rooms on the ground floor share the terrace with adjacent rooms. Unfortunately, the hotel has less garden space than most Buda pensions. However, there is a solarium, and the restaurant (serving only dinner) offers outdoor dining in summer.

XII. Béla király út 47, 1121 Budapest. ℰ **1/274-4000**. Fax 1/395-8377. www.bobbio.hu. 22 units. 63€ ($75) double; 72€–84€ ($86–$100) suite. Plus 3% VAT. Rates include breakfast. Rates 20% lower in low season. AE, MC, V. Free parking. Bus: 28 from Moszkva tér to Béla király út. **Amenities:** Restaurant (dinner only); bar; sauna; limited room service; laundry service; dry cleaning. In room: TV, minibar.

Hotel Panda   The Hotel Panda is on Pasaréti Square, in a pleasant neighborhood in the Buda Hills. There are a grocery store and several other businesses in the busy little square. The hotel reception is friendly and efficient. Unfortunately, the desirability of the rooms varies greatly. Rooms facing the front (10 in all) have terraces, with southern exposure and nice views. Rooms elsewhere in the hotel, with smaller windows and without terraces, can get a bit stuffy. Each bathroom has a window; all have bidets. While the larger suites are quite big, the smaller ones are identical in size to normal double rooms.

II. Pasaréti út 133, 1026 Budapest. ℰ **1/275-0133** or 1/275-0134. Fax 1/394-1002. www.budapesthotelpanda.hu. 28 units. 60€ ($72) double; 71€ ($85) suite. Rates include breakfast. Rates 15% lower in low season. AE, MC, V. Limited free parking. Bus: 5 from Március 15 tér or Moszkva tér to Pasaréti tér (the last stop). In room: TV, minibar.

INEXPENSIVE

Vadvirág Panzió ⍟ (Value   A good 10-minute walk from the bus stop, the Vadvirág (the name means wildflower) is in a gorgeous part of the Buda Hills just a few blocks behind the Béla Bartók Memorial House. Sloping gardens and terraces surround the pension. Inside, the hallways are decorated with prints by the late Hungarian-born op artist Victor Vasarely. The rooms are all different; most are small but tastefully furnished. Half the rooms have balconies; some have refrigerators. Room no. 2 is the best in the house: It's a small suite with a balcony. There's a sauna (10€/$12 per hour) and a small restaurant with plenty of outdoor seating.

II. Nagybányai út 18, 1025 Budapest. ℰ **1/275-0200**. Fax 1/394-4292. www.hotels.hu/hotelvadvirag. 15 units. 55€–80€ ($66–$96) double. Rates include breakfast. MC, V. Parking available in private garage for 10€ ($12) per day or for free on street. Bus: 5 from Március 15 tér or Moszkva tér to Pasaréti tér (the last stop). **Amenities:** Bar; sauna; laundry service. In room: TV, minibar, safe.

7 Margaret Island

EXPENSIVE

Danubius Grand Hotel Margitsziget ⍟⍟   This is one of only two hotels on Margaret Island, Budapest's most popular park. Though two bridges connect the island with the rest of the city, vehicular traffic (except one city bus) is forbidden except for access to the hotels. Located on the northern tip of lovely Margaret Island, in the middle of the Danube, this hotel was originally built in 1873. Destroyed in World War II, it was restored and reopened in 1987, and has a Bauhaus style and a lovely country hunting lodge feel to it, with lots of dark wood, green leather chairs, and marble floors and columns. An underground tunnel connects the hotel to the adjacent Thermal Hotel Margitsziget. While the majority of guests don't come for the official spa treatment, a number of spa-related facilities at the Thermal Hotel can be used free of charge, including the swimming pool, the sauna, and the thermal bath. The rooms are standard for a four-star hotel, and each is slightly different, some with balconies. Many of the rooms have retained the original light fittings and other features, but a few of them only have showers. The fitness room, sauna, and pools were recently modernized to meet the highest standards. The formal Széchenyi Restaurant serves International/Hungarian cuisine, including special diet dishes and kosher meals on request, along with live gypsy music. There is also terrace dining. There are several bars, including the lively Dreher Bierstube. Hotel is smoke-free.

XIII. Margitsziget, 1138 Budapest. ℭ 800/448-4321 in North America or 1/889-4700. Fax 1/889-4939. www. danubiushotels.com. 164 units. 135€–148€ ($162–$177) single; 154€–168€ ($184–$201) double; 178€–228€ ($213–$273) suite. Breakfast and VAT included. Spa facilities usage included in the rate. AE, DC, MC, V. Parking 13€ ($16) per day. **Amenities:** Restaurant; 3 bars; access to Thermal Hotel's swimming pool, thermal bath, spa, and sauna; shops; Jacuzzi; car rental; business center; salon; 24-hr. room service; laundry service; dry cleaning service; travel agency; wireless Internet in public areas; rooms for those w/limited mobility. *In room:* A/C, TV, dataport, minibar, coffeemaker, safe, phone.

8 Youth Hostels

There is intense competition in Budapest between the leading youth hostel companies and various privately run hostels. The leading company is **Travellers' Youth Way Youth Hostels,** also known as **"Mellow Mood Ltd."** (ℭ 1/413-2062; www.mellow mood.hu). They run three year-round hostels: **Marco Polo** (ℭ 1/413-2555; www. marcopolohostel.com), **Mellow Mood Central Hostel** (ℭ 1/411-1310; www. mellowmoodhostel.com), and the **Hostel Fortuna** (ℭ 1/215-0600; www.fortuna hostel.hu), and six summer-only hostels.

Young representatives from Travellers' and from some of the privately run youth hostels sometimes meet international trains arriving in Budapest. Some representatives even board Budapest-bound international trains at the Hungarian border crossing so that they can work the backpacking crowd before the train reaches Budapest. Your best bet is to book a bed in advance at one of our recommended hostels; if you haven't, you can make phone calls upon your arrival to try to secure a hostel bed or you can try your luck with the hostel hawkers. Since they make a commission on every customer they bring in, the hostel representatives tend to be pushy and say whatever they think you want to hear about their hostel. Shop around and don't let yourself be pressured. Most hostels that solicit at the station have a van parked outside. The ride to the hostel is usually free, but you may have to wait a while until the van is full.

Mellow Mood operates a youth hostel placement office at Keleti Station (ℭ 1/ 343-0748), off to the side of track 9 and track 6, near the international waiting room. This office, open daily 7am to 8pm, can help you book a bed in one of Travellers' hostels or in other hostels.

The main office of the **Hungarian Youth Hostel Federation (Magyar Ifjúsági Szállások Szövetsége)** is located at Molnár utca 3 (near Ferenciet tere, Blue line; ℭ 1/411-2390; www.youthhostels.hu). They can provide you with a full list of youth

(Value) Staying in Private Rooms

It is becoming less and less common, but private rooms in private apartments are definitely an option for budget travelers in Hungary. When you book a private room, you get a room in someone's apartment. You'll usually share the bathroom either with the hosts or with other guests. Breakfast is not included, but the host will often offer a continental spread (bread, butter, jam, coffee or tea) for around 800 Ft to 1,200 Ft ($4–$6). You may also have limited kitchen privileges (ask in advance to be sure). Some landlords will greet you when you arrive, give you a key, and seemingly disappear; others will want to befriend you, help you change money, show you around, and sometimes even cook for you.

Most rooms are quite adequate and some are even memorable, but any number of reasons may cause you to dislike your accommodations: Location in a noisy neighborhood, a tiny bathroom, and wretched coffee are among the complaints we've heard from the occasional displeased traveler. The great majority of guests, though, are satisfied; certainly, staying in a private room provides a window into everyday Hungarian life that you can't really find anywhere else (except, perhaps, in some of the family-run pensions).

You can book rooms through accommodations agencies (for example, **Ibusz** (C) **36/1-485-2700;** www.ibusz.hu). Prices vary slightly between agencies, but, generally speaking, an average room will cost between 4,500 Ft and 6,500 Ft ($23–$33) for two people, or 5,000 Ft ($25) for a single, plus a 3% tourism tax. High-end rooms in fashionable neighborhoods can cost significantly more. Most agencies add a 30% surcharge (to the first night only) for stays of less than 4 nights. When booking a room, make sure you know its exact location on a map and that you know how to get there. There's scarcely an address in Budapest that cannot be reached by some form of public transportation, so regard with skepticism anyone who tells you that you must take a taxi. In peak season you may need to shop around a bit for the location you want, but you can always find a room somewhere. Arriving at an agency early in the day will afford the best selection. We do not recommend booking by phone before arriving; you will get the best service, rates, and idea of the style of various apartments by talking to the agent in person.

In Keleti Station, where most international trains arrive, you are likely to be approached by all sorts of people offering you private rooms. Many are honest folks trying to drum up some personal business, though the more aggressive ones can be intimidating if not downright annoying; dismiss the aggressive types. Keep in mind that when the middleman (the agency) is eliminated, prices tend to be slightly better, so you might consider taking a room from one of these people, especially if you arrive late at night when the agencies are closed or if long lines at the agencies drive you to despair. Trust your judgment and don't let anyone pressure you. Feel free to haggle over prices.

hostels in Hungary, including those in Budapest, and book your hostel stay. You can also pick up an IYHF card (no photo required) for 2,300 Ft ($8.10). There is a useful youth travel agency run by **Mellow Mood Ltd.,** located at VII. Baross tér 15 (② 1/413-2062; www.mellowmood.hu), that also books hostel stays from its office. To reach the agency, get off at Baross utca on tram no. 4 or 6. This agency is open Monday through Friday from 8am to 4pm. Both of these companies' websites have information and e-mail addresses for various hostels. Though you cannot reserve online through the agencies, you can contact the hostels directly through their e-mail to book a bed or room.

In July and August a number of university dormitories and other empty student lodgings are converted into hostels, many managed by Travellers'. Their locations (as well as their condition) have been known to change from year to year, so we haven't reviewed any of them in this guide. The youth hostels and budget lodgings listed below are all open year-round unless the review says otherwise.

INNER CITY & CENTRAL PEST

Marco Polo Hostel ⚐ *Value*   Although this place calls itself a youth hostel, it is really more like a budget hotel. This is no backpackers' haunt as we noticed that most of the guests were well-dressed middle-aged Europeans. Given the central location and the clean, modern rooms (the hostel opened in 1997), this is a very good deal. There is no curfew and no lockout. Open year-round, the hostel is operated by Mellow Mood Ltd. There are safes available at the front desk.

VII. Nyár u. 6, 1072 Budapest. ② 1/413-2540. Fax 1/413-6058. www.marcopolohostel.com. 46 units (36 double units, 5 quad units, 5 12-bed units; all with shower and toilet). 8,500 Ft ($43) per person in double unit, 5,800 Ft ($29) per person in quad, 4,500 Ft ($23) per person in 12-bed unit. Rates include breakfast. 10% discount for IYHF members. No credit cards. Parking available for a fee. Metro: Blaha Lujza tér (Red line). **Amenities:** Restaurant; communal kitchen; tour desk; Internet access available; car-rental desk; free bus from Keleti Railway Station; coin-op washers and dryers. *In room:* TV in double and quad rooms, hair dryer and iron available at reception.

Yellow Submarine Lotus Youth Hostel ⚐⚐   This private hostel, open year-round, is centrally located across the street from Nyugati train station, on the very busy Teréz körút. It is within walking distance of all central Pest attractions. The hostel is on the third floor of a residential building. There is nothing more than a small sign downstairs by the mailbox to let you know you are in the right place. Ring the bell and you will be buzzed in. You need not repeat this ritual more than once, as all guests are given keys. There is no curfew. The rooms are clean and spacious, but the bathrooms can get a bit grimy. Rooms are mixed sex. Each guest gets a locker; locks are provided with a deposit. Guests are "expected" to be quiet after 10pm, but it only takes one bad egg to spoil the mix. English-language newspapers are provided daily and the "Sub" features a common area equipped with cable TV, Internet access, cold drinks, a lending/swapping library, and public phones. The same firm is in the process of opening a new hostel not far, in the central Andrássy boulevard area.

VI. Teréz krt. 56 (3rd floor), 1066 Budapest. ②/fax 1/331-9896. www.yellowsubmarinehostel.com. 7 units (2 10-bed units, 2 2–4 bed units, 1 8-bed unit, 1 6-bed unit, and 1 2-bed unit). 2,900 Ft ($15) for bed in 10-bed unit, 3,000 Ft ($15) for bed in the others, except 7,500 Ft ($38) for bed in 2-bed unit. Rates include breakfast. AE, MC, V. No parking available. Metro: Nyugati pu. (Blue line). **Amenities:** Communal kitchen; laundry service.

CENTRAL BUDA

Hotel Citadella   Budapest's most famous (or at least its oldest) budget hotel, this tired old establishment is located inside the Citadella, the 19th-century Habsburg garrison that commands a panoramic view over the city from the top of Gellért Hill.

Once upon a time it was a one-of-a-kind place where young folks from the East and West came and hung out together high up on the hill in an old fortress. However, the hostel has become more commercialized and more run-down, and it no longer seems special or unique to us. The rooms, luxuriously large, are well worn but clean, with high ceilings and remarkable views. The public bathrooms are merely passable. Nearby you'll find an expensive restaurant, a nightclub, and a casino.

XI. Citadella sétány, 1118 Budapest. ☎ 1/466-5794. Fax 1/386-0505. 12 units (1 dorm unit with 14 beds and toilet and shower, 11 quad units with shower only). 11,300 Ft ($57) for a double unit (2 people in a quad unit); 16,500 Ft ($83) for a quad unit; 2,054 Ft ($10) for dorm bed. Breakfast 1,000 Ft ($4.50) extra. No credit cards. Free parking. Bus: 27 from Móricz Zsigmond körtér to the Citadella.

OUTER PEST

Aquarium Youth Hostel 𝒜𝒜 (Value)   This hostel (formerly known as Ananda) is run by an interesting South American fellow named Jairo Bustos, who operated at least two other hostels of the same name in Budapest in the early 1990s. The hostel is well located just a few minutes by foot from Keleti Railway Station (where most international trains arrive), on the corner of Alsóerdósor utca and Péterfy Sándor utca. Like most other centrally located, privately run youth hostels in town, Aquarium is sited in a residential building (a classic Pest apartment house), and there is little evidence from the street of its existence within (just a small buzzer that says HOSTEL). The hostel has extremely clean rooms (mixed-sex) and a friendly, engaging staff. Guests are given large lockers in which to store gear, and there is a TV in the common room. There is no curfew. The hostel is frequented in equal parts by tired rail travelers arriving at Keleti Station and by meditation-vegetarian types who have been drawn by Mr. Bustos, a magnetic personality who is somewhat famous among certain circles of locals and Euro travelers.

VII. Alsóerdósor u. 12 (2nd floor). ☎/fax 1/322-0502. 4 units (1 double and 3 4-bed units). 3,000 Ft ($15) per person in the 4-bed unit; 10,000 Ft ($50) per unit for the 1 double. No credit cards. No parking available. Metro: Keleti pu. (Red line). **Amenities:** Coin-op washers and dryers; communal kitchen; free Internet access.

Station Guesthouse 𝒜𝒜 (Finds)   Opened in 1997 in a large house in a drab neighborhood in outer Pest (on the train tracks, just minutes from the suburban Zugló Railway Station), this year-round hostel proudly boasts a nonstop party atmosphere. Don't come here for a quiet place to stay. For many guests, the time spent at this hostel is a principal part of their time spent in Budapest. The hostel is not run by a hostel chain, and the informative staff is fiercely proud of its independence—they treat you as guests in their house. The rooms (mixed-sex) are standard dorm rooms. The well-stocked bar is open—and in use—24 hours a day. The common room has a pool table (free use) and walls filled with murals and other creations by the guests. There is live music (rock, blues, jazz), principally performed by hostel guests. The hostel has a fully equipped kitchen (there is a grocery store nearby), and the facilities are surprisingly clean given the somewhat hedonistic atmosphere. Internet access is available at 20 Ft (10¢) per minute. There is a TV and there are safe lockers.

XIV. Mexikói út 36/b. ☎ 1/221-8864. Fax 1/383-4034. www.stationguesthouse.hu. 11 units (attic floor space for mattresses; 3 6-bed units; 2 4-bed units; 3 3-bed units; 2 2-bed units). 2,300 Ft ($12) per mattress in attic; 2,800 Ft ($14) per bed in 6-bed units; 3,100 Ft ($16) per bed in 4-bed units; 3,600 Ft ($18) per bed in 3-bed units; 3,600 Ft ($18) per bed in 2-bed units. All rates listed above are for the 1st night, with a 100 Ft (50¢) discount per night for up to 5 additional nights. No discount for IYHF members. No credit cards. Plenty of parking available on street and in the yard. Bus: No. 7 (Red) from Keleti Station to Hungaria krt.; walk under railway embankment, and turn right on Mexikói út. **Amenities:** Bar; communal kitchen; laundry service.

Where to Dine in Budapest

Budapest features an increasingly diverse range of restaurants to go along with those more traditional eateries that have stood the test of time. Ethnic restaurants have appeared on the scene in the last decade; you'll find Japanese, Korean, Indian, Middle Eastern, Greek, and Mexican restaurants in the city. Of course, most tourists understandably want to sample authentic Hungarian food while in Budapest. Each restaurant has its own story and character. In this city, traditional fare runs the gamut from greasy to gourmet; there are few palates that can't be pleased here. Budapest has gained a reputation for good dining at reasonable prices, so live it up.

However, one warning: While this country is landlocked, many restaurants pride themselves of their fresh seafood delights. Many Hungarians probably hark back to a time when the sea was a part of this land, and some even think that the sea is closer than it actually is. The fact is, such a promise is hard to keep; **we recommend staying away from imported seafood.** At traditional Hungarian restaurants you will find delightful local fish: **Szeged** or **Tisza** fish soups are delicious, and far better than a far-from-fresh seafood platter.

WHERE TO EAT *Étterem* is the most common Hungarian word for restaurant and is applied to everything from cafeteria-style eateries to first-class restaurants. A *vendéglő*, or guesthouse, is a smaller, more intimate restaurant (literally an "inn"), often with a Hungarian folk motif;

a *csárda* is a countryside *vendéglő* (often built on major motorways and frequently found around Lake Balaton and other holiday areas). An *étkezde* is an informal lunchroom open only in the daytime, while an *önkiszolgáló* means self-service cafeteria; these are typically open only for lunch. Stand-up *büfés* (snack counters) are often found in bus stations and near busy transportation hubs. A *cukrászda* or *kávéház* is a classic central European coffeehouse, where lingering over a beverage and pastry has developed into an art form.

There are also a variety of establishments that, though primarily designed for drinking, also serve meals. A *borozó* is a wine bar; these are often found in cellars (they are likely to include in their name the word *pince* [cellar] or *barlang* [cave]), and generally feature a house wine. A *söröző* is a beer bar; these places, too, are often found in cellars. Sandwiches are usually available in *borozós* and *sörözős*. Finally, a *kocsma* is a sort of roadside tavern. Kocsmas are found on side streets in residential neighborhoods; the Buda Hills are filled with them. Most kocsmas serve a full dinner, but the kitchens close early.

MUSIC Live Gypsy music is a feature in many Hungarian restaurants, although you'll find it primarily in restaurants that cater to travelers. Generally speaking, what you find in restaurants is not authentic Gypsy music, but an ersatz pop variety. If a member of the band plays a number at your table, good manners dictate that you give a tip; the appropriate amount varies with the price category of

---

(Tips   **Reserve a Table Online**

Reserving a table at Budapest restaurants is not always an easy task, especially for a Friday night when small restaurants like Café Kör (see p. 101) fill up very quickly. Many travelers chose to reserve in advance on **budapestweek.com**. The site itself has been rather neglected in recent times, but the reservation network works well. Choose the restaurant, number of guests, smoking or not smoking. Within a day, you'll get a confirmation, after the friendly Rozsa confers with the restaurant for availability.

---

the restaurant itself (1,000 Ft–2,000 Ft/ $4.50–$9 is a fair starting point). It is perfectly acceptable, however, for you to politely decline his or her offer to play for you.

PRICE CATEGORIES   For the purposes of this book, we have classified restaurants as follows: A restaurant is Very Expensive if the average main course costs more than $25; Expensive, between $20 and $25; Moderate, between $15 and $25; and Inexpensive, $15 and under. Remember that all things are relative—an "Expensive" meal in Budapest may not cost much more than a cup of coffee with a pastry in Rome.

In the listings below, few restaurants outside the "Very Expensive" and "Expensive" categories accept credit or charge cards, and even some in these two categories don't accept them. You can assume that English-language menus are available in all "Very Expensive" and "Expensive" restaurants and in most "Moderate" restaurants.

Sometimes waiters will mention "specials" that don't appear on the menu, and in some of the more expensive new establishments, chefs are proudly willing to adjust their menu in accordance with your taste. It is customary to ask the price before ordering such a special. Also, some restaurants don't list drinks on the menu, while others list them but omit the prices. Again, feel free to inquire about the price before ordering.

WARNING   The U.S. Embassy circulates a list of restaurants that engage in "unethical business practices" such as "excessive billing," using "physical intimidation" to compel payment of excessive bills, and "assaulting customers" for nonpayment of excessive bills. If you don't want to encounter the "restaurant mafia," avoid these places. The current list includes **Városközpont** (accessible by outside elevator), Budapest V district, Váci utca 16; **La Dolce Vita**, Október 6. utca 8; **Nirvana Night Club**, Szent István krt. 13; **Ti'Amo Bar,** Budapest IX district, Ferenc körút 19–21; **Diamond Club**, Budapest II district, Bimbó út 3; and **Pigalle Night Club,** Budapest VIII district, Kiss József utca 1–3.

You can always check the embassy website for updated information: visit http://budapest.usembassy.gov/tourist_advisory.html.

---

1 Restaurants by Cuisine

CAFES & BISTROS

Cafe Incognito ⊛ (The Inner City & Central Pest, p. 123)

Darshan Cafe and Udvar (The Inner City & Central Pest, p. 124)

Old Amsterdam (The Inner City & Central Pest, p. 124)

Paris, Texas (The Inner City & Central Pest, p. 124)

Key to Abbreviations: $$$$ = Very Expensive $$$ = Expensive $$ = Moderate $ = Inexpensive

COFFEEHOUSES

Angelika Cukrászda (Central Buda, p. 122)

Auguszt Cukrászda ✵✵ (Central Buda, p. 123)

Centrál Kávéház ✵✵✵ (The Inner City & Central Pest, p. 120)

Gerbeaud's ✵✵ (The Inner City & Central Pest, p. 121)

Lukács Cukrászda ✵ (The Inner City & Central Pest, p. 121)

Művész Kávéház ✵ (The Inner City & Central Pest, p. 121)

Parlament Kávéház ✵✵ (The Inner City & Central Pest, p. 122)

Ruszwurm Cukrászda ✵✵ (The Castle District, p. 123)

Szamos Marcipán Budai Cukrázda ✵ (The Buda Hills, p. 123)

FRENCH

La Fontaine ✵ (The Inner City & Central Pest, $$$, p. 97)

Le Jardin de Paris ✵ (Central Buda, $$, p. 114)

Lou Lou ✵ (The Inner City & Central Pest, $$$, p. 100)

GREEK

Taverna Dionysos (The Inner City & Central Pest, $$, p. 106)

HUNGARIAN CONTEMPORARY

Arcade ✵✵ (Central Buda, $$, p. 113)

Articsóka (The Inner City & Central Pest, $$, p. 100)

Baraka ✵✵ (The Inner City & Central Pest, $$$, p. 97)

Bock Bisztró ✵✵ (Northern Buda & Óbuda, $$, p. 120)

Box utca ✵✵ (The Inner City & Central Pest, $$, p. 101)

Buena Vista ✵ (The Inner City & Central Pest, $$, p. 101)

Café Kör ✵ (The Inner City & Central Pest, $$, p. 101)

Café Miró ✵ (The Castle District, $, p. 117)

Café Pierrot ✵✵ (The Castle District, $$$, p. 116)

Fészek ✵ (The Inner City & Central Pest, $$, p. 101)

Firkász ✵✵ (The Inner City & Central Pest, $$, p. 102)

Gerloczy Kávéház ✵ (The Inner City & Central Pest, $$, p. 102)

Gresham Kávéház ✵ (The Inner City & Central Pest, $$, p. 102)

Hemingway ✵ (Central Buda, $$, p. 114)

Jankó Kortárs Magyar Étterem ✵ (The Castle District, $$, p. 116)

Kéhli Vendéglő ✵✵ (Northern Buda & Óbuda, $$$, p. 119)

Képiro ✵ (The Inner City & Central Pest, $$, p. 103)

Kisbuda Gyöngye ✵✵ (Northern Buda & Óbuda, $$$, p. 119)

M ✵✵ (The Inner City & Central Pest, $$, p. 104)

Menza ✵ (The Inner City & Central Pest, $$, p. 104)

Ocean Bar and Grill ✵✵ (The Inner City & Central Pest, $$, p. 104)

Remiz ✵✵ (The Buda Hills, $$$, p. 115)

Rivalda Café & Restaurant ✵ (The Castle District, $$, p. 116)

Robinson Restaurant ✵✵ (Beyond Central Pest, $$$, p. 112)

Spoon Café & Lounge ✵✵ (The Inner City & Central Pest, $$, p. 106)

Tabáni Terasz ✵✵ (Central Buda, $$, p. 114)

Tom George ✵ (The Inner City & Central Pest, $$, p. 106)

VistaCafé Restaurant (The Inner City & Central Pest, $$, p. 105)

Zebrano ✵ (The Inner City & Central Pest, $$, p. 107)

HUNGARIAN TRADITIONAL

Alabárdos ✵ (The Castle District, $$$$, p. 115)

Alföldi Kisvendéglő ✵ (The Inner City & Central Pest, $, p. 108)

> *Tips* **Check, Please: Paying Your Bill & Tips on Tipping**
>
> In restaurants in Budapest, the customer has to initiate the paying ritual. You may find that your waiter has disappeared by the time you're ready to settle up. Call over any restaurant employee and ask to pay. The waiter whose job it is to collect payment (maybe your waiter, maybe not) will eventually (don't hold your breath) be sent to your table with the bill, which is usually nestled in a small booklet. If you think the bill is mistaken, don't be embarrassed to question it; locals commonly do this. Waiters readily correct the bill when challenged.
>
> **Always ask if a service charge is already included**, as is often the case. If service charge is included, no tip is necessary (though locals usually round the bill up to make payment easier). If no service charge is included, **add 10% to the bill (15% for exceptional service**—though note that the waiter very rarely gets a share of the tip). Place the entire amount in the booklet, which you may then leave on the table. If you want to split your bill, the waiters are happy to do so; try to let them know in advance, while ordering your meal.
>
> In smaller, less formal lunchroom-type places, waiters will often remain at your table after delivering the bill, waiting patiently for payment. In these face-to-face encounters, state the full amount you are paying (bill plus tip), and the waiter will make change on the spot.

Aranyszarvas ✦ (Central Buda, $$, p. 113)

Bagolyvár ✦ (Beyond Central Pest, $$, p. 112)

Csarnok Vendéglő ✦ (The Inner City & Central Pest, $, p. 108)

Csendes Étterem ✦ (The Inner City & Central Pest, $, p. 108)

Ezüstponty ✦✦✦ (The Buda Hills, $$, p. 118)

Gundel ✦✦ (Beyond Central Pest, $$$$, p. 109)

Horgásztanya Vendéglő ✦ (Central Buda, $$, p. 114)

Kacsa Vendéglő ✦✦✦ (Central Buda, $$$$, p. 113)

Kisharang Étkezde ✦ (The Inner City & Central Pest, $, p. 109)

Kispipa Vendéglő ✦ (The Inner City & Central Pest, $$, p. 103)

Makkhetes Vendéglő ✦ (The Buda Hills, $, p. 118)

Náncsi Néni Vendéglője ✦✦ (The Buda Hills, $$$, p. 117)

Szeged Vendéglő (Central Buda, $$, p. 114)

Szép Ilona ✦ (The Buda Hills, $$, p. 118)

Új Sipos Halászkert (Northern Buda & Óbuda, $$$, p. 119)

INDIAN

Govinda Vegetariánus Étterem ✦ (The Inner City & Central Pest, $, p. 108)

Salaam Bombay ✦✦ (The Inner City & Central Pest, $$, p. 105)

Shalimar (The Inner City & Central Pest, $$, p. 106)

ITALIAN

Páva ✦✦ (The Inner City & Central Pest, $$$, p. 100)

Pomo D'oro ✦ (The Inner City & Central Pest, $$, p. 105)

Lou Lou ☞ FRENCH   Located on a quiet side street in the financial district, not far from Parliament, this small (just eight tables) candlelit cellar space was opened in 1996 by Károly Rudits, who formerly ran the kitchen at the Kempinski hotel. The decor is rustic and tasteful, with Roman yellow walls and a vaulted ceiling. The lengthy menu is in English. If you want to splurge, opt for the grilled prawns or veal. Fresh-fish dishes are the specialty of the house. Lou Lou features an extensive wine list. A house wine is available and is a good choice. As we were going to press this restaurant was going through a substantive renovation, so by the time you venture here, a "new look" and changes to the menu are expected.

Vigyázó F. u. 4. ℂ 1/312-4505. Reservations recommended. All soups 840 Ft ($4.20); appetizers 1,680 Ft–2,880 Ft ($8.40–$14); main courses 2,340 Ft–5,400 Ft ($12–$27). AE, MC, V. Mon–Fri noon–3pm; Mon–Sat 7pm–midnight. Metro: Deák tér (all lines) or Kossuth tér (Red line).

Páva ☞☞ ITALIAN   The restaurant of Budapest's truly world-class hotel must be elegant and suave at the same time, and this one is both. While the atmosphere here is a tad stiff, the dining experience is memorable. Make sure you leave yourself a lot of time to enjoy the Páva, however, which serves really great Italian cuisine: this is a 3-hour, six-course meal, and if you are lucky the friendly Italian restaurant manager Andrea Colla will guide you through a dinner in which four kinds of wines are served. We started with warm baby artichoke with provolone cheese and arugula served with a light balsamic dressing. Then came the best part of the feast: a porcini and truffle cappuccino with wild mushrooms and taleggio toast which was basically a mushroom soup, but exquisite and truly memorable. Next was a pumpkin and scampi risotto, which was followed by a bitter and truly unsavory grenade apple and Campari gratiné. It was supposed to guide us into the main course, but it just didn't work. The roasted duck breast with wild mushrooms served with folded ravioli was excellent, however, and it was a pleasure just dining in this building: one of Budapest's most beautiful.

Roosevelt tér 5–6. ℂ 1/268-5100. Reservations recommended. 6-course menu 9,800 Ft ($49), with wines 18,000 Ft ($90). AE, DC, MC, V. Mon–Sat 6–10pm. Metro: Deák tér (all lines) or Kossuth tér (Red line).

MODERATE

Articsóka HUNGARIAN CONTEMPORARY   An exceptionally well-designed establishment, Articsóka is actually a complex consisting of a restaurant, a cafe, a roof terrace, an art gallery, and a theater that was once a favorite among Hungarian show-biz and media celebrities. The Moorish interior has a careful, harmonious design. The restaurant offers a combination of tasty food, a polite staff, and at times, entertainment. The menu includes Hungarian, vegetarian, seafood, and international delicacies. While the restaurant prides itself as being "Mediterranean," we saw little evidence of this. The house recommended hardy local specialties. We tasted a traditional Hungarian goulash, followed by roast tenderloin of pork stuffed with gooseliver purée in ham and a pearl-onion sauce, and a leg of lamb, Pékné-style. The meats were tender, and food acceptable; but it didn't shine as being a unique cuisine in a city whose culinary palette has expanded in recent years. On occasional evenings there are free theater performances at the small theater that seats some 120. Check out the programs in advance on the restaurant website.

VI. Zichy Jenő u. 17. ℂ 1/302-7757. www.articsoka.hu. Reservations recommended, especially for the roof terrace. Soup 750 Ft–850 Ft ($3.75–$4.25); starters 1,200 Ft–2,300 Ft ($6–$12); main courses 2,500 Ft–3,900 Ft ($13–$20). AE, MC, V. Daily noon–midnight. Metro: Opera (Yellow line).

Box utca 🎯🎯 HUNGARIAN CONTEMPORARY   A unique sports bar and restaurant dreamed up by Hungarian boxing legend and national hero, István "Ko-Ko" Kovács. An Olympic and professional world boxing champion, Ko-Ko (as he is affectionately known by Hungarians) was truly brilliant, somewhat of a psychological prankster. In creating Box utca, he has applied his crafty wits to the culinary world. He's decorated his restaurant with a wide array of memorabilia, pictures, and newspaper clippings from his climb to fame. The far end of the restaurant is more intimate than the street-front seats, and on a non-sports night the atmosphere has little to do with a traditional sports bar or restaurant, save for the television screens. We were as impressed by the food as we were by the atmosphere; Vegetarians will enjoy the huge clam-shape pasta with forest mushrooms topped with a spinach and cheese sauce, while meat eaters can try the duck ragout with forest mushrooms, a blueberry sauce, and croquettes. A curious crowd inhabits this place, from the swanky to the young and restless. Have dessert in the cigar room, which has wireless high-speed Internet access and more memorabilia.

VI. Bajcsy Zs. út 21. ⓒ 1/354-1444. Reservations recommended. Soup 650 Ft–790 Ft ($3.25–$3.95); starters 1,450 Ft–1,750 Ft ($7.25–$8.75); main courses 1,550 Ft–3,750 Ft ($7.75–$19). AE, DC, MC, V. Mon–Fri 8am–midnight; Sat–Sun 10am–midnight. Metro: Arany János (Blue line).

Buena Vista 🎯 HUNGARIAN CONTEMPORARY   Located in one of the best places to hang out in the summer months, on Liszt Ferenc square. While the food is good, the look and feel of the place doesn't seem to know if it wants to be a cool and hip hangout for stars or those who want to be seen, or a traditional Hungarian restaurant. The interior decor is stark and simple, and service pleasant. The restaurant prides itself on its wide variety of Hungarian wines.

VI. Liszt Ferenc tér 4–5. ⓒ 1/344-6303. www.buena-vista.hu. Reservations recommended. Soup 690 Ft ($3.45); starters 990 Ft–1,990 Ft ($4.95–$9.95); main courses 1,690 Ft–4,990 Ft ($8.45–$25). AE, DC, MC, V. Mon–Fri 8am–1am; Sat–Sun 11am–1am. Metro: Oktogon (Yellow line).

Café Kör 🎯 HUNGARIAN CONTEMPORARY   This centrally located restaurant began as a coffeehouse in 1995, and in subsequent years it developed both in terms of its space and in cuisine to the comfortable and reliable restaurant that it is today. Just a stone's throw away from the Basilica, the owners developed Café Kör based on models of simple decor and attentive cuisine seen in other international capitals. The restaurant has become increasingly popular due to its proximity to four- and five-star hotels, notably the Hotel Four Seasons Gresham Palace. We ate strips of duck breast with honey, apple, and green pasta which ended up being a tad dry. The roast salmon with lemon balm sauce was, again, acceptable and even good, but not exceptional. We recommend this restaurant because you will always be satisfied, although not necessarily overly impressed.

V. Sas u. 17. ⓒ 1/311-0053. Reservations recommended. Soup 490 Ft–680 Ft ($2.50–$3.50); starters 730 Ft–2,300 Ft ($4.95–$9.95); main courses 1,600 Ft–3,580 Ft ($8.45–$25). No credit cards. Mon–Sat 10am–11pm. Metro: Bajcsy-Zsilinsky út (Yellow line).

Fészek 🎯 *Value* HUNGARIAN CONTEMPORARY   Owned by the same folks who own the better-known Kispipa Vendéglő (see below), Fészek is located in the quiet, interior courtyard of a building at the corner of Dob utca and Kertész utca. The outdoor dining experience here is without equal in the busy center of Pest. A small, easy-to-miss sign on the street is the only advertisement. Pass through a dim lobby to enter the restaurant. Savory wild game and freshwater fish dishes are the house specialties. Be sure to reserve ahead of time since Fészek is invariably crowded.

VII. Kertész u. 36. © 1/322-6043. Reservations recommended. Soup 300 Ft–800 Ft ($1.50–$4); main courses 1,100 Ft–2,900 Ft ($5.50–$15). No credit cards. Daily noon–midnight. Tram: 4 or 6 to Király utca.

Firkász *Value* HUNGARIAN CONTEMPORARY   A reminder that traditions can live on and become reborn in the form of new and lively places like Firkász. "Tradition is our future" is their motto of sorts, one that the immaculately dressed manager Gergely Sallai takes very seriously. There is a turn-of-the-last-century feeling to the restaurant, and yet it remains contemporary. This place has the roots of a magical place that keeps old-style traditions alive. The eatery is decorated with a wealth of wine bottles, and the walls are pasted with early-20th-century newspapers, old pictures, telephones, or clocks. It is the favorite eatery of the finest young Hungarian film-director, the 30-year-old Kornél Mundruczó, who is an almost daily regular here, in the old-world style. Some regulars venture in for a drink or meal at the bar, while others are seated and watch the lively accordion player, or a tad tipsy or more gathering of tourists. The restaurant serves a wide selection—60 to 80 strong—of Hungarian wines. We had a tender and rich deer ragout with mashed potatoes, but choose from a vast selection of Hungarian specialties like Szeged Goulash, gooseliver, or wild game.

XIII. Tátra u. 18. © 1/450-1118. Reservations recommended. Soup 590 Ft–1,390 Ft ($2.95–$6.95); starters 990 Ft–2,390 Ft ($4.95–$12); main courses 1,999 Ft–4,690 Ft ($10–$23). MC, V. Daily noon–midnight. Tram: 4 or 6 to Jászai Mari tér.

Gerloczy Kávéház *Value* HUNGARIAN CONTEMPORARY   A reader and her amusing story lead us to this centrally located coffeehouse-restaurant that bakes divine bread and greets you with the sounds of a classical harp. The restaurant itself is a two-story former bank building that also has a long history as a coffeehouse. It lost that function during World War II. Now a little over a year old, it already feels as if it is steeped in tradition. Our reader described grinning with joy as she began to eat her toasted ewe's cheese salad. She was particularly enchanted by the playfully sassy style of the waiters, describing being inadvertently *ooh la la*-ed by a fish platter traveling past her table. The waitress escorting it even twirled and did a curtsey with the dish in front of her and her mother before heading off to its destination. We weren't curtsied, but in fact tried that fish platter and were somewhat disappointed at its lack of freshness—the only part of our meal that didn't completely impress us, though. It is comfortably located, welcoming, and nice for a light meal and a good wine.

V. Gerloczy u. 1. © 1/235-0953. Reservations recommended. Soup 490 Ft–780 Ft ($2.45–$3.90); starters 690 Ft–1,760 Ft ($3.45–$8.80); main courses 1,300 Ft–2,780 Ft ($6.50–$14). MC, V. Mon–Fri 7am–11pm; Sat–Sun 8am–11pm. Metro: Deák tér (Red line).

Gresham Kávéház HUNGARIAN CONTEMPORARY   Housed in the luscious Hotel Four Seasons Gresham Palace, despite the name, this is not a coffeehouse. Not even close, and in the name of the true traditional coffeehouses and the pillars of those traditions, we even take offence to the name. That is not to say that we would not like to see a coffeehouse here, in fact, we would. This is a restaurant, and the management makes no bones about it. They even told us that is not recommended to come here simply for a coffee. Hermetically sealed as the architecture of the hotel is, this restaurant is actually the "breakfast room" for hotel guests. We tried the gooseliver here, and can say that it competes with the famed Gundel restaurants: it is served with traditional lecso and potatoes. The Argentine sirloin steak served with spinach was also excellent, as it should be. You can also find traditional fare like chicken paprikas with galuskas, spaghetti, or chicken breast or more lavish plates like a glazed duck breast served with polenta, wild mushroom, and baby onions.

V. Roosevelt tér 5–6. ⓒ 1/268-5110. Reservations recommended. Soup 1,200 Ft ($6); starters 2,100 Ft–3,200 Ft ($10.50–$16); main courses 2,600 Ft–3,800 Ft ($13–$19). AE, DC, MC, V. Daily 6:30am–10:30pm, except Thurs–Sat open until 11pm, Sunday open 6:30-11pm. Metro: Deák tér (Red line) or tram 2 to Roosevelt tér.

Iguana Bar & Grill 🍴🍴 *Kids* MEXICAN   Colorfully decorated and always buzzing with activity, you might have trouble finding a seat at this buzzing restaurant. This is a real hangout for Budapest expatriates, but also draws younger crowds and families. The decor includes a fare of old Mexican posters, reproductions from Diego Rivera oddities, and strangely, even a reproduction of an old master painting of the Last Supper. Opened in 1997, Iguana continues to be on the map for those who are looking for home-style service and reliable, good-ol' Mexican food: quesadillas, chilies, fajitas, burritos, enchiladas, plus vegetarian options. For those who are adventuresome, try the enticing fajitas made of marinated strips of tenderloin, chicken, and shrimp. The fajitas are grilled on a sizzling hot steamy iron platter with onions and peppers. Jenö's Quesadilla (formerly Gino's) is my special treat, which includes a red pepper next to it on the menu and is puportedly named after a Budapest expatriate. You might also try the Iguana Beer, made especially for the restaurant by a small Csepel Island brewery.

Zóltán u. 16. ⓒ 1/331-4352. www.iguana.hu. Reservations recommended. Appetizers 600 Ft–1,200 Ft ($3–$6); main courses 1,800 Ft-3,300 Ft ($9–$16.50). AE, DISC, MC, V. Daily 11:30am–12:30am (Fri–Sat until 1:30am). Metro: Kossuth tér (Red line).

Képiro 🍴 HUNGARIAN CONTEMPORARY   Centrally located, the restaurant is decorated with the buoyant reproductions of the contemporary Hungarian artist Ákos Birkás and offers reliable contemporary Hungarian dishes. A magical beef marinade, made from the juice of various meats, is used to varying effect; it masks a lack of pizazz in the terrine of gooseliver, but the Képiro beef tenderloin baked with sweetbreads and goat cheese melts wonderfully in your mouth, and tastes somewhat of lamb! The warm appetizer of grilled tiger prawns served with avocado noodles and leek is another solid choice. The "chocolate symphony" with pomegranate, served with truffle *millefeuille,* a white-chocolate brownie roll, and marble chocolate will leave you whirling.

V. Képiro u. 3. ⓒ 1/266-0430. www.kepirorestaurant.com. Reservations recommended. Soups 650 Ft–1,000 Ft ($3.25–$5); starters 1,390 Ft–2,950 Ft ($7–$14.75); main courses 2,200 Ft–4,450 Ft ($11–$22.25). AE, MC, V. Daily noon–3pm and 6–11pm. Metro: Kálvin tér (Blue line).

Kispipa Vendéglő 🍴 *Value* HUNGARIAN TRADITIONAL   Unobtrusively located on a residential street in Erzsébetváros, behind the old Jewish district, Kispipa (Little Pipe) is a cozy, well-lit establishment. The cream-colored walls are lined with vintage Hungarian poster advertisements, and piano music contributes to the relaxed atmosphere. The menu is extensive; wild-game dishes are the house specialty. Five "complete menu" deals offer soup, a main course, and a dessert for a very reasonable price. Kispipa, in former times one of Budapest's few private restaurants, has played a small part in modern Hungarian history: The political party FIDESZ (Young Democrats), now the main opposition party, was founded here (illegally, no less) in 1988. Until recently, Kispipa was closed during the entire summer, but it is now open year-round.

VII. Akácfa u. 38. ⓒ 1/342-2587. Reservations recommended. Main courses 1,700 Ft–4,000 Ft ($8.50–$20). AE, DISC, MC, V. Mon–Sat noon–1am. Metro: Oktogon (Yellow line).

M ✫✫ HUGARIAN CONTEMPORARY French cuisine and atmosphere are blended with Hungarian flavors in this restaurant that serves its water in Communist-era jugs—and what it saves on the furnishings, it invests in good, simple and fresh foods. The decor here is as simple as it gets, with curtains and flowers literally drawn on the walls in simple lines. Next to the popular cafe square at Liszt Ferenc Tér, the atmosphere is homelike with Spanish or French music playing quietly in the background. Miklós Sulyok, the owner of this restaurant, is well known in the liberal circles of Budapest politics and cohorts among the poets, writers, and artists of the capital. This small two-floor restaurant has a very snug atmosphere and even serves homemade bread. The menu changes on a daily basis, and let this be a surprise for the visitors. We enjoyed a grilled Viking steak served with sausages and potatoes on a large wooden plate. The chef makes a point of creating meals on a whim, based on what he finds fresh at the market. Because of the home-style nature of this restaurant, some of the plates may not always be available . . . but the chef will always be able to dream something up for you.

VII. Kertész utca 48. ℂ **1/342-8991.** www.rajzoltetterem.hu. Soups 650 Ft–750 Ft ($3.25–$3.75); starters 1,350 Ft–1,550 Ft ($6.75–$7.75); main courses 1,250 Ft–2,550 Ft ($6.25–$13). No credit cards. Daily noon–midnight. Metro: Oktogon.

Marquis de Salade RUSSIAN/AZERI This little place turns out a wide assortment of dishes from a variety of different cuisines. Unfortunately, the English-language menu is a tad unreadable, but if you get through the poor translation of the text you will soon realize that the restaurant employs an eclectic mix of cooks from areas around the world, resulting in a sophisticated yet earthy selection of offerings that reflect this diversity. Located on the edge of Pest's theater district, it is a favorite luncheon spot of Hungarian actors.

VI. Hajós u. 43. ℂ **1/302-4086.** Appetizers 800 Ft–1,700 Ft ($4–$8.50); starters 1,200 Ft–15,000 Ft ($6–$75); main courses 2,500 Ft–3,900 Ft ($13–$20). MC, V. Daily 11am–1am. Metro: Arany János u. (Blue line).

Menza ✫ ⓥalue HUGARIAN CONTEMPORARY It's not surprising that this restaurant is the brainchild of the same team that started exporting Communist-era shoes to Europe as a kind of nostalgia item. The place, decorated in pastel orange and greens, exudes creativity, which is probably why Hungarian experimental theater's true star Anna-Maria Láng of the Krétakör group once recommended it as her top pick. Run by the youngish entrepreneur Roland Radványi, the decor here is decidedly retro and reminiscent of the '60s or '70s without the accompanying disco beats. The food, on the other hand, is traditional but sumptuous. We started with the clear beef soup with carrots, vegetables, and dumplings (surprisingly not served with horseradish). The appetizers were more exciting: duck liver pâté or the adventuresome bone marrow—taken right out of the bone in front of you—served with a salad and garlic toast. For the main course, we tried the exquisite chicken breast with plumbs and red onions, as well as the divine duck breast with cabbage pasta: we recommend both.

VI. Liszt Ferenc tér 2. ℂ **1/413-1482.** Reservations recommended. Soups 560 Ft–690 Ft ($2.80–$3.45); starters 850 Ft–1,190 Ft ($4.25–$5.95); main courses 1,390 Ft–2,790 Ft ($6.95–$14). AE, MC, V. Daily 10am–midnight. Metro: Oktogon (Yellow line).

Ocean Bar and Grill ✫✫ HUGARIAN CONTEMPORARY In a landlocked country all too impressed by seafood, this is your best bet if you want to get the freshest in town. "It's like eating at home in London . . . it's light and fresh," London-based costume designer John Cowell told us of his visit to this restaurant during the Budapest shoot of the motion-picture *Aragon*. With seafood imported from Norway three times a week this restaurant that is located adjacent to the Marriott Hotel and the Danube is a favorite among film crews not only for its food but for its service and pleasant ambience. The service is fast, even a tad too fast, as we had to emphasize the fact that we enjoy contemplating an empty plate in order to enjoy each course. The interior is sparsely decorated, and in a unique element in Budapest, has an open kitchen. There are two large aquariums with African cichlids, while a third has exotic saltwater fish with living corals to give the space a lively and colorful vibe. We started our meal with a Bergen fish soup, and a cream soup with salmon, cod, and shrimp. Our main dish was a sumptuous mega platter of seafood that included salmon, scallops, swordfish, mussels, cod, prawns, and tuna. Don't forget dessert, in our case a chocolate delight served with a passion-fruit coulis and vanilla ice cream.

V. Petőfi tér 3. © 1/266-1826. www.oceanbargrill.com. Reservations recommended. Soups 900 Ft–1,990 Ft ($4.50–$9.95); starters 1,690 Ft–2,790 Ft ($8.45–$14); main courses 2,390 Ft–7,000 Ft ($12–$35). AE, MC, V. Daily noon–midnight. Metro: Vörösmarty tér (Yellow line).

Pomo D'oro ⊙ ITALIAN The concept behind this restaurant delves around the simple, but all powerful, tomato. As the story goes, the menu reads, in the 16th and 17th centuries it was an aphrodisiac used by alchemists in various curative potions. That's why it became customary for men to offer seedling tomato plants to young women. So you can imagine that suddenly the tomato sauce that we ate on our entree at the Pomo D'oro seemed to take on a new meaning. The two-story restaurant itself is large and massive, made of walls of stone. We started with a platter that included a wonderful imported Burrata cheese, Parma ham, and bruschetta, while the main course included pastas with meats and seafood, a rendezvous of seafood specialties. The Bolognese pasta was sumptuous, while the story of the "Priest Strangler" dish was far more interesting than its heavy yet bland taste. The king prawns and blue mussels, however, were tasty and fresh. The atmosphere was quiet and intimate.

V. Arany János u. 9. © 1/302-6473. www.pomodorobudapest.com. Reservations recommended. Soups 750 Ft–1,890 Ft ($3.75–$9.45); starters 990 Ft–1,750 Ft ($4.95–$8.75); main courses 1,480 Ft–4,990 Ft ($7.40–$25). MC, V. Mon–Fri 11am–midnight; Sat–Sun noon–midnight. Metro: Arany János u. (Blue line).

Salaam Bombay ⊙⊙ INDIAN "I wanted to create an Indian restaurant . . . but in Europe, without emphasizing the typical statues, tandori or butter chicken . . ." said the ambitious Firdosh Irani, the managing director of this recently opened restaurant. And this is exactly what he did. Irani came to Budapest in 1994 via New York, and has been in the Indian cuisine business for over 30 years. And it shows, since this restaurant probably gives you the best value that your money can buy in Budapest, as well as a unique look at a more contemporary and varied Indian menu than we are accustomed to. The interior of the restaurant was designed in India, and created in Budapest. Psychedelic colors pervade the space, with shells, sand, and bamboo sticks leaving it both exotic and sparsely contemporary at the same time. We started with the unusual and sumptuous chicken momo, which was basically steamed dumplings stuffed with chicken and served with a spicy tantra sauce. The chicken rolls cooked in a creamy almond sauce were also the favorite of this gourmet taster. As the food kept on coming, the many varied hot and piquant tastes melded one after another into a crescendo. Irani, who is emphatic and passionate about introducing a new look to Indian dining, emphasizes that times are changing, and he is changing with them.

V. Mérleg u. 6. 𝄽 1/411-1252. www.salaambombay.hu. Soups 500 Ft–600 Ft ($2.50–$3); starters 700 Ft–950 Ft ($3.50–$4.75); main courses 1,500 Ft–3,200 Ft ($7.50–$16). MC, V. Daily noon–3pm and 6–11:30pm. Metro: Deák tér (Red line).

Shalimar INDIAN   Among the first Indian restaurants opened in Budapest, this cellar-styled venue was developed by Amar Sinha, who arrived in the Magyar capital as a young man and has stayed in Budapest ever since. The restaurant generally serves North Indian fare, Mughlai cuisine, using almost 60 different spices to prepare. The atmosphere is friendly but a bit outdated. Sinha is looking at ways to renew his restaurant: not a simple task since it has developed a clientele among expatriates, tourists, and Hungarians alike who have relied on Shalimar for its simplicity and good, reliable food. We started with an Indian Cobra beer, followed by a chicken makhani, koma beef, lamb with spinach, and lentils. Don't forget the naan bread, baked in a tandoor clay oven, fired with charcoal.

VII. Dob u. 50. 𝄽 1/352-0305. Reservations recommended. Soup 690 Ft ($3.45); starters 880 Ft–4,150 Ft ($4.40–$21); main courses 1,730 Ft–2,950 Ft ($8.65–$15). AE, MC, V. Daily noon–4pm for lunch, 6–11pm for dinner. Tram: 4 or 6 to Király utca.

Spoon Café & Lounge 𝄽𝄽 HUNGARIAN CONTEMPORARY   Start your evening off at this romantic floating restaurant on the Danube with a Kir Royale, made of bols crème de casis. The suave restaurant with a romantic view of the Chain Bridge is attractive to the MTV generation and is frequented by young professionals, expatriates, and tourists alike. The nifty boat (it even has an elevator for those who are completely lazy, and plenty of terrace space when the weather permits) is owned by the same restaurateur who runs Robinson Restaurant near Heroes' Square, and even serves a similar fare. On the left when entering is a more intimate and sparse space, while to the right is a lively dining area adorned with a tropical aquarium, TV screens, and two sit-down bars. Our food was served on different-shaped plates; the gooseliver pâté with fig marinated in Tokay wine and caramelized purple onion jam is a fine starter. The maize cream soup with St. Jacques mussels was excellent, as was the Angus Argentine steak with Gorgonzola sauce with grilled vegetables. We took advantage of their many cocktails, at which point we sparked up a conversation with our friendly neighbors. This is a perfect place to go in a group. The bathrooms here are also noteworthy, with a terrific view of the Danube.

V. Vigadó tér 3. kikötő (facing the Inter-Continental Hotel). 𝄽 1/411-0933. www.spooncafe.hu. Reservations recommended. Soup 550 Ft–1,600 Ft ($2.75–$8); starters 790 Ft–2,890 Ft ($3.95–$15); main courses 2,790 Ft–5,690 Ft ($14–$29). AE, DC, MC, V. Daily 10am–1:30am. Tram: 4 or 6 to Király utca. Metro: Vörösmarthy tér (Yellow line).

Taverna Dionysos GREEK   This restaurant is a faithful rendition of a Greek tavern, located on Pest's Danube embankment. It serves an extensive fish menu, souvlaki, lobster, and shrimp in a Mediterranean environment. The restaurant is located in a typically whitewashed building, and you are served on blue-and-white tablecloths. You'll find good, authentic Greek fare here, at reasonable prices. Weather permitting, sidewalk dining overlooking the Danube is available, but call in advance to reserve.

V. Belgrád rakpart 16. 𝄽 1/318-1222. Reservations recommended. Soups 490 Ft–820 Ft ($2.45–$4.10); starters 540 Ft–1,920 Ft ($2.70–$9.60); main courses 1,690 Ft–10,990 Ft ($8.45–$55). AE, MC, V. Daily noon–midnight. Metro: Ferenciek tere (Blue line).

Tom George 𝄽 *Overrated* HUNGARIAN CONTEMPORARY   One of Budapest's most trendy restaurants frequented by both suave Hungarians and visitors as well, particularly the English crowds. The palette runs from contemporary Indian to Japanese, with a generous selection of sushi. The interior is spacious, the lighting atmospheric, and the general feeling emanates "coolness." If you are with a small group, reserve the rounded tables at the far end of the restaurant that seat eight comfortably. While we do recommend this restaurant, the only problem is the service. Despite a high proportion of waiters, the service can be gruelingly slow and the waiters less than enlightening. We started with an Indian Lentil soup with creamy veggies, followed by a fresh, light green salad. We finished our meal with a tender Argentine sirloin steak, and watched enviously as a variety of beautiful-looking sushi was served to the next table!

V. Október 6 utca 8. ℂ 1/266-3525. Reservations recommended. Soups 680 Ft–1,650 Ft ($3.40–$8.25); starters 1,650 Ft–3,580 Ft ($8.25–$18); main courses 2,500 Ft–7,600 Ft ($13–$38). AE, MC, V. Daily noon–midnight. Metro: Ferenciek tere (Blue line).

VistaCafé Restaurant HUNGARIAN CONTEMPORARY   This is a convenient place for a hardy meal, right in the center of town and adjacent to one of the city's most frequented travel agencies, Vista. The restaurant's manager is László Gulyás, who returned to Hungary, homesick, after working in the service sector in Graz and Munich. It is airy, with high ceilings and the works of local contemporary artists hanging on the walls. The menu includes dishes like filet of pork coated with spinach and bacon, tenderloin a la Rossini with almond potato croquettes, or the dish that we had: crispy port roast Bereg style. There is also a season-specific menu which changes monthly. Our dish was as heavy as you can imagine with fried onion rings and served with potatoes. Try to take a walk after this meal! Nightly a live pianist entertains with jazz or Latin beats, and there are also Internet machines, so you can also check your e-mail.

VI. Paulay Ede 7. ℂ 1/268-0888. www.vistacafe.hu. Reservations recommended Wed–Thurs evenings. Soups 480 Ft–680 Ft ($2.40–$3.40); starters 520 Ft–1,250 Ft ($2.60–$6.25); main courses 1,450 Ft–2,690 Ft ($7.25–$14). AE, DC, DISC, MC, V. Daily 9–11pm. Metro: Deák tér (Red line).

Zebrano ☆ HUNGARIAN CONTEMPORARY   Located inside of the boutique Andrássy hotel, Zebrano is a stylish addition to a stretch of Andrássy út that has relatively few dining options. The place recently underwent a makeover, and now has a sort of '70s old-school retro decor, with wood laminate tables, an orange-and-black color scheme, and the kind of iron floor that would be found in a warehouse. Seating is in comfy leather chairs, and tables are nicely spaced out giving each plenty of space and privacy. The orange bar sits in front of a glass wall with a waterfall flowing over it, separating the restaurant from the hotel. The restaurant emphasizes its Asian-influenced dishes, like its Indonesian chicken and orange duck salad, but the menu here is truly international in scope, offering dishes that span the globe, like borscht; a starter plate with pâté, caviar, prosciutto, and gravelax; a Mediterranean seafood platter; and a Cajun chicken breast with black-bean sauce. The dessert list is small, but the tasty lemon-flavored cheesecake is worth a calorie splurge. The wine list offers few wines by the glass. It is also mostly Hungarian, which denies diners the chance to sample foreign wines with their foreign-accented foods. The menu, which changes seasonally, is a bit pricey for most Hungarians, but the place attracts many workers from nearby embassies and businesses, particularly for its quick three-course business lunches, which are guaranteed to be served in under 30 minutes.

VI. Andrássy út 111. ℂ 1/462-2189. Appetizers 2,000 Ft–4,100 Ft ($10–$21); soup 750 Ft–1,500 Ft ($3.75–$7.50); main courses 2,200 Ft–5,700 Ft ($11–$29). AE, DC, MC, V. Mon–Fri 11:30am–2:30pm and 6pm–12:30am; Sat 6pm–2:30am. Metro: Bajza utca (Yellow line).

INEXPENSIVE

Alföldi Kisvendéglő ☆ HUNGARIAN TRADITIONAL   The spicy, paprika-laced tastes of the Hungarian Plain are presented well in this time-tested Pest eatery. There is a comprehensive menu of traditional Hungarian fare, which is in English but continues to have lots of funny mistakes. Our host explained, "We are not linguists!" They concentrate on true Hungarian cuisine. When we visited, waiter Imre Bárkovits was celebrating 31 years working at the restaurant. He recommended the classic Szeged fisherman's soup, which is a meal in and of itself, containing three different kinds of fish. They serve Balaton fish, white sea fish, lamb, and the age-old specialties, chicken and veal paprikas. Choose between the rustic interior or weather permitting, sidewalk tables on a busy road. The waiters are formal, and can be a bit old school. As per tradition.

V. Kecskeméti u. 4. ℃ **1/267-0224.** Soup 720 Ft–950 Ft ($3.60–$4.75); starters 575 Ft–1,776 Ft ($3.40–$7.50); main courses 990 Ft–1,640 Ft ($4.95–$8.20). MC, V. Daily 11am–midnight. Metro: Kálvin tér (Blue line).

Csarnok Vendéglő ☆ *Finds* HUNGARIAN TRADITIONAL   On the Inner City's quiet Hold utca (Moon St.), the Csarnok Vendéglő is located between Szabadság tér and Bajcsy-Zsilinszky út, not far from the United States Embassy. Its name comes from the wonderful early-20th-century market hall *(csarnok)* next door. One of the few restaurants in this part of the Inner City, it's even more notable for its uniformly low prices. The menu features typical Hungarian Vendéglő fare, heavy as usual on meat dishes. Try the catfish stew, with *túrós csusza* (pasta with cottage cheese and sour cream) for a side dish. Somewhat cramped outdoor seating is available on the sidewalk, but sit inside for the full effect of the Hungarian decor.

V. Hold u. 11. ℃ **1/269-4906.** Main courses 600 Ft–1,500 Ft ($3–$7.50). No credit cards. Mon–Sat 9am–11pm; Sun noon–10pm. Metro: Arany János utca (Blue line).

Csendes Étterem ☆ HUNGARIAN TRADITIONAL   Located on the Múzeum körút section of Pest's Inner Ring boulevard, just a few minutes' walk from the main tourist area around Váci utca, the Csendes Étterem (Quiet Restaurant) features inexpensive Hungarian, Slovak, and Transylvanian dishes. Try the pork cutlet a la Bakony, which is a rich, creamy mushroom stew with plenty of sour cream and *galuska* (small noodles) for garnish. The restaurant has a decidedly rustic look, with exposed wooden rafters, wooden booths, and tasteful equestrian posters decorating the walls. The English-language menu is full of amusing errors. Csendes is a student hangout; ELTE University is just down the street.

V. Múzeum krt. 13 (enter from side street, Ferenczy István utca). ℃ **1/267-0218.** Soup 290 Ft–390 Ft ($1.45–$1.95); main courses 1,000 Ft–1,350 Ft ($5–$6.75). No credit cards. Mon–Sat noon–10pm. Metro: Astoria (Red line) or Kálvin tér (Blue line).

Govinda Vegetariánus Étterem ☆ INDIAN   A sparsely decorated New Age–style spot, this restaurant that was once called Gandhi serves interesting vegetarian food in a tranquil, smoke-free environment. The eatery, decorated with paintings of Indian gods and murals, operates on a self-service system where you can choose from different dishes, each at a set price. You can also choose from two daily menu options written on a blackboard. Choices might include stuffed squash with Indian ragout and brown rice; or a potato-pumpkin casserole with garlic Roquefort sauce, steamed cabbage, and spinach soufflé. Or you can simply go for a soup (cream of cauliflower perhaps, or lentil) and the salad bar, though the salads lack variety. Seating is

greatly influenced by his visits to French wineries. "I visited the best châteaus in Médoc, worked on the harvest, and had tastings," he said. Soon after, he began making his own wine. "At this time, in 1992, it was absolutely the beginning," he said. "I bought barrels, and I put my ideas, and my taste into this cooperation with my partners." In those days Malatinszky was working 20 hours a day, and things weren't always easy. "Winemaking technology was very simple then. Everything was made by hand, without temperature control, and there were no stainless steel tanks, only wood casks," he said. "I built an absolutely modern winery, and there weren't any similar wineries."

It's clear to both winemakers and wine drinkers here in Hungary that the best wine is yet to come. "I'm expecting enormous development in the following 10 years, because we are now over the biggest investments," said Figula Jr.

Wine Primer: Hungary has 22 wine regions and cultivates more than 93 varieties of wine grapes, producing the full spectrum of reds, whites, roses, and sparkling wines. Unfortunately for the rest of the world—but lucky for the wine-loving tourist—many of the best Hungarian wines are still kept for the domestic market. Curious wine drinkers should take note that several varietals are indigenous to Hungary, such as Furmint, Hárslevelű, Juhfark, Királyleányka, and Kadarka.

Best Regions for Whites: The majority of wine produced in Hungary is still white, and each region produces its own recognizable styles. Somló produces some of the country's best whites, which are usually acidic. Hungarians like to say that if you've ever tasted a Somlói, you'll never forget it. Tokaj produces world famous dessert wines. The Balaton regions, particularly Badacsony, make excellent whites, as does Gyöngyös in the Mátraalja region.

Best Regions for Reds: Due to the international preference for red wine that has emerged over the past decade or so, Hungary has been producing increasingly greater amounts of reds. Villány is known as the Bordeaux of Hungary. Szekszárd, Sopron, and Eger also produce fine reds. But great reds also come from regions better know for their whites, like Balatonlelle.

Names To Watch For: Hungary's best winemakers are household names among Hungarian wine lovers. The country has thousands of producers, these are a few of the best: József Bock, Vylan, Ede Tiffán, Mihály Figula, Huba Szeremley, Attila Gere, Béla Fekete, Tibor Gál, István Tóth, Ferenc Takler, Mátyás Szőke, St. Andrea (György Lőrincz), Vilmos Thummerer, Franz Weninger, János Konyári, Csaba Malatinszky, Légli Ottó, Oremus, Királyudvar, István Szepsy, Degenfeld, and Ferenc Vesztergombi.

EXPENSIVE

Robinson Restaurant ✶✶ HUNGARIAN CONTEMPORARY   The setting could not be more romantic and harmonious, with live music and tasteful décor around you as you dine overlooking the small but tranquil lake in City Park. Robinson is one of Budapest's most dynamic and well-situated restaurants, near both Heroes' Square and the Museum of Fine Arts. The food is varied, ranging from traditional classics like chicken paprika served with egg dumplings, to more exotic seafood dishes like the savory giant prawn on garlic-spinach bed with green curry. We had a perfectly done, tender ripened Angus sirloin steak with onion rings and French potato hot-pot, which was on the daily menu. Vegetarian and children's menus are available, and a coffee shop (also overlooking the lake) is on the second floor.

XIV. Városligeti tó. ℭ 1/422-0224. www.robinsonrestaurant.hu. Reservations recommended. Soup 790 Ft–890 Ft ($3.95–$4.45); starters 1,990 Ft–2,890 Ft ($9.95–$14); main courses 2,790 Ft–5,980 Ft ($14–$30). AE, DC, MC, V. Daily noon–4pm and 6pm–midnight. Metro: Hősök tere (Yellow line).

MODERATE

Bagolyvár ✶ Kids HUNGARIAN TRADITIONAL   Bagolyvár (Owl Castle) offers something unique for the budget traveler—a taste of Gundel, Budapest's most famous (and most expensive) restaurant, at less than wallet-flattening prices. In founding this restaurant, George Lang wanted to offer Hungarian "home-style" cooking to the general public at a reasonable price, and thus was born his second Budapest eatery, located just next door to Gundel in City Park. The Bagolyvár menu is limited to half a dozen main courses (supplemented by daily specials), which include roast veal with green beans and layered Savoy cabbage. We started with a sorrel cream soup with a grated hard-boiled egg, which was refreshingly light and a fine example of really good home cooking. The filet mignon with prime port bacony-style with gnocchi was excellent, but so heavy as to leave you literally sweating. The decor and ambience are pleasant and unpretentious, giving the feeling of a traditional Hungarian csárda. Some may get offended, however, at the blatant institutional sexism in the tradition of this otherwise good restaurant. The menu indicates that George Lang "created a kitchen with home cooking in which exclusively women are at work . . ." This harks back to notions that might well be forgotten. Imagine, for instance, an eatery in Alabama suddenly becoming "white-only" out of nostalgia. The parallel is extreme, but I think the logic is appropriate. The building is itself a nice example of Art Nouveau by the outstanding architect of the time, Károly Kós, whose other excellent project is the Budapest Zoo, right next door. Highchairs are available for young children. Outdoor dining is available in the restaurant's garden, next to a small pond, weather permitting.

XIV. Állatkerti út 2. ℭ 1/468-3110. Reservations recommended. Soup 580 Ft–890 Ft ($2.90–$4.45); starters 820 Ft–2,600 Ft ($4.10–$13); main courses 1,260 Ft–3,610 Ft ($6.30–$18). AE, DC, MC, V. Daily noon–11pm. Metro: Hősök tere (Yellow line).

4 Central Buda

VERY EXPENSIVE

Kacsa Vendéglő ✶✶✶ HUNGARIAN TRADITIONAL   Translated as "Duck Inn," this elegant, charming restaurant gives you a first-rate dining experience that feels both luxurious and homey. The space is located on Fő utca, the main street of Watertown, the Buda neighborhood that lies between Castle Hill and the Danube. Enticing main courses include roast duck with morello cherries, haunch of venison with grapes, and fresh pikeperch from Balaton. Other enticing dishes on the menu include grilled frogs' legs on a bed of vegetables with white wine, smoked salmon, or the delicious grilled forest mushrooms with cognac sauce and wild rice. The restaurant, which has functioned as an eatery for some 160 years, is run by Áron Rozsnyai, who obviously loves what he does, and he does it well. A trio of string players in the space completes a perfectly choreographed dining experience.

Fő u. 75. (℃ 1/201-9992. Reservations recommended. Soup 800 Ft–1,300 Ft ($4–$6.50); starters 1,800 Ft–4,100 Ft ($9–$21); main courses 1,600 Ft–6,500 Ft ($8–$33). AE, MC, V. Daily noon–1am. Metro: Batthyány tér (Red line).

MODERATE

Aranyszarvas (♠ HUNGARIAN TRADITIONAL   Aranyszarvas (The Golden Stag) is located in a historic building in central Buda's Tabán district, just below and to the south of Castle Hill. There's indoor seating in a dining room with a restrained wild-game motif, but on pleasant nights customers dine on the outdoor terrace. A string trio is available to serenade, but must be requested in advance. As the name and decor suggest, this restaurant serves wild game, and the menu lists a variety of reasonably priced dishes, such as hunter's saddle of hare, Serbian wild boar, and venison stew. The fake flowers and greenery, and somewhat dated atmosphere take away from the authentic nature of this traditional-style eatery. The venue does have a history. "I eat here, as my grandparents did years ago," said Zoltán Tihanyi, whose grandfather was sent away from the area under the Communist regime. "I come here and in some way meet them at this very place. . . . I assert the fact that we returned to where we came from."

I. Szarvas tér 1. (℃ 1/375-6451. Reservations recommended. Soup 650 Ft–890 Ft ($3.25–$4.45); starters 1,100 Ft–2,900 Ft ($5.50–$15); main courses 2,100 Ft–3,500 Ft ($11–$18). AE, MC, V. Daily noon–11pm. Bus: A number of buses serve Döbrentei tér, including no. 8 from Március 15 tér.

Arcade (♠♠ HUNGARIAN CONTEMPORARY   A modern interior decorated with the contemporary Hungarian artworks of El Kazovskij, Mulasics, and Nadler, this is a pleasant retreat at the foot of the Buda hills. Hungarian contemporary dancer and doctor Kata Juhász, who enjoys good wines, directed us to this venue which serves a unique palette of seafood and a selection of Hungarian and international cuisine. The starter was truly special, being a wonderfully marinated salmon with a red-pepper sauce: an unusual, yet very positive selection in a country where marinated or smoked salmon is a rarity. As a main course we enjoyed a medallion of Hungarian pork with red-wine-seasoned chestnut and fruit, an adventuresome mix that worked. A snazzy little touch is the small elevator that delivers the food from the kitchen to our waiter before being bandied to our table. We liked this place for its cozy and creative atmosphere.

XII. Kiss János altábornagy u. 38. (℃ 1/225-1969. Reservations recommended. Soup 890 Ft ($4.45); starters 850 Ft–2,970 Ft ($4.25–$15); main courses 1,870 Ft–4,990 Ft ($9.35–$25). MC, V. Mon–Sat noon–4pm and 6pm-midnight. Metro: Déli pályaudvar, then take 59 tram.

Hemingway (♠ HUNGARIAN CONTEMPORARY   Situated adjacent to a small pond dubbed a lake, this restaurant has been a staple in Budapest for some time. Recommended to us by Gábor Izbéki, the well-respected editor of the local daily paper *Metro,* the interior of the venue gives off a Mediterranean feel to it with the live music adding to the soothing, authentic atmosphere. We started with a chopped smoked salmon with white cheese and exquisitely marinated tomatoes. The starter was the real treat here, with a perfect mix of bursting tastes. The main course—a beefsteak with garlic, prunes, and pasta served in melted blue cheese sauce, seemed somewhat lacking in creativity after a divine entree. In the summer, eat outside on the terrace overlooking the water.

XI. Kosztolányi D. tér 2, Feneketlen tó. 🕿 1/381-0522. www.hemingway-etterem.hu. Soup 590 Ft–650 Ft ($2.95–$3.25); appetizers 1,690 Ft–2,590 Ft ($8.45–$13); main courses 1,790 Ft–3,290 Ft ($8.95–$16). AE, DC, MC, V. Daily noon–midnight. Bus: Take bus 7 toward Buda from ferenciek tér to Feneketlen tó, a small "lake."

Horgásztanya Vendéglő 🕿 HUNGARIAN TRADITIONAL   Just a short block from the Danube, on the main street of Buda's Watertown neighborhood (Víziváros), the Horgásztanya Vendéglő is a family-style fish restaurant of reliable quality and modest prices for this part of town. Don't worry, non–fish eaters will enjoy dining here, too: The extensive menu lists a variety of Hungarian specialties. The decor is traditional Hungarian, catering to tourists.

I. Fő u. 27. 🕿 1/212-3780. Soup 390 Ft–1,590 Ft ($1.75–$7.15); main courses 1,300 Ft–2,490 Ft ($5.85–$11). No credit cards. Daily noon–11pm. Metro: Batthyány tér (Red line).

Le Jardin de Paris 🕿 FRENCH   In the heart of Buda's Watertown, just across the street from the modern-looking Institut Français is this wonderful little French bistro, celebrating its 15th year in existence. A cozy cellar space, it is decorated with an eclectic collection of graphic arts, posters, and lithographs. The restaurant is not about nouvelle cuisine, but prides itself for its '70s-style French bistro-like atmosphere and cuisine. The menu features a variety of French specialties, and the wine list offers both French as well as Hungarian vintages. Presentation is fine, the service is excellent, while the food is adequate. As you eat by candlelight a lone pianist keys away French *chansons* and jazz tunes. We tried a delicious assortment of house pâtés, including goose, duck, and a mixed variety. The lamb was tender, stuffed with acidy olives, served with broccoli, cauliflower, and potatos. There's outdoor seating in a garden area in summer.

I. Fő u. 20. 🕿 1/201-0047. Reservations recommended. Soup 900 Ft–1,900 Ft ($4.50–$9.50); starters 1,600 Ft–3,500 Ft ($8–$18); main courses 1,650 Ft–4,650 Ft ($8.25–$23). AE, DC, MC, V. Daily noon–midnight. Metro: Batthyány tér (Red line).

Szeged Vendéglő HUNGARIAN TRADITIONAL   Come to this classic vendéglő for a taste of Szeged, the southern Hungarian city that is admired for its zesty cuisine, among other reasons (see p. 259 for more information on Szeged). The house specialties are spicy fish dishes, including the famous fish soup, *Szeged halászlé*. The restaurant is a touch old school, but the food is good and hearty. Ersatz Gypsy music is performed nightly. The restaurant is just down the street from the Hotel Gellért, not far from one of Buda's busiest transportation hubs, Móricz Zsigmond körtér.

XI. Bartók Béla út 1. 🕿 1/209-1668. Soup 500 Ft–600 Ft ($2.50–$3); main courses 1,500 Ft–3,000 Ft ($7.50–$15). V. Daily noon–11pm. Tram: 47 or 49 from Deák tér to Hotel Gellért.

Tabáni Terasz 🕿🕿 HUNGARIAN CONTEMPORARY   This restaurant has the feel of a peasant home spruced up with contemporary paintings and other touches. The chef prepares delicious traditional fare pared with healthy vegetables, including a Hungarian gooseliver ragout in its own fat, served with vegetables and purple onions. The steak and bacon stuffed with goat cheese and served with pan-fried potatoes was generous, beautifully prepared and presented. In the summer months, we recommend sitting outside on the terrace. In the off season the interior dining is cozy and intimate.

I. Apród utca 10. 🕿 1/201-1086. www.tabaniterasz.hu. Soup 690 Ft–890 Ft ($3.45–$4.45); starters 1,550 Ft–2,500 Ft ($7.75–$13); main courses 1,650 Ft–3,300 Ft ($8.25–$17). AE, MC, V. Daily noon–midnight. Bus: A number of buses serve Döbrentei tér, including no. 8 from Március 15 tér.

INEXPENSIVE

Marxim *(Kids)* PIZZA On a gritty industrial street near Moszkva tér, Marxim's chief appeal lies not in its cuisine but in its decor, which attracts visitors from far and wide. The motif is Marxist nostalgia (the entrance is marked by a small neon red flag), but with a nod to the macabre side of the old system. The cellar space is a virtual museum of barbed wire, red flags, banners, posters, and cartoons recalling Hungary's dark past. Several years ago, Marxim was unsuccessfully prosecuted under a controversial law banning the display of the symbols of "hateful" political organizations. Amazingly, this is one of very few places in Budapest where you can still see this kind of stuff, so thoroughly have symbols of the Communist period been erased. (Another place, of course, is Szoborpark [Statue Park]; see "Where Have All the Statues Gone," on p. 137 for details.) The loud, very smoky cellar space is more of a bar than a restaurant. A number of draft beers are available on tap.

II. Kisrókus u. 23. (C) **1/316-0231.** Pizza 590 Ft–1,290 Ft ($2.95–$6.45); pasta 520 Ft–890 Ft ($2.60–$4.45). No credit cards. Mon–Thurs noon–1am; Fri–Sat noon–2am; Sun 6pm–1am. Metro: Moszkva tér (Red line).

5 The Castle District

VERY EXPENSIVE

Alabárdos *(G)* HUNGARIAN TRADITIONAL In the heart of the Castle District, Alabárdos—which means a medieval "guard"—offers Hungarian-style cuisine in an intimate, elegant setting. The historic building that houses the restaurant has several medieval details; 15th-century arches can be seen in the courtyard. The atmosphere inside is hushed and elegant, although slightly pretentious. They appreciate "appropriately" dressed guests at this conservative establishment. The walls are judiciously decorated in a medieval motif, with comfortable leather chairs. A guitarist performs unobtrusively. Meals are served on Zsolnay porcelain in the summer, and Herend in the winter, the two most famous Hungarian manufacturers. The menu is extensive. We had tarragon roast lamb chops served with beans, tomatoes, and goat cheese, which was tender, tasty, and elegantly served. Weather permitting, outdoor dining is available in the courtyard.

I. Országház u. 2. (C) **1/356-0851.** www.alabardos.hu. Reservations required. Soup 1,400 Ft ($7); starters 1,900 Ft–2,900 Ft ($9.50–$15); main courses 3,500 Ft–9,500 Ft ($18–$48). AE, DC, DISC, MC, V. Daily noon–midnight; Saturday open for lunch noon–4pm. Bus: Várbusz from Moszkva tér or no. 16 from Deák tér to Castle Hill. Funicular: From Clark Ádám tér to Castle Hill.

Arany Kaviár *(GG)* RUSSIAN This venue is a lavishly decorated Russian restaurant that brings back memories of the Belle Epoque Russia of the time of the Czar. Serving truly magnificent caviar, we think that this is the kind of place the characters of Tolstoy could have frolicked, feasted, sang, and danced in. The plush interior is decorated with Russian samovars, icons, and paintings depicting cold winter landscapes. If your pocketbook can afford it, treat yourself to a wide variety of rather pricey caviars, including Russian Astrakhan Beluga Caviar, or even more exotic Iranian varieties. Meals take a long time, and are interrupted by swigs of fine vodka, which you should only drink cold. We had a lavish cold-starter plate, rich with fish, caviar, king prawns, and other seafood delights. The strips of beef prepared to Count Stroganoff's original recipe, which served as our main dish, was almost an aside. By the time it was served, our spirits were deep in the cool Russian interior. The slowly served starters, drinks, and sumptuous fireworks of different tastes served as appetizers fulfilled its mission: to serve delicate foods as a hardy meal.

l. Ostrom u. 19. © 1/201-6737. www.aranykaviar.hu. Reservations required. Soup 850 Ft– 1,800 Ft ($4.25–$9.00); starters 1,050 Ft–3,500 Ft ($5.25–$18); main courses 3,500 Ft–9,500 Ft ($18–$48). AE, DC, DISC, MC, V. Daily noon–midnight. Bus: Várbusz from Moszkva tér.

EXPENSIVE

Café Pierrot ⒢⒢ HUNGARIAN CONTEMPORARY   An intimate, comfortable restaurant serving excellent cuisine. Café Pierrot was originally established as a real coffeehouse style cafe, while over the years it developed to become elegant establishment that it is today. Following recent renovations, the atmosphere feels like a high-class wine cellar decorated with contemporary artworks, soft lighting, and fresh orchids. We started with a gooseliver trilogy, which included a brûlée, a liver terrine and grilled. If the Gundel's grilled gooseliver is the barometer by which to be measured, then Pierrot lost out, being less tender and a little bit chunky. The marinated venison steak, however, was truly delicious, and the place was also beautifully presented. The menu also includes tempting dishes like oven roasted duck breast or roasted guinea fowl breast. The back part of the restaurant is more intimate, while the frontal area is closer to the action. A pianist plays every evening after 6pm.

l. Fortuna u. 14. © 1/375-6971. www.pierrot.hu. Reservations recommended. Soups 990 Ft–1,190 Ft ($4.95–$5.95); starters 1,590 Ft–3,290 Ft ($7.95–$16); main courses 2,690 Ft–5,890 Ft ($13–$29). AE, DC, MC, V. Daily 11am–midnight. Bus: Várbusz from Moszkva tér.

MODERATE

Jankó Kortárs Magyar Étterem ⒢ HUNGARIAN CONTEMPORARY   The brainchild of chef Lajos Takács, this is a beautifully decorated and conceived venue. Within the restaurant there is a contemporary art gallery and a separate piano bar. We visited the gallery while waiting for our main course, and wandered off to the piano bar for a romantic candlelit dessert and coffee. Let your imagination venture, and you could be sitting in Rick's American Café from the classic film *Casablanca*. This restaurant wins big when it comes to the space, its design and conception. A great place for a date! When it comes to the culinary delights served here, the restaurant makes a rare attempt at "new" Hungarian cuisine. The food is beautifully presented, and game is served with fruit, and unusual sauces are blended and experimented with. The only problem is that the dishes lack the zest of the traditional fare, and in their foray into re-creation, end up being a tad bland. We ate fresh goat cheese with chives, for instance, which lacked flavor but made for a beautiful display. The mangalica pork with lemon sauce was tasty and even a tad exotic with fruit added to the mix. The waiters were truly kind; reserved, somewhat awkward folk trying to be charismatic. Jankó is a suave place, with great potential.

l. Hess András tér 4. © 1/488-7416. www.janko.hu. Reservations recommended. Soups 850 Ft–1,500 Ft ($4.25–$7.50); starters 1,400 Ft–1,950 Ft ($7–$9.75); main courses 1,900 Ft–4,900 Ft ($9.50–$25). MC, V. Daily noon–midnight. Bus: Várbusz from Moszkva tér.

Rivalda Café & Restaurant ⒢ HUNGARIAN CONTEMPORARY   Rivalda serves up contemporary, creative food with a side of Hungarian history and personality. In the late 17th century Francis Joseph I established a casino with a theater where this restaurant now stands. And Rivalda, without a doubt, retains the theatrical charm: a sole saxophonist plays his lonely tunes, dwarfed by the château-yellow backdrop at the far end of the restaurant; theater lights and riggings adorn the ceilings; and the walls are painted with the backdrops of plays and caricatures of famous Hungarian actors. We started with the escargot baked in garlic and cheese, just browned slightly, followed by a tender but nondescript rack of lamb on a bed of sautéed spinach, with pine-nut sauce and dried fruit couscous. Agnes Weininger, the Canadian restauranteur at the helm, has become known for her creations, including the recently published story of a long-distance love affair with her Greek knight in shinning armor.

I. Szinház u. 5–9. ✆ **1/489-0236**. www.rivalda.net. Reservations recommended. Soups 925 Ft–1,100 Ft ($4.60–$5.50); starters 1,700 Ft–1,950 Ft ($8.50–$9.75); main courses 1,900 Ft–4,500 Ft ($9.50–$23). AE, MC, V. Daily 11:30am–11:30pm. Bus: Várbusz from Moszkva tér.

INEXPENSIVE

Café Miró ✿ HUNGARIAN CONTEMPORARY   Located in the heart of the castle area, this restaurant and coffee and pastry shop is an ideal place to stop in between visiting museums and getting to know the area. Miró, named affectionately after the 20th-century surrealist painter, also serves an assortment of salads and warm dishes, the most popular being a spring salad with chicken, Roquefort cheese, and avocado slices. We had the mozzarella and spinach turkey breast served with potato croquettes, which was palatable. The service here is not top-notch either; being either slow (we waited more than three-quarters of an hour for our meal), or without a smile. It is, however, the most convenient and comfortable place for a brief respite in this area.

I. Úri u. 30. ✆ **1/201-5573**. Soups 790 Ft–990 Ft ($3.95–$4.95); starters 1,390 Ft–1,590 Ft ($6.95–$7.95); main courses 1,790 Ft–2,890 Ft ($8.95–$14). No credit cards. Daily 9am–midnight. Bus: Várbusz from Moszkva tér.

6 The Buda Hills

EXPENSIVE

Náncsi Néni Vendéglője ✿✿ (Finds) HUNGARIAN TRADITIONAL   Decorated with turn-of-the-20th-century Budapest, and now even contemporary vistas of Hungary, this popular but remote restaurant (Aunt Nancy's Inn) is located high in the green Buda Hills. There's outdoor garden dining in the summer, with live accordion music at night. The menu features typical Hungarian dishes, prepared with great care. The creatively thought up liver in grape sauce marinated in cherry is second only to the gooseliver served at Gundel. Their cottage cheese dumplings are also the very best in town. The restaurant is near St. Christoph Villa and the Petneházy Country Club Hotel, both recommended hotels. It's like a night in the country.

II. Ördögárok út 80. ✆ **1/397-2742**. Reservations recommended for dinner. Soup 590 Ft–1,050 Ft ($2.95–$5.25); starters 650 Ft–1,820 Ft ($3.25–$9.10); main courses 1,450 Ft–7,777 Ft ($7.25–$39). AE, MC, V. Daily noon–11pm. Tram: 56 from Moszkva tér to the last stop, then change to bus no. 63 to Széchenyi utca.

Remiz ✿✿ (Value) HUNGARIAN CONTEMPORARY   Remiz was born at a time when many entrepreneurs were opening little food shops, while others, like Remiz owner Alice Meződi, wanted to bring dining out of the Socialist era. The "Remiz" is literally the place where trams spend the night, and the venue for this restaurant that was opened in 1992. Meződi and her husband József, the lead singer of the classic Hungarian rock band Apóstol, are also magnets for creative dinner guests, including Hungarian actor András Kern, actress Enikő Eszenyi, choreographer Iván Markó, and the elder-statesman Hungarian film director Miklós Jancsó. A pianist and trumpet player effortlessly play melodies in the tram-shaped restaurant, which is decorated with early-20th-century posters. Try an assortment of gooseliver specialties, classic chicken paprikas, or a tender veal filet with bolete mushrooms that will leave you satisfied, and just curious enough to ask Alice to tell you some stories.

II. Budakeszi út 5. ℰ **1/275-1396.** www.remiz.hu. Reservations recommended. Soup 780 Ft–1,240 Ft ($3.90–$6.20); starters 980 Ft–2,620 Ft ($4.90–$13); main courses 1,980 Ft–3,520 Ft ($9.90–$18). AE, DC, MC, V. Daily 9am–midnight. Bus: 158 from Moszkva tér (departs from Csaba utca, at the top of the stairs, near the stop from which the Várbusz departs for the Castle District).

MODERATE

Ezüstponty ✸✸✸ *Finds* HUNGARIAN TRADITIONAL   A true and tested traditional Hungarian fish and game restaurant that enjoys a history of some 150 years on the very same spot. The author's favorite Hungarian restaurant, this unassuming and magical place allows you to enjoy a wide variety of home-style dishes served in an old-world atmosphere. The building itself feels like a rustic woody country house that is awakened nightly with live traditional Hungarian music played on the violin and guitar. It is decorated with paintings of sailboats, old photographs, and Budapest street scenes. Austere waiters serve a menu that is long and varied, but the true specialty remains the heavy but sumptuous carp soup Szeged-style with haslets, served in a small stew pot. Best consumed with fresh hot peppers, toast, and butter, the soup is rich, textured, and always fresh. The no-nonsense manager recommended us a Wels goulash, which was a rich fish paprikas served with galuska, sour cream, and bacon bits. No visitor should come to Budapest without visiting this place at least once, because then—and only then—can you truly return knowing that you have tasted authentic, traditional, and hardy Hungarian cuisine.

XII. Némethvölgy út 96. ℰ **1/319-1632.** Reservations recommended. Soup 480 Ft–750 Ft ($2.40–$3.75); starters 940 Ft–2,350 Ft ($4.70–$12); main courses 1580 Ft–3,450 Ft ($7.90–$17). AE, DC, MC, V. Daily 11am–11pm. Tram: 59 from Déli Pályaudvar.

Szép Ilona ✸ HUNGARIAN TRADITIONAL   The marks of a now not-so-recent history have been left intact in this unassuming restaurant. In fact, this is one of the few restaurants that have maintained their Communist-era facades. The simple words "Szép Ilona" on a burgundy background now have a dated look, but one that is instantly recognizable to anybody who remembers the days before the systemic changes in Hungary. This is also a place of legends. The famous 19th-century Hungarian writer János Arany recounted that Hungary's much praised 15th-century King Matthias began a love affair with "Ilona," the daughter of a forester, in this very location in the then woody hills of Buda. Appropriately, thus, the restaurant was called "Szép Ilona," or translated, "Beautiful Ilona." This cheerful, unassuming restaurant with a 150-year-old history now serves a mostly local clientele, boasting a good selection of Hungarian specialties; try the *borjúpaprikás galuskával* (veal paprika) served with *galuska* (a typical central European style of dumpling), or smoked pork with risotto. There's a small sidewalk-side garden for summer dining, where you can enjoy the peaceful, wooded, and fresh summer air. And since Szép Ilona is located in a pleasant Buda neighborhood, after your meal, you can take a stroll through the tree-lined streets.

II. Budakeszi út 1–3. ℰ **1/275-1392.** Soup 420 Ft–800 Ft ($2.10–$4.00); starters 600 Ft–2,200 Ft ($3–$11); main courses 980 Ft–3,470 Ft ($4.90–$17). MC, V. Daily 11:30am–10pm. Bus: 158 from Moszkva tér (departs from Csaba utca, at the top of the stairs, near the stop from which the Várbusz departs for the Castle District).

INEXPENSIVE

Makkhetes Vendéglő ✸ *Finds* HUNGARIAN TRADITIONAL   In the lower part of the Buda Hills, Makkhetes (the name means "7 of Acorns," a Hungarian playing card) is a rustic little neighborhood eatery. The crude wood paneling and absence of ornamentation give it a distinctly country atmosphere. The regulars (the waiters seem to know everyone who enters) start filing in at 11:30am for lunch. The food is good and the portions are large. You won't go wrong with the *paprika csirke galuskával* (chicken paprika with dumplings). Outdoor dining is available.

XII. Németvölgyi út 56. ℂ **1/355-7330.** Soup 420 Ft–760 Ft ($1.65–$3.10); main courses 990 Ft–2,400 Ft ($3.80–$9.90). No credit cards. Daily 11am–10pm. Tram: 59 from Moszkva tér to Kiss János altábornagy utca stop (then walk up hill to the right on Kiss János altábornagy utca).

7 Northern Buda & Óbuda

EXPENSIVE

Kéhli Vendéglő ✻✻ HUNGARIAN CONTEMPORARY   Housed in a historic Óbuda building, Kéhli is an upscale traditional Hungarian restaurant with a cozy dining room and an enclosed garden. Located behind the Corinthia Aquincum Hotel in Óbuda's old city, the restaurant can be a bit difficult to find—ask a local when you get into the general vicinity. One of the house specialties is Szinbád's Favorite, named for the famous pirate introduced to Hungary by the early-20th-century novelist Gyula Krúdy; the dish consists of pork stuffed with chicken liver rolled in bacon and served in a paprika-and-mushroom sauce. The restaurant used to be frequented by the novelist, who is famous for his appetizing descriptions of hedonistic meals he enjoyed on the premises. Another dish worth sampling is the Szeged fish soup, which is among the best we have tasted. The roast gooseliver with garlic, which is another house specialty, is over-rated and a tad bland, however. The really adventurous should try the beef bone marrow served with pepper and paprika on slices of toast for an appetizer. Dinner is accompanied by live Gypsy music, and in our case opera singer Erzsébet Morvay Pálma spontaneously broke out in song, bringing the whole restaurant to applause.

III. Mókus u. 22. ℂ **1/250-4241.** Reservations recommended. Soup 580 Ft–1,260 Ft ($2.90–$6.30); starters 980 Ft–2,020 Ft ($4.90–$10); main courses 1,480 Ft–6,980 Ft ($7.40–$35). AE, MC, V. Daily noon–midnight. Train: HÉV suburban railway from Batthyány tér to Árpád híd.

Kisbuda Gyöngye ✻✻ HUNGARIAN CONTEMPORARY   Tucked away in a quiet side street in a residential Óbuda neighborhood, the Kisbuda Gyöngye ("Pearl of Little Buda") is favored by Hungarians and visitors alike. The restaurant has its origins in a building that stood not far away called Kisbuda, built in the 14th century, which was transformed into a bar and artists' hub of sorts by Alice Meződi and her musician husband József Meződi of the classic Hungarian rock band Apostol. When Kisbuda was closed in 1992, the founders created this heir, the Kisbuda Gyöngye. The heavy yet warm wooden interior was created from odd antique furniture, bed-boards and such. The hand-painted mural on the ceiling was impressive, and you are sure to enjoy the highly entertaining pianist who adds to the early-19th-century, intimate atmosphere. During the summer this cozy restaurant also features an interior garden shaded by a wonderful old, gnarly tree. The gourmet menu features a delightful palette of standard Hungarian and international offerings. Try the marvelous *pâté de foie gras*-plate for a starter, then indulge into the savory deer steak with apple sauce.

III. Kenyeres u. 34. ℂ **1/368-9246.** www.remiz.hu. Reservations highly recommended. Soup 880 Ft–1180 Ft ($4.40–$5.70); starters 2,400 Ft–3,800 Ft ($12–$19); main courses 1,400 Ft–2,600 Ft ($7–$13). AE, DC, MC, V. Mon–Sat noon–midnight. Bus: 60 or tram 17 from Margit híd (Buda side).

Új Sipos Halászkert HUNGARIAN TRADITIONAL   In its own handsome building on Óbuda's dignified main square, this restaurant consists of several rooms that radiate a comfortable air of worn elegance. Though the exterior of the restaurant receives a fresh paint job from time to time, and the word "Új" (new) was added to the restaurant's name a few years ago, the interior is, to our eyes, unchanged, which is just fine with us. The menu specializes in Hungarian seafood dishes. A string trio enhances the atmosphere, and there is a small interior garden area.

III. Fő tér 6. © 1/388-8745. Reservations recommended. Soup 550 Ft–1,950 Ft ($2.75–$9.75); main courses 1,900 Ft–4,700 Ft ($9.50–$24). MC, V. Daily 11am–midnight. Train: Suburban HÉV line to Árpád híd.

MODERATE

Bock Bisztró ★★ HUNGARIAN CONTEMPORARY Although it's located inside of the Corinthia Grand Royal Hotel, this place is no hotel restaurant, and is even operated independently from the hotel. On an average night, a few hotel guests wander in, but the crowd is mainly wine-loving locals. Partially owned by József Bock (one of the country's premier winemakers), the kitchen is run by Executive chef Lajos Biro (also of Múzeum Étterem) and turns out a delicious combination of Spanish, Italian, and Hungarian dishes. The menu includes lots of light snacks—perfect for accompanying one of the more than 50 wines by the glass that they pour—such as several types of bruschettas, tapas, and various cheese and cured meat combinations. Starters are more substantial, continue with the Mediterranean influence, and often reflect the chef's creativity with common Hungarian ingredients. The sautéed goose-liver, for example, pairs the Hungarian delicacy with cold, sweet ginger parfait. Other options are deer carpaccio, ravioli with paprika cream sauce, frogs' legs almondine, and a delicious horseradish soup with ham chips. Main courses include several game, duck, and lamb dishes served in typically large Hungarian portions. Service here is detail oriented, and servers are eager to recommend different wines with each course. The creative Mediterranean-influenced Hungarian menu here is nicely executed, enticing you to return for another meal and a few more glasses of different wines.

VII. Erzsérbet krt. 43–49. © 1/321-0340. Reservations recommended. Appetizers 950 Ft–1,900 Ft ($4.75–$9.50); soup 550 Ft–700 Ft ($2.75–$3.50); main courses 2,100 Ft–3,700 Ft ($11–$19). MC, V. Mon–Sat 11am–11pm. Tram: 4 or 6 to Király utca.

8 Traditional Coffeehouses

Like Vienna, imperial Budapest was famous for its coffeehouse culture. Literary movements and political circles alike were identified in large part by which coffeehouse they met in. Sándor Petőfi, the revolutionary poet of 1848 fame, is said to have instructed his friend János Arany, another leading Hungarian poet of the day, to write to him in care of the Pilvax Coffee House, as he spent more time there than at home. Although Communism managed to dull this cherished institution, a handful of classic coffeehouses miraculously survived the tangled tragedies of the 20th century, and, with just a few exceptions, all have been carefully restored to their original splendor.

All the classic coffeehouses offer delicious pastries and coffee in an atmosphere of luxurious—if occasionally faded—splendor. Many offer small sandwiches, some serve ice cream, and some feature bar drinks. Pastries are displayed in a glass. Table sharing is common, and lingering for hours over a single cup of coffee or a pastry is perfectly acceptable, and is in fact encouraged by the free daily papers provided by the house.

THE INNER CITY & CENTRAL PEST

Centrál Kávéház ★★★ This is the closest to the Viennese coffeehouse culture in Budapest, and is a perfect replica of the original establishment that stood on the premises from 1887. Although there is a superb restaurant here as well, this place is best

My, what an inefficient way to fish.

Ring toss, good. Horseshoes, bad.

Faster! Faster! Faster!

We take care of the fiddly bits, from providing over 43,000 customer reviews of hotels, to helping you find our best fares, to giving you 24/7 customer service. So you can focus on the only thing that matters. Goofing off.

travelocity
You'll never roam alone.

known as a coffeehouse. The house was restored by one of Hungary's own homegrown successful businessman, Imre Somody—one of the country's very few new millionaires who seem willing to recycle profits by investing in the country's general wealth. This place is perfectly located in the Inner City, and is always busy with an interesting mix of the local university crowd from ELTE and CEU, celebrity intellectuals, and the ever-present travelers, who have taken to the place immediately. Watch at the right end of the smoky section as you enter where a table is perpetually reserved for local writer Géza Csemer, who is more than a regular here. The coffeehouse's calm green interior also allows you to check out the free copies of various newspapers over a coffee and a fresh croissant. You can visit as early as 8am; this is the only place open at that time of the day in the area. A simple espresso at Centrál costs 310 Ft ($1.60).

V. Károlyi Mihály u. 9. ✆ 1/266-2110. www.centralkavehaz.hu. AE, DISC, MC, V. Daily 8am–midnight. Metro: Ferenciek tere (Blue line).

Gerbeaud's ✸✸ (Kids)   Gerbeaud's is probably Budapest's most famous coffeehouse. Founded in 1858, it has stood on its current spot since 1870. Whether you sit inside amid the splendor of the late-19th-century furnishings, or outside on one of Pest's liveliest pedestrian-only squares, you will surely enjoy the fine pastries that made the name Gerbeaud famous; we especially recommend their moist plum pies *(szilvás lepény)*. Gerbeaud's reputation and location ensure that it's filled to capacity throughout the year, although many locals complain that the value-for-money ratio has become disappointing. Given its history, however, you cannot afford to have at least one coffee here during your stay. In good weather, try getting a table outside on bustling Vörösmarty tér where you can watch kids (yours perhaps?) play around (and on) the square's fountain.

V. Vörösmarty tér 7. ✆ 1/429-9000. www.gerbeaud.hu. AE, DC, DISC, MC, V. Daily 9am–9pm. Metro: Vörösmarty tér (Yellow line).

Lukács Cukrászda ✸   A faithful reproduction of a vintage coffeehouse, this large, airy establishment was created decades after a coffeehouse of the same name closed its doors. It marked one of the early efforts to bring back the lively coffee-shop life of the capital, as the Lukács has been operating since 1912 on the grand Andrássy boulevard. It is just a few minutes' walk from Oktogon, and not far away from Heroes' Square. It is a perfect stop on a stroll from downtown to the Museum of Fine Arts or a walk in the City Park. This is more of a quiet hideaway, less frequented than most traditional coffeehouses, but the ambience is peaceful and made all the more comfy with the piano player's soothing notes. A drawback of the Lukács is that it shares its entrance with a bank. Nevertheless, it is a great place to sit in air-conditioned splendor and write postcards over a long, slow cup of joe.

VI. Andrássy út 70. ✆ 1/302-8747. DC, DISC, MC, V. Mon–Fri 9am–8pm; Sat–Sun 10am–8pm. Metro: Opera (Yellow line).

Művész Kávéház ✸   Just across Andrássy út from the Opera House, Művész (Artist) was one of Budapest's finest traditional coffeehouses; it was around even in Communist times. The lush interior features marble tabletops, crystal chandeliers, and mirrored walls. Despite its old-world grandeur, however, Művész retains a casual atmosphere. Elaborate ice-cream sundaes are a favorite with locals and travelers alike. There are tables on the street, but sit inside for the full coffeehouse effect.

VI. Andrássy út 29. ✆ 1/352-1337. No credit cards. Daily 9am–noon. Metro: Opera (Yellow line).

Our Favorite Sweets

Hungary is a land of sweet teeth, and the country's confections will satisfy even the most rabid cravings.

Found only in Hungary, **Dobos torta** is a light chocolate layer cake with a caramelized frosting. **Ischler** is a delightful Viennese specialty—two shortbread cookies with apricot jam filling, double-dipped in dark chocolate. **Meggyes rétes,** a sour cherry strudel, is a traditional favorite. And just when you thought the sour cherry strudel was unbeatable, along comes the heavenly poppy-seed strudel, **Mákos rétes.**

Kakaós csiga is a chocolate snail: buttery and flaky rolled pastry sprinkled with chocolate. They're available in bakeries everywhere (but not in cafes). A **kifli** is a cross between a croissant and a roll. The **Szegedi** variety (named for Szeged, the southeastern city from whence it comes) has a sweet almond glaze. It's available at cafes or bakeries, but you might have to travel to Szeged for an authentic taste.

Sold from kiosks that sell nothing else, **kürtőskalács** is a delicious, melt-in-your-mouth honey bread quite unlike anything else you've ever tasted. It is traditionally made with dough wrapped around a cylindrical piece of wood shaped like a rolling pin and baked in an extremely hot oven. It's not available in regular shops or cafes.

It's a mystery why Ben and Jerry haven't figured this one out yet: Hungarian **cinnamon ice cream (fahej)** is to die for. And if you come across the rarest of its varieties, cinnamon rice ice cream **(fahejes rizs),** by all means try it.

Parlament Kávéház 🍷🍷 Situated adjacent to Hungary's Parliament buildings, this coffeehouse is decorated with an impressive rounded painting of the Parliament buildings, and even a ceiling mural. Spending a few hours here you are likely to bump into politicians, public figures, or alternately hoards of tourists making a stop here before or after taking a tour of the Parliament buildings. We spotted Hungary's first Minister of Equal Opportunity and now a Socialist European Union parliamentarian, the elegant Katalin Lévai, speaking emphatically talking as she sipped a coffee here as she characteristically twirled and played with what looked like a necklace over and over again. We also saw the spokesman for the former conservative government spokesman Gábor Borokai plotting his next move. This is a place where serious people go to talk shop. Tourists and journalists, meanwhile, observe attentively.

V. Vértanúk tere 1. ✆ 1/269-4352. No credit cards. Mon–Sat 8am–8pm. Metro: Kossuth tér (Red line).

CENTRAL BUDA

Angelika Cukrászda The Angelika Cukrászda is housed in a historic building next to St. Anne's Church on Buda's Batthyány tér. The sunken rooms of this cavernous cafe provide the perfect retreat on a hot summer day. The place includes a grill restaurant outside and a complex of terraces on three levels in the summer months. Now you will find a perfect view of the Parliament building and the Chain Bridge. The stained-glass windows and marble floors contrast beautifully with the off-white canvas upholstery and cast-iron furniture. You can choose from among a selection of excellent pastries, coffees, and teas. There is a small gallery inside the coffeehouse, where artworks are displayed. Be wary of your bill; we had the unpleasant experience of being over-charged by an errant and arrogant waiter, who was quickly reprimanded by the owner when we complained.

I. Batthyány tér 7. No credit cards. Daily 9am–midnight. Metro: Batthyány tér (Red line).

Auguszt Cukrászda 🍴🍴 We highly recommend this true and tested coffeehouse, established in 1870 and remarkably still run by the family of the founder. The latest of four generations of confectioners, József Auguszt, who now runs the coffee shop, came to greet us with his chef's hat eager explain his family's long-standing Budapest tradition. While not in the same place the coffeehouse even existed in some form or another during the Communist era, save for the harshest years of the 1950s. In 1951 it was nationalized, the same year that József was born. As was the tradition of the Communists with entrepreneurial types, they sent the family off to the countryside, in their case, a small town in northeastern Hungary called Taktaszada. A year after Hungary's 1956 revolution things became easier, they returned to Budapest and the family opened the coffeehouse in its current location. József continues the family tradition of creating a new cake for his father's birthday. Some years, they work, some years they don't. The E-80, named after his father Elemér Auguszt, was created on his father's 80th birthday, and has become a staple of the shop. József is now working on the King's Cake, or the cake of Kings! His father will be 93 years old. . . .

II. Fény utca 8. 🕻 1/316-3817. www.augusztcukraszda. No credit cards. Tues–Sat 10am–6pm. Metro: Batthyány tér (Red line).

Szamos Marcipán Budai Cukrázda 🍴 Traditional coffeehouse and confectionary nestled in the pleasant airy hills of Buda. The confectionary, a favorite of locals, prides itself in the use of fresh base materials and traditional recipes. A wealthy assortment of cakes can also be ordered here, including their famous marzipan cakes.

XII. Böszörményi út 44. 🕻 1/355-1728. No credit cards. Daily 10am–7pm. Metro: Apor Vilmos tér stop of 56 tram from Déli Pályaudvar (Red line).

THE CASTLE DISTRICT

Ruszwurm Cukrászda 🍴🍴 *Kids* More than a century old, the Ruszwurm is an utterly charming little place, with two rooms outfitted with small tables and chairs, and shelves lined with antiques. It is owned by the Szamos dynasty of pastry and marzipan chefs (you can visit their museum in Szentendre; see p. 220). It can be very difficult to find a free table here, and the four out front on the sidewalk seem forever occupied. You must try the unsurpassable *krémes,* a two-layered crisp pastry confection with vanilla cream filling. Another favorite here is the Dobos torta, a multilayered cake with a thin caramel crust on top.

I. Szentháromság u. 7. 🕻 1/375-5284. No credit cards. Daily 9am–8pm in high season, 10am–7pm in low season. Bus: Várbusz from Moszkva tér or no. 16 from Deák tér to Castle Hill. Funicular: From Clark Ádám tér to Castle Hill.

9 Cafes & Bistros

Cafe Incognito 🍴 Sophisticated but informal, Incognito opens far out onto the street in summer. There's a full bar.

VI. Liszt Ferenc tér 3. 🕻 1/342-1471. Mon–Tues noon–midnight; Wed–Fri noon–2am; Sat 2pm–2am; Sun 2pm–midnight. Metro: Oktogon (Yellow line).

Darshan Cafe and Udvar   Darshan is a small, always crowded hangout with a hip Indian ambience. Pass through a gate strung with bells to reach the complex of shops, cafes, and dance spots in the small courtyard. You may want to look around in the Indigo Record shop (alternative music) or browse over the impressive, artsy Hungarian T-shirt collections while waiting for your beer to arrive; at 400 Ft to 650 Ft ($1.80–$2.90) for half a liter on tap, this is definitely a bargain on a hot summer day. Featured on the menu is a delicious Eastern variation on a traditional Hungarian dish known as *főzelek*—part casserole, part stew, and entirely vegetarian. Enjoy.

Krúdy Gyula u. 7. © 1/266-5541. Mon–Thurs 11am–1am; Fri 11am–2pm; Sat 6pm–2am; Sun 6pm–midnight.

Old Amsterdam   A great success off the Inner Ring, Old Amsterdam is a favorite of everyone from international business types to young, hip travelers. The establishment has a genuine Dutch cafe quality, with an extensive selection of the best beers in Europe, including Belgian fruit beers of all kinds, and a menu offering an assortment of Dutch cheeses.

Királyi Pál u. 14. © 1/266-3649. Mon–Fri 10am–midnight; Sat–Sun noon–midnight. Metro: Kálvin tér (Blue line).

Paris, Texas   Paris, Texas, prides itself on being the first nightlife spot to have opened up on the now buzzing Ráday utca, which was converted a few years ago into a pedestrian-only street, and is now lined with bars and cafes. The clientele is largely composed of students, and they linger into the small hours of the morning. This is a cozy place to eat, drink, and talk. The walls of three adjacent rooms are lined with old photographs, providing a window into the local culture of the 1910s and 1920s. In the summer there is outdoor seating.

IX. Ráday u. 22. © 1/218-0570. Mon–Fri 10am–3am; Sat–Sun 1pm–3am. Metro: Kálvin tér (Blue line).

7

Exploring Budapest

Historic Budapest is surprisingly small, and many sights listed in the following pages can be reached by foot from the city center. Take the time to stroll from one place to the next—you'll find yourself passing magnificent, if often run-down, examples of the city's distinctive architecture.

1 The Top Attractions

PEST

MUSEUMS

Museums are closed on Mondays, except where noted. Most museums offer substantial student and senior discounts. Many also offer a family rate. Inquire at the ticket window.

Holokauszt Emlékközpont (Budapest Holocaust Memorial Center) ✐✐ This center, a beautiful and moving memorial to the Jews murdered during World War II, opened in 2004 and became the first government-funded Holocaust Memorial Center in central Europe. The center is built around an old, eclectic-style synagogue building that was designed by Leopold Baumhorn (1860-1932), the most prolific architect of synagogues at the turn-of-the-20th-century. The space has a permanent exhibition and a research center. The temporary exhibitions tend to be small or multimedia photography exhibitions. A memorial wall lists the names of Holocaust victims.

IX. Páva u. 39. ✆ 1/455-3333. www.hdke.hu. Admission is free. Tues–Sun 10am–6pm. Metro: Ferenc körut (Blue line).

Nemzeti Múzeum (Hungarian National Museum) ✐✐ The Hungarian National Museum, an enormous neoclassical structure built from 1837 to 1847, was one of the great projects of the early-19th-century Age of Reform, a period that also saw the construction of the Chain Bridge and the National Theater (no longer standing), as well as the development of the modern Hungarian national identity. The museum was a major site during the beginning of the Hungarian Revolution of 1848 and 1849; on its wide steps on March 15, 1848, the poet Sándor Petőfi and other young radicals are said to have exhorted the people of Pest to revolt against the Habsburgs. The very presence of such an imposing structure in the capital of Hungary, and its exhibits, which proudly detail the accomplishments of the Magyars, played a significant role in the development of 19th-century Hungarian nationalism.

The museum's main attraction is the replica of the so-called crown of St. Stephen (King Stephen ruled 1000–38). The original was moved to its new location, the Parliament building, as part of Hungary's millennium celebrations in 2000. In 1978 former U.S. Secretary of State Cyrus Vance ceremoniously returned the crown to Hungary from the United States, where it had been stored since the end of World War II. Few Hungarians would assert, however, that the two-tiered crown on display ever

Budapest Attractions

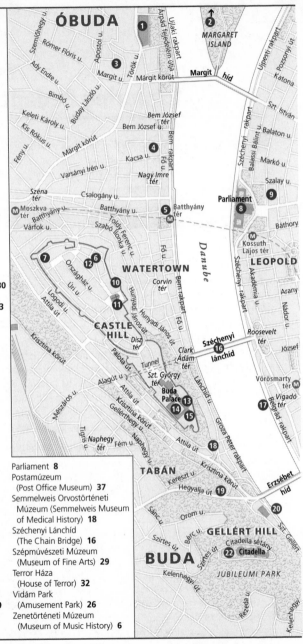

INFORMATION
Tourinform **33, 39**

SPA BATHING
Gellért Baths **23**
Király Baths **4**
Lukács Baths **1**
Palatinus Baths **2**
Rácz Baths **19**
Széchenyi Baths **27**

TRANSPORTATION HUBS
Deák tér Metro Station **36**
HÉV Suburban Rail Station **5**
Vigadó tér Boat Landing **17**

(i) Information
(M) Metro

0   1/4 mi

actually rested on Stephen's head: Its lower part was evidently a gift to King Géza I (1074–77), and its upper part was built for Stephen V, who reigned almost 250 years after the first Stephen's death. The two main museum exhibits on view are "The History of the Peoples of Hungary from the Paleolithic Age to the Magyar Conquest," which features various objects and documents that illustrate the history of Hungarians from their migration from Siberia to their arrival in the country now known as

A New Direction for the Museum of Fine Arts

In 2004, then 43-year-old László Baán took the helm of the **Museum of Fine Arts** (★★, promising to bring the museum into the 21st century. On his first day on the job, the self-professed technocrat removed comely advertising billboards that surrounded the dirty building facade, initiated the creation of a multiple-language website, and pledged to follow a policy of openness that would usher the institution back onto the international stage. He has since initiated the re-design of the museum, which will include a store, more modernist-era representation, and an ambitious plan to increase the exhibition space itself.

Until recently, the museum had only created a handful of exhibitions that attracted large numbers of viewers. Blockbuster-type exhibitions are now on the agenda. Báan would like to promote the collection, and better "sell" his museum, and bring it to international levels.

He points to the Leonardo da Vinci sculpture as a gem, the only one recognized as being from the hands of the master. He also notes the Spanish collection of the museum, said to be the most important in continental Europe outside of Spain and Portugal. A third strong point of the museum is its impressive prints and drawings collection, Báan says.

The Museum of Fine Arts in Budapest was established in 1906 with the Esterházy collection, amassed by one of Hungary's leading and wealthiest families. The collection included hundreds of old master paintings, including the Esterházy Madonna of 1508, by the Italian painter Raphaello, works by Veronese, Duccio, and El Greco, and 8,000 prints and drawings. The museum now has more than 100,000 artifacts, including more than 6,000 modern and old master paintings, a Greco-Roman collection of antiquities, a wealthy collection of Spanish art, and a host of fine French Impressionist works.

The museum is not without challenges. It faces lawsuits seeking the return of artworks left with the museum for safekeeping during World War II. Legal woes aside, the museum is enjoying a healthy new life under Baan's direction and in March 2006 celebrated its own centennial with Hungary's largest-ever art exhibition (themed around King Sigismund of Luxembourge). In the meantime, some 2,500 artworks that once belonging to Hungarians are still in the hands of Russia, who consider these works of art 'trophy art," refusing to return the World War II–era war loot. Restitution claims seem to be stuck in the legal system.

See the listing in this section for more information.

Hungary, and **"The History of the Hungarian People from the Magyar Conquest to 1989"** ⚜, which includes artifacts and documents relating the story of the Hungarian people from their arrival in this area up to the system change in 1989. "The Hungarian Royal Insignia" is a smaller permanent exhibit.

VIII. Múzeum krt. 14. ⓒ 1/338-2122. www.hnm.hu. Free admission. Tues–Sun 10am–6pm (to 5pm in winter). Metro: Kálvin tér (Blue line).

Néprajzi Múzeum (Ethnographical Museum)   Directly across Kossuth tér from the House of Parliament, the vast Ethnographical Museum is located in the stately neo-Renaissance/eclectic former Hungarian Supreme Court building. The ornate interior rivals that of the Opera House. A ceiling fresco of Justitia, the goddess of justice, by the well-known artist Károly Lotz, dominates the lobby. Although a third of the museum's holdings are from outside Hungary, you'll want to concentrate on the Hungarian items. The fascinating permanent exhibition, "From Ancient Times to Civilization," features everything from drinking jugs to razor cases to chairs to clothing.

V. Kossuth tér 12. ⓒ 1/473-2400. www.neprajz.hu. Free admission for permanent exhibits. 1,200 Ft ($6) for temporary shows. Tues–Sun 10am–6pm. Metro: Kossuth tér (Red line).

Szépművészeti Múzeum (Museum of Fine Arts) ⚜⚜   Planned at the time of the 1896 millennial celebration of the Magyar Conquest, the Museum of Fine Arts opened 10 years later in this neoclassical behemoth on the left side of huge Heroes' Square, at the edge of City Park. The museum is the main repository of foreign art in Hungary and it houses one of central Europe's major collections of such works. A significant part of the collection was acquired in 1871 from the Esterházys, an enormously wealthy noble family who spent centuries amassing great art. There are eight sections in the museum: Egyptian Art, Antiquities, Baroque Sculpture, Old Masters, Drawings and Prints, 19th-Century Masters, 20th-Century Masters, and Modern Sculpture. Most great names associated with the old masters—Tiepolo, Tintoretto, Veronese, Titian, Raphael, Van Dyck, Brueghel, Rembrandt, Rubens, Hals, Hogarth, Dürer, Cranach, Holbein, Goya, Velázquez, El Greco, and others—are represented here. It has been said, though, that while the museum suffers no shortage of works by the old masters, it can boast precious few outright masterpieces. Delacroix, Corot, and Manet are the best-represented 19th-century French artists in the museum. See "A New Direction for the Museum of Fine Arts" box in this section.

XIV. Hősök tere. ⓒ 1/469-7100. Free admission for permanent collection; other exhibits 1,000 Ft–1,800 Ft ($5–$9). Tues–Sun 10am–5:30pm. Free guided tours in English at 11am Tues–Fri, Sat 11am and 3pm. Metro: Hősök tere (Yellow line).

HISTORIC SQUARES & BUILDINGS

Hősök tere (Heroes' Square) ⚜⚜ *Kids*   Situated at the end of Pest's great boulevard, Andrássy út, and at the entrance to its most famous park, City Park (Városliget), the wide-open plaza of Hősök tere (Heroes' Square) is one of the symbols of the city. During the country's Communist era, Socialist holidays were invariably celebrated with huge military reviews in the square. In 1989 a rally here on the day of the reburial of Imre Nagy (who was the prime minister of Hungary during the Hungarian Revolution and who was executed after the 1956 uprising against the Soviet-backed regime) attracted 300,000 people to the square.

The square, like the park beyond it, was laid out for the 1896 Magyar Conquest millennial celebration. In its center stands the 35-m-high (118-foot-high) Millennial Column; arrayed around the base of the column are equestrian statues of Árpád and the six other Magyar tribal leaders who led the conquest. Behind the column, arrayed along a colonnade, are 14 heroes of Hungarian history, including King Stephen I, the country's first Christian king (first on left); King Matthias Corvinus, who presided over Buda's golden age in the 15th century (sixth from right); and Lajos Kossuth, leader of the 1848–49 War of Independence (first on right). The statues were restored in 1996 in honor of the 1,100th anniversary of the Magyar Conquest. Kids adore looking at the equestrian statues, and the square is close to many kid-friendly activities. Two of Budapest's major museums, the Museum of Fine Arts and the Exhibition Hall, flank Heroes' Square.

Take the metro to Hősök tere (Yellow line).

Magyar Állami Operaház (Hungarian State Opera House) ๑๑   Completed in 1884, the Opera House, on Pest's elegant Andrássy út, is the crowning achievement of famous Hungarian architect Miklós Ybl. Budapest's most celebrated performance hall, the opera house boasts a fantastically ornate interior featuring frescoes by two of the best-known Hungarian artists of the day, Bertalan Székely and Károly Lotz. Both inside and outside are dozens of statues of such greats as Beethoven, Mozart, Verdi, Wagner, Smetana, Tchaikovsky, and Monteverdi. Home to both the State Opera and the State Ballet, the Opera House has a rich and evocative history, which is related on the guided tours given daily at 3 and 4pm (these can be arranged in English). Well-known directors of the Opera House have included Gustav Mahler and Ferenc Erkel. See p. 203 for information on performances. The only way to tour the

> **Fun Fact Striking a Sour Note**
>
> A political scandal marked the Hungarian State Opera House's opening performance in 1884. Ferenc Liszt had written a piece to be performed especially for the event, but when it was discovered that he had incorporated elements of the "Rákóczi March," a patriotic (and anti-Habsburg) Hungarian melody, he was prevented from playing it.

interior is on a guided tour, which costs 2,400 Ft ($12). The blatant discrimination here is that if you have the same tour in Hungarian, the price is a mere 500 Ft ($2.50). They claim it is because of the translation, but with the plethora of young language speakers, this is a weak excuse. After all, travel to other European cities, and most would condemn this practice.

VI. Andrássy út 22. ✆ 1/331-2550. www.opera.hu. Tour 2,400 Ft ($12). Tours given daily at 3 and 4pm (available in English). Metro: Opera (Yellow line).

Parliament ๑   Budapest's great Parliament building, completed in 1902, was built to the eclectic design of Imre Steindl. It mixes a predominant neo-Gothic style with a neo-Renaissance dome. Standing proudly on the Danube bank, visible from almost any riverside vantage point, it has been from the outset one of Budapest's symbols, though until 1989 a democratically elected government had convened here exactly once (just after World War II, before the Communist takeover). Built at a time of extreme optimism and national purpose, the building was self-consciously intended to be one of the world's great houses of Parliament, and it remains one of the largest state buildings in Europe. The main cupola is decorated with statues of Hungarian kings.

On either side of the cupola are waiting rooms leading into the respective houses of Parliament. The members of Parliament are said to gather in these waiting rooms during breaks in the session to smoke and chat—note the cigar holders on the side of the doors. The waiting room on the Senate side (blue carpet) is adorned with statues of farmers, peasants, tradesmen, and workers. The figures that decorate the waiting room on the Representatives' side (red carpet) are of sailors, soldiers, and postal officials. The interior decor is predominantly neo-Gothic. The ceiling frescoes are by Károly Lotz, Hungary's best-known fresco artist. Note the large carpet from the small Hungarian village of Békésszen-tandrás, which is purportedly the biggest handmade carpet in Europe. The Parliament is also home to the legendary crown jewels of St. Stephen, which were moved here from the National Museum as part of the Hungarian millennium celebration.

V. Kossuth tér. ✆ 1/441-4415, www.parlament.hu. Admission (by guided tour only): 60-min. tour in English 2,300 Ft ($12), 1,150 Ft ($5.75) students. Tickets are available at Gate X. Tours are given Mon–Fri 10am and noon, 2pm (but not on days in which Parliament is in session, which is usually Tues and Wed, or during protocol events); Sat 4pm; Sun at 2pm. Metro: Kossuth tér (Red line).

CHURCHES & SYNAGOGUES

Bazilika (St. Stephen's Church) ⚜

Although not a basilica in the technical sense of the word, Hungarians like to call St. Stephen's "the Basilica" in honor of its sheer size: It's the largest church in the country. It took over 50 years to build the Bazilika (the collapse of the dome in 1868 caused significant delays); three leading architects, two of whom (József Hild and Miklós Ybl) died before work was finished, presided over its construction. The church was considered so sturdy that important documents and artworks were stored in it during the World War II bombings. In 2003 a full-scale renovation of the church and neighboring square was completed, and now the cleaned-up front of the church graces the colorful and grand Szent István tér (St. Stephen's Sq.), where travelers sip their coffee in open-air cafes. The bust above the main entrance is of King Stephen, Hungary's first Christian king. Inside the church, in the Chapel of the Holy Right (Szent Jobb Kápolna), you can see Hungarian Catholicism's most cherished—and bizarre—holy relic: Stephen's preserved right hand. Organ concerts are sometimes held here, although reparations to the organ have made them intermittent. Daily Mass is held at 7am and 8am at the Szent Jobb Chapel, and 5:30 and 6pm in the Basilica; Sunday Mass at 8, 9, and 10am, noon, and 6 and 7:30pm.

Moments **A Heavenly View**

The tower of the St. Stephen's Church offers great views of the city. The climb is not recommended for the weak of knees or lungs, but a newly installed elevator will whisk you up in no time.

V. Szent István tér 33. ✆ 1/317-2859. www.basilica.hu. Church free; treasury 300 Ft ($1.50); tower 500 Ft ($2.50). Church daily 7am–6pm, except during services; treasury daily 9am–5pm (10am–4pm in winter); Szent Jobb Chapel Mon–Sat 9am–5pm (10am–4pm in winter), Sun 1–5pm; tower Apr–Oct Mon–Sat 10am–6pm (closed Nov–Mar). Metro: Arany János utca (Blue line) or Bajcsy-Zsilinszky út (Yellow line).

Belvárosi Plébániatemplom (Inner City Parish Church) ⚜

The Inner City Parish Church, standing flush against the Erzsébet Bridge in Pest, is one of the city's great architectural achievements. It is also the oldest building in Pest. The 12th-century Romanesque church that was first built on this spot was constructed inside the remains of the walls of the Roman fortress of Contra-Aquincum. In the early 14th century, a Gothic church was built where the Romanesque church once stood, and this medieval church, with numerous additions and reconstructions reflecting various architectural trends, still stands today. Both Gothic and baroque elements can be observed on the exterior, and the interior niches are built in both styles. Inside, you'll also find a *mihrab* (prayer niche) dating from the Turkish occupation, when the church was temporarily converted into a mosque. The painting on the altar is the work of the 20th-century artist Pál Molnár, whose work can also be seen in St. Anne's Church. The church was almost torn down when the Erzsébet Bridge was built in the late 19th century. Fortunately, an alternative plan won out, calling for the new bridge to wind around the church in a serpentine fashion (this interesting construction is best viewed from Gellért Hill). Daily Mass is held at 6:30am and 6pm; Sunday Mass at 9am, 10am, noon, and 6pm.

V. Március 15 tér. © 1/318-3108. Free admission. Mon–Sat 6am–7pm; Sun 8am–7pm. Metro: Ferenciek tere (Blue line).

Dohány Synagogue ⋆ Built in 1859, this is Europe's largest synagogue and the world's second-largest synagogue. Budapest's Jewish community still uses it. The architecture has striking Byzantine and Moorish elements; the interior is vast and ornate, with two balconies and the unusual presence of an organ. An ambitious restoration was completed in recent years, funded in large part by a foundation set up by the American actor Tony Curtis, who is of Hungarian-Jewish descent. The building's original splendor is now apparent.

The synagogue has a rich but tragic history. Adolf Eichmann arrived with the occupying Nazi forces in March 1944 to supervise the establishment of the Jewish ghetto and the subsequent deportations. Up to 20,000 Jews took refuge inside the synagogue complex, but 7,000 did not survive the bleak winter of 1944–45. These victims are buried in the courtyard, where you can also see a piece of the original brick ghetto wall. The National Jewish Museum is inside the synagogue complex (see p. 136 for information on the museum).

VII. Dohány u. 2–8. Admission 600 Ft ($3). Mon–Thurs 10am–5pm; Fri 10am–2pm; Sun 10am–2pm. Services are held Fri 6pm and Sat 9am. Metro: Astoria (Red line) or Deák tér (all lines).

BUDA
MUSEUMS
Budapesti Történeti Múzeum (Budapest History Museum) ⋆ This museum, also known as the Castle Museum, is the best place to get a sense of the once-great medieval Buda. It might be worth splurging for a guided tour—even though the museum's descriptions are written in English, the history of the palace's repeated construction and destruction is so confusing and arcane that it's difficult to really understand what you're seeing without a tour guide.

"The Medieval Royal Palace and its Gothic Statues" exhibit consists almost entirely of rooms and artifacts uncovered during the post–World War II excavation and rebuilding of the palace. In this exhibit the rooms and halls themselves are more notable than the fragments and occasional undamaged pieces of statues, stone carvings, earthenware, and the like. The "History of Budapest Since 1686" exhibit is worth visiting for its photographs.

I. In Buda Palace, Wing E, on Castle Hill. © 1/224-3700. Admission 900 Ft ($3.15). Audio guided tours by qualified staff in English for serious history buffs, at a whopping 800 Ft ($27), are available. May 15–Sept 15 daily 10am–6pm; Nov 1–Feb 28 Wed–Mon 10am–4pm. Bus: Várbusz from Moszkva tér or 16 from Deák tér to Castle Hill. Funicular: From Clark Ádám tér to Castle Hill.

Nemzeti Galéria (Hungarian National Gallery) ⋆ A repository of Hungarian art from medieval times through the 20th century, the Hungarian National Gallery is an enormous museum—you couldn't possibly view the entire collection during a single visit. The museum was founded during the great reform period of the mid–19th century and was moved to its present location in Buda Palace in 1975. Hungary has produced some fine artists, particularly in the late 19th century, and this is the place to view their work. The giants of the time are the brilliant **Mihály Munkácsy** ☙☙, whose masterpieces include *The Lintmakers, Condemned Cell,* and *Woman Carrying Wood;* László Paál, a painter of village scenes, including *Village Road in Berzova, Path in the Forest at Fontainbleau,* and *Depth of the Forest;* **Károly Ferenczy** ☙☙, whose mastery of light is seen in *Morning Sunshine* and *Evening in March;* and Pál Szinyei Merse, a plein-air artist whose own artistic developments paralleled those of the early French Impressionists (check out *Picnic in May*). Some other artists to look for are Gyula Benczúr, who painted grand historical scenes; Károly Lotz, best known as a fresco painter (you can see his creations at the Opera House and Matthias Church), who is represented at the museum by a number of nudes and several fine thunderstorm paintings; and Bertalan Székely, a painter of historical scenes and landscapes. József Rippl-Rónai's canvases are premier examples of Hungarian post-Impressionism and Art Nouveau (see *Father and Uncle Piacsek Drinking Red Wine* and *My Grandmother*), while Tivadar Csontváry Kosztka, the "Rousseau of the Danube," is considered by some critics to be a genius of early modern art.

I. In Buda Palace, Wings B, C, and D, on Castle Hill. ✆ **1/375-5567.** Free admission to permanent collection. Variable entrance for temporary exhibitions. Tues–Sun 10am–6pm. Bus: Várbusz from Moszkva tér or 16 from Deák tér to Castle Hill. Funicular: From Clark Ádám tér to Castle Hill.

A FAMOUS CHURCH

Mátyás Templom (Matthias Church) ☙   Officially named the Church of Our Lady, this symbol of Buda's Castle District is popularly known as Matthias Church after the much-loved 15th-century Renaissance king who was the main donor of the building and who was twice married here. The structure that originally stood here dates to the mid–13th century. However, like other old churches in Budapest, Matthias Church has an interesting history of destruction and reconstruction, and was constantly being refashioned in the architectural style that was popular at the time of reconstruction. The last two Hungarian kings (Habsburgs) were crowned in this church: Franz Joseph in 1867 (Liszt wrote and performed his *Coronation Mass* for the occasion) and Charles IV in 1916. The church interior is decorated with works by two outstanding 19th-century Hungarian painters, Károly Lotz and Bertalan Székely. Organ concerts are held here every other Friday evening in July and August at 8pm. Daily Mass is held at 8:30am, 12:30pm, and 6pm; Sunday Mass at 8:30am, 9:30am, noon, and 6pm.

I. Szentháromság tér 2. ✆ **1/355-5657.** Admission 600 Ft ($3). Daily 9am–6pm. Bus: Várbusz from Moszkva tér or 16 from Deák tér Castle Hill. Funicular: From Clark Ádám tér to Castle Hill.

SPECTACULAR VIEWS

Gellért Hegy (Gellért Hill) *Moments*   Gellért Hill, towering 230m (754 ft.) above the Danube, offers the single best panorama of the city. The hill is named after the iron-fisted Italian Bishop Gellért, who assisted Hungary's first Christian king, Stephen I, in converting the Magyars. Gellért became a martyr when vengeful pagans killed him by rolling him down the side of this hill in a barrel. An enormous statue of Gellért now stands on the hill, with the bishop defiantly holding a cross in his outstretched hand.

On top of Gellért Hill you'll find the **Liberation Monument,** built in 1947 supposedly to commemorate the Red Army's liberation of Budapest from Nazi occupation, though many believe that Admiral Horthy, Hungary's wartime leader, had planned the statue prior to the liberation to honor his fighter-pilot son, who was killed in the war. A mammoth statue, it's one of the last Socialist Realist memorials you'll find in Hungary. The statue's centerpiece, a giant female figure holding a leaf aloft, is affectionately known as *Kiflis Zsuzsa* (*kifli* is a crescent-shaped roll eaten daily by many Hungarians, while Zsuzsa, or Susie, is a common girl's name). Hungarian children like to call the smaller flame-holding figure at her side *Fagylaltos fiú* (the boy with the ice-cream cone).

Also atop Gellért Hill is the **Citadella** (© 1/365-6076), a symbol of power built for military control by the Austrians in 1851, shortly after they crushed the Hungarian War of Independence of 1848 and 1849. It costs 1,200 Ft ($6) to enter the Citadella, which is open daily from 9am to 7pm. There are several exhibitions to see here, but the main attraction is the great view. To get here, take bus no. 27 from Móricz Zsigmond körtér or hike up on any of the various paved pathways that originate at the base of the hill.

Halászbástya (Fisherman's Bastion)   The neo-Romanesque Fisherman's Bastion, perched on the edge of Buda's Castle District, near Matthias Church and the Hilton Hotel, affords a marvelous panorama of Pest. Built in 1905, it was intended mainly for decorative purposes, despite its military appearance. In recent years, the local city-council has imposed a fee to pass on the lookout portion of this site, to the annoyance of many tourists. Looking out over the Danube to Pest, you can see (from left to right): Margaret Island and the Margaret Bridge, Parliament, St. Stephen's Basilica, the Chain Bridge with the Hungarian Academy of Sciences and the Gresham Palace behind it, the Vigadó Concert Hall, the Inner City Parish Church, the Erzsébet Bridge, and the Szabadság Bridge. To get to the Halászbástya, take the Várbusz from Moszkva tér or bus no. 16 from Deák tér, or funicular from Clark Ádám tér to Castle Hill.

ÓBUDA
ROMAN RUINS

The **ruins of Aquincum** ⊛, the once-bustling capital of the Roman province of Pannonia, are spread throughout the southern part of Óbuda. Unfortunately, the various sites are far away from one another, and the layout of modern Óbuda is quite antipedestrian (the main Budapest-Szentendre highway cuts right through Óbuda), so it's difficult to see everything. Fortunately, two major sites are right across the road from one another, near the Aquincum station of the suburban HÉV railroad. The ruined **Amphitheater of the Civilian Town** is directly beside the HÉV station. It's open all the time and you're free to wander through (you should be aware that homeless people sometimes set up shelter within the walls). Across the highway from the amphitheater stand the ruins of the Civilian Town. Everything is visible from the roadside, except for the collection at the **Aquincum Museum,** which is located at III. Szentendrei u. 139 (© 1/250-1650; www.aquincum.hu). This neoclassical structure was built at the end of the 19th century in harmony with its surroundings. The museum exhibits coins, utensils, jewelry, and pottery from Roman times. Its most unique exhibit is a portable water organ (a rare and precious musical instrument) from A.D. 228. Entry to the museum is 700 Ft ($3.50). It's open from May to September, Tuesday through Sunday from 10am to 5pm, and from October to April, Tuesday through Sunday 9am to 5pm. Take the HÉV suburban railroad from Batthyány tér to Aquincum.

BRIDGING PEST & BUDA
Széchenyi Lánchíd (The Chain Bridge)   ⊛*(Moments)*   The Chain Bridge is, along with Parliament and the Castle, one of the dominant symbols of Budapest. It was built

Impressions

How much beauty there is in the Chain Bridge, what elegant silence, haughty humility, charming lightness, and archaic melancholy!

—Antal Szerb, 20th-century Hungarian writer

in 1849. As the first permanent bridge across the Danube, it paved the way for the union of Buda, Óbuda, and Pest into a single city. Prior to 1849, people relied on a pontoon bridge that had to be dismantled when ships passed and could be swept away in stormy weather. The initiative for the Chain Bridge came from the indefatigable Count István Széchenyi, the leading figure of Hungarian society during the mid-19th-century Age of Reform. A Scotsman named Adam Clark, for whom the square on the Buda side of the bridge is named, came to Budapest to supervise the massive project; he chose to remain in the city until his death many years later. The bridge was blown up by the retreating Nazis in World War II, but was rebuilt immediately after the war. Located in the heart of the city, it's best admired at night, when it's lit up like a chandelier until midnight. It is closed to motor vehicles on some weekends in the summer, when pedestrians, artists, craftspeople, vendors, locals, and tourists take over. But it's always an easy walk across if you're heading to Castle Hill—or merely want a midriver view of the city.

2 More Museums & Sights

PEST

Bélyegmúzeum (Postal Stamp Museum)   This may seem like an attraction of decidedly limited appeal, but generations of philatelists the world over have admired the artistic creations of Hungary's postal system, the Magyar Posta, as have we. You don't have to be a stamp collector to enjoy a visit. This wonderful little museum has rack after rack of the country's finest stamps—over 12 million in total! The "Madonna with Child" in **Rack 49,** which was mistakenly printed upside-down, is said to be Hungary's most valuable stamp. The stamps of **Rack 65** demonstrate how runaway inflation devastated Hungary in the 1940s. Variations on Lenin and Stalin can be seen in **Racks 68 to 77,** and **Racks 70 to 80** ✈✈ contain numerous brilliant examples of Socialist Realism. The staff is extremely friendly and well informed.

VII. Hársfa u. 47. ⓒ 1/341-5526. www.belyegmuzeum.hu. Admission 200 Ft ($1). Apr–Oct Tues–Sun 10am–6pm; Nov–Mar Tues–Sun 10am–4pm. Tram: 4 or 6 to Wesselényi utca.

Iparművészeti Múzeum (Museum of Applied Arts) ✈   It's worth a trip to the Museum of Applied Arts just to see the marvelous building that houses the collection. The museum was designed by Ödön Lechner in the 1890s. Lechner, whose most famous creation is the Town Hall in the Great Plain city of Kecskemét (p. 256), was an incredibly adventurous architect who combined traditional Hungarian folk elements with the Art Nouveau style of his time. If you're impressed by this structure, pay a visit to the former Post Office Savings Bank on Hold utca, another fine example of Lechner's work (see "Walking Tour 3: Leopold Town & Theresa Town," in chapter 8, "Strolling Around Budapest"). The museum's ceramic decoration comes from the famous Zsolnay factory in Pécs. Permanent exhibits, which are made up of antique decorative arts from all over Europe, are divided into five sections: furniture;

textiles; metalwork; ceramics, porcelain, and glass; and an eclectic display of books, leather, and ivory. Much of the museum's space is given to temporary exhibitions.

IX. Üllői út 33–37. ℂ **1/456-5100.** www.imm.hu. Admission 600 Ft ($2.25). Tues–Sun 10am–6pm. Metro: Ferenc körút (Blue line).

Ludwig Múzeum (Ludwig Museum of Contemporary Art) 🖈 Located in the recently opened Palace of Art, overlooking the Danube, this was formerly the Museum of the Hungarian Workers' Movement. Now converted to a more politically correct purpose, it houses a less-than-inspiring and poorly curated permanent exhibition of contemporary Hungarian and international art. The collection consists primarily of American pop art and central European contemporary works. It includes several late Picassos, Andy Warhol's *Single Elvis,* and a still functional Jean Tinguely, as well as an eclectic mix of Hungarian works by artists like Imre Bukta, Beáta Veszely, and Imre Bak. Like the Kunsthalle in Vienna, this museum is sometimes worth visiting for the various temporary exhibitions of contemporary works, mostly by alternative European artists.

IX. Komor Marcell u. 1. ℂ **1/555-3444.** www.ludwigmuseum.hu. Free admission for permanent collection. Sun, Tues, Fri 10am–6pm; Wed noon–6pm; Thurs noon–8pm; Saturday 10am–8pm; closed Mondays. Tram: 2 or 2A.

Nemzeti Zsidó Múzeum és Levéltár (National Jewish Museum and Archives) This museum is located in the Dohány Synagogue complex (p. 132). A tablet outside informs visitors that Theodor Herzl, the founder of Zionism, was born on this spot. The four-room museum is devoted to the long history of Jews in Hungary. Displays include Sabbath and holiday items (including some gorgeous examples of the famous Herend porcelain company's Passover plates), and ritual and everyday artifacts. The last room contains a small, moving exhibit on the Holocaust in Hungary.

VII. Dohány u. 2–8. ℂ **1/342-8942.** Admission 1,000 Ft ($5). Mon–Thurs 10am–5pm; Fri and Sun 10am–2pm. Metro: Astoria (Red line) or Deák tér (all lines).

Postamúzeum (Post Office Museum) 🖈 *Finds* The exhibits here are of limited interest, but the building itself and the apartment in which the museum is situated— the opulently furnished former Sexlehner family flat—are simply dazzling. Chandeliers dangle from the frescoed ceilings, and intricately carved wood moldings trim the walls.

VI. Andrássy út 3. ℂ **1/269-6838.** Admission 200 Ft ($1), free admission on Sun. Tues–Sun 10am–6pm. Metro: Bajcsy-Zsilinszky út (Yellow line) or Deák tér (all lines).

Terror Háza (House of Terror) 🖈🖈 The former headquarters of the ÁVH secret police, this building is witness to some of the darkest days of 20th-century Hungary and is now a chilling museum, one of the best in Hungary. It was set up as a memorial to the victims of both Communism and Fascism, and is an attempt to recapture life under successive oppressive regimes in Hungary. The building was the headquarters of the Nazis in 1944, and many individuals were tortured and murdered in the eerie cellars of this building. The Communist secret police were next to use the venue as a place for their own torture and oppression. The tearing down of the ugly exterior facade has been the subject of much debate, however, and for political reasons it has remained the sore thumb of the grand Andrássy boulevard.

VI. Andrássy út 60. ℂ **1/374-2600.** www.houseofterror.hu. Admission 1,200 Ft ($6). Tues–Fri 10am–6pm; Sat–Sun 10am–7:30pm. Metro: Oktogon (Yellow line).

A JEWISH CEMETERY
Kozma Cemetery *Finds* The city's main Jewish cemetery is in the eastern end of the Kőbánya district, a long tram ride from the center of town. An estimated half-million

Where Have All the Statues Gone?

Ever wonder where all the vanished Communist statues went after the fall? Over a decade and a half ago, Budapest and the rest of Hungary were filled with monuments to Lenin, to Marx and Engels, to the Red Army, and to the many lesser-known figures of Hungarian and international Communism. Torn rudely from their pedestals in the aftermath of 1989, they sat in warehouses for a few years gathering dust, until a controversial plan for a **Socialist Statue Park (Szoborpark Múzeum)** was realized. The park's inconvenient location and the relatively small number of statues on display (reflecting nothing of their former ubiquity) make the park less enticing than it could be. In addition, the best examples of the genre, dating from the Stalinist period of the late 1940s and 1950s, were removed from public view long before 1989 and were presumably destroyed long ago.

Located in the XXII district (extreme Southern Buda) on Balatoni út (© 1/424-7500; www.szoborpark.hu), the park is a memorial to an era, to despotism, and to bad taste. The museum gift shop sells all sorts of Communist-era memorabilia, such as T-shirts, medals, and cassettes of Red Army marching songs. The park is open daily from 10am to dusk and admission is 600 Ft ($3). To get to the park, take the black-lettered bus no. 7 from Ferenciek tere to Etele tér. Board a yellow Volán bus (to Érd) for a 20-minute ride to the park. Or, for a premium, you can take the new and convenient direct bus service from Deák tér for 2,450 Ft ($12) (admission ticket to the park included). The timetable varies almost monthly, but 11am and 3pm departures remain constant for July and August.

people are buried here. A vast, peaceful place, the cemetery is still in use today. Ornate Art Deco tombs stand proudly near the main entrance, their faded grandeur a testament both to the former status of those buried beneath them and to the steady passage of time. The cemetery is the site of Hungary's most moving Holocaust memorial, a set of nine walls with the names of victims etched into it. About 6,500 names appear—a small portion of the 600,000 Hungarian Jews estimated to have perished in the war. Survivors and relatives have penciled in hundreds of additional names.

X. Kozma u. 6. Free admission. Mon–Thurs 8am–4pm; Fri and Sun 8am–2pm. Tram: 37 from Blaha Lujza tér to the next to last stop.

BUDA

Hadtörténeti Múzeum (Museum of the History of Warfare)   Housed in a former barracks in the northwestern corner of the Castle District, this museum houses exhibits that relate the history of warfare in Hungary from the time of the Turkish occupation to the 20th century. The Turkish weaponry display is particularly interesting. Unfortunately, all the uniforms, decorations, models, weapons, maps, and photographs are accompanied by Hungarian text only. **Toy soldiers** ⓖ are available in the gift shop.

I. Tóth Árpád sétány 40. © 1/325-1647. www.militaria.hu. Free admission. Apr–Sept Tues–Sun 10am–6pm; Oct–Mar Tues–Sun 10am–4pm. Bus: Várbusz from Moszkva tér or 16 from Deák tér to Castle Hill. Funicular: From Clark Ádám tér to Castle Hill.

Fun Fact **Did You Know...?**

- A network consisting of 10km (6¼ miles) of tunnels, built in the Middle Ages for military purposes, lies underneath Buda's Castle District.
- Budapest was the site of the European continent's first underground metro line, which you can still ride today (the Yellow line).
- Budapest did not become a unified city until 1873, when Pest, Buda, and Óbuda merged.
- The retreating Nazis blew up all of Budapest's bridges in the final days of World War II.
- The Red Army liberated Pest from Nazi occupation on January 18, 1945, but did not manage to liberate Buda until February 13.
- The Swedish diplomat Raoul Wallenberg, stationed in Budapest, saved thousands of Jews from Nazi deportation by issuing fake passports and setting up "safe houses," only to disappear himself into the Soviet gulag after the city's liberation.
- Budapest's Jewish population (about 80,000) is the largest of any European city outside Russia.

Kőzépkori Zsidó Imaház (Medieval Jewish Prayer House) *Finds*   This tiny medieval Sephardic synagogue was unexpectedly discovered in the 1960s during general excavation work in the Castle District. It dates to approximately 1364, when Jews were allowed to return to the Castle District after having been expelled from the district by King Lajos 4 years earlier. After the massacre of Buda's Jews in the late 17th century (following the defeat of the occupying Turks by a Habsburg-led Christian army), the synagogue was turned into an apartment and, over the ensuing centuries, forgotten. A nearby excavation unearthed the ruins of another, much larger, synagogue dating from 1461; all that remains of it are a keystone, on display now inside this synagogue, and three stone columns standing in the courtyard here. Some Hebrew gravestones are also on display behind a grate in the entryway; the small one in the center of the front row dates from the 3rd century A.D. The English-speaking caretaker will give you a free informal tour if you express an interest. You can pretty much see the whole place from the entry; consider your admission fee a contribution to the museum.

I. Táncsics Mihály u. 26. © **1/355-8849.** Admission 400 Ft ($2). May–Oct Tues–Sun 10am–6pm. Bus: Várbusz from Moszkva tér or 16 from Deák tér to Castle Hill. Funicular: From Clark Ádám tér to Castle Hill.

Semmelweis Orvostörténeti Múzeum (Semmelweis Museum of Medical History)   This museum, which traces the history of medicine from ancient times to the modern era, is located in the former home of Ignác Semmelweis, Hungary's leading 19th-century physician. Semmelweis is hailed as the "savior of mothers" for his role in identifying the cause of puerperal (childbed) fever and preventing it by advocating that physicians wash their hands between patients, an uncommon practice at the time. The museum, spread over four rooms, displays everything from early medical instruments to anatomical models to old medical textbooks. There's also a faithfully reconstructed 19th-century pharmacy. Descriptions are in Hungarian only, but many exhibits are self-explanatory. In the Semmelweis Memorial Room, two book-cases display the eminent scholar's collection of medical texts. Keen eyes might notice the seven volumes of Osler's *Modern Medicine,* written long after Semmelweis' death; they were a gift from former U.S. President George Bush to the late József Antall, who became the prime minister of Hungary after the first democratic elections in 1990. Antall had previously been director of the Semmelweis Museum.

I. Apród u. 1–3. © 1/375-3533. Free admission. Tues–Sun 10:30am–6pm. Take any bus or tram to Döbrentei tér (for example, bus 8 from Március 15 tér).

A MUSLIM SHRINE
Gül Baba Türbéje (Tomb of Gül Baba) ☆ *Finds*   The unfortunate Turkish dervish Gül Baba died at dinner in 1541. It was no ordinary meal either, but a gala in Matthias Church celebrating the conquest of Buda. Gül Baba was a member of a Turkish order that was involved in horticulture and that specifically focused on developing new species of roses. Today his tomb, which is located in a wonderfully steep, twisting neighborhood at the beginning of the Hill of Roses (Rózsadomb) district, is maintained as a Muslim shrine by the Turkish government. The descriptions are in Hungarian and Turkish, but an English-language pamphlet is available on request. The tomb, set in a park and sur-rounded by lovely rose gardens, is the northernmost Muslim shrine in Europe. The recently restored museum, which relates the story of Gül Baba's life, was reopened in 1997 in an official ceremony attended by Turkey's President Demirel.

II. Mecset u. 14. © 1/355-8764. Admission 400 Ft ($2). Tues–Sun 10am–6pm. Tram: 4 or 6 to the Buda side of Margaret Bridge; the most direct route to Gül Baba tér is via Mecset utca, off Margaret utca.

ÓBUDA
Varga Imre Gyűjtemény (Imre Varga Collection)   Imre Varga is Hungary's best-known contemporary sculptor. This small museum, just off Óbuda's Fő tér, shows a good cross section of his sensitive, piercing work. Historical subjects on dis-play inside the museum range from the pudgy, balding figure of Imre Nagy, reluctant hero of the 1956 Hungarian Uprising, to the dapper, capped Béla Bartók. The museum also has a garden where Varga's sad, broken figures stand forlornly or sit on benches resting their weary feet; live cats prance around in the garden, enhancing the mysterious atmosphere. For an example of the sculptor's work in a public context, see the statue of Imre Nagy near Parliament.

III. Laktanya u. 7. © 1/250-0274. Admission 500 Ft ($2.50) for adults, 250 Ft ($1.25) for students and seniors. Tues–Sun 10am–6pm. Train: HÉV suburban railroad from Batthyány tér to Árpád híd.

Victor Vasarely Museum   This museum, devoted to the works of the late Hungar-ian-born founder of op art, was opened in 1987 after the artist donated some 400 works to the Hungarian state. A huge, airy place, it extends over two floors. On dis-play is a full range of the artist's colorful, geometric art.

III. Szentlélek tér 6. © 1/250-1540. Free admission for the permanent collection. It is advised to call in advance, since the museum closes occasionally for private events. Daily 10am–5:30pm. Train: HÉV suburban railroad from Batthyány tér to Árpád híd.

AN ARCHITECTURAL WONDER
Leo Frankel Synagogue   Still in use today, the Leo Frankel Synagogue is about as bizarre an architectural creation as Budapest has to offer. This seemingly normal apartment building looks no different from its neighbors—until you notice the Star of David and the menorah carved into its facade. But that's just the beginning: The

synagogue, which was built in 1887 and 1888, is lodged inside the building and completely fills the interior courtyard. In 1928 it was surrounded by a six-story apartment house. This was done both to protect the synagogue from anti-Semitic violence and to provide accommodations for 51 Jewish families, including the families of the synagogue's rabbis and cantors. During World War II, Nazi invaders used the synagogue as a stable, rendering it absolutely unusable. Since the 1990 regime change, the synagogue has been restored twice, most recently in 2000.

Insider Tip: The whole scene is best viewed from above; climb the stairs or take the antique elevator to gain perspective. An official tour of the synagogue is available through Chosen Tours (p. 149).

II. Frankel Léo u. 49. 🕐 **1/326-1445.** Suggested admission 600 Ft ($3), but any donation gratefully accepted. Mon–Fri 9am–1pm by prior arrangement. Services Fri nights and Sat mornings. Tram: 17 from the Buda side of Margaret Bridge (2 stops).

3 Parks, Gardens & Playgrounds

Hungarians love to stroll in the park, and on weekends and summer afternoons, it seems as if the whole of Budapest is out enjoying what Hungarians lovingly refer to as "the nature."

Popular **Margaret Island (Margit-sziget)** has been a public park since 1908. The long, narrow island, connected to both Buda and Pest via the Margaret and Árpád bridges, is barred to most vehicular traffic. In addition to three important ruins—the Dominican Convent, a 13th- to 14th-century Franciscan church, and a 12th-century Premonstratensian chapel—attractions on the island include the Palatinus Strand open-air baths (p. 152), which draw upon the famous thermal waters under Margaret Island; the Alfréd Hajós Sport Pool; and the Open-Air Theater. Sunbathers line the steep embankments along the river, and bikes are available for rent (see "By Bike," under "Getting Around" in chapter 4). There are several snack bars, open-air restaurants, and even clubs. Despite all this, Margaret Island remains a quiet, tranquil place. In any direction off the main road, you can find well-tended gardens or a patch of grass under the shade of a willow tree for a private picnic. Margaret Island is best reached by bus no. 26 from Nyugati tér, which runs the length of the island, or tram no. 4 or 6, which stops at the entrance to the island midway across the Margaret Bridge. *Warning:* These are popular metro lines for pickpockets. See "Staying Safe" in chapter 2, on p. 21.

City Park (Városliget) ⅌ is an equally popular place to spend a summer day, and families are everywhere. Heroes' Square, at the end of Andrássy út, is the most logical starting point for a walk in City Park. Built in 1896 as part of the Hungarian millennial celebrations, the square has been the site of some important moments in Hungarian history. The lake behind the square is used for boating in summer and for ice skating in winter (p. 153). The Vajdahunyad Castle, located by the lake, is an architectural mishmash if there ever was one. The castle was built as a temporary structure in 1896 for the millennial celebration in order to demonstrate the different architectural styles in Hungary; it was so popular that a permanent structure was eventually designed to replace it. It is now home to the **Agricultural Museum,** the largest of its kind in Europe, which has especially interesting exhibitions on Hungary's grape and wine industries. Admission to the museum is 900 Ft ($4.50); it's open in summer, early fall, and late spring Tuesday through Friday and Sunday from 10am to 5pm, Saturday 10am to 6pm; in late fall, winter, and early spring Monday through Friday

Óbuda and Margaret Island

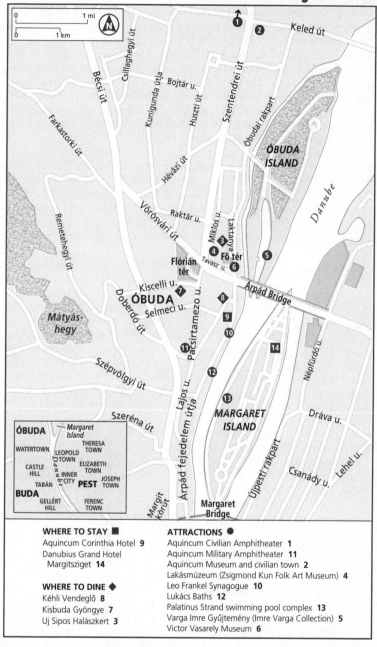

10am to 4pm, Saturday and Sunday to 5pm. Take the Yellow line of the metro to Széchenyi fürdő to get to the museum. The park's **Animal Garden Boulevard (Állatkerti körút),** the favorite street of generations of Hungarian children, is where the zoo, the circus, and the amusement park are all found (see "Especially for Kids," below). Gundel, Budapest's most famous restaurant, is also here, as are the Széchenyi Baths, which boast a splendid outdoor pool. The southern end of City Park is considerably less crowded, with fewer buildings. The **Transport Museum** is among the few attractions here. The nearby **Petőfi Csarnok** is the venue for a variety of popular cultural events, concerts, and flea market fairs. The Yellow metro line makes stops at Hősök tere (Heroes' Square), at the edge of the park, and at Széchenyi fürdő, in the middle of the park.

There are numerous parks and nature reserves in the **Buda Hills.** You can ride the Children's Railroad through the hills or take the János Hill chairlift to its highest point (p. 145). The Buda Hills are a great place to explore on your own; you'll hardly ever stray too far from a bus or tram line, and yet you'll feel as if you're in the countryside, far from a bustling capital city. Moszkva tér is the best place to start an excursion into the hills. Pick up tram no. 56 or bus no. 21, 22, or 28; get off when you see an area you like.

Tucked away throughout Budapest you will find some charming playgrounds. The Hungarian word for playground is *játszótér* (or *játszó kert*). **Károly kert** *⋆⋆*, a wonderful little enclosed park in the southern half of the Inner City, is bordered by Ferenczy István utca, Magyar utca, and Henszlmann Imre utca. Enter the park through a wrought-iron gate. Once inside, you'll find swings and seesaws, an enclosed miniature soccer field, a sandbox with a slide, and a nice stretch of green grass to run on. In the middle of all this is a fountain surrounded by flowers. The equipment is not as modern as what you'll find at some of the city's other playgrounds, but the park has a distinct old-world charm. Indeed, it once belonged to the adjacent Károlyi mansion, which was the home of Mihály Károlyi, who served briefly as Hungarian prime minister in 1918. The mansion was recently restored to its old splendor and functions as the Museum of Hungarian Literature (© 1/317-3611, ext. 203). Its location in the Inner City makes it a convenient destination. The museum is open Tuesday to Sunday from 10am to 6pm. Admission is 400 Ft ($2).

The playground in the **Millenáris Park,** right behind the Mammut Shopping Mall in Buda's Széna tér, would probably be preferred more by the kids. The playground is located in a reconstructed industrial heritage site that was once home to the famous Ganz Company, which produced carriages and engines for the Hungarian railroads beginning in the 19th century. Parents can watch their kids playing in this safe and creative playground from the shade of trees, next to an impressive system of decorative waterfalls and fountains.

Another fine playground is located not far from Buda's busy transportation hub, Móricz Zsigmond körtér. At the intersection of Villányi út and Tas Vezér utca (directly across the street from the Hotel Flamenco), this playground is entirely self-enclosed (no dogs allowed), clean, well maintained, and very large, with lots of modern equipment.

Other good playgrounds can be found in VII. Almássy tér, between Blaha Lujza tér and Oktogon, and at Hild tér, in a small park near the Pest side of the Chain Bridge.

Margaret Island, for all its charm, lacks a decent playground. The best one it has to offer is just off the main road to the left after you pass the stadium at the head of the island.

If you find yourself in Buda's Watertown district (perhaps on our Watertown walking tour; see p. 173) and you want to make a little play stop, there is a small, colorful neighborhood playground in a quiet, residential area on Franklin utca, between Donáti utca and Iskola utca.

Another neighborhood playground is found in **Pillangó Park,** just across the street from the Pillangó utca metro station (Red line). This playground is situated in the midst of a huge Socialist-era housing development in outer Pest. The architecture is not pretty, but this is how most people live in Budapest, so it's worth a look. The playground features a manually operated merry-go-round for the little ones, and another nearby playground has a cable swing for bigger kids.

Rainy day desperation? Take the kids to the Moszkva tér McDonald's or to IKEA (Red line metro to Örs vezér tere), both of which have decent indoor play spaces.

4 Especially for Kids

The following attractions are for kids of all ages, since just about everyone loves a train ride in the hills, a spin on a Ferris wheel, or a good puppet show. Three attractions here—the zoo, the amusement park, and the circus—are located in City Park (Városliget), along the famed Animal Garden Boulevard (Állatkerti körút). You could easily spend a whole child-oriented day here.

In addition to the information below, see the information on the Palatinus Strand outdoor swimming-pool complex (p. 173) and horse and pony riding in the Buda Hills (p. 153). Also see the latter half of the preceding section, "Parks, Gardens & Playgrounds," above for the lowdown on the best of Budapest's playgrounds.

MUSEUMS

Csodák Palotája (Palace of Wonders) *Kids*   The Csodák Palotája is an interactive science center featuring dozens of fun, educational exhibits, including laser displays, optical puzzles, and mazes—in one large room. This place is best for kids over 3 years old.

XIII. Váci út 19. ⓒ 1/350-6131. www.csodapalota.hu. Admission 600 Ft ($3). Tues–Fri 9am–5pm; Sat–Sun 10am–6pm. Closed in Aug. Metro: Lehel tér (Blue line). From the metro station, walk north on Váci út (in direction of Bulcsu utca and Déval utca).

Természettudományi Múzeum (Museum of Natural History) *Kids*   Using the natural history of the Carpathian Basin, the exhibits here trace human development from the earliest times to the emergence of civilized society. The museum features a large "discovery room" on the first floor, in which all the exhibits are interactive. Participation is both educational and fun. The museum is nicely situated next to Orczy Kert (Orczy Garden), a large park featuring over 100 different species of trees and a small lake. Until after World War II, the park belonged to the Hungarian Military School, which now houses the museum.

VIII. Ludovika tér 2. ⓒ 1/210-1085. www.nhmus.hu. Free admission. Wed–Mon 10am–6pm, closing 1 hr. earlier in winter. Metro: Nagyvárad tér (Blue line).

FAMILY FUN IN CITY PARK

Állatkert (Zoo) *Kids*   Opened in 1866, the zoo is located near the circus and the amusement park on City Park's famous Animal Garden Boulevard, a favorite spot of Hungarian youngsters for 130 years. Although the zoo has been modernized several times, it still retains the sad flavor of an old-style, fairly inhumane zoo. Nice attractions here are the pony rides and two important examples of Art Nouveau architecture: the main entrance gate and the elephant house. Two recently renovated greenhouses, the largest of their kind in central Europe, contain spectacular tropical plants.

XIV. Állatkerti krt. 6–12. ℂ 1/273-4900. www.zoobudapest.com. Admission 1,300 Ft ($6.50) adults, 900 Ft ($4.50) children 2–14, free for children under 2. Kids under 14 must be accompanied by a parent. Mon–Thurs 9am–5pm; Fri–Sun 9am–7pm (varies according to month, verify with website). Metro: Hősök tere or Széchenyi fürdő (Yellow line).

Közlekedési Múzeum (Transport Museum) ⓐ *Kids*   Located near the Petőfi Csarnok in the little-visited southeastern corner of City Park, this wonderful museum, which celebrated its 100th anniversary in 1999, features large-scale 1:5 models of various kinds of historic vehicles, especially trains. The museum also exhibits vintage motorcycles and bicycles, early model cars, and antique horse buggies. A model train set runs every 15 minutes on the mezzanine level; follow the crowds. On weekends a film on aviation history is shown at 11am. The gift shop features all sorts of transportation-related trinkets. An aviation exhibit is housed in the Petőfi Csarnok, an all-purpose community center nearby.

XIV. Városligeti krt. 11. ℂ 1/273-3840. Free admission for permanent collection, temporary exhibitions cost 400 Ft ($2) adults, 200 Ft ($1) children. Tues–Sun 10am–5pm, until 6pm on Sun. Trolleybus: 74 from Károly körút (pick it up on Dohány utca, across the street from Dohány Synagogue) or 72 from Podmaniczky utca, near Nyugati Station.

Vidám Park (Amusement Park) ⓐ *Kids*   Popular with Hungarian families, Vidám Park (literally "Happy Park"), unlike Disneyland or Copenhagen's Tivoli Gardens, is eminently affordable. Two rides in particular are not to be missed: the merry-go-round and the Ferris wheel. The 100-year-old **merry-go-round** *(Körhinta)* ⓐⓐ, constructed almost entirely of wood, was recently restored to its original, delightful grandeur. The riders must actively pump to keep the horses rocking. Authentic Wurlitzer music plays, and as the carousel spins round and round, it creaks mightily. The **Ferris wheel** *(óriáskerék)* ⓐⓐⓐ is also wonderful, although it has little in common with the rambunctious Ferris wheels of the modern age. A gangly, bright-yellow structure, it rotates at a liltingly slow pace, gently lifting you high into the sky for a remarkable view. Vidám Park also features Europe's longest wooden roller coaster.

Note: Parents must pay for a ticket for themselves and one for their child when accompanying a child who is too young to go on a ride by him- or herself. Next door is a toddlers' amusement park (Kis Vidám Park), although several rides in the Vidám Park are also suitable for toddlers.

XIV. Állatkerti krt. 14–16. ℂ 1/363-8310. www.vidampark.hu. Admission 300 Ft ($1.50) adults; free for children under 120cm tall (about 4 ft.); rides 300 Ft–600 Ft ($1.50–$3); your best bet is to buy a stack of 20 tickets (plus 2 "free" extra tickets) on entry for 6,000 Ft ($30). Mar–Nov Mon–Fri 10am–8pm, Sat–Sun to 8pm summer hours; see website for other periods. Metro: Széchenyi fürdő (Yellow line).

A RAILROAD & CHAIRLIFT
Gyermekvasút (Children's Railroad) ⓐⓐ *Kids*   Hungarian children, specially trained and under adult supervision, run this scenic narrow-gauge railway, making a trip on the railroad especially exciting for youngsters. The youthful engineers are dressed in miniature versions of the official MÁV (Hungarian State Railways) uniforms, with all the appropriate paraphernalia. The railway was built in the late 1940s and was formerly run by the Young Pioneers, the youth movement of the Communist Party, although these days it has no political affiliation. The train slowly winds 11km (6¾ miles) through the Buda Hills, providing numerous panoramas along the way.

You can board at either terminus, or anywhere along the way. To get to the Hűvösvölgy terminus, take tram no. 56 from Moszkva tér to the last stop. To get to the Széchenyi-hegy terminus, take the same no. 56 tram from Moszkva tér two stations to the railroad *(fogaskerekű vasút)* station (the railroad station is called Városmajor, and it is across the street from the Hotel Budapest, on Szilágyi Erzsébet fasor in Buda). One-way travel time on the railway is 45 minutes.

Call the Széchenyi hegy terminus. ℂ 1/395-5420. www.gyermekvasut.com. A one-way trip costs 400 Ft ($2) adults, 150 Ft (75¢) children ages 6 to 14; a round-trip ticket is 800 Ft ($4) adults, 300 Ft ($1.50) children. In the summer, trains run every hour or so Mon–Fri 10am–5pm; and Sat–Sun 10am–6pm. Winter hours of operation are Mon–Fri 9am–4pm, Sat–Sun 10am–5pm.

János-Hegy Libegő (János Hill Chairlift) ᴿ ⁿᵈˢ   This somewhat primitive chairlift takes you up János Hill to a spot that's a steep 10-minute walk from Budapest's highest point. At the top is the neo-Romanesque *Erzsébet Kilátó* (**Lookout Tower**), built in 1910. It costs 400 Ft ($1.80) to climb the tower (well worth it for the view), which is open daily from 8am to 5pm. You'll find a nondescript snack bar at the tower. You can ride the chair back down, hike back down to the no. 158 bus, or, if you have a map of the Buda Hills, hike out to any number of other bus connections. Call Tourinform (ℂ 1/317-9800) for more information on the bus lines.

XII. Zugligeti út 93. ℂ 1/394-3764. A one-way chairlift trip costs 450 Ft ($2.25) adults, 200 Ft ($1) children; a round-trip ticket is 900 Ft ($4.50) adults, 400 Ft ($2) children. The lift operates daily 10am–4pm. Take bus 158 from Moszkva tér to the last stop.

ENTERTAINMENT: THE CIRCUS, PUPPET THEATERS & FOLK DANCING

Nagy Cirkusz (Great Circus)   It's not the Big Apple Circus, but kids love it just the same. Budapest has a long circus tradition, though most Hungarian circus stars still opt for the more glamorous and financially rewarding circus life abroad. This is a traditional circus, with clowns, animals, jugglers, acrobats, and so on. When buying

Bábszínházak (Puppet Theaters)

Kids from around the world love **Hungarian puppet theater**. The shows are all in Hungarian, but with such standard fare as Hungarian versions of *Cinderella, Peter and the Wolf,* or local favorites *Misi Mókus, Marcipán cica,* and *János Vitéz,* no one seems to have trouble following the plot. The audience is an important part of the show: For instance, Hungarian children shriek *"Rossz farkas!"* ("Bad wolf!") at every appearance of the villain in *Peter and the Wolf.*

Budapest has two puppet theaters, with the season running from October to mid-June. Tickets are extremely cheap, usually in the 600-Ft-to-1,100-Ft ($3–$5.50) range. The **Budapest Puppet Theater (Budapesti Bábszínház)** is at VI. Andrássy út 69 (ℂ 1/321-5200); the nearest metro station is Oktogon (Yellow line). The **Kolibri Puppet Theater (Kolibri Bábszínház)** is at VI. Jókai tér 10 (ℂ 1/353-4633); Jókai tér is halfway between the Oktogon and Opera stations of the Yellow metro line. Shows start at various times throughout the day (days vary, so call in advance) with the first show usually at 10am and the last at 5pm, and tickets are available all day at the box offices.

tickets, it's helpful to know that *porond* means ring level and *erkély* means balcony. The box office is open daily from 10am to 7pm.

XIV. Állatkerti krt. 7. ℂ 1/343-9630. www.maciva.hu. Tickets 1,200 Ft–1,900 Ft ($6–$9.50) adults, 900 Ft–1,500 Ft ($4.50–$7.50) children, free for children under 4. Performances: On weekdays except Mon and Tues at 3pm; 3 performances on Sat, with a morning show at 10:30am in addition to the regular 3pm and 7pm shows; 2 shows on Sun, at 10:30am at 3pm. Metro: Hősök tere or Széchenyi fürdő (Yellow line).

IN-LINE SKATING & ICE SKATING
Also see p. 153 for more on ice skating.

Görzenál Roller Blading   If your kids enjoy in-line skating, skateboarding, or trampolining, this is the place for them. Rental skates are available for 600 Ft ($3). You can spend as much time as you like here; no one will kick you out after an allotted time.

III. Árpád fejedelem út 2000. ℂ 1/250-4800. Admission 400 Ft ($2) Mon–Thurs, 600 Ft ($3) Fri–Sun. Sun–Thurs 9am–8pm; Fri–Sat 9am–9pm. Bus: 6 from Nyugati pu. Train: HÉV suburban railway from Batthyány tér to Árpád fejedelem.

Jégpálya (Ice Ring) Pólus Center   Pólus Center rink is a decent-size ice rink in a shopping mall.

XV. Szentmihályi u. 131. ℂ 1/419-4070. Admission 400 Ft ($2) for 1 hr.; 300 Ft ($1.50) to rent skates. Mon 9–10am and 11am–3pm; Tues and Fri 9am–4pm; Wed–Thurs 9am–3pm; Sat–Sun 10am–5pm. Trolleybus: 6 from Keleti Station.

5 For the Music Lover

Three museums in Budapest celebrate the contributions of great Hungarian musicians.

The greatest Hungarian composer of the 19th century, and one of the country's most famous sons, was undoubtedly **Ferenc (Franz) Liszt** (1811–96). Although Liszt spent most of his life abroad, he maintained a deep interest in Hungarian culture and musical traditions, as evidenced by his well-known "Hungarian Rhapsodies." Liszt is well known for creating the musical idiom known as the symphonic poem with his *Les Preludes* (1848). He served as the first president of Budapest's Academy of Music, which is named after him. To top it all off, Liszt was also one of the great virtuoso pianists of his century.

If Liszt was the towering figure of 19th-century Hungarian music, **Béla Bartók** (1881–1945) and **Zoltán Kodály** (1882–1967) were the giants of the early 20th century. The founders of Hungarian ethnomusicology, Bartók and Kodály traveled the back roads of the country in the early 1900s, systematically recording not only Hungarian and Gypsy folk music, but also music of the whole Carpathian Basin region. Peasant folk music had been an important part of the region's rural culture for hundreds of years, but by the early 20th century, there were not many musicians playing and the music was in danger of being lost. In addition to saving a wealth of music from oblivion, Bartók and Kodály made some important discoveries in their research, noting both the differences and the interrelationships between Hungarian and other folk music traditions (especially Gypsy music), which had fused considerably over time. Both men were composers, and the influence of the folk music they so cherished can easily be heard in their compositions. Kodály established the internationally acclaimed Kodály method of musical education and lived to become the grand old man of Hungarian music, while Bartók died relatively young in the United States, an impoverished, embittered refugee from Fascism.

Regularly scheduled concerts are given at the museums below; see the listings for details. For a complete concert schedule, check Budapest's free bimonthly *Koncert Kalendárium,* available at most four- and five-star hotels, and tourist information centers.

Bartók Béla Emlékház (Béla Bartók Memorial House)   This little museum, high in the Buda Hills, occupies Béla Bartók's final Hungarian home and exhibits artifacts from Bartók's career as well as some of the composer's original furniture. The house has been decorated to reflect the time period and atmosphere in which the composer lived, and is run by the composer's heirs. On publication, the museum was undergoing extensive renovations that will extend the museum. Every year on September 26, the date of Bartók's death, the Bartók String Quartet performs in the museum. Concerts are also given on Friday evenings in spring and autumn, and occasionally on Sundays as well.

II. Csalán u. 29. ℂ 1/394-2100. www.bartokmuseum.hu. Museum 600 Ft ($3); concert tickets 1,000 Ft–2,500 Ft ($5–$13). Tues–Sun 10am–5pm. Bus: 5 from Március 15 tér or Moszkva tér to Pasaréti tér (the last stop).

Liszt Ferenc Emlékmúzeum (Ferenc Liszt Memorial Museum)   Located in the apartment in which Liszt spent his last years, this modest museum features several of the composer's pianos, including a child's Bachmann piano and two Chickering & Sons grand pianos. Also noteworthy are the many portraits of Liszt done by the leading Austrian and Hungarian artists of his time, including two busts by the Hungarian sculptor Alajos Stróbl. Concerts are performed here on Saturdays at 11am.

VI. Vörösmarty u. 35. ℂ 1/322-9804. Admission 400 Ft ($1.60). Guided group tours in English for a whopping 7,200 Ft ($36), if arranged in advance. Mon–Fri 10am–6pm; Sat 9am–5pm. Metro: Vörösmarty utca (Yellow line).

Zenetörténeti Múzeum (Museum of Music History)   Various instruments and manuscripts are displayed in this museum, which is housed in a historic building in Buda's Castle District. You'll find a reproduction of Béla Bartók's workshop as well as the Bartók Archives. For lack of sponsorship, this gorgeous concert venue has been silent since mid-2000, to the deep regret of local music aficionados. Perhaps by the time you arrive, the museum will again be hosting concerts.

I. Táncsics M. u. 7. ℂ 1/214-6770, ext. 250. Admission 400 Ft ($2). Tues–Sun 10am–6pm. Bus: Várbusz from Moszkva tér or 16 from Deák tér to Castle Hill. Funicular: From Clark Ádám tér to Castle Hill.

6 Organized Tours

BUS TOURS

Ibusz (ℂ 1/485-2700; www.ibusz.hu), with decades of experience, offers 11 different boat and bus tours, ranging from basic city tours to special folklore-oriented tours. Unfortunately, the tours are pretty sterile and boring, and we actually think you're better off taking a walking tour or a different boat tour (see below). Ibusz operates year-round, with an abbreviated schedule in the off season. All buses are air-conditioned, and all guides speak English. Some sample offerings are a 3-hour **Budapest City Tour** for 5,000 Ft to 10,000 Ft ($25–$50; free for children under 12), and a 2-hour Parliament Tour (you'll be inside the building for 2 hr.) for 7,500 Ft ($38). There's a free hotel pickup service that will pick you up 30 minutes before departure time. For a full list of tours, pick up the Ibusz *Budapest Sightseeing* catalog, available at all Ibusz offices, Tourinform, and most hotels. Tours can be booked at any Ibusz office and at most major hotels, or by calling Ibusz directly at ℂ 1/485-2700. All major credit cards are accepted.

Queeny Bus Ltd (© 1/247-7159, 1/246-4755 or 70/338-1159; www.queenybus.hu) offers bus tours on an open-air bus that departs from major hotels, at the Basilica under a green parasol with a sign indicating CITY TOUR, or at the Museum of Ethnography. The company offers three basic tours. The first departs from the Museum of Ethnography, will set you back 8,500 Ft ($43) and is a 4-hour tour taking you to City Park, Parliament, the diplomatic quarter, and the Gellért Hill. It departs at 9am on Monday, Wednesday, and Thursday to Sunday, and at 11am on Tuesday to Sunday. The second tour departs from the Basilica, sets you back 6,000 Ft ($30), and takes you to the Basilica, Parliament, Heroes' Square, the Castle District, the Danube shores, and the diplomatic quarter. Departs daily at 10am, 11am, and 2:30pm. A third tour, lasting two hours and departing from the Basilica at 11am and 2:30pm, will set you back 4,800 Ft ($24) and takes you on a tour of highlights of the city from May to September.

VARIOUS

EUrama Travel Agency (© 1/327-6690; www.eurama.hu) offers a series of 12 tours including city tours, walking tours, Jewish Budapest, an Etyek wine tour, one of the Hungarian puszta, a folklore evening, a Danube Bend tour, and one around Lake Balaton. Prices vary between 5,000 Ft ($25) and 17,000 Ft ($85), and run from 1½ hours to 10 hours. Children under 12 receive a 50% discount.

BOAT TOURS

A boat tour is a great way to absorb the scope and scale of the Hungarian capital, and a majority of the city's grand sights can be seen from the river. The Hungarian state company **MAHART** operates daily 2-hour sightseeing cruises on the Danube, using two-story steamboats. The Budapest office of MAHART is at V. Belgrád rakpart (© 1/318-1704; www.mahartpassnave.hu). Boats depart frequently from Vigadó tér (on the Pest waterfront, between the Erzsébet Bridge and the Chain Bridge, near the Budapest Marriott hotel) on weekends and holidays in the spring and every day in summer. Additionally, MAHART offers chartered boat tours (for large groups) up and down the Tisza River in eastern Hungary from April 1 to October 15. These tours are booked through separate agencies in the towns of departure (Tokaj, Kisköre, Tiszasege, Szolnok, Szeged, and many others along the river). Ask at MAHART for further information and for the telephone numbers necessary for booking.

Legenda, at XI. Fraknó u. 4 (© 1/266-4190; www.legenda.hu), a private company founded in 1990, offers several boat tours on the Danube, using two-story steamboats. The daytime tour, called "Duna Bella," operates daily at 2:30pm, year-round, with additional daily trips during the summer. The 2-hour ride includes a stop at Margaret Island, with a walk on the island. Tickets cost 3,600 Ft ($18). The nighttime tour, departing daily at 8:15pm, is called "Danube Legend" and is more than a bit hokey, but worth it for the view of the city all lit up. "Danube Legend" tickets cost 4,200 Ft ($21). On both trips your ticket entitles you to two free glasses of wine or beer and unlimited soft drinks. A shorter variation of the daytime tour, without the stop on the island, runs from mid-April to mid-October. All boats leave from the Vigadó tér port, Pier 7. Tickets are available through most major hotels, at the dock, and through the Legenda office. Look for the company's brochure at Tourinform.

The **Operetta Ship,** departing from at Vigadó tér (© 20/332-9116, 1/318-1223, or 1/488-0475; www.operetthajo.hu), offers a unique candlelit boat tour that includes performers of the Hungarian State Opera House singing famous operas, operettas, Italian and Spanish songs, musicals, instrumental solos, and Hungarian folklore. During the tours, you will hear famous excerpts from Strauss, Mozart, Lehar, Gershwin, Puccini, and more. The boat tour runs from April until October, and operates Monday to Wednesday, Friday, and Sunday from 8 to 10pm. The boat tour with a dinner included costs 12,500 Ft ($63), or 8,500 Ft ($43) without the meal. There is also a "music" sightseeing tour guided in English, German, or Hungarian, that costs 4,000 Ft ($20).

WALKING TOURS

Several new companies offer walking tours of historic Budapest. We recommend "The Absolute Walking Tour in Budapest" offered by **Absolute Walking Tours** ✦ (✆ 06-30/211-8861; www.discoverhungary.com). The tours, conducted by knowledgeable and personable guides, start at pickup point 1 outside the Evangelical Church in Deák tér (all metro lines) at 9:30am and 1:30pm or at pickup point 2 on the front steps of the Műcsarnok at Hősök tere (Yellow line) at 10am and 2pm from mid-May through September. From October through mid-December and February through mid-May, tours start daily at 10:30 and 11am only, in January on weekends only, from the same departure points that are listed above for the high-season tours. Students get a 500 Ft ($2.50) discount. Tickets are 4,000 Ft ($20), free for children under 12. Show this book (or the company's flyer, on display at many tourist haunts) and you'll get a 500 Ft ($2.50) discount. Buy your ticket from the tour guide at the start of the tour. Tours last anywhere from 3½ to 5 hours, depending on the mood of the group, and take you throughout both central Pest and central Buda. Wear your best walking shoes and leave the heavy knapsack at your hotel.

Budapest Walks (✆ 1/340-4232) is another company offering walking tours. It features four tours: "Highlights of Pest," "Gems of Buda Castle," "Music Budapest," and "Fine Arts Museum and the City Park." Tours are conducted daily from May through September only. The Castle Hill tour starts at 2pm (Mon, Tues, Thurs, and Sat), and meets in front of the Matthias Church in Buda's Castle District; the Pest tour starts at 2pm Tuesday and Thursday, and meets in front of Café Gerbeaud, in Pest's Vörösmarty tér. Both tours last 2½ hours; the Pest tour is 3,200 Ft ($14), 4,500 Ft ($20) with a tour of Parliament included; the Buda tour is 3,800 Ft ($17). "Music Budapest" is offered Monday and Friday at 2pm for 4,500 Ft ($20); meet at the Opera House. "Fine Arts Museum and the City Park" is offered Wednesday and Saturday at 2pm for 3,200 Ft ($14); meet in front of the Fine Arts Museum in Hősök tere (Heroes' Sq.).

SPECIALTY TOURS

Chosen Tours (✆/fax 1/355-2202) specializes in tours related to Jewish life and heritage in Budapest. The 1½- to 2-hour guided walking tour of Pest's historic Jewish Quarter is a good introduction to that fascinating neighborhood. Tours are conducted from April through October and run Monday through Friday and Sunday, beginning at 10am in front of the Dohány Synagogue, on Dohány utca. The walking tour costs 2,420 Ft ($11). You should reserve a space on the tour ahead of time. Chosen Tours offers a 1-hour, air-conditioned bus tour of Jewish sights in Buda as an add-on to the walking tour. Called "Budapest Through Jewish Eyes," the combination tour ticket costs 3,740 Ft ($17). Reserve your space early. Other tours, available for private bookings, include a tour of Jewish art and a trip to Szentendre, as well as tours catering to individual needs and interests (such as Jewish "roots" tours). The company offers a free pickup service from select hotel locations.

7 Spa Bathing & Swimming: Budapest's Most Popular Thermal Baths

Hungarians are great believers in the medicinal powers of thermal bathing. Even if you are unsure about the health benefits, it's hard to deny that time spent in thermal baths is enjoyable and relaxing. The baths of Budapest have a long and proud history, stretching back to Roman times. The bath culture flourished while the city was under Turkish occupation, and several still-functioning bathhouses—Király, Rudas, and Rácz—are among the architectural relics of the Turkish period. In the late 19th and early 20th centuries—Budapest's "golden age"—several fabulous bathhouses were built: the extravagant and eclectic Széchenyi Baths in City Park, the splendid Art Nouveau Gellért Baths, and the solid neoclassical Lukács Baths. All of these bathhouses are still in use and are worth a look even for nonbathers. Most baths in Budapest have recently instituted a complicated new pricing system (dubbed the "refund system") that charges according to the time that you have spent in the baths. Previously, a single admission ticket bought you an unlimited visit. Now, you are generally required to pay for the longest possible duration (4 hr. or more) when you enter the bathhouse and you are refunded on the basis of the actual time that you spent on the premises when you exit. You are given a chip card upon entry; keep careful track of the card because if you lose it you are assumed to have stayed for the maximum time and you will not receive a refund.

THE BEST BATHHOUSES

Gellért Baths 🏛🏛   Budapest's most spectacular bathhouse, the Gellért Baths are located in Buda's Hotel Gellért, the oldest Hungarian spa hotel and an Art Nouveau jewel. Enter the baths through the side entrance. The exterior of the building is in need of restoration, but once inside the lobby, you'll be delighted by the details. The unisex indoor pool is without question one of Europe's finest, with marble columns, majolica tiles, and stone lion heads spouting water. The two single-sex Turkish-style thermal baths, off to either side of the pool through badly marked doors, are also glorious, though in need of restoration. In the summer months, the outdoor roof pool attracts a lot of attention for 10 minutes every hour on the hour, when the artificial wave machine is turned on. There are separate nude sunbathing decks for men and women, but you'll have to figure out where they are. In general, you need patience to navigate this place.

XI. Kelenhegyi út 4. ☎ 1/466-6166. Admission to the thermal bath costs 3,000 Ft ($15) for 4 hr. or more; a 15-min. massage is 2,300 Ft ($12). Lockers or cabins are included. Admission to all pools and baths, without a cabin and only communal dressing rooms, is 2,500 Ft ($13) adults and children, for 4 hr. or more. Prices and the lengthy list of services, including the complicated refund system, are posted in English. The thermal baths are open in summer daily 6am–7pm; in winter Mon–Fri 6am–7pm, Sat–Sun 6am–5pm, with the last entrance an hour before closing. Take tram 47 or 49 from Deák tér to Szent Gellért tér.

Király Baths 🏛🏛   The Király Baths are one of Budapest's most important architectural monuments to Turkish rule. This is a place where Hungarian culture meets the Eastern culture that influenced it. The bath itself, built in the late 16th century, is housed under an octagonal domed roof. Sunlight filters through small round windows in the ceiling. The water glows. The effect is perfectly tranquil. In addition to the thermal baths, there are sauna and steam room facilities. Bring a towel if you like, since you will not receive one until the end of your treatment. Upon exiting the baths, help yourself to a cotton sheet from the pile near the base of the stairs. Wrap yourself up

Tips   Thermal Bathing 101

Thermal bathing is an activity steeped in ritual. For this reason, and because bathhouse employees tend to be unfriendly relics of the old system, many foreigners find a trip to the baths stressful or confusing at first. As with any ritualistic activity, it helps to spend some time observing before joining in. Even then, you are likely not to know what to do or where to go. The best advice is to try to enjoy the foreignness of the experience—why else do we leave home?

The most confusing step may well be the first: the ticket window, with its endless list of prices for different facilities and services, often without English translations. Chances are you're coming to use one of the following facilities or services: *uszoda* (pool); *termál* (thermal pool); *fürdő* (bath); *gőzfürdő* (steam bath); massage; and/or sauna. There is no particular order in which people move from one facility to the next; do whatever feels most comfortable. Towel rental is *törülköző* or *lepedő*. An entry ticket generally entitles you to a free locker in the locker room *(öltöző);* or, at some bathhouses, you can opt to pay an additional fee for a private cabin *(kabin)*. At the Király, everyone gets a private dressing room and an employee locks and unlocks the rooms (p. 150).

Remember to pack a bathing suit—and a bathing cap, if you wish to swim in the pools—so you won't have to rent vintage 1970 models. In the single-sex baths, nude bathing is the custom and the norm. Towels are provided, but usually as you re-enter the locker area after bathing. You may want to bring your own towel with you into the bathing areas if this makes you uncomfortable. Flip-flops are also a good idea. Soap and shampoo are only allowed in the showers, but should be brought out to the bath area so that you can avoid having to return to the comparatively cold locker room prematurely. You will, most likely, want to wash your hair after soaking in the sulphuric waters. Long hair must be tied back when bathing. Leave your eyeglasses in your locker as they will get fogged up in the baths.

Generally, extra services (massage, pedicure) are received after a bath. Tipping is tricky; locker room attendants do not expect tips (except perhaps at the Gellért) but would welcome a tip in the 200-Ft-to-400-Ft range ($1–$2) while masseurs and manicurists expect a tip in the 200-Ft-to-600-Ft range ($1–$3).

There are drinking fountains in the bath areas, and it's a good idea to drink plenty of water before a bath. And don't bathe on an empty stomach; the hot water and steam take a heavy toll on the unfortified body, especially for those unaccustomed to the baths. Most bathhouses have snack bars in the lobbies where you can pick up a cold juice or sandwich on your way out. After the baths, you will be thirsty and hungry. Be sure to replenish yourself.

and lounge with a cup of tea in the relaxation room, where you can also receive a pedicure or massage.

Women can use the baths on Monday, Wednesday, and Friday from 7am to 5pm. Men are welcome on Tuesday, Thursday, and Saturday from 9am to 7pm.

I. Fő u. 84. ✆ 1/201-4392. Admission to baths 1,100 Ft ($5.50) for 1½ hr. only. Metro: Batthyány tér (Red line).

Rudas Baths 🌟🌟 Near the Erzsébet Bridge, on the Buda side of the city, is another of Budapest's classic Turkish baths. These baths are for men only, though both sexes are admitted to the swimming pool. During early mornings the crowd is predominantly composed of older men, and according to local lore, the place becomes something of a pickup spot after 9am. The first baths were built on this site in the 14th century, although the Rudas Bathhouse itself dates to the late 16th century. It boasts an octagonal pool and domed roof; some of the small window holes in the cupola have stained glass, while others are open to the sky, allowing diffused light to stream in. You'll find most of the same services and facilities here that you would at Király: a thermal bath, a sauna, and a steam bath.

I. Döbrentei tér 9. ✆ 1/356-1322. Admission to thermal baths 1,000 Ft ($5) for 1½ hr. only (!), swimming pool 800 Ft ($4). Weekdays 6am–8pm; weekends 6am–1pm. Bus: 7; get off at the Buda side of the Erzsébet Bridge, turn left, and venture down to the riverside.

Széchenyi Baths 🌟🌟 Part of an immense health spa located in the City Park, the Széchenyi Baths are perhaps second only to the Gellért Baths in terms of facilities and popular appeal. Ivy climbs the walls of the sprawling pool complex here. On a nice day, crowds of bathers, including many families and tourists, visit the palatial unisex outdoor swimming pool. Turkish-style thermal baths are segregated and are located off to the sides of the pool. Look for the older gentlemen concentrating intently on their chess games, half-immersed in the steaming pool. Prices are all posted in English, and the refund system is described.

XIV. Állatkerti út 11–14, in City Park. ✆ 1/363-3210. www.szechenzifurdo.hu. Admission to the thermal baths is 2,000 Ft ($10), dressing cabins are extra. Daily 6am–7pm, except Sat–Sun in winter, when the complex closes at 5pm. Metro: Széchenyi fürdő (Yellow line).

OTHER BATHING CHOICES

Rácz bathhouse, located at I. Hadnagy u. 8–10 (✆ 1/356-1322), near the Erzsébet Bridge in Buda, has been closed for renovation for some time. They have not announced new hours or prices, but it was previously open 6:30am to 7pm Monday through Saturday. The bathhouse was previously open on Monday, Wednesday, and Friday for women only, and Tuesday, Thursday, and Saturday for men only.

Lukács bath and swimming pool, at II. Frankel Leo u. 25–29 (✆ 1/326-1695), is open Monday through Friday from 6am to 7pm, and Saturday and Sunday from 6am to 4pm. The entrance fee is 1,500 Ft ($7.50). Take tram no. 4 or 6 to the Buda side of the Margaret Bridge; walk from there.

More modern spa facilities are available at the two Thermal Hotels: **Helia** (p. 84) and **Corinthia Aquincum** (p. 86).

AN OUTDOOR POOL COMPLEX

Palatinus Strand 🌟🌟 *Finds* In the middle of Margaret Island is Budapest's best-located *strand* (literally "beach," but better translated, in this context, as "outdoor pool complex"). It's a fantastic place, fed by the Margaret Island thermal springs. There are three thermal pools, a vast swimming pool, a smaller artificial wave pool, a water slide, segregated nude-sunbathing decks, and large, grassy grounds. Other facilities include Ping-Pong tables, pool tables, trampolines, and dozens of snack bars: in other words, a typical Hungarian *strand.* The waters of the thermal pools are as relaxing as at any of the other bathhouses (but the older bathhouses offer a much more memorable experience). **Warning:** Beware of pickpockets on the bus to the complex.

XIII. Margit-sziget. (C) 1/340-4505. Admission adults, 1,500 Ft–1,900 Ft ($7.50-$9.50) Mon–Fri. May to mid-Sept daily 8am–7pm. Last entry at 6pm. Take bus 26 from Nyugati pu.

8 Outdoor Activities & Sports

BIKING   Although we are avid cyclists, we don't generally recommend biking in Budapest due to unruly drivers and fast-moving traffic. That said, see "Getting Around" in chapter 4, "Getting to Know Budapest," for some biking options.

GOLF   For information, contact the **Hungarian Golf Club,** V. Bécsi út 5 ((C) 1/317-6025; www.golfhungary.hu). The nearest course is located on Szentendre Island, 25 minutes north of Budapest by car. Call the course directly at (C) 26/392-465. For putting practice, the **19th Hole Golf Driving Range** is located at II. Adyliget, Feketefej u. 6 ((C) 1/354-1510).

HORSEBACK RIDING   Riding remains a popular activity in Hungary, land of the widely feared Magyar horsemen of a bygone era. A good place to mount up is the **Petneházy Lovasiskola (Riding School),** at II. Feketefej u. 2 ((C) 1/397-5048; www.petnehazy-lovascentrum.hu). As far out in the Buda Hills as you can go without leaving the city limits, the school is located in open country, with trails in the hills. Riding on the track with a trainer costs 2,500 Ft ($13) for 30 minutes; open riding with a guide is 4,500 Ft ($23). There are also pony rides for children at 1,500 Ft ($7.50) for 15 minutes, and there are 30-minute horse-cart rides at 10,000 Ft ($50) for a group of up to 10 people. The Petneházy Country Club is down the road. At the stable is a great little *csárda* (inn/restaurant), recently renovated; you might want to have lunch here. The stable is open year-round Friday, Saturday, and Sunday from 9am to 5pm. Take bus no. 56 (56E is fastest) from Moszkva tér to the last stop, then bus no. 63 to Feketefej utca, followed by a 10-minute walk.

The **Hungarian Equestrian Tourism Association,** located at V. Ferenciek tere 4 ((C) 1/317-1644; fax 1/267-0171; www.equi.hu), might also serve your riding interests.

IN-LINE SKATING & ICE SKATING   There are several options for both in Budapest. The ice rinks mentioned on p. 146 are very appropriate for children. The oldest and most popular ice rink is in Városliget, on the lake next to Vajdahunyad castle. However, since it is an open-air facility, it is open only from mid-October till the end of February. Hours are Monday through Friday 9am to 1pm and 4 to 8pm; Saturday 9am to 1pm, 2 to 6pm, and 7 to 10pm; Sunday 10am to 1pm and 4 to 8pm. The fee is 300 Ft ($1.50) on weekdays and 600 Ft ($3) on weekends. Skates rent for 500 Ft ($2.50) an hour. International visitors should also have their passports for ID when renting. Adults and children can rent in-line and ice skates at all the rinks.

SQUASH   City Squash Courts (Országos Fallabda Központ), at II. Marczibányi tér 13 ((C) 1/325-0082), has four courts. An easy walk from Moszkva tér (Red metro line), their hourly rates—per court—are 3,600 Ft ($16) for 1 hour of play during peak hours (Mon–Fri 5–10pm) and 2,800 Ft ($13) for 1 hour of play at other times. Racquets can be rented for 500 Ft ($2.25); balls can be purchased. The courts are open daily from 7am to midnight. The **Hotel Marriott Squash Court,** at V. Apáczai Csere

J. u. 4 (© **1/266-4290**), also rents out court time for 2,800 Ft ($13) per hour from 9am to 4pm, and for 3,900 Ft ($18) per hour from 6 to 9am and 4 to 10pm. Racquets rent for 500 Ft ($2.25).

TENNIS   If you plan to play tennis in Budapest, bring your own racquet along since most courts don't rent equipment; when it is available, it's usually primitive.

Many of Budapest's luxury hotels, particularly those removed from the city center, have tennis courts that nonguests can rent. The **MTK Sport Complex,** in Buda at XI. Bartók Béla út 63 (© **1/209-1595**), boasts 13 outdoor clay courts. The fee is a very reasonable 500 Ft ($2.50) per hour during the day or 1,200 Ft ($6) per hour at night, under floodlights. Three outdoor courts are covered by a tent year-round; from October through April, all courts are covered and the price of play throughout the day is 2,200 Ft ($11) per hour. Equipment is not available for rental. The facility is open daily from 6am to 10pm. Móricz Zsigmond körtér, a transportation hub served by countless buses and trams, is only 5 minutes from the center by foot.

8

Strolling Around Budapest

Budapest is a city to see by foot. The following walking tours are intended to introduce you to the texture and color of the city. On these walking tours, special attention is paid to the hidden Budapest, the glorious details that make this the memorable city that it is. Many of the city's top attractions—the Buda Palace and Parliament, the National Gallery, and the National Museum among them—are included on these tours, but dozens of minor sites—vintage pharmacies and quiet courtyards, market halls and medieval walls—are visited as well.

See chapter 3, "Suggested Budapest & Hungary Itineraries," for ways to incorporate these walking tours into a 1- or 2-day visit.

WALKING TOUR 1	PEST'S INNER CITY

Start:	Deák tér.
Finish:	Danube Promenade.
Time:	3 to 4 hours (excluding museum stops).
Best Times:	Tuesday through Saturday.
Worst Times:	Monday, when museums are closed, and Sunday, when stores are closed.

The city of Pest, like most medieval cities, was surrounded by a protective wall. The wall is long gone, though some remnants still exist, which we'll see on this tour. The historic center of the city, inside the walled area, is still known as the Belváros, or Inner City. The Erzsébet Bridge divides the Inner City into two parts: The busier northern half features luxury hotels along the Danube Promenade (Dunakorzó) and boutiques and shops along the pedestrian-only Váci utca; the quieter southern half is largely residential, though it is home to the main buildings of Eötvös Loránd University and a number of lovely churches. The southern half has undergone something of revitalization since the 1996 extension of Váci utca, and is no longer quite as sleepy as it once was. Pest's Inner Ring Boulevard (Kiskörút) wraps around both halves, tracing the line of the former medieval city wall. This walking tour spends equal time in each half of the Inner City, visiting museums, churches, stores, courtyards, and a great market hall en route. We'll end with a leisurely stroll down the Danube Promenade.

Begin at Deák tér, where all three Budapest metro lines converge. If you have any questions about theater tickets, activities, or excursions, now would be a good time to pop in to:

❶ **Tourinform**
Located at V. Sütő u. 4, Budapest's main tourist information bureau has helpful information on lodging, cultural programs, and excursions.

Alternatively, you could start with a visit to the:

❷ Underground Railway Museum

This museum is located in the underground passage beneath Deák tér. Here, you can see a beautifully preserved train from the European continent's first underground system, built in Budapest in 1896.

From nearby Szomory Dezső tér, head down Fehérhajó utca toward Szervita tér, formerly Martinelli tér. Ahead of you, you'll notice Váci utca, the crowded pedestrian street. The tour will return there later; for now, turn left onto:

❸ Szervita tér

On this street you will find the early-18th-century baroque Servite Church, the column of the Virgin Mary, and the former Török Banking House, with its colorful Secessionist mosaic.

Continue now down Városház utca (City Hall St.), which begins to the left of the church. Dominating this street is the 18th-century:

❹ City Hall

This is the largest baroque edifice in Budapest. It was originally designed as a hospital by Anton Martinelli.

The lime-green neoclassical building at Városház u. 7 is the 19th-century:

❺ Pest County Hall

After a visit to the inner courtyards, you will see, as you emerge onto busy Kossuth Lajos utca, the Erzsébet Bridge to your right, with the northern slope of Gellért Hill behind it.

Directly across the street (reached via the underpass) is the:

❻ Franciscan Church

A church has stood here as early as the 13th century, but the present church dates from the 18th century. The relief on the building's side depicts Miklós Wesselényi's heroic rescue effort during the awful Danube flood of 1838. Next door, a shop sells religious artifacts, including hand-painted icons from Bulgaria, Ukraine, and Russia. The name of the shop is **Ecclesia**, at V. Ferenciek tere 7–8

(© 1/317-3754), and it is open Monday through Friday 9:30am to 5:30pm and Saturday 9:30am to 1pm.

Continuing south on Ferenciek tere, the striking neoclassical building with the colorful dome is the:

❼ Eötvös Loránd University (ELTE) Library

This is an 18th-century building with beautiful carved wooden bookcases along the walls.

Continue straight on Károlyi Mihály utca; the next big square is:

❽ University Square (Egyetem tér)

This square is home to the ELTE Law School; the baroque University Church, with a copy of the *Black Madonna* of Czestochowa above the altar; and the Sándor Petőfi Literary Museum, a veritable shrine to Hungarian literary heroes (almost all are largely unknown outside Hungary).

Continue down to the far end of the square, where you'll find:

❾ A small monument to the 1838 Danube flood

The monument can be seen on the wall at the corner of Szerb utca and Király Pál utca; a map shows the extent of the flooding. Notice that the entire Inner City was underwater!

Return to the top of the square and turn right onto Henszlmann Imre utca. After ½ block, on your left you will see:

❿ Károly kert

This beautifully maintained neighborhood park has benches in the shade, swings, a miniature soccer field, and a lovely fountain with begonias growing around it. The park is filled with the sounds of children all day long.

Exit the park onto Magyar utca and turn left, then right onto Ferenczy István utca. Emerge onto busy Múzeum körút, and turn right again. Take a quick detour into the quiet courtyard of Múzeum körút 21, where you will find a well-preserved section of:

Walking Tour 1: Pest's Inner City

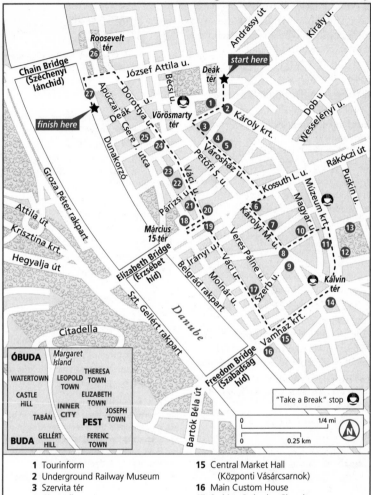

1 Tourinform
2 Underground Railway Museum
3 Szervita tér
4 City Hall
5 Pest County Hall
6 Franciscan Church
7 Eötvös Loránd University (ELTE) Library
8 University Square (Egyetem tér)
9 Monument to 1838 Danube Flood
10 Károly kert
11 Medieval City Wall
12 Hungarian National Museum
13 Központi Antikvárium
🔵 Múzeum Kávéhaz
14 Calvinist Church

15 Central Market Hall
   (Központi Vásárcsarnok)
16 Main Custom House
17 Serbian Orthodox Church
18 Inner City Parish Church
19 Váci utca
20 Pharmacy
21 Zsolnay, Herend and Ajka shops
22 Vali Folklor
23 Margit Kovács ceramic relief
24 Philantria Flower Shop
25 Corvina Könyvklub (Corvina Book Club)
🔵 Gerbeaud's
26 Roosevelt tér
27 Danube Promenade (Dunakorzó)

⓫ Pest's medieval city wall

Most of the city wall is long gone, but this part is in good shape and dates back to the 15th century.

Back out on Múzeum körút, you will note, across the street, the massive neoclassical:

⓬ Hungarian National Museum

Legend has it that the fiery poet Sándor Petőfi recited his incendiary "National Song" on the museum steps on the first day of the 1848 anti-Habsburg Hungarian Revolution. The museum's most famous exhibit, the legendary Hungarian crown jewels of King Stephen, was moved to the House of Parliament as part of the millennium frenzy; in the museum, you can see a replica of the regalia. The jewels have an astonishing history nonetheless: a complex tale of theft, subterfuge, and rescue. Spirited out of Hungary before the Soviet liberation of 1945, they ended up in U.S. government hands. President Jimmy Carter's secretary of state, Cyrus Vance, ceremoniously returned them to the Hungarian government in 1978. The National Museum is one of those museums where, depending on your interest in historical artifacts, you can spend 10 minutes or 10 hours.

 TAKE A BREAK
Don't miss your chance to pop in for a coffee at the **Parlament Kávéház**, at V. Vértanuk tere 1.

This part of Múzeum körút has long been known for its *antikvária*, stores selling rare books and maps. At Múzeum krt. 13–15, you'll find the:

⓭ Központi Antikvárium

Another *antikvárium*, called Honterus, is ahead at Múzeum krt. 35.

 TAKE A BREAK
Make a stop at the **Múzeum Kávéház**, Múzeum krt. 12 (℡ 1/ 267-0375), which is suitable either for a Hungarian lunch or just coffee and pastries.

Continue south down Múseum krt. until you hit Kálvin tér, named for the 19th-century:

⓮ Calvinist Church

The colorful ceramic tiles that grace this church's roof make it an easily identifiable landmark in the Budapest landscape. Medieval Pest's Kecskeméti Gate stood on Kálvin tér, on the site of the bridge passage between the two buildings of the Hotel Mercure Korona. Turn right at Kálvin tér onto Kecskeméti utca, passing in front of the hotel, and then take your first left onto tiny Bástya utca. Walk several blocks down this quiet residential street, until it comes to a T-intersection at Veres Pálné utca. On that corner, at the rear of a shabby playground, you will find another fine piece of Pest's medieval town wall. Now turn left onto Veres Pálné utca and return to the körút.

You're now on the Vámház (Customs House) körút section of the Inner Ring. Just ahead of you on the right is the graceful green span of the Szabadság (Freedom) Bridge, with the Gellért Hotel towering over Buda's Danube bank. Proceed toward the river to the:

⓯ Central Market Hall (Központi Vásárcsarnok)

This is the largest and most spectacular of Budapest's late-19th-century market halls. Renovated and reconstructed in the late 1990s, the bright, airy hall houses a wide assortment of fresh-produce vendors who dispense dairy products, meat and poultry, vegetables, and fruit. Escalators lead to a mezzanine level where traditional folk items are sold. Fast-food and drink booths are also upstairs. While the new market hall is clean and extremely pleasant, it clearly lacks the homey grit and verve of a traditional market, such as the outdoor market in Szeged (see chapter 14, "Southern Hungary: The Great Plain & the Meczek Hills").

Next door to the market is the eclectic-style former:

⑯ Main Customs House

Now a university economics building (pop in to the lobby to admire the statue of Karl Marx), the house overlooks the Danube—from here, you can admire the full span of the Szabadság Bridge, our favorite of Budapest's seven bridges.

Now turn left onto the pedestrian-only Váci utca and start off toward the southern end of the Inner City. Take a short detour at Szerb utca (turn right), named for the lovely 18th-century:

⑰ Serbian Orthodox Church

This church is separated from the street by a small garden. Interestingly, the paintings on the iconostasis reflect the Italian Renaissance instead of the more typical Byzantine style. Return to Váci utca and continue walking north.

At Szabadsajtó utca, turn left toward the Danube. Passing under the Erzsébet Bridge, you're now back in the northern, more crowded half of the Inner City. Towering above you is the:

⑱ Inner City Parish Church

Built and rebuilt numerous times since the 12th century, this church displays Gothic and baroque elements on the exterior. Inside, there are niches built in both Gothic and baroque styles, as well as a *mihrab* (prayer niche) dating from the Turkish occupation, when the church was temporarily converted into a mosque.

Pass under the archways of the ELTE Arts Faculty building (walking away from the river), and stop at the next street:

⑲ Váci utca

This is the more crowded half of this pedestrian-only street.

At Váci u. 34, on the corner of Kígyó utca (Snake St.), is a wonderful old:

⑳ Pharmacy

This pharmacy is furnished with antique wooden cabinets and drawers.

Nearby, on Kígyó utca, you'll find:

㉑ Retail shops for Zsolnay and Herend porcelain and Ajka crystal

We are partial to the delightfully gaudy Zsolnay porcelain, from the southern city of Pécs. Even if you don't intend to buy, these shops are worth a peek.

Proceed down Váci utca. You'll probably make various stops at the shops along the way, and you should definitely visit the courtyard of Váci u. 23, which houses:

㉒ Vali Folklor

This tiny shop offers a fine assortment of authentic secondhand Hungarian folk costumes, as well as tapestries, ceramics, and figurines. Its extended collection also features Communist-era badges, pins, and medals from throughout eastern Europe. Small though it is, this store truly stands tall above the atrocious kitsch that you'll find in stores in these parts.

Make a left down Régiposta utca. Across the street from McDonald's, above the door of Régiposta u. 13, is a lovely but faded:

㉓ Margit Kovács ceramic relief of a horse and coach.

Kovács was Hungary's greatest ceramic artist. A superb museum dedicated to her work can be visited in the small town of Szentendre, on the Danube Bend (p. 220).

Double back to Váci u. and stop at no. 9 to look at the Art Nouveau interior of the:

㉔ Philantria Flower Shop

Note the whimsical carved moldings here, as well as wall murals in the style of Toulouse-Lautrec.

Váci utca ends in Vörösmarty tér, one of Pest's loveliest squares, which has a number of attractions in addition to the monumental statue of the great Romantic poet Mihály Vörösmarty, author of "The Appeal," Hungary's "second national anthem." Nearby, at Vörösmarty tér 1, second floor, room 201, is the:

㉕ Corvina Könyvklub (Corvina Book Club)

This is the place to find the latest English-language translations of Hungarian literature. This offbeat warehouse store, buried deep in an administrative building in the heart of the Inner City, and identifiable to the public only by the banner hanging in its second-floor window, is the central outlet of the Corvina Press.

Across the square, ½ block away, at Deák Ferenc u. 10, is the American Express office. But certainly the best-known feature of Vörösmarty tér is its legendary coffeehouse:

TAKE A BREAK
Gerbeaud's, at Vörösmarty tér 7, was founded in 1858 and has been at this site since 1870. The decor and the furnishings are classic turn-of-the-century, and the pastries are among the city's best. In summertime try any of the fresh-fruit strudels *(gyümölcs rétes).*

Walk down Dorottya utca to the next stop:
㉖ Roosevelt tér
The place is described in detail in "Walking Tour 3: Leopold Town & Theresa Town," later in this chapter. The Buda

Palace looms on Castle Hill directly across the river, which is spanned here by the Széchenyi Chain Bridge.

Here, where the statue of the great 19th-century educator József Eötvös stands, is the beginning of the fabled:
㉗ Danube Promenade (Dunakorzó)
Gone are the traditional coffeehouses that lined the length of the promenade between the Chain Bridge and the Erzsébet Bridge during the late 19th century. In their place rise luxury hotels, the most monstrous of which is the Budapest Marriott, a concrete behemoth. Nevertheless, all of Budapest still comes to stroll here: Join the throngs, equal parts native and traveler. The glorious unobstructed view of Buda across the river remains as beautiful as it ever was. Castle Hill towers above Watertown, whose many steeples pierce the sky. Along the promenade you'll find artists, musicians, vendors, and craftspeople, not to mention various hustlers and lowlifes.

WALKING TOUR 2 **THE CASTLE DISTRICT**

Start:	Roosevelt tér, Pest side of Chain Bridge.
Finish:	Tóth Árpád sétány, Castle District.
Time:	3 to 4 hours (excluding museum visits).
Best Times:	Tuesday through Sunday.
Worst Time:	Monday, when museums are closed.

A limestone-capped plateau rising impressively above the Danube, Castle Hill was first settled in the 13th century; it remains the spiritual capital of Hungary. The district has been leveled more than once, most recently by the 1945 Soviet shelling of Nazi forces. It was always painstakingly rebuilt in the prevailing style of the day, shifting from Gothic to baroque to Renaissance. After World War II, an attempt was made to incorporate various elements of the district's historic appearance into the general restoration. Castle Hill, a UNESCO World Cultural Heritage site, consists of two parts: the Royal Palace itself and the so-called Castle District, a mostly reconstructed medieval city. The Royal Palace now houses a number of museums, including the Hungarian National Gallery. The adjoining Castle District is a compact, narrow neighborhood of cobblestone lanes and twisting alleys; restrictions on vehicular traffic enhance the tranquillity and the old-world feel. Prime examples of every type of Hungarian architecture, from early Gothic to neo-Romanesque, can be seen. A leisurely walk in the Castle District will be a warmly remembered experience.

Walking Tour 2: The Castle District

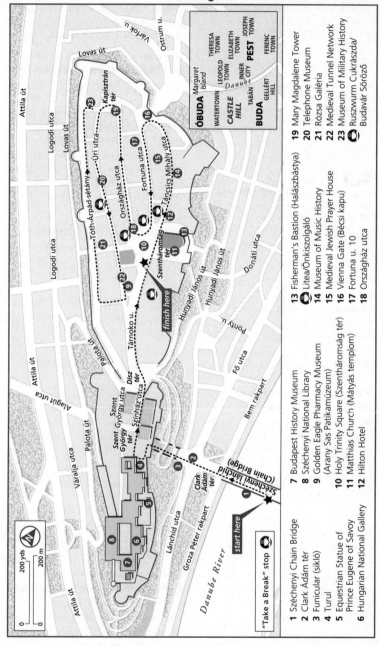

"Take a Break" stop

200 yds
200 m

start here

finish here

1 Széchenyi Chain Bridge
2 Clark Ádám tér
3 Funicular (sikló)
4 Turul
5 Equestrian Statue of
  Prince Eugene of Savoy
6 Hungarian National Gallery
7 Budapest History Museum
8 Széchenyi National Library
9 Golden Eagle Pharmacy Museum
  (Arany Sas Patikamúzeum)
10 Holy Trinity Square (Szentháromság tér)
11 Matthias Church (Mátyás templom)
12 Hilton Hotel
13 Fisherman's Bastion (Halászbástya)
  Litea/Önkiszolgáló
14 Museum of Music History
15 Medieval Jewish Prayer House
16 Vienna Gate (Bécsi kapu)
17 Fortuna u. 10
18 Országház utca
19 Mary Magdalene Tower
20 Telephone Museum
21 Rózsa Galéria
22 Medieval Tunnel Network
23 Museum of Military History
  Ruszwurm Cukrászda/
  Budavár Söröző

To get an accurate picture of the dimensions and grandeur of Castle Hill, start the walking tour in Pest's Roosevelt tér, on the:

❶ Széchenyi Chain Bridge

One of the outstanding landmarks of Budapest, the first permanent bridge across the Danube was originally built in 1849. Sadly, that first bridge was destroyed by Nazi dynamite during World War II. The 1949 opening ceremony for the reconstructed bridge was held 100 years to the day after its original inauguration.

Walk across the bridge. Arriving in Buda, you're now in:

❷ Clark Ádám tér

This square was named for the Scottish engineer who supervised the building of the bridge and afterward made Budapest his home.

From Clark Ádám tér, take the:

❸ Funicular (sikló)

The funicular will transport you up to the Royal Palace in just a minute or two (see "Getting Around" in chapter 4, "Getting to Know Budapest"). Dating from 1870, it too was destroyed in World War II and was not rebuilt until 1986. You can also walk up the steep stairs to Castle Hill.

Whichever method of ascent you choose, when you arrive at the top, turn and look left at the statue of the:

❹ Turul

This mythical eagle is perched on the wall looking out over the Danube to Pest. The eagle is said to have guided the ancient Magyars in their westward migration.

The main courtyard of the palace, from which the museums are entered, is on the building's far side, but first go down the nearby stairs to see the:

❺ Equestrian Statue of Prince Eugene of Savoy

Prince Eugene was one of the leaders of the united Christian armies that ousted the Turks from Hungary in the late 17th

century. Inside the palace are a number of museums. You might want to visit them now or return after the walking tour.

The first museum is the:

❻ Hungarian National Gallery

This museum houses much of the greatest art ever produced by Hungarians. Don't miss the works of the 19th-century artists Mihály Munkácsy, László Paál, Károly Ferenczy, Pál Szinyei Merse, Gyula Benczúr, and Károly Lotz. Nor should you overlook József Rippl-Rónai, the great Art Nouveau painter of the turn-of-the-20th-century period.

Proceed to the:

❼ Budapest History Museum

The highlights here are the Gothic rooms and statues that were uncovered during the post–World War II excavation and rebuilding of the Royal Palace. The rooms and all their contents, dating back as far as the 14th century, were buried for hundreds of years.

Next we have the:

❽ Széchenyi National Library

The library is named for Ferenc Széchenyi (not his more famous son István, after whom the Chain Bridge is named), who founded the institution in 1802. It now houses the world's greatest collection of "Hungarica," with some four million holdings.

Now proceed to Wing A of the Buda Palace, where you'll find the:

❾ Golden Eagle Pharmacy Museum (Arany Sas Patikamúzeum)

Renaissance and baroque pharmacy relics are displayed in this odd little museum.

Just ahead on Tárnok utca is:

❿ Holy Trinity Square (Szentháromság tér)

This central square of the Castle District is where you'll find the Holy Trinity Column, or Plague Column, dating from the early 18th century, and the:

⑪ Matthias Church (Mátyás templom)

Officially called the Church of Our Lady, this symbol of the Castle District is universally known as Matthias Church because the Renaissance monarch, Matthias Corvinus, one of Hungary's most revered kings, was the major donor of the church and was married twice inside it. There's an ecclesiastical art collection inside. Organ concerts are held Tuesday and Friday evenings in the summer.

Next door to the church is the:

⑫ Hilton Hotel

The Castle District's only major hotel, the Hilton tastefully incorporates two ruins into its award-winning design: a 13th-century Dominican church, with a tower rising above the hotel, and the baroque facade of a 17th-century Jesuit college, which makes up the hotel's main entrance. During the Socialist years, this was one of the very few Western-style hotels accompanied by a casino, until the systemic changes after which four- and five-star hotels have mushroomed in numbers. Summer concerts are held in the Dominican Courtyard.

Behind the Hilton is the:

⑬ Fisherman's Bastion (Halászbástya)

This sprawling neo-Romanesque structure was built in 1905 on the site of an old fish market (hence the name), and affords a marvelous panorama of Pest. Looking out over the Danube to Pest, you can see (from left to right): Margaret Island and the Margaret Bridge, Parliament, St. Stephen's Basilica, the Chain Bridge, the Vigadó Concert Hall, the Inner City Parish Church, the Erzsébet Bridge, and the Szabadság Bridge. Avoid the overpriced restaurant inside the Fisherman's Bastion.

TAKE A BREAK
You may want to stop at **Litea**, a bookstore and tearoom located in the Fortuna Passage, opposite the Hilton. You can browse, then sit and enjoy a cup of tea while looking over your selections. If it is lunch you desire, head to the **Café Miró**, opposite the Matthias Church on Úri utca (p. 117), where you can have a light lunch, coffee, tea or a sumptuous pastry.

Because the entire length of each of the Castle District's north-south streets is worth seeing, the tour will now take you back and forth between the immediate area of Szentháromság tér and the northern end of the district. First, head down Táncsics Mihály utca, to Táncsics Mihály u. 7, the:

⑭ Museum of Music History

Beethoven stayed here for a spell in 1800, when this structure was a private home. The museum now houses the archives of the great composer Bartók. The building next door, at Táncsics Mihály u. 9, served for many years as a prison. Among those incarcerated here were Mihály Táncsics, the 19th-century champion of free press after whom the street is named, and Lajos Kossuth, the leader of the 1848 to 1849 anti-Habsburg revolution. Táncsics utca was the center of Buda's Jewish community during medieval times. During general postwar reconstruction work in the 1960s, the remains of several synagogues were uncovered.

Continue walking down the street to Táncsics Mihály u. 26, where you'll find the:

⑮ Medieval Jewish Prayer House

This building dates from the 14th century. In the 15th and 16th centuries, the Jews of Buda thrived under Turkish rule. The 1686 Christian reconquest of Buda was soon followed by a massacre of Jews. Many survivors fled Buda; this tiny Sephardic synagogue was turned into an apartment.

After exiting the synagogue, retrace your steps about 9m (30 ft.) back on Táncsics Mihály utca, turn left onto Babits Mihály köz, and then turn left onto Babits Mihály sétány. This path will take you onto the top of the:

⑯ Vienna Gate (Bécsi kapu)

This is one of the main entrances to the Castle District. From the top of the gate, you can look out onto the fashionable Rose Hill (Rózsadomb) neighborhood in the Buda Hills. The enormous neo-Romanesque building towering above Bécsi kapu tér houses the National Archives. Bécsi kapu tér is also home to a lovely row of houses (nos. 5–8).

From here, head up Fortuna utca to the house at:

⑰ Fortuna u. 10

This is certainly one of the district's most photographed houses. It dates from the 13th century but has been restored in Louis XVI style. The facade incorporates medieval details.

Continue to Fortuna u. 4, where you'll find the charming, unassuming:

⑱ Országház utca

This is one of two streets in the Castle District that are best suited for viewing a mysterious Hungarian contribution to Gothic architecture: niches of unknown function that were built into the entryways of medieval buildings. When uncovered during reconstruction, the niches were either preserved or incorporated into the designs of new, modern structures. Niches can be seen in Országház u. nos. 9 and 20, while no. 28 has enormous wooden doors.

Walk down Országház utca until it ends in Kapisztrán tér, site of the:

⑲ Mary Magdalene Tower

Once part of a large 13th-century church, the tower is the only section that survived World War II.

Now take Úri utca back in the direction of the Royal Palace. In a corner of the courtyard of Úri u. 49, a vast former cloister, stands the small:

⑳ Telephone Museum

The museum's prime attraction is the actual telephone exchange (7A1-type rotary system) that was in use in the city from 1928 to 1985.

Continue down Úri u. and make a right onto Szentháromság u., and walk to no. 13 where you'll see:

㉑ Rózsa Galéria

No doubt you've noticed the presence in the Castle District of a large number of art galleries. Hungarian naive and primitive art is on display at this gallery. Works of art can be had for, on average, 100,000 Ft ($100).

Head back to Úri u. and find no. 9, the entrance to the:

㉒ Medieval Tunnel Network

The network weaves its way through the almost 15km (9 miles) of rock beneath the Castle District. The only part of this network that you can actually see is home to the Buda Wax Works, an unimpressive, tacky exhibit on the "legends" of early Hungarian history.

Úri utca ends back in Dísz tér. Take tiny Móra Ferenc utca (to the right) to Tóth Árpád sétány, the promenade that runs the length of the western rampart of the Castle District. This is a shady road with numerous benches. At its northern end, appropriately housed in the former barracks at Tóth Árpád sétány 40, is the:

㉓ Museum of Military History

This museum is dedicated to the history of Hungary's military endeavors, including World War I and World War II. For those looking for the exhibits on the 1956 Revolution, many of these exhibits have been transferred to the Terror House museum.

The walking tour ends back near Szentháromság tér, where you can catch the Várbusz down to Moszkva tér. Alternatively, from Dísz tér you can get bus no. 16 to Deák tér.

WINDING DOWN
The **Ruszwurm Cukrászda,** Szentháromság u. 7, has been here since 1827. This little coffeehouse and pastry shop is the only one of its kind in the Castle District. Its pastries are among the

city's best. Just down the street, at Úri u. 13, is **Budavár Söröző,** a good spot for a snack, espresso, or beer. It has just two tiny tables inside and three or four outside on the sidewalk.

WALKING TOUR 3   LEOPOLD TOWN & THERESA TOWN

Start: Kossuth tér, site of Parliament.
Finish: Művész Coffeehouse, near the Opera House.
Time: About 3 hours (excluding museum visits and the Opera House tour).
Best Times: Tuesday through Sunday. Note that if you want to visit the Parliament building, you should secure your ticket in advance.
Worst Time: Monday, when museums are closed.

In 1790 the new region developing just to the north of the medieval town walls of Pest was dubbed Leopold Town (Lipótváros) in honor of the emperor, Leopold II. Over the next 100 years or so, the neighborhood developed into an integral part of Pest, housing numerous governmental and commercial buildings: Parliament, government ministries, courthouses, the Stock Exchange, and the National Bank were all built here. This tour will take you through the main squares of Leopold Town. You'll also walk briefly along the Danube and visit a historic market hall. Along the way, you can stop to admire some of Pest's most fabulous examples of Art Nouveau architecture, as well as the city's largest church. Then you'll cross Pest's Inner Ring boulevard, leaving the Inner City, and head up elegant Andrássy út, on the edge of Theresa Town (Terézváros). There you'll see some wonderful inner courtyards and finish the tour with a visit to the dazzling State Opera House (try to arrive here by 3 or 4pm if you'd like to tour the Opera House).

Exiting the Kossuth tér metro (Red line), you'll find yourself on the southern end of:

❶ Kossuth tér
Walk toward Parliament, passing the equestrian statue of the Transylvanian prince Ferenc Rákóczi II, hero of an early-18th-century anti-Habsburg revolt. Exiled after the failure of his revolt, Rákóczi wandered from Poland to France and then to Turkey, where he remained until his death. A small monument in front of the statue commemorates the victims of the October 1956 Hungarian uprising, a major part of which played out right in this square.

You can't miss, on your left, one of the symbols of Budapest, the neo-Gothic:

❷ House of Parliament
Unless you've only just arrived in Budapest, you certainly will have seen this massive structure hugging the Danube. The Parliament building, designed by Imre Steindl and completed in 1902, had been used only once by a democratically elected government prior to 1989. Since 2000, in addition to its government functions, it has also been home to the fabled Hungarian crown jewels. Unfortunately, you can enter only on guided tours (the half-hour tour is worthwhile for the chance to go inside). See p. 131 for tour times and information.

The grandiose, eclectic-style building across the street from Parliament was the former Supreme Court. The building now houses the:

❸ Ethnographical Museum

This museum boasts more than 150,000 objects in its collection. The "From Ancient Times to Civilization" exhibition contains many fascinating relics of Hungarian life. See p. 129 for more information.

Continue walking in front of Parliament, and walk past the statue of 1848 revolutionary hero Lajos Kossuth. Notice Kossuth, eyes fixed on the distance, pointing directly toward the Parliament building. Now walk around to the side of Parliament and enter the small park by the Danube at the northern end of Kossuth tér. There's a sensitive Imre Varga statue of Mihály Károlyi, first president of the post–World War I Hungarian Republic. Across the Danube, to your left, you can see Castle Hill and the church steeples of Watertown (Víziváros) beneath it. The bridge visible to your right is the Margaret Bridge.

Here, you have two options. The more intrepid, and those traveling without children, can turn left, go down the stairs, and scurry across the busy two-lane road to the river embankment. Walk south along the blustery embankment; after completing this circumnavigation of Parliament, cross back and come up the set of stairs. Others can simply circle back to the southern end of Parliament. You'll find a small statue of a seated, somber-looking Attila József, the much-loved interwar working-class poet, whose tragic suicide (by jumping under a train at Lake Balaton) is imitated from time to time in Hungary. Cross the tram tracks and, walking away from the river, pass the metro entrance and continue through Vértanúk tere ("Square of Martyrs"). Here stands:

❹ Imre Varga's statue of Imre Nagy

Nagy was the reformist Communist who led the failed 1956 Hungarian Uprising. He was executed in 1958, 2 years after the Soviet-led invasion. This statue, *Witnesses to Blood,* was erected in 1996, 7 years after the reburial of Nagy attracted some 300,000 Hungarians to Hősök tere (Heroes' Sq.). Like the nearby statue of Kossuth, the statue of Nagy has his gaze

fixed on Parliament in the distance while he is crossing a symbolic bridge.

Now walk a few blocks down Nádor utca and turn left onto Zoltán utca. The massive yellow building on the right side of Zoltán utca is the former Stock Exchange, now headquarters of Hungarian Television. There are plans to move the television headquarters to a new building, but these plans constantly fail due to financial reasons. The front of the television building is on:

❺ Freedom Square (Szabadság tér)

Directly in front of you is the Soviet Army Memorial, built in 1945 to honor the Soviet-led liberation of Budapest and topped by the last Soviet Star remaining in post-Communist Budapest. The monument is surrounded by metallic gates after it was vandalized on several occasions. The American Embassy is at Szabadság tér 12, also surrounded by a whole spider web of comely metallic gates of its own, also scarring the stately environment.

Paying careful attention to the often-unruly traffic here, walk diagonally through the square, aiming for its southeast corner, site of the eclectic:

❻ Hungarian National Bank (Magyar Nemzeti Bank)

Leaving Szabadság tér via Bank utca, you can enter the National Bank through a side entrance. Its well-preserved, ornate lobby reminds one more of an opera house than a bank; its air-conditioned sky-lit main hall has rows of soft, comfortable chairs where you can take a breather.

Continue on Bank utca, making the first left onto Hold utca (Moon St.), formerly known as Rosenberg házaspár utca, for Ethel and Julius Rosenberg. Next door, to the rear of the National Bank and connected to it by a small footbridge, is the spectacular and newly restored:

❼ Former Post Office Savings Bank (Posta Takarékpénztár)

The bank was built in 1901 to the design of Ödön Lechner, the architect who endeavored to fuse Hungarian folk elements with the Art Nouveau style popular at this time.

Walking Tour 3: Leopold Town & Theresa Town

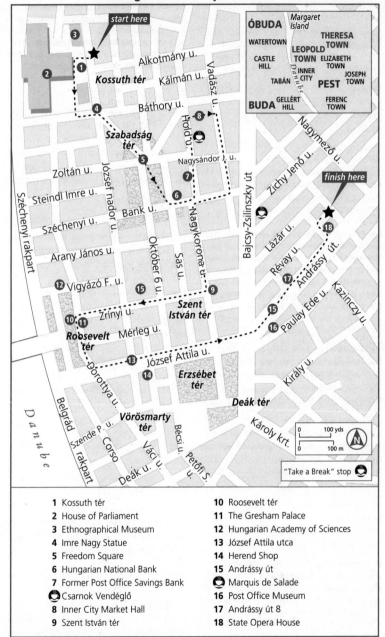

start here

ÓBUDA Margaret Island

WATERTOWN   THERESA TOWN
CASTLE HILL   LEOPOLD TOWN ELIZABETH TOWN
         INNER CITY
TABÁN   JOSEPH TOWN
         PEST
BUDA GELLÉRT HILL   FERENC TOWN

Alkotmány u.

Kossuth tér   Kálmán u.

Vadász u.

Báthory u.

Hold u.

Szabadság tér

Nagysándor J. u.

Zoltán u.

József nádor u.

Steindl Imre u.

Bank u.

Széchenyi u.

Arany János u.

Október 6 u.

Sas u.

Nagykorona u.

Vigyázó F. u.

Zrínyi u.

Szent István tér

Roosevelt tér

Mérleg u.

József Attila u.

Erzsébet tér

Vörösmarty tér

Deák tér

Széchenyi rakpart

Belgrád rakpart

Szende P. u.

Corso

Deák u.

Váci u.

Bécsi u.

Petőfi S. u.

Dorottya u.

Károly krt.

Nagymező u.

Zichy Jenő u.

finish here

Bajcsy-Zsilinszky út

Lázár u.

Révay u.

Andrássy út

Paulay Ede u.

Király u.

Kazinczy u.

Danube

0   100 yds
0   100 m

"Take a Break" stop 🅖

1 Kossuth tér
2 House of Parliament
3 Ethnographical Museum
4 Imre Nagy Statue
5 Freedom Square
6 Hungarian National Bank
7 Former Post Office Savings Bank
🅖 Csarnok Vendéglő
8 Inner City Market Hall
9 Szent István tér

10 Roosevelt tér
11 The Gresham Palace
12 Hungarian Academy of Sciences
13 József Attila utca
14 Herend Shop
15 Andrássy út
🅖 Marquis de Salade
16 Post Office Museum
17 Andrássy út 8
18 State Opera House

TAKE A BREAK
On the corner of Hold utca and Nagysándor József utca is **Csarnok Vendéglő**, Hold u. 11. This unassuming little restaurant, visited mainly by neighborhood residents, is good for a typical Hungarian lunch. The restaurant's name is taken from the nearby:

❽ Inner City Market Hall (Belvárosi Vásárcsarnok)

Built in 1897, this cavernous market hall has been newly restored. The market (which closes at 4pm) is one of the city's liveliest; pick up some fruit in season.

Emerge from the Market Hall onto Vadász utca and turn right. Passing Nagysándor József utca, look right for a great view of the colorful tiled roof of the former Post Office Savings Bank you recently passed. Turn right on Bank utca (the metro station you see on your left is Arany János utca; Blue line) and left on Hercegprímás utca. After a few blocks, you'll find yourself in:

❾ Szent István tér

This is the site of the famous St. Stephen's Basilica, Budapest's largest church, seating some 8,500 people. Built between 1851 and 1905, it is well worth a stop. In the Szent Jobb Kápolna, behind the main altar, you can see an extraordinary and gruesome holy relic: Stephen's preserved right hand, which is paraded around town annually on St. Stephen's Day, August 20. Monday-night organ concerts are held in the church in summer. The once-run-down square in front of the church has been recently rehabilitated and is now a great place to spend some time. See p. 131 for more information.

Head down Zrínyi utca, straight across the square from the church entrance. As you pass Október 6 utca, you might want to make a slight detour to Bestsellers, an English-language bookstore owned by the Central European University at no. 11. Bestsellers stocks travel books, especially on eastern Europe. Alternately, you may want to stop at the corner of Zrínyi utca and Nádor utca and walk into the building of the Central European University itself; downstairs

you will find their other bookstore, which has a more academic stock of works by central and east European scholars, including works on the political, economic, and cultural changes in the region. Returning now to the Danube, you'll find yourself emerging into:

❿ Roosevelt tér

This square lies at the head of the famous Chain Bridge. Built in the revolutionary year 1848 to 1849, the bridge was the first permanent span across the Danube. Roosevelt Square itself is really too full of traffic to be beautiful, but there are several important and lovely buildings here, including:

⓫ The Gresham Palace

Built in 1907, this is one of Budapest's best-known Art Nouveau buildings, and houses Budapest's most exclusive hotel: the Hotel Four Seasons Gresham Palace. During the copious and successful renovations that took place before the opening of the hotel, developers had to wrestle with challenges of their own. The proposed building of a parking lot spawned one of the first successful civic protest movements in town since the 1989 change in regime. A group of environmental activists chained themselves to the 100-year-old trees in the park in front of the building, defeating the plan to cut them down and transform the graceful park into a parking lot for the hotel. The hotel instead enjoys an underground garage.

To your right, as you face the river, is the neo-Renaissance facade of the:

⓬ Hungarian Academy of Sciences

Like the Chain Bridge, this building was the brainchild of 19th-century Count István Széchenyi (often called "the Greatest Hungarian"), who completed it in 1864. A statue of Széchenyi adorns the square. Guards prevent access beyond the academy's lobby, but it's worth a peek inside. A statue of Ferenc Deák, architect of the 1867 Compromise with Austria, is in a shady grove in the square's southern end, by the Atrium Hyatt Hotel.

Turn left away from the river onto bustling:

⑬ József Attila utca

This street was named for the poet whose statue embellishes Kossuth tér. You're now walking along a portion of the Inner Ring (Kiskörüt), which separates the Inner City (Belváros), to your right, from Leopold Town (Lipótváros), to your left.

At József nádor tér, you may want to stop in at the:

⑭ Herend Shop

Herend china is perhaps Hungary's most famous product, and this museum-like shop is definitely worth a look.

Continue up József Attila utca. You'll pass Erzsé-bet tér, site of Budapest's main bus station, just before reaching Bajcsy-Zsilinszky út. Endre Bajcsy-Zsilinszky, a heroic leader of Hungary's wartime anti-Fascist resistance, was executed by the Arrow Cross (Hungary's Nazi party) on Christmas Eve 1944. Crossing Bajcsy-Zsilinszky út, you'll find yourself at the head of stately:

⑮ Andrássy út

Lined with trees and a wealth of beautiful apartment buildings, this is *fin de siècle* Pest's greatest boulevard, which is recognized as a World Heritage Site by UNESCO. Andrássy út is the home to a lively cafe-and-bar scene, as well as a number of small museums. There are colorful terraces, and delicious cakes and ice cream are sold under the shade of the huge trees all the way up to Oktogon.

Returning now to Andrássy út, look for no. 3, a building with a stunning entryway, which is the:

⑯ Post Office Museum

The museum's main attraction is clearly the opulently appointed apartment in which it's located. Imagine: This is how the wealthy of Andrássy út used to live! The frescoes in the entryway are by Károly Lotz, whose frescoes also decorate the Opera House and Matthias Church, in the Castle District. See p. 136 for more information.

Cross over to the even-numbered side of Andrássy. Stop to peek into other entryways and courtyards. Be sure to take a look in the vestibule of:

⑰ Andrássy út 8

Here you'll find more ceiling frescoes and painted-glass courtyard doors; the courtyard is typical of this kind of Pest apartment building. Next door, Andrássy út 12 is a building that used to belong to the once-feared Interior Ministry, and was the site of torture and other mistreatment of "political criminals." Ironically, given its ugly past, the building has a gorgeous entryway and an inner courtyard with frescoes covering the walls. An officer sometimes guards the entrance; sightseers are usually allowed to poke their heads in.

Continue on Andrássy út until you reach the neo-Renaissance:

⑱ State Opera House

Designed by Miklós Ybl and built in 1884, the Opera House survived the siege of Budapest at the end of World War II nearly unscathed. In fact, its huge cellars provided shelter for thousands during the bombing. Turning left on Hajós utca, walk around the Opera House. There are a number of music stores on Hajós utca. The street directly behind the Opera House, Lázár utca, affords an unusual view of the Bazilika. And if you are lucky, you can hear performers practicing through open windows on Dalszinház utca. English-language Opera House tours (the only way, short of attending a performance, that you can get a look inside the building) are daily at 3 and 4pm year-round and start at the front entrance. See p. 130 for more details.

You'll find the Opera station of the Yellow metro line just in front of the Opera House.

⑲ The House of Terror Museum

A highly politicized museum which is dedicated to those who survived two terror regimes: the Communist and Fascist regimes. The museum is meant to be a memorial to the victims, and at the same time to present a picture of what life was like for Hungarians in those turbulent times. When it was opened, the museum—which is probably Hungary's most technologically advanced—was much criticized for its emphasis or over-emphasis on the Communist-era crimes, vs. those of the Fascists. History is revisited in a different light in Hungary, and depending on whom you are talking to, they will have another view of both the present and the past.

WALKING TOUR 4   THE JEWISH DISTRICT

Start:	Dohány Synagogue.
Finish:	Wesselényi utca.
Time:	About 2 hours (excluding museum visit).
Best Times:	Sunday through Friday.
Worst Time:	Saturday, when the museum and most shops are closed.

The Jewish district in Pest has a long and ultimately tragic history. It first sprang up in medieval times just beyond the Pest city wall (which stood where today's Inner Ring boulevard stands), because Jews were forbidden to live inside the town. Later, Pest expanded beyond its walls, and the Jewish district actually became one of the city's more centrally located neighborhoods. The huge synagogues that you'll see on this tour give some idea of the area's former vitality. Under German occupation in World War II, the district became a walled ghetto, with 220,000 Jews crowded inside; almost half perished during the war. Sadly, the neighborhood is now more or less in a state of decay; buildings are crumbling, garbage is strewn about, and graffiti covers the walls. Nevertheless, this compact little neighborhood is filled with evocative sights.

Halfway between Astoria (Red metro line) and Deák tér (all metro lines) is the:
❶ Dohány Synagogue
This striking Byzantine building, Europe's largest synagogue and the world's second-largest, was built in 1859 and is still used by Budapest's Neolog (Conservative) Jewish community. The synagogue is newly cleaned and restored. See p. 132 for more details.

The small, free-standing brick wall inside the courtyard, to the left of the synagogue's entrance, is a piece of the original:
❷ Ghetto Wall
This wall kept Budapest's Jews inside this district during World War II. This is not actually where it stood, however; it was situated on Károly körút, the nearby stretch of the Inner Ring boulevard.

To the left of the wall, on the spot marked as the birthplace of Theodor Herzl, the founder of modern Zionism, is the:

❸ National Jewish Museum
On display are artifacts and art from the long history of Hungarian Jewry. The last of the four rooms is given over to a moving exhibit on the Holocaust in Hungary. (**Note the open hours:** May–Oct only, Mon–Thurs 10am–5pm, Fri 10am–3pm, and Sun 10am–1pm.) The synagogue courtyard can be entered through the rear of the complex on Wesselényi utca.

Inside the courtyard is the still-expanding:
❹ Holocaust Memorial
Designed by Imre Varga, a wonderful contemporary Hungarian sculptor, the memorial is in the form of a weeping willow tree. Thin metal leaves, purchased by survivors and by descendants to honor relatives who were victims, are slowly filling the many branches. The courtyard behind the memorial is called the Raoul Wallenberg Memorial Park, in honor of the Swiss diplomat who saved thousands

Walking Tour 4: The Jewish District

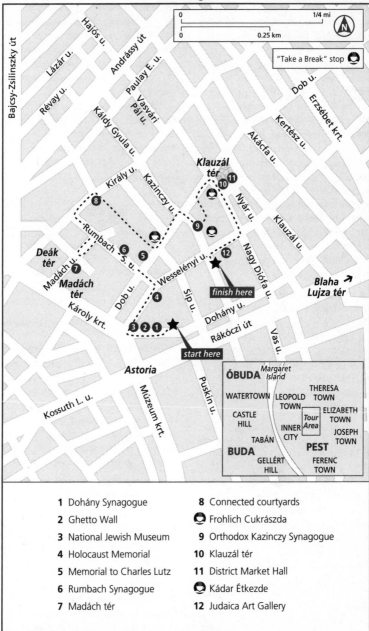

1 Dohány Synagogue
2 Ghetto Wall
3 National Jewish Museum
4 Holocaust Memorial
5 Memorial to Charles Lutz
6 Rumbach Synagogue
7 Madách tér

8 Connected courtyards
🍵 Frohlich Cukrászda
9 Orthodox Kazinczy Synagogue
10 Klauzál tér
11 District Market Hall
🍵 Kádar Étkezde
12 Judaica Art Gallery

of Jewish lives in wartime Budapest. The names of some of Budapest's "righteous Gentiles" are inscribed on four pillars.

Now head down Rumbach utca. On the right, against a cement wall near the corner of Rumbach utca and Dob utca, is the rather bizarre-looking:

❺ Memorial to Charles Lutz

Lutz was the Swiss consul who aided Wallenberg's heroic attempts to save Budapest's Jews from the Nazi death camps. The inscription from the Talmud reads: "Saving one soul is the same as saving the whole world." The author of these words would not, in fact, be writing them today were it not for the heroic work of Mr. Lutz. We have not forgotten.

Another, rather lonely, memorial to Wallenberg stands on Szilágyi Erzsébet fasor, far away in Buda.

Half a block farther on Rumbach utca is the:

❻ Rumbach Synagogue

This handsome but decrepit yellow-and-rust-colored building is, in its own way, as impressive as the Dohány Synagogue. Built in 1872 by the Vienna architect Otto Wagner, this Orthodox synagogue is no longer in use. You can't go inside, but the facade itself is worth seeing.

Continue down Rumbach utca and make a left on Madách út to look at the giant archway of:

❼ Madách tér

In the 1930s a plan was drawn up for the creation of a great boulevard similar in form and style to Andrássy út. World War II put an end to the ambitious project, and the grand Madách tér leads only to itself now. Looking through the arch on a clear day, you get an unusual view of Gellért Hill, crowned by the Liberation Monument. Several new art galleries can be found on Rumbach utca and Madách út.

Head back to Rumbach utca and proceed down that street. Take a right onto Király utca, which forms the northern border of the historic Jewish district. At Király u. 13, head through the long series of:

❽ Connected courtyards

These courtyards emerge onto Dob utca, back in the heart of the Jewish district. This kind of complex—residential buildings connected by a series of courtyards—is typical of the Jewish district. As you can readily see, these courtyards are in extremely poor condition, dirty and rundown with graffiti-covered walls and abandoned apartments, though the appearance in recent years of several flashy retail shops may presage a general improvement.

TAKE A BREAK
Frohlich Cukrászda, Dob u. 22, is the only functioning kosher cukrászda (sweet shop) left in the district. Here, you can purchase pastries, rolls, or ice cream. (Be aware that the shop closes for 2 weeks at the end of Aug.)

Half a block to the left off Dob utca on Kazinczy utca, at no. 29, is the:

❾ Orthodox Kazinczy Synagogue

Built in 1913 and still active, this synagogue is being slowly and beautifully restored. It has a well-maintained and lively courtyard in its center. There are a number of apartments in which members of the Orthodox community live. While hundreds of travelers visit the Dohány each day, far fewer make the trip here.

Go all the way through the courtyard, emerge onto Dob utca, turn right, and head into:

❿ Klauzál tér

This is the district's largest square and its historic center. A dusty park and renovated playground fill the interior of the square.

At Klauzál tér 11, you'll find the:

⓫ District Market Hall (Vásárcsarnok)

One of the half-dozen or so great steel-girdered market halls built in Budapest in the 1890s, this one is rather run-down and now houses a Skála grocery store.

The entrance area is filled with smaller vendors selling fruit or vegetables.

TAKE A BREAK
You have two lunch options in Klauzál tér and its immediate vicinity, each with a markedly different character. **Hanna Kosher Restaurant,** back at the Kazinczy Synagogue, is the city's only strictly kosher restaurant. It's open daily for lunch and offers a somewhat pricey multicourse prix-fixe lunch. Buy your ticket at the window and wash your hands at the sink on the way in. Men should keep their heads covered inside. **(Note:** Meals can't be purchased on Sat—they have to be prepaid the

day before, though they can be eaten on Sat.) **Kádár Étkezde,** at Klauzál tér 9, is a simple local lunchroom (Tues–Sat 11:30am–3:30pm) serving a regular clientele ranging from young paint-spattered workers to elderly Jews.

Now head back out on Nagydiófa utca to Wesselényi utca, where you can end the walking tour at Wesselényi u. 13, the:

⑫ Judaica Art Gallery
Here you'll find Jewish-oriented books, both new and secondhand (some are in English). Clothing, ceramics, art, and religious articles are also for sale.

WALKING TOUR 5   TABÁN & WATERTOWN (VÍZIVÁROS)

Start: The Pest side of the Erzsébet Bridge.
Finish: The Buda side of the Margaret (Margít) Bridge.
Time: About 2 to 3 hours (excluding museum visits).
Best Time: Any time.
Worst Time: There is no bad time to visit.

This tour will take you through a narrow, twisting neighborhood along the Buda side of the Danube. Tabán, the area between Gellért Hill and Castle Hill, was once a vibrant but very poor workers' neighborhood. The neighborhood was razed in the early 20th century for "sanitary reasons"; only a handful of Tabán buildings still stand below the green expanse of parks where the rest of Tabán once was. The neighborhood directly beneath Castle Hill, opposite the Inner City of Pest, has been called Víziváros (Watertown) since the Middle Ages. Historically home to fishermen who made a living on the Danube, Víziváros was surrounded by walls in Turkish times. The neighborhood still retains a quiet integrity; above busy Fő utca (Main St.), which runs one street up from and parallel to the river along the length of Watertown, you'll wander along aged, peaceful lanes.

Begin the walking tour on the Pest side of the:
❶ Erzsébet Bridge
The nearest metro stations are Ferenciek tere (Blue line) and Vörösmarty tér (Yellow line). The original Erzsébet Bridge was completed in 1903, but like all the city's bridges, it was destroyed by the Germans in World War II; the present bridge was constructed in 1964. Note how the bridge skirts around the Inner City Parish Church, which dates to the 12th century.

Cross the bridge on the right side with the flow of traffic. In order to do this, you'll need to be in front of the church; there's a staircase opposite, leading up to the bridge.

In front of you is Gellért Hill; the statue of Bishop Gellért bears his cross defiantly on the mountainside. From here, the legend goes, vengeful 11th century pagans, recalling the cruelties of the conversion to Christianity, forced the Italian bishop, who had aided King Stephen's crusade, into a barrel and rolled him to his death in the river far below.

Upon reaching Buda, descend the steps, and, passing the statue of Queen Erzsébet, note the tablet commemorating the anti-Fascists who, on this spot in 1944, blew up a statue of Gyula Gömbös, a leading Hungarian Fascist politician of the interwar period. You're now at the bottom of the historic Tabán district. Walk away from the bridge, toward the yellow church whose steeple is visible above the trees. Your first stop here in Buda is the:

❷ Tabán Parish Church

You can enter this church, which was built in 1736. Inside, you'll find a copy of a 12th-century carving called the *Tabán Christ*. The original is in the Budapest History Museum (inside the Buda Palace; see p. 132).

Exit the church and walk past it. You'll now see in front of and above you the southern end of the Buda Palace. Watertown is the long, narrow strip of Buda that lies on a slope between Castle Hill and the Danube. Before proceeding to it, note the tile-roofed Stag House on Szarvas tér, diagonally across the street. One of Tabán's few remaining old buildings, it now houses the Aranyszarvas Restaurant. Cross to the side of the street that the Stag House is on. From here, you can see across busy Attila út (the street that runs behind Castle Hill) two graffiti-covered pillarlike chunks of the:

❸ Berlin Wall

The presence of the pieces of the wall here recall the pivotal role that Hungary played in the fall of East German Communism. Thousands of East German vacationers crossed the border from Hungary into Austria after the iron curtain was dismantled here in the late summer of 1989. This exodus helped spark the popular movement that led ultimately to the collapse of the East German regime and the breaching of the Berlin Wall.

Continue now down Apród út. The rust-and-white building at Apród út 1–3 is the:

❹ Semmelweis Medical History Museum

Named after one of Hungary's greatest physicians, the museum has exhibits related to a variety of medical fields and contains furnishings from the 19th-century Szentlélek Pharmacy.

Proceed down the street to:

❺ Ybl Miklós tér

This narrow square on the Danube is named for Hungary's most celebrated architect. The lovely building at the square's southern end is the former Várkert (Castle Garden) Kiosk; it's now a casino. The patio ceiling here is covered with *sgraffito*, a decoration created by carving into a coating of glaze to reveal the color below. Directly across the street from Miklós Ybl's statue is the Várkert Bazar. This once-beautiful place is now in a frightful state of disrepair, but you can still admire the ornate archways and stairs. If current plans are followed through, this area will be considerably developed in the coming years.

Walk the length of the old Bazar to *Lánchíd utca* (Chain Bridge Street), so named because it leads into Clark Ádám tér, the Buda head of the Chain Bridge. Walking away from the river, take the steep set of stairs on your left up to quiet, canyonlike:

❻ Öntőház utca

In summer the terrace gardens of these residential buildings thrive. Flowers, small trees and shrubs, ivy, and grape vines are cultivated with care.

Turn right, winding back down to Lánchíd utca toward:

❼ Clark Ádám tér

This is a busy traffic circle named for the Scottish engineer who supervised the building of the Chain Bridge in 1848 and 1849. Clark grew so fond of Budapest during his assignment that he remained in the city until his death.

Immediately to your left is the:

❽ Funicular *(sikló)*

The funicular goes up to the Buda Palace. In front of the funicular is the "Zero Kilometer Stone," the marker from which all highway distances to and from Budapest are measured.

Walking Tour 5: Tabán & Watertown (Víziváros)

1 Erzsébet Bridge
2 Tabán Parish Church
3 Berlin Wall
4 Semmelweis Medical History Museum
5 Ybl Miklós tér
6 Öntőház utca
7 Clark Ádám tér
8 Funicular (sikló)
9 Tunnel
10 Fő utca (Main Street)
11 Jégverem utca
12 Hunyádi János út
13 Institut Français
🍴 Horgásztanya Vendeglő/ Le Jardin de Paris
14 Capuchin Church
15 Corvin tér
16 Iskola utca (School Street)
17 Bem rakpart
18 Szilágyi Dezső tér
19 Batthyány tér
20 St. Anne's Church
21 The Vásárcsarnok (Market Hall)
🍴 Angelika Cukrászda
22 St. Elizabeth's Church
23 Nagy Imre tér
24 Király Baths
25 Chapel of St. Florian
26 Öntödei (Foundry) Museum
27 Bem József tér
28 The Buda side of the Margaret Bridge

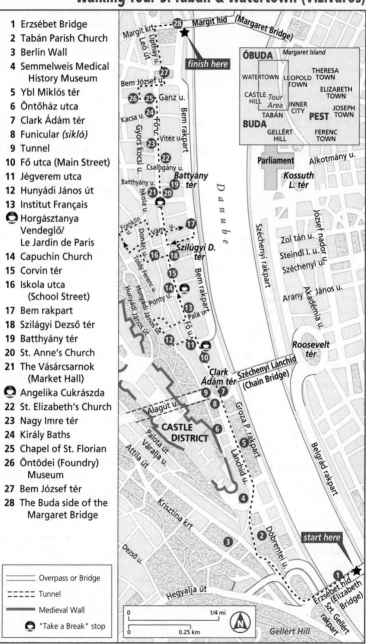

Overpass or Bridge
Tunnel
Medieval Wall
🍴 "Take a Break" stop

175

Straight across the square from the Chain Bridge is:

⑨ The Tunnel

Built between 1853 and 1857, the tunnel connects Watertown with Christina Town (Krisztinaváros) on the other side of Castle Hill. The joke of the day was that the tunnel was built so that the precious Chain Bridge could be placed inside when it rained. Just across the street from the tunnel, a set of stairs marks the beginning of the long climb up to Castle Hill.

Passing straight through the square, you'll find yourself at the head of Watertown's:

⑩ Fő utca (Main Street)

You'll be either on or near this long, straight street for the remainder of this walking tour. As you pass Jégverem utca, make a little detour toward the river to examine the solid wood door at Jégverem u. 2. Note the small door cut out of the larger one, presumably a gatekeeper's door in days gone by, when the main doors were kept closed except for carriages and the like.

Now head left on:

⑪ Jégverem utca

At Kapucinus utca, you'll get a marvelous view of the steep old tile rooftops down the street.

Proceed up the stairs to the next street:

⑫ Hunyadi János út

Walk through the absurdly tall, narrow doorway of Hunyadi János út 9. Peek into the courtyard to see the crude wooden construction of the inner terrace landings. Hunyadi János út 4, across the street, has a dazzling enclosed atrium above the inner courtyard; its timeless beauty sharply contrasts against the sheer horror of the dungeonlike cellar, clearly visible beneath you.

At the intersection with Szalag utca, turn right and then right again on Szőnyeg utca, back toward Fő utca. Bear left on Pala utca. Crossing Kapucinus utca, continue down the steps. Here

are the rooftops you viewed from a distance a short while ago. Emerge onto Fő utca, where you'll see the site of the monstrous:

⑬ Institut Français

Note also the reconstructed remains of a medieval house across the street from this French cultural center.

TAKE A BREAK
At the **Horgásztanya Vendéglő (The Fisherman's Den)**, I. Fő u. 29, Hungarian seafood is served in a rustic setting, and **Le Jardin de Paris** (p. 114), I. Fő u. 20, a delightful French bistro.

Across the street from Horgásztanya is the former:

⑭ Capuchin Church

This is the first of several Watertown churches included on this tour. Note the Turkish door and window frames on the church's southern wall.

Just past this church is:

⑮ Corvin tér

Several interesting buildings, including the home of the Hungarian State Folk Ensemble, are located here. If the timing is right, you might hear a rehearsal through the open windows. Note the row of very old baroque houses at the top of the square. There is presently a major archaeological dig going on at this square.

Head above Corvin tér to:

⑯ Iskola utca (School Street)

Turn right on Iskola utca and left up the Donáti lépcső (stairs) to Donáti utca; a clay frieze of two horsemen adorns the residential building to the left, opposite the stair landing. Turn right and walk to the next set of stairs, Toldy lépcső. Turn left up the stairs and right onto Toldy Ferenc utca, a residential street lined with old-fashioned gas lampposts. This street is so tranquil that the only other travelers are likely to be following this very walking tour. Notice the gorgeous brick secondary school on your right (Toldy Ferenc Gimnázium); a plaque notes *"itt tanított Antall József"* ("József Antall [first post-Communist prime minister] taught here"). Just before Iskola utca is a wonderful little playground, the perfect place to stop if you've been dragging any youngsters along with you.

Now turn right on Iskola utca, then left onto Vám utca. Cross Fő utca, heading to the:

⓱ Bem rakpart

This is the Danube embankment. Directly across the river is Parliament. The next bridge on your left is the Margaret Bridge, where this walking tour will end.

Turn right now and you'll immediately find yourself in:

⓲ Szilágyi Dezsó tér

The neo-Gothic Calvinist Church here dates from the end of the 19th century. The composer Béla Bartók lived at Szilágyi Dezsó tér 4 in the 1920s. The Danube bank near this square is the site of a piece of Hungary's darkest history: Here, the Arrow Cross (Nyilas), the Hungarian Nazis, massacred thousands of Jews in 1944 and 1945, during the last bitter winter of World War II. Many were tied together into small groups and thrown alive into the freezing river.

Returning now to Fő utca, turn right and continue on toward Watertown's main square, Batthyány tér. You may want to stop in at the Herend Village Pottery shop at Bem rakpart 37, on the ground floor of the housing block. You'll find several attractions along:

⓳ Batthyány tér

One of this area's principal sights is the 18th-century:

⓴ St. Anne's Church

One of Hungary's finest baroque churches, St. Anne's was almost destroyed in the early 1950s because the Hungarian dictator Mátyás Rákosi (known as "Stalin's most loyal disciple") thought that when Stalin visited him at his office in Parliament, he would be loath to look across the Danube at a Buda skyline dominated by churches. Fortunately, Rákosi's demented plan was never realized.

Also on the square is:

㉑ The Vásárcsarnok (Market Hall)

One of several markets built in 1897, this building now houses a large, well-stocked grocery store (which is even open on Sun!). The interior is worth a look. Two doors down is the former White Cross Inn, a rococo building, which, like St. Anne's, dates from the 18th century. The legendary philanderer Casanova is said to have spent a night here, hence the name of the ground-floor nightclub. Next door, at Batthyány tér 3, above the first-floor windows of the building, are several enchanting but shamefully dirty clay friezes.

Continue along Fő utca. The next church on your right is:

㉒ St. Elizabeth's Church

Presently closed for renovations, this church has a fine baroque interior. The frescoes date from the 19th century.

Continue along Fő utca. You're now approaching the northern border of Watertown; larger streets—such as Batthyány utca and Csalogány utca—now bisect Fő utca. You can no longer see Castle Hill. The next square is:

㉓ Nagy Imre tér

A small park hidden behind a Total gas station, this square is named for the reform Communist leader who played a leading, if slightly reluctant, role in the 1956 Hungarian Revolution. The prisonlike building on the corner is the Military Court of Justice, where Nagy was secretly tried and condemned to death in 1958, thus providing Hungary with yet another martyr. Nagy's reburial in June 1989 was a moment of great national unity, and a statue of Nagy was later erected near Parliament (p. 129). The main entrance to the Military Court of Justice is on Fő utca.

Two blocks farther up Fő utca, at Fő u. 82–86, are the:

㉔ Király Baths

This 16th-century bathhouse is one of the city's major reminders of the period of Turkish rule. Even if you're not going in to bathe, you should take a peek at the gorgeous interior. The baths are open on different days for men and women (p. 150).

Next door, at the corner of Fő utca and Ganz utca, is the baroque:

㉕ Chapel of St. Florian

Today this is a Greek Orthodox church; it's nice if not spectacular—have a look inside the vestibule.

Turn left on Ganz utca, passing through the small park between the baths and the church. At the end of Ganz utca is the:

㉖ Öntödei (Foundry) Museum

This museum is housed inside the original structure of the famed Abraham Ganz Foundry (started in 1845). From the exterior, painted a creamy yellow with a rusty-red trim, it's hard to imagine the vast barnlike interior. The collection of antique cast-iron stoves is the highlight of the exhibits.

Turn right onto Bem József utca, a street with several small fishing and Army-Navy–type supply stores, and head back down toward the Danube. You'll find yourself in:

㉗ Bem József tér

This square is named after the Polish general who played a heroic role in the Hungarian Revolution of 1848 and 1849. On October 23, 1956, the square hosted a rally in support of the reform efforts in Poland. The rally, and the subsequent march across the Margaret Bridge to Parliament, marked the beginning of the famous 1956 Hungarian Uprising.

Turn left onto Lipthay utca, which is parallel to the river. Admire the buildings on your left along this street before ending the tour at:

㉘ The Buda side of the Margaret Bridge

Here, you can pick up the no. 4 or 6 tram and head to either Buda's Moszkva tér (Red metro line) or across the river to Pest's Outer Ring boulevard.

Budapest Shopping

Globalization has hit the Hungarian capital and at breakneck speed. From name-brand items to stylish secondhand shops, Budapest offers a far wider array of shopping experiences than just a few years ago.

In some ways, Budapest has become metropolitan in terms of shopping. Once ruled by countless small monotonous shops and boutiques offering a scanty selection of goods, today local Budapest citizens and travelers alike crowd an ever-growing number of gigantic malls and shopping centers.

Still, buyer beware: Quality and value are not always on the agenda. So while most mainstream locals wallow in the lowly atmosphere of the giga-malls, fashion driven and retro-loving highbrows have returned—ironically—back to the small shops. Overcoming bankruptcy due to the influx of the mega-malls, these shops—stylish, modern, and cool—have become the center of attention once again. Scroll through a wide selection of some of these stores offered in this chapter or venture out on your own.

FOLKLORE Travelers seeking folklore objects do not have to look far. A chain called Folkart has shops (one is called Népművészeti bolt, another is called Háziipari bolt) that boast great selections of handmade goods at unbeatable prices. Popular items include pillowcases, pottery, porcelain, dolls, dresses, skirts, and sheepskin vests. Antiques shops, running along Falk Miksa Street in downtown Budapest, feature a broad selection of vintage furniture, ceramics, carpets, jewelry, and accessories.

Other sources of authentic folk items are the ethnic Hungarian women who come to Budapest with bags full of handmade craftwork from Transylvania, a region of Romania heavily populated with ethnic Hungarians. Keep your eyes open for these vendors, who sell their goods on the street and are unmistakable in their characteristic black boots and dark-red skirts, with red or white kerchiefs tied around their heads. Their prices are generally quite reasonable, and bargaining is customary. The police half-heartedly drive the vendors from one neighborhood to the next, and they congregate where they can.

PORCELAIN Another popular Hungarian item is porcelain, particularly from the country's two best-known producers, Herend and Zsolnay. Although both brands are available in the West, you'll find a better selection and substantially lower prices in Hungary.

HUNGARIAN FOOD Typical Hungarian foods also make great gifts. Hungarian salami is world-famous. Connoisseurs generally agree that Pick Salami, produced in the southeastern city of Szeged, is the best brand. Herz Salami, produced locally in Budapest, is also a very popular product (though not as popular as Pick). You should be aware that some people have reported difficulty in clearing U.S. Customs with salami; bring it home at your own risk. Another typical Hungarian food product is chestnut paste *(gesztenye püré)*, available in a tin or block wrapped in foil; it's used primarily as a pastry filling but can also top desserts and ice cream. Paprika paste *(pirosarany)* is another product that's tough to find outside Hungary. It usually comes in a bright-red tube. Three types are available: hot *(csípős)*, deli-style *(csemege)*, and sweet *(édes)*. All these items can be purchased at grocery stores *(élelmiszer)* and delicatessens *(csemege)*. Another product to look for is Szamos brand marzipan. Szamos Confectioners, a recently reestablished family business that was originally founded in 1935, is also said to make the best ice cream in the country. They're based in Szentendre, with a shop in Budapest at V. Párisi u. 3 (© **1/317-3643**). See "Appendix B: Hungarian Cuisine" for more food information.

WINES Illustrious local traditional wines and spirits have matured. The sweet white Tokaji Aszú, Tokaji Eszenzia, and Tokaji Szamorodni, mouthwatering Egri Bikavér, Villányi Cuveé, Szekszárdi Bikavér, and Kékfrankos are the most representative. The transcendent Pálinka—a strong fruit brandy—is a Hungarian treasure that soothes the stomach and bullies the brain. The black spirit that cures all, Unicum, the trademark product of Zwack, is a bitter liqueur made of herbs.

MARKETS If you love markets, you're in for a treat. There are numerous markets here: flea markets *(használtáru piac)*, filled not only with every conceivable kind of junk and the occasional relic of Communism, but also with great quantities of mostly low-quality new items like clothing, cassettes, and shoes; and food markets *(vásárcsarnok, csarnok, or piac)*, which sell row after row of succulent fruits and vegetables, much of it freshly picked and driven in from the surrounding countryside. You can find saffron and several varieties of dried mushrooms for surprisingly low prices at these markets.

1 The Shopping Scene

MAIN SHOPPING STREETS The hub of the tourist-packed capital is the first pedestrian shopping street in Budapest, Váci utca. It runs from the stately Vörösmarty tér in the center of Pest, across Kossuth Lajos utca, all the way to Vámház krt. High-end locals and travelers alike throng Váci utca as well as the boutique- and shop-filled roads bisecting pedestrian streets and courtyards. Váci utca was formerly known throughout the country as *the* street for good bookshops. Sadly, only one remains. The street is now largely occupied by Euro-fashion clothing boutiques (where high prices prevail) and an overwhelming number of folklore/souvenir shops, as well as cafes and bars (many of which are overpriced tourist traps).

Another popular shopping area for travelers is the **Castle District** in Buda, with its abundance of overpriced folk-art boutiques and art galleries. A healthy selection of Hungarian wines from historical local viticulture regions can also be found in the intimate labyrinthine cellar of the **House of Hungarian Wines**.

While Hungarians might window-shop in these two neighborhoods, they tend to do their serious shopping elsewhere. One of their favorite streets is Pest's **Outer Ring (Nagykörút)**, which extends into **West End Center**, central Europe's largest multifunction shopping mall, located just behind the Nyugati Railway Station. Another bustling shopping street is Pest's **Kossuth Lajos utca**, off the Erzsébet Bridge, and its continuation, **Rákóczi út**, which extends all the way out to Keleti Railway Station. **Andrássy út**, from Deák tér to Oktogon, is also a popular, though much more upscale, shopping street. Together with the adjacent **Liszt Ferenc tér** and **Nagymező**

utca, Andrássy út is also the most popular hub for nightlife, with numerous coffee shops, bars, and restaurants. In Buda, Hungarian crowds visit the shops of **Margit körút** and the neighborhood around the transportation hub **Móricz Zsigmond körtér,** where the Buda Skála department store is located. Hidden among the herd of cafes and restaurants of the lively **Ráday utca,** small interior design boutiques and shops present unique presents and doodads. You can often pay by credit card in the most popular shopping areas.

HOURS   Most stores are open Monday through Friday from 10am to 6pm and Saturday from 9am or 10am to about 1pm. Some stores stay open an hour or two later on Thursday or Friday, and some close for an hour at lunchtime. Most shops are closed on Sunday, except for those in downtown Pest. Shopping malls are open on weekends, sometimes as late as 9pm or 10pm.

TAXES & REFUNDS   Refunds on the 10% to 25% **value-added tax (VAT),** which is built into all prices, are available for most consumer goods purchases of more than 50,000 Ft ($250), VAT included (look for stores with the "Tax-Free" logo in the window). The refund process, however, is elaborate and confusing. In most shops, the salesperson can provide you with the necessary documents: the store receipt, a separate receipt indicating the VAT amount on your purchase, the VAT reclaim form, and the mailing envelope. The salesperson should also be able to help you fill out the paperwork. Use a separate claim form for each applicable purchase. If you are departing Hungary by plane, you can collect your refund at the **IBUSZ Agency** at Ferihegy Airport. You have to do this right after checking in but *before* you pass security control. Otherwise, hold on to the full packet until you leave Hungary and get your forms certified by Customs when you land. Then, mail in your envelope and wait for your refund. Two wrinkles: You must get your forms certified by Customs within 90 days of the purchase, and you must mail in your forms within 183 days of the date of export certification on the refund claim form. For further information, contact **Global Refund (Innova-Invest Pénzügyi Rt.),** IV. Ferenciek tere 10, 1053 Budapest (© **1/411-0157;** fax 1/411-0159; www.globalrefund.com).

SHIPPING & CUSTOMS   You can ship a box to yourself from any post office, but the rules on packing boxes are as strict as they are arcane. The Hungarian postal authorities prefer that you use one of their official shipping boxes, for sale at all post offices. They're quite flimsy, however, and have been known to break open in transit.

Very few shops will organize shipping for you. Exceptions to this rule include most Herend and Zsolnay porcelain shops, Ajka crystal shops, and certain art galleries, which employ the services of a packing-and-shipping company, Touristpost. Touristpost offers three kinds of delivery: express, air mail, and surface. At the moment, it seems that the service is not available directly to the public but functions only through these particular shops. You may inquire further at **Touristpost,** III. Meggyfa u. 31 (© **1/ 388-7465;** www.touristpost.hu). Though the service is costly (for example, 30,000 Ft/$135 for 60 lb.), you will still likely be paying less for fine porcelain and crystal purchased in Hungary than you would at home.

Hungarian Customs regulations do not limit the export of noncommercial quantities of most goods. However, the export of some food staples, like coffee (1kg) is strictly regulated (but rarely enforced). The limit on wine and spirits is 1 liter each, and 500 cigarettes may be exported. For more on Customs, see p. 12.

2 Shopping A to Z

ANTIQUES

With a rich selection of specialized shops carrying antique artifacts from keys to precious furniture, Budapest will please all bric-a-brac-adoring travelers. Nevertheless, when shopping for antiques, you should know that Hungary forbids the export of items that are designated "cultural treasures." Some purchases come with a certificate allowing export; with other purchases, the buyer has the responsibility of going to the correct office (in the Museum of Applied Arts) and applying for the certificate. Our advice is to buy only from those shops that supply the certificate for you; a journey through Hungarian bureaucracy—like any other bureaucracy—can be a withering experience.

Although it no longer has a monopoly on the sale of antiques, the state-owned trading house contingent **BÁV** (Bizományi Kereskedőház és Záloghitel Rt.; www.bav.hu) continues to control the lion's share of the antiques market in Hungary. Here's a partial list of addresses, contact information, and products for BÁV shops:

- The shop at II. Franken Leo u. 13 (© **1/315-0417**) specializes in vintage paintings, jewelry, and furniture.
- The shop at V. Bécsi u. 1 (© **1/266-2087;** fax 1/317-2548), near Deák tér, is the largest of the shops, specializing in antique furniture, chandeliers, carpets, and paintings.
- The shop at V. Ferenciek tere 10 (© **1/318-3733**) specializes in carpets and jewelry.
- The shop at V. Szent István körút 3 (© **1/473-0666**), on Pest's shopping Outer Ring, showcases antique furniture, carpets, and jewelry.
- The shop at VI. Andrássy út 43 (© **1/342-9143**), near the Opera House, specializes in antique art, furniture, carpets, porcelain, and silver.
- The shop at V. Párizsi u. 2 (© **1/318-6217**), stocks rare jewelry gems.
- The shop at IX. Tűzoltó u. 14 (© **1/215-6657**) specializes in furniture.

Located on the pedestrian beehive Váci utca, **Detre & Ferency Antikvitás,** at V. Váci utca 51 (© **1/317-7743**), draws in wide-eyed enquirers through its exquisitely furnished enormous windows. The shop specializes in world-famous Hungarian porcelains—Herend and Zsolnay, jewelry, silver, and bronze knickknacks in addition to unique glassworks. Auctions are held twice per year.

The **Empire Antique Gallery,** at Apáczai Csere János u. 4 (© **1/266-8210**), a family-owned treasure chest operating shops in Lima, Peru, and Ecuador, is located in the lush environment of the Budapest Marriott Hotel's foyer. Showcased are valuable porcelain, jewelry, silverware, numismatic medals, and paintings.

Ecclesia Szövetkezet, at V. Ferenciek tere 7 (© **1/317-3754**), next door to the Franciscan church, has authentic hand-painted icons from Russia, Bulgaria, and Ukraine, starting at around 20,000 Ft ($90); contemporary hand-painted copies start as low as 5,000 Ft ($23).

In general, Hungary has yet to find its way in creating its new artistic voice, one that finds a representative mix between all zones—past, present, and future. A few have succeeded. The **Pintér Antik Diszkont** at V. Falk Miksa u. 10 (© **1/311-3030**) stocks a widespread selection of vintage furniture, porcelain and decorative in its daedal interior, a small post-bomb shelter salon, while the **Pintér Szonja Contemporary Gallery**—located within the antiques shop—displays groundbreaking contemporary Hungarian artworks.

Anna Antiques   Carefully packed from wall-to-wall, this beautiful shop presents a nice selection of furniture and pottery while also excelling in hand-embroidered textiles. Take your time and find out more about the objects on display from the charming shop-owner. Open Monday through Friday 10am to 6pm, Saturday 10am to 3pm. V. Falk Miksa u. 18-20. ✆ **1/302-5461**. Tram: 4 or 6.

Bardoni Eurostyle Antiques   With its stay-a-while atmosphere, the store is decorated as a chic but congested living room. Bardoni carries characteristic Art Nouveau, Bauhaus, and Art Deco furniture and decoratives. Open Monday through Friday 10am to 6pm, and Saturday 10am to 2pm. V. Falk Miksa u. 12. ✆ **1/269-0090**. www.bardoni.hu. Tram: 4 or 6.

Mihálka Gallery   In this centrally located cramped gallery you'll find a wide array of 18th- and 19th-century vintage furniture, paintings, objets d'art, and interior decoratives. Open Monday through Friday 10am to 6pm, Saturday 10am to 2pm. V. Bajcsy Zsilinszky út 20. ✆ **1/302-8650**. www.mihalka.hu. Metro: Arany János u. (Blue line).

The **Ecseri Flea Market** (see "Markets," later in this chapter) also deserves mention here, as numerous private antiques dealers operate booths at this one-of-a-kind open-air market.

ART GALLERIES

Budapest is home to a developing—and still fairly quick-changing—art gallery scene. Uniquely, many art galleries are also auction houses, and vice versa. A new generation of Hungarian collectors has developed, and significant interest from European and international collectors has really fueled the development of the Hungarian modern-art market. The market for antiques is also dynamic as many objects that gathered dust over the Communist era have once again entered the market. Contemporary art, meanwhile, has made less headway in the past few years, and remains an area for future development.

Many galleries are antique-contemporary hybrid ventures that feature anything from fine art to vintage books. Export rules apply to antiques and all works of art considered to be Hungarian cultural treasures, although that list has become less expansive than it once was. Before completing a purchase, confirm that you'll be allowed to take the work out of the country; gallery proprietors should have the requisite documentation on hand.

Galleries tend to keep normal store hours (Mon–Fri 10am–6pm and Sat 10am–1 or 2pm, sometimes as late as 6pm). They're concentrated in two areas: the Inner City of Pest and Buda's Castle District. If you want to browse, the art and antiques area of Budapest runs along Falk Miksa, from Jászai Mari tér down to the parliament. A host of art galleries and antiques shops can be found along this route. The art gallery with the best taste in furniture and modern paintings is the Ernst Gallery, located adjacent to Budapest's best coffeehouse, the Centrál Coffee House.

ACB   A contemporary art–oriented gallery, ACB was founded in 2003 by a group with a business-in-art mentality and hosts frequently changing exhibitions of Hungarian and international artists. The gallery also features the eclectic, dynamic paintings, digital prints, photos, and videos collected by the founders, now described as the Irokéz Collection. Open Monday through Friday 2 to 6pm. VI. Király u. 74. ✆ **1/413-7608** or 1/413-7609. www.acbgaleria.hu.

Dorottya Gallery   Albeit oppressively austere to some, the Dorottya Gallery—which is associated with the Ernst Museum—compiles excellent contemporary installations, photographs, and media art. Open Monday through Thursday 1 to 7pm, and Friday through Sunday 11am to 7pm. V. Dorottya u. 8. ✆ **1/266-0223**. Metro: Vörösmarty tér (Yellow line).

Ernst Gallery   The gallery features fine and applied arts from Hungary and around Europe. The Ernst Gallery, the most posh gallery in town, is run by a dynamic duo of the Austrian-born Ernst Wastl and his Greek-born wife, Eleni Korani. They put together exhibitions, discover "unknown" Hungarian artists, and whatever they put their hands onto ends up being the talk of the town. The gallery also exhibits and sells fine furniture and a wealthy collection of rarities including vintage art books, posters, and other curiosities. Open Monday through Friday 10am to 7pm, and Saturday 10am to 2pm. V. Irányi u. 27. ✆ 1/266-4016 or 1/266-4017. www.ernstgaleria.hu. Metro: Ferenciek tér (Blue line).

Godot Gallery   Located beside the cafe of the same name, Godot opened its door to the arty crowd in 1999 in order to present a new, dynamic space for contemporary Hungarian art. Exhibitions follow distinctly anti-mainstream themes, and this is reflected in the uneven quality of the works displayed. Open Monday through Friday 10am to 6pm. VII. Madách I. u. 8. ✆ 1/322-5272. www.godot.hu. Metro: Deák tér (all lines).

kArton Gallery   Run by the art institution kArton, kArton and its sister **raktArt** gallery feature a colorful segment of contemporary visual art—focusing under-appreciated genres like comics, illustrations, and cartoons. Open Monday through Friday 1 to 6pm, and Saturday 10am to 2pm. V. Alkotmány u. 18. ✆ 1/472-0000. www.karton.hu. Metro: Ferenciek tere (Blue line).

K.A.S. Gallery   The Studio of Contemporary Artists, K.A.S. is run by the go-getter art curator Ilona Nyakas. It is a small, cozy space smack in the touristy epicenter of the pedestrian shopping street. The Gallery presents the works of young local artists. Open Monday through Friday noon to 5:30pm. V. Váci u. 36. ✆ 1/318-2084. Metro: Ferenciek tere (Blue line).

Kieselbach Gallery and Auction House   Established and directed by art historian Tamás Kieselbach, the Kieselbach gallery functions as a gallery and auction-house. It also puts on museum-type shows that present artworks from private collections at biannual non-selling exhibitions. The gallery specializes in paintings from Hungarian artists between 1850 and 1950. Auctions are held twice a year. Open Monday through Friday 10am to 6pm, and Saturday and Sunday 10am to 1pm. V. Szent István körút 5. ✆ 1/269-3148 or 1/269-2210. www.kieselbach.hu. Tram: 4 or 6 to Jászai Mari tér.

Liget Gallery   Curator and art critic Tibor Várnagy has run this gallery since 1983. The Liget (Grove) gallery in the City Park features nonprofit exhibitions, an open, easygoing artistic space for performances, film screenings, and concerts. Highlights are the socially conscious artwork of local talents. Open Wednesday through Monday 2 to 6pm. XIV. Ajtósi Dürer sor 5. ✆ 1/351-4924. www.c3.hu/~ligal. Metro: Hősök tere (Yellow line).

Mû-terem Gallery and Auction House   Established and directed by art historian Judit Virág and her husband, István Törö, this gallery also functions as an auction house. Similar to their main competitors, the Kieselbach Gallery, this gallery also puts on museum-type shows presenting artworks from private collections. Paintings by 19th- and 20th-century Hungarian artists are found here, a gallery that regularly produces record-setting prices for artists. Auctions are held twice a year. Open Monday through Friday 10am to 6pm, and Saturday and Sunday 10am to 1pm. V. Falk Miksa u. 30. ✆ 1/269-3148 or 1/269-2210. www.mu-terem.hu. Tram: 4 or 6 to Jászai Mari tér.

Nagykázi Galéria és Aukcióház   Hungarian and international artists, furniture, and classical European artworks are found in this gallery and auction house. Up to ten auctions are held yearly. Open Monday through Friday 10am to 6pm, and Saturday and Sunday 10am to 2pm. V. Balaton u. 8. ✆ . www.nagyhazi.hu. Tram: 4 or 6 to Jászai Mari tér.

⟮Finds⟯ Hungarian Art Market: From Bust to Boom

Over the past decade and a half, Hungarian artworks, including those of modern Hungarian masters such as Jószef Rippl-Ronai, Béla Iványi Grünwald, Béla Kádár, and Armand Shöenberger, have been gaining popularity among both Hungarian and international collectors.

As a result after a decade-old transition from communism to a market-driven economy in Hungary, the art market has gone from bust to boom as collectors discover the works of classical and modern Hungarian artists. Even in the U.S., paintings are fetching record-breaking prices. In the spring of 2005, a Jozsef Rippl-Ronai (1861-1927) painting called *Girl with a Cage* (1891-92) was auctioned off to Budapest-based art dealer Ernst Wastl of Ernst Gallery (see listing in this section) for a whopping $590,400.

The market within Hungary itself has been particularly active. Many artworks are returning to Hungary after having been dispersed during World War II, or the subsequent Communist era. Before World War II, Hungarian private collectors amassed notable collections, although many of these were pillaged by Nazi Germany and later Soviet Russia after the war. (Many of Hungary's pre-war cultural treasures to this day are thought to be in Russia, and their return is the subject of protracted and heated negotiations between the two countries, which seem to be getting nowhere.)

You can see this feeding frenzy for Hungarian art at spring and fall auctions in Budapest, which fill to capacity (with some also bidding on the phone from international locations). Visitors watch in awe as records are broken almost on a yearly basis. Paintings that only a decade ago may have fetched $15,000, can now fetch ten times that, especially if you are talking about internationally renowned artists like Mihály Munkácsy.

The auction-house scene in Hungary has become so popular that in contrast to North America or Europe, most of the important private galleries have created a dual system of being both auction houses and galleries. See the art galleries listed in this section, and call or inquire in person for their auction schedules.

Stúdió Gallery The frequently changing exhibitions feature the works of Hungarian art students. If you're looking for the zest of the new-art trend, don't miss out on this studio. Open Monday through Saturday 2 to 6pm. V. Képíró u. 6. ℂ **1/267-2033.** Metro: Kálvin tér (Blue line).

Várfok Gallery An art dealer by the name of Károly Szalóky has an ambitious plan to transform Várfok utca in the Castle District into a street of contemporary Hungarian art galleries. He has already opened two new galleries on the street, **Spiritusz** and **XO Gallery** (ℂ 1/214-0373). The main gallery—Várfok—features a fine mix of old and novel Hungarian artwork. Open Tuesday through Saturday 11am to 6pm. I. Várfok u. 14. ℂ **1/213-5155.** www.varfok-galeria.hu. Take the Castle Shuttle bus from Moszkva tér.

ART SUPPLIES

Hobbyművész   Feeling crafty? Jam-packed with do-it-yourself decor equipment, this craft-chain store offers jewelry, painting, drawing, and candle-creating accessories in every style, form, and size. Open Monday through Friday 11am to 7pm, Saturday 10am to 3pm. II. Margit körút 3. © **1/212-2807.** www.hobbymuvesz.hu. Tram: 4-6. Two other shops in the city center are at VIII. Üllői út 36, © **1/212-1938,** and VI. Nagymező u. 45–47, © **1/311-7040.**

Kéregvirág—RAKU Bt.   Serving and boosting creative ideas, this store features handmade "barkflower-paper" decoratives and accessories. Kéregvirág goodies include paper-flower ornaments, boxes, sachets, and office equipment. XXII. Vasút u. 1. © **1/207-3216.** www.keregvirag.hu. Bus: 3.

Neoart   For the amateur and professional artist, Neoart offers a wide selection of watercolors, oil paints, and acrylic paints, as well as brushes, drawing materials, canvas, and paper. Open Monday through Friday 9am to 5pm. VI. Bajcsy köz. 3. © **1/353-3750.** Metro: Arany János u. (Blue line).

BEAUTY & HEALTH

Bio-Mania   Combatting chemically "infected" products and unhealthy lifestyles, the store features bio-produced medicinal and health-supportive products in addition to cosmetics. Open weekdays from 10am to 6pm. XIII. Pannónia u. 57. © **20/477-4569.** www.bio-bolt.hu. Metro: Lehel tér (Blue line).

Ilcsi Beautifying Herbs   All women want beauty—some have it and some know how to "create" it. Mrs. Daniel Molnár and son, Ferenc Molnár—creators of Ilcsi—know. Over 130 products—made from 65 to 70 herbs, fruits, vegetables, and water—build the base of this enterprise, one that strengthens the legend of the beauty of Hungarian girls. Be sure to make an appointment well in advance in one of the many shops listed on www.ilcsi.com. Open weekdays from 7am to 7pm. V. Nagymező u. 19. © **1/312-8339.** Metro: Oktogon or Opera (Yellow line).

Lush   Lush creates outstanding, environmentally friendly soaps out of purely organic materials such as pine, lavender, orange, avocado, or banana. Take a long, relaxing balmy bubble bath in French Kiss, Hot Milk, Turbo Bubble, or Blue Skies aroma-bars. Other Lush stores can be found in MOM Park and Árkád shopping malls. Open Monday through Friday 10am to 7pm, Saturday 10am to 2pm. V. Szent István krt. 1. © **1/472-0530.** www.lush.hu. Take tram 4 or 6.

Rossmann   A mainstream brand of cosmetics, perfumery, and pharmaceuticals, Rossman operates 150 outlets around the country. They carry more than your ordinary drugstore, so you can find quick birthday gifts like cheap CDs, home décor, and even munchies for your favorite pet. Open Monday through Friday 8am to 7pm, Saturday 9am to 2pm. V. Kossuth L. u. 12. No phone.

BOOKSTORES

Bestsellers   Bestsellers is Budapest's first English-language bookstore (opened in 1992). With its spacious and bright interior, the shop is a popular meeting spot for English-speaking travelers. The store has a wide selection of fiction, as well as a reasonably good collection of travel books, including books on Hungary. A wide selection of newspapers and magazines is also available. (***Note:*** The owner also runs **Király Books,** at I. Fő u. 79, which has a fair selection of guidebooks, maps, and language books in mostly English and French; call © **1/214-0972.**) Open Monday through

Friday 9am to 6:30pm, Saturday 10am to 5pm, Sunday 10am to 4pm. V. Október 6 u. 11. ℂ **1/312-1295.** Metro: Arany János utca (Blue line).

Biblioteka Antikvárium   At the head of Andrássy út, near Bajcsy-Zsilinszky út, this is one of central Pest's better *antikvária* (old and rare bookshops). The store has a fine selection of English-language books, and a variety of maps, prints, and engravings adding to the stock of over 25,000 volumes. Open Monday through Friday 10am to 6pm, Saturday 9am to 1pm. VI. Andrássy út 2. ℂ **1/475-0240.** Metro: Deák tér (all lines).

Central European University Bookstore   This store features books covering a wide variety of disciplines. The selection of books on central and eastern European politics and history is particularly notable since the Central European University Press publishes a great variety of books on all topics central European (visit www.ceu press.com). Open Monday through Friday 10am to 6pm. V. Nádor utca 9. ℂ **1/327-3097.** Metro: Kossuth tér (Red line) or Arany János utca (Blue line).

Honterus Antikvárium és Aukciós Ház Kft.   Located near the Központi Antikvárium, across the street from the Hungarian National Museum (Nemzeti Múzeum), this shop has more prints and maps on display than any other antikvárium in town—suitably, since the shop was named after János Honter, a renowned Transylvanian map master. There's a shelf of mostly arcane, out-of-date English-language academic books as well as a stack of *National Geographic* magazines. Broadening its activity, the shop hosts auctions specializing in Hungarian literary curios. Open Monday through Friday 10am to 6pm, Saturday 10am to 2pm. V. Múzeum krt. 35. ℂ **1/267-2642.** www.honterus.hu. Metro: Astoria (Red line) or Kálvin tér (Blue line).

Írók Boltja 🎯🎯   The "Writers' Bookshop"—a true literary center with a rich history, first-rate literary events, and inspired window displays—is a mecca for writers, readers, and curious bystanders. In the first half of the last century the store was the popular Japanese Coffee House, a popular literary coffeeshop, then became the Spark Bookstore around 1955, during the Communist era. The shop's name was changed around 1958, and was state-run until 1991, when 14 employees became the co-owners during the privatization of state-owned business. It is now practically an institution, and Hungarian authors such as Péter Nádas, Péter Eszterházy, and Nobel-prize winner Imre Kertész have read here. Almost all events are held in Hungarian, but the store has a nice selection of English-language books, plus a cozy in-store coffee corner. Open Monday through Friday 10am to 6pm, Saturday 10am to 1pm. VI. Andrássy út 45. ℂ **1/322-1645.** www.irokboltja.hu. Metro: Oktogon (Yellow line).

Központi Antikvárium   Central Antikvárium is the city's oldest and largest old and rare bookstore. Indeed, it is said to be the largest of its type in all of central Europe. Opened in 1881 across the street from the Hungarian National Museum on "Antikvárium Row" (Múzeum krt. was the antikvárium street during the pre–World War I era, home to 37 different shops at that time), this shop has books, prints, maps, and a shelf of assorted knickknacks. Open Monday through Friday 10am to 6.30pm, Saturday 10am to 2pm. V. Múzeum krt. 13–15. ℂ **1/317-3514.** Metro: Astoria (Red line) or Kálvin tér (Blue line).

Libri Studium Könyvesbolt   This is the only bookstore—among the dozen Libri bookstore chains—left on Váci utca, which was formerly home to many, many bookstores. This is a good option for those in search of English-language books (mostly Corvina books) about Budapest or Hungary. Coffee-table books, guidebooks, fiction and poetry in translation, and scholarly works are available. There's also a good selection of maps, including the hard-to-find Cartographia trail map of the Buda Hills *(A Budai Hegység).* Open Monday through Friday 10am to 6:30pm, and weekends 10am to 3pm. V. Váci u. 22. © 1/318-5680. www.libri.hu. Metro: Vörösmarty tér (Yellow line) or Deák tér (all lines).

Litea: Literature & Tea Bookshop   Situated in the Fortuna courtyard, opposite the Hilton Hotel, this bookshop/teahouse stocks a wide range of books on Hungary; CDs and cassettes of the works of Hungarian composers; and cards, maps, and other quality souvenirs for serious enthusiasts of Hungarian culture. Take your time browsing, order a cup of tea, sit, and have a closer look at the books that interest you. This calm, no-obligation-to-buy atmosphere is a rare find. Open daily 10am to 6pm. I. Hess András tér 4. © 1/375-6987. www.litea.hu. Bus: Várbusz from Moszkva tér, bus 16 from Deák tér, or funicular from Clark Ádám tér, to Castle Hill.

Red Bus Bookstore   A paperback sanctuary specializing in classical literature, thrillers, and fiction, this pocket-size purely English-language secondhand bookstore is the perfect place to pop in for quick book trade or to find some hidden literary gems. Look out for the bobtail opening hours: Monday through Friday 11am to 7pm, Saturday between 10am and 2pm. V. Semmelweis u. 14. © 1/337-7453. Metro: Astoria (Red line).

COINS
Globe Numizmatikai Galéria   This small shop, not far from Deák tér and a block from the CEU Bookshop, in a quiet part of the Inner City, has a variety of coins and antique paper money for sale. Of particular note (no pun intended) are the Roman coins, a reminder of the far reach of the Roman Empire. Open Monday through Thursday 9:30am to 3pm, Friday 9:30am to 2pm. V. Nádor u. 5. © 1/337-7940. Metro: Deák tér (all lines).

DEPARTMENT STORES & MALLS
A plethora of new American-style malls has sprung up in Budapest over the past decade and a half, and has proven immensely popular to Budapesters. **Duna Plaza,** XII. Váci út 178 (© 1/465-1666; www.dunaplaza.net), was the first mall built and boasts 120 different shops (including a Virgin Records Megastore), a nine-screen "Hollywood Multiplex," snack bars and pubs, and the best bowling alley in the city. Duna Plaza is open daily 10am to 9pm; the entertainment complex closes later than the rest of the mall.

Pólus Center, at XV. Szentmihályi út 131 (© 1/415-2114; www.polus.com), is home to **TESCO,** the British supermarket chain (the only place in town, we believe, where Marmite is sold!), as well as to countless other shops. Wings in the mall have flashy American street names: Rodeo Drive, Sunset Boulevard, Wall Street. Open weekdays 10am to 8pm, weekends 10am to 6pm. A mall shuttle bus, bus 173 orbus no. 73 (red-lettered), departs for Polus Center from Keleti train station.

Tips Looking for Coins

In addition to visiting Globe Numizmatikai Galéria (see above), coin enthusiasts might also want to visit the several coin shops across the street from the Dohány utca Synagogue, near Astoria (Red line metro).

Built in Polus Center's proximity, **Asia Center** at XV district. Szentmihályi út 167–169 (📞 **1/688-8888**; www.asiacenter.hu), opened its doors in 2003 to myriad Asian-produced products from clothing to furniture. The second wing of the mall will be completed by 2008. Take Polus mall shuttle or no. 73 (red-lettered) departing from Keleti train station.

WestEnd City Center at VI district. Váci út 1–3 (📞 **1/238-7777**), the behemoth mall opened in 2000 right behind Nyugati Railway Station, has generated much concern about the future of downtown shops and boutiques, and has led to the demise of numerous small businesses in the immediate area of the Outer Ring boulevard. Within its 400 some-odd shops, however, a rich selection of stores makes it a must-see for shoppers. Take a breather from shopping and relax on the open-air garden roof-terrace. It is open daily from 8am to 11pm.

Opened in 2002, **Árkád,** District X. Örs vezér tere 25 (📞 **1/433-1400**; www. arkad.hu) is the youngest mall in the city. The thronged German-owned mall comprises some of the most trendy stores from Marks & Spencer, C&A, Mexx, Nike, and Zara. The large circular cafe/restaurants in the heart of the mall tend to rapidly fill up in the afternoon. Take the Red line metro to Örs Vezér tér.

On Buda, **Mammut,** next to **Millenáris,** the entertainment park that was built on the site of the old Ganz industrial area, is a 1998 construction. With a glass passageway connecting the two wings, the mall was extended in 2001, and thus comprises over 300 shops. It is located at II. Lövőház u. 2–6 (📞 **1/345-8024**; www.mammut.hu), incorporating Fény utca market, near Moszkva tér (Red line metro), and is open Monday through Saturday 10am to 9pm, and Sunday 10am to 6pm.

EuroCenter Óbuda District III, Bécsi út 154 (📞 **1/437-4660**; www.eurocenter-obuda.hu) and **Új Udvar,** District III. Bécsi út 38–44 (📞 **1/437-8200**; www.uj-udvar.hu), are mediocre malls in Buda mostly targeted at locals. Shops have individual opening hours although both malls are generally open Monday through Friday 10am to 9pm. Take tram no. 18 from the Buda side of the Margit Bridge.

Built near the Budapest Congress Center, among the most recent malls is the **MOM Park,** District XII. Alkotás utca 53 (📞 **1/487-5500**; www.mompark.hu), a spacious, sophisticated new conglomerate. Home to one of three Palace Cinemas (operating the first digital multiplex in central Europe), plus a chic interior design boutique called Goa and a trendy Italian shoe shop by designer Alberto Zago. Open daily 7am to midnight. Take tram no. 61 or 59 from Moszkva tér.

With a handful of small shops and boutiques, **Budagyöngye,** District II, Szilágyi Erzsébet fasor 121 (📞 **1/275-0839**; www.budagyongye.com), is hardly the "pearl of Buda" as its name implies, but it manages to adequately cater the needs of its regular local crowd. It's open Monday through Friday from 9am to 7pm, Saturday 9.30am to 2pm, and Sunday 10am to 1.30pm. Take bus no. 56 or tram no. 61 from Moszkva tér.

The humdrum **Europark,** District XIX. Üllői út 201 (📞 **1/347-1549**; www. europark.hu); **Campona,** District XXII. Nagytétényi út 37–43 (📞 **1/424-3000**; www. campona.hu); and the functional **Csepel Pláza,** District XXI. Rákóczi Ferenc út 154–170 (📞 **1/425-8111**; www.csepelplaza.net) are all located in the outskirts of Budapest and hard to get to without a car.

Sprawling Örs vezér tere, the eastern terminus of the Red metro line, is home to Budapest's branch of the internationally known Swedish furniture store **IKEA,** District XIV. Örs vezer tere (📞 **1/460-3100**; www.ikea.hu), and the city's first quasi-American-style mall, **Sugár.** The mall is open Monday through Friday from 9am to

6pm and weekends from 9am to 2pm. Individual shops within the mall set their own hours.

Closer to the center of the city, try the retro evergreen **Skála Metro,** at Nyugati tér across from Nyugati Station, or the equally popular **Buda Skála,** on Október 23 utca, near Móricz Zsigmond körtér. Both are open Monday through Friday from 10am to 6pm and on Saturday from 9am to 1pm.

At Váci utca 16, the **Fontana Department Store** houses the latest in men's and women's international designer fashions. There's an elegant perfumery and a cafe on the top floor. Open Monday through Friday from 10am to 7pm and Saturday until 3pm. Farther along the street at Vörösmarty tér 3, **Luxus Áruház** (© **1/318-2277**) specializes in mainly men's and women's fashion and accessories.

FASHION & SHOES

We list just a few options, assuming that you'll discover the rest on your own. For discount clothes, see "Markets," later in the chapter.

Ciánkáli   Called the Anti-Fashion Shop, this "high-quality" secondhand shop chain sells vintage junk and alternative-punk modish collections and accessories. They also display a large selection of funky brand-new items. Look for the wide selection of leather clothing. Open Monday through Friday 10am to 7pm, Saturday 10am to 2pm. VII. Dohány u. 68. © **1/341-0540.** Metro: Blaha Lujza tér (Red line).

Emilia Anda   Mixing organic materials like silk with plastic or paper, the noted young designer Emilia Anda's clothes make heads turn. Her studies in architecture paved the way for creating her inimitable lustrous get-ups, one that stands out in the Hungarian fashion world. Open Monday through Friday noon to 6pm, Saturday 11am to 2pm. V. Váci u. 16/b. No phone. Metro: Vörösmarty tér (Yellow line).

Iguana   Looking for some sparkling oversized grandma-glasses or perhaps crazy '60s or '70s cult accessories? A shrine for retro-rats, the shop stocks rows of peace jackets, trousers, bags, and jewelry. Listen to or purchase some of their all-star euphoric secondhand CDs. Open Monday through Friday 11am to 7pm, Saturday 10am to 2pm. VIII. Krúdy Gyula u. 9. No phone. www.iguanaretro.hu. Metro: Kálvin tér (Blue line). There is a second store at XI. Tompa u. 1. No phone. Tram: 4 or 6.

Katti Zoób   Celebrated Hungarian fashion designer Zoób's high-end couture ranges from slick, eccentric, yet harmonious businesswomen's outfits to smart and naughty on-the-go-wear and accessories. The shop, located in the capacious MOM Park, is open Monday through Saturday 10am to 8pm, Sunday 10am to 6pm. XII. Alkotás u. 53. © **1/487-5609.** www.kattizoob.com. Tram: 59 or 61.

Katalin Hampel   Put on the Hungarian design map with her unique marriage of traditional Hungarian clothing with a modern flair, Katalin Hampel designs women's clothing marked by delicate precision of handmade embroidery. Open Monday through Friday 10am to 6pm, Saturday 10am to 1pm. V. Váci u. 8. © **1/318-9741.** www.tangoantique. com. Metro: Vörösmarty tér (Yellow line).

La Boutique   Showcasing the products of significant high-end shoe designers, the shop specializes in men's shoes and the prices match Western designer label prices. Open Monday through Friday 10am to 7pm, and Saturday 10am to 4pm. VI. Andrássy út 16. © **1/302-5646.** Metro: Opera (Yellow line).

Látomás   Run by 25 suave-creative designers, the shop is a fresh addition to the growing Hungarian fashion marketplace. The sexy, chic, and unique hats, jewelry, and

Extreme Fashion! Budapest's Avant-Garde Designers

While Hungary can't compete with the fashion capitals of Paris, New York, or Milan, some trailblazers in the Hungarian fashion world are setting the foundations again. They remember Hungary's pre-war glamour, when Budapest was termed the "Paris of Eastern Europe," a notion quashed by years of Communism and its attacks on creative self-expression. Now, several established designers like **Tamás Náray** and **Katti Zoób** are catering to the new upperclass with some posh, pricey designs.

Tamás Király, meanwhile, is a true creative visionary who puts on shows everywhere from New York to London—including several with the noted designer Vivienne Westwood. Király is more of a fashion artist than a "label" designer. He creates designs that could come out of some fantasy dreamscape, and he takes part in numerous "performances." Don't be surprised if you see a model walking around Budapest with bizarre metallic structures, followed by another in a costume and on crutches, with another eating cotton candy off of the body of yet another model. If you see one of these avant-garde fashion performances, it is likely that the event was dreamed up by Tamás Király. If you decide to buy one of the creations, though, you may be disappointed. They are probably not for sale. Király truly lives on the outer edges of the classical "fashion world," all while being in the center of a unique creative world. He considers himself, meanwhile, the "most free designer in the universe."

For more on the Budapest fashion scene, visit Pep! Magazine's website, **www.pepmagazin.hu** (click "English") or the Budapest fashion blog **www. bpfashion.hu** (English version promised for mid-2006).

For information on Budapest Fashion Weeks, see **www.budapestfashion week.com** and **www.fashionweek.hu**.

accessories are intended mostly for women—although men might find some must-have's as well. Browse through their spicy secondhand clothing stock as well. Open Monday through Friday 11 to 7pm, Saturday 11am to 3pm. VII. Dohány u. 20. No phone. Tram: 4 or 6.

Manu-Art   Handmade by local designers, these warm clothes are likely to cheer up those who work in the cool outdoors. Odd fluffy sheep, crazy snails, or curlicue non-figurative designs suit all ages. Open Monday through Friday 10am to 7pm, Saturday 10am to 2pm. You'll find a second store in the busy Mammut mall (same phone). V. Károly krt. 10 © **1/266-8136.** Metro: Astoria (Red line).

Náray Tamás   Situated in the posh Ybl Palace, across from the Central Kávéház, this elegant and spacious shop sells the creations of one of Hungary's most celebrated designers, Tamás Náray. The clothes are tasteful, yet the materials used have much to be desired. The cutting-edge status of the collection is reflected in the extreme price range. Monday through Friday noon to 8pm, Saturday 10am to 2pm. V. Károlyi M. u. 12. © **1/266-2473.** Metro: Ferenciek tere (Blue line).

Retrock A group of young contemporary designers swimming against the mainstream fashion-current established this colorful boutique comprising one-of-a-kind clothes and accessories. Sanctuary for extreme fashion aficionados. Open Monday through Friday 10:30am to 7:30pm, Saturday 10:30am to 4:30pm. V. Ferenczy István u. 28. (✆ 1/318-1007. www.retrock.com. Metro: Astoria (Red line).

Tisza Cipő A former Soviet-era brand, Tisza Shoes has been smartly resuscitated into a retro shoe brand that shot up on the must-have shoes in Hungary. It is now enjoying its laid-back high-end segment market position. Open Monday through Friday 10am to 6pm, Saturday 10am to 2pm. VII. Károly körút 1. (✆ 1/266-3055. www.tisza cipo.hu. Metro: Astoria (Red line).

V50 Design Art Studio ⚡ Fashion designer Valeria Fazekas has an eye for clothes that are both eye-catching and elegant. Her hats are works of art. Prices are reasonable, but she does not accept credit cards. She has a second shop at V. Belgrád rakpart 16, where she can often be found working late into the night in the upstairs studio. Both shops are open Monday through Friday 10am to 6pm, Saturday 10am to 2pm. V. Váci u. 50. (✆ 1/337-5320. Metro: Ferenciek tere (Blue line).

Vakondgyár Hungarian youth fashion, this T-shirt boutique chain features outrageous shirts designed by a whimsical young artist. Starting with the mole figure—the cute key character that gave the brand its name—the shirts' self-indulgent designs include fanciful insects, goofy Hungarian cartoon characters, and other New Age logo-like creations in a cacophony of color. Open Monday through Friday 10am to 6pm, Saturday 10am to 1pm. V. Magyar u. 52. (✆ 20/222-5295. Metro: Kálvin tér (Blue line).

FOLK CRAFTS

Except for a few specialty shops like the ones listed below, the stores of the formerly state-owned **Folkart Háziipar** should be your main source for Hungary's justly famous folk items. Almost everything sold at these stores is handmade—from tablecloths to miniature dolls, from ceramic dishes to sheepskin vests. You can shop with the knowledge that a jury has examined all items for authenticity. Look for the distinctive label (or sticker) that will let you know that you are looking at a Folkart product: a circle with a bird in the center, surrounded by the words FOLKART/ NÉPMŰVÉSZETI HUNGARY. The private folk-art shops lining Váci utca and the streets of the Castle District tend to be much more expensive than Folkart, and their products, unlike Folkart's, often tend toward the kitschy (though with some notable exceptions).

The Art of MAG Design Jewelry

Nine gifted jewelry artists joined forces in 2001 and now offer quality jewelry under the label **MAG Design**, managed and directed by the friendly Péter Lipták. Best in show: Klára Abaffy combines silver with various exotic materials; Eszter Zámori works with gold, silver, and colourful precious stones (and some pieces make slight sounds as you move); and Gyöngyvér Gaál once combined miniature flowers with silver, coral, and polyester. See the MAG Design wares and talk to Peter in the **VAM Design Gallery**, which is open Monday to Friday from 8am to 6pm (Tuesdays from 1pm to 4pm), at Váci utca 62-64 ((✆ 30/984-3616).

Folkart's main store, **Folkart Centrum,** has been relocated to the upper end of the mall at V. Váci u. 58 (© **1/318-4697**) and is open daily 10am to 7pm.

One outstanding private shop on Váci utca is **Vali Folklór,** in the courtyard of Váci u. 23 (© **1/337-6301**). A soft-spoken man named Bálint Ács runs this cluttered shop. Ács travels through the villages of Hungary and neighboring countries buying up authentic folk items. He's extremely knowledgeable about the products he sells, and he enjoys speaking with customers (in German or English). When he is not around, his elderly mother keeps shop (she doesn't speak English). The most appealing items here are the traditional women's clothing and the jewelry boxes. From time to time, the store features marvelous, genuine Russian icons. The store has recently expanded its collection to include a great variety of now-hard-to-find Soviet and east European Communist-era pins, medals, and badges, with fair prices. Bálint Ács' mother can tailor clothing for your size in 3 to 4 days. Open Monday through Friday 10am to 6pm, Saturday and Sunday 10am to 7pm (sometimes closed on weekends; call ahead).

Holló Folkart Gallery, at V. Vitkovics Mihály u. 12 (© **1/317-8103**), is an unusual gallery selling handcrafted reproductions of original folk-art pieces from various regions of the country. Beautiful carved and painted furniture is for sale, as are small mirrors, decorative boxes, traditional decorative pottery, and wooden candlesticks. Open Monday through Friday from 10am to 6pm, Saturday 10am to 2pm.

FOR KIDS

Kenguru Kuckó   Providing a holistic supply of mandatory kids' gear, the shop has an extensive selection of clothing, toys, books, and accessories. Choose and schedule one of their entertaining children's events for the weekend. Open on weekdays from 10am to 6pm. II. Margit krt. 34. © **1/212-4780**. Metro: Nyugati Pályaudvar (Blue line).

Kis Herceg Gyermekdivat (Little Prince Children's Fashion)   Infant and children's clothes and shoes are sold here. You'll find everything from swimsuits to ski jackets in bright sunny colors and adorable prints. Open Monday through Friday 9am to 5pm, Saturday 9am to 1pm. VI. Andrássy u. 55. © **1/342-9268**. Metro: Oktogon (Yellow line).

GIFTS & HOME DECOR

Ban Sabai   Assisting in creating a sensual and warm home, Ban Sabai—meaning calm, perfect home—features various lush gift or interior design objects brought from mystical Thailand. Open Monday through Friday 10:30am to 7pm, Saturday 10am to 2pm. VI. Jókai u.5. © **1/707-6564**. Metro: Oktogon (Yellow line).

BoConcept   Variability—a keyword in interior design—is the essence of this high-class Danish design store. True to its masterful Danish design roots, this store offers a stylish selection of couches, chairs, beds, and accessories. Get organized. Fashionably. Open Monday through Friday 10am to 7pm, Saturday 10am to 5pm, Sunday 11am to 3pm. Óbuda Gate Shopping Center. II. Árpád Fejedelem útja 26-28. www.boconcept.hu. © **1/346-3040**. Tram: 17, or bus 60 or 86.

BomoArt   This jam-packed shop stocks unique handmade paper "artworks"—boxes, stationery, and diaries. Seductive nature-inspired decorative accessories further stimulate visitors to set the inner creator free. V. Régiposta u. 14. © **1/318-7280**. Metro: Deák tér (all lines) or Astoria (Red line).

Demko Feder   The best way of ensuring a calm, quality night's rest is to pamper yourself with the praised pure wool, bio bedding products of Demko Feder. The company specializes in ultra-comfortable pillows, back-sparing bed interiors, and other interior design products. Open Monday through Friday 10am to 6pm, Saturday 10am to 1pm. V. József Attila u. 20. © **1/212-4408**. www.demko.hu. Metro: Deák tér (all lines).

Goa Love   Taking over Provence design—continuing to feature furnishings for the home in the spirit of Provence—this charming interior decorating and design shop specializes in singular wedding presents and Japan ceramics. Open Monday through Friday 10am to 6pm, and Saturday 10am to 2pm. VII. Király u. 19. © **1/352-8449**. Metro: Deák tér (all lines).

Roomba Home Culture   Created by talented brothers Oszkár and Bence Vági, this novel furniture and design shop offers sizzling trendy yet reasonably priced designs, decorations, and accessories. V. Arany János u. 29. © **1/374-0570**. Metro: Arany János u. (Blue line).

MARKETS
Markets in Budapest are very crowded, bustling places. Beware of pickpockets; carry your valuables under your clothing in a money belt rather than in a wallet (see "Staying Safe" on p. 21 in chapter 2, "Planning Your Trip to Budapest").

OPEN MARKETS (PIAC)
Ecseri Flea Market   According to a local rumor you can find anything at this busy flea market—from eviscerated bombshells to dinosaur eggs. True? Well, you seem to believe it once inside. You are greeted by rows of wooden tables chock-full of old dishes, toys, linens, and bric-a-brac as you enter this market at Nagykörösi út 156. From the tiny cubicles in the narrow corridors, serious dealers market their wares: Herend and Zsolnay porcelain, Bulgarian and Russian icons, silverware, paintings, furniture, clocks, rugs, prewar dolls and stuffed animals, antique clothing, and jewelry. Due to all the tourist attention—mostly during the weekend—the prices of the market have increased severely although some bargains can still be made. Antiques buyers: Be aware that you'll need permission from the Museum of Applied Arts to take your purchases out of the country (p. 182). Haggling is standard and necessary. Purchases are in cash only. The market runs Monday through Friday 8am to 2pm, Saturday 6am to 2pm, Sunday 8am to 1pm. XIX. Nagykörösi út. © **1/280-8840**. Take bus 54 from Boráros tér.

Józsefvárosi Piac   The market closest to the city center, the Józsefvárosi piac is informally known as "Four Tigers," an allusion to the tremendous presence of Chinese vendors. The piac, situated on the side of a railroad yard, near the Józsefváros Station, is not really a flea market, since most of the goods are not secondhand. But you'll find bargains aplenty: Chinese silk, Turkish dresses, Russian caviar, vodka, the occasional piece of Stalinist memorabilia, toy tanks, Romanian socks, slippers, and chalky-tasting chocolate. Also for sale are dishes, clocks, pens, combs, clothes, tea, and east European condoms. All prices are negotiable. Dozens of languages are spoken in the tightly packed, crowded lanes of this outdoor market, which operates daily from 6am to 6pm. Feel free to flex your bargaining muscles here. VIII. Kőbányai út. © **1/313-8890**. Take tram 28 from Blaha Lujza tér (Red line metro) or 36 from Baross tér (Keleti Station, Red line metro), and get off at Orczy tér.

PECSA Flea Market   Located in the area of the open-air stage at Petäfi Csarnok, this market is little known by travelers. In the midst of the enchanting Városliget (City Park), this market features a wide array of offerings, from vintage to brand-new bric-a-brac, antique jewelry, books, clothing, and electronic equipment. This place is where you can find a bargain, where few tourists have ventured to date. Open on weekends from 7am to 2pm. XIV. Zichy Mihály út 14. © **1/363-3730**. www.pecsa.hu. A short walk in the park from Hősök tere (Heroes' Square) (Yellow line).

FRUIT & VEGETABLE MARKETS (*CSARNOK* OR *PIAC*)

There are five vintage market halls *(vásárcsarnok)* in Budapest. These vast cavernous spaces, architectural wonders of steel and glass, were built in the 1890s in the ambitious grandiose style of the time. Three are still in use as markets and provide a measure of local color you certainly won't find in the grocery store. Hungarian produce in season is sensational, and you'll seldom go wrong with a kilo of strawberries, a cup of raspberries, or a couple of peaches.

The **Központi Vásárcsarnok (Central Market Hall)**, at IX. Vámház körút 1–3 (© **1/217-6067**), is the largest and most spectacular market hall. Located on the Inner Ring (Kiskörút), just on the Pest side of the Szabadság Bridge, it was impeccably reconstructed in 1995. This bright, three-level market hall is a pleasure to visit. Fresh produce, meat, and cheese vendors dominate the space. Keep your eyes open for inexpensive saffron and dried mushrooms. The mezzanine level features folk-art booths, coffee and drink bars, and fast-food booths. The basement level houses fishmongers, pickled goods, a complete selection of spices, and Asian import foods, along with a large grocery store. The market is open Monday 6am to 5pm, Tuesday through Friday 6am to 6pm, Saturday 6am to 2pm. The nearest metro station is Kálvin tér (Blue line).

The recently restored **Belvárosi Vásárcsarnok (Inner City Market Hall)**, at V. Hold utca 13 (© **1/476-3952**), is located in central Pest in the heart of the Lipótváros (Leopold Town), behind the Hungarian National Band at Szabadság tér. It houses a large supermarket and several cheesy discount clothing shops, in addition to a handful of independent fruit-and-vegetable vendors. The market is open Monday 6:30am to 5pm, Tuesday through Friday 6:30am to 6pm, Saturday from 6:30am to 2pm. Take the metro either to Kossuth tér (Red line) or Arany János utca (Blue line).

The **Rákóczi téri Vásárcsarnok**, at VIII. Rákóczi tér 7–9 (© **1/313-8442**), was badly damaged by fire in 1988 but was restored to its original splendor and reopened in 1991. There's only a small area of private vendors; the rest of the hall is filled with retail booths. Open Monday 6am to 4pm, Tuesday through Friday 6am to 6pm, Saturday 6am to 1pm. Take the metro to Blaha Lujza tér (Red line) or tram no. 4 or 6 directly to Rákóczi tér.

In addition to these three large classic market halls, Budapest has a number of neighborhood produce markets. The **Fehérvári úti Vásárcsarnok**, at XI. Kőrösi J. u. 7–9 (© **1/385-6563**), in front of the Buda Skála department store, is the latest classic food market in Budapest to be renovated. Some of the charm is lost, but such is progress. Just a block from the Móricz Zsigmond körtér transportation hub, it's open Monday 6:30am to 5pm, Tuesday through Friday from 6:30am to 6pm, Saturday 6:30am to 1pm. Take tram no. 47 from Deák tér to Fehérvári út, or any tram or bus to Móricz Zsigmond körtér.

The **Fény utca Piac,** on II. Fény utca, just off Moszkva tér in Buda, formerly a nondescript neighborhood market, underwent an ambitious reconstruction in 1998 in connection with the building of the Mammut shopping mall, to which it is now attached. Unfortunately, the renovation has meant higher rental fees, which have driven out most of the small independent vendors. Except for a small area on the first floor designated for vendors, the new market retains little of the old atmosphere.

Open Monday 6am to 5pm, Tuesday through Friday 6am to 6pm, Saturday 6:30am to 1pm. Take the metro to Moszkva tér (Red line).

Lehel tér Piac, at VI. Lehel tér (© **1/288-6898**), is another neighborhood market, whose reconstruction was completed in 2003. The market features a wide selection of fresh food and meats, cheap Hungarian trademark products as well as rinky-dink clothing, kitchen appliances, and flowers. Unfortunately, the reconstruction, as in the other cases, has diminished the neighborhood charm we used to love so much. Interestingly for history buffs, the designer of the controversial architecture—resembling a tacky, colorful adventure park—is none other than László Rajk, the son of the Communist Party official of the same name whose trial and execution for conspiracy in 1949 represented the beginning of the dark era of Stalinist paranoia and terror in postwar Hungary. The market is open Monday through Friday 6am to 6pm, Saturday 6am to 2pm. Take the metro to Lehel tér (Blue line).

MUSIC

Akt.Records   Once known as Afrofilia, this cozy shop in the heart of Budapest stocks an impressive collection of minimal, hip-hop, electro, jazz, and folklore records. Open Monday through Friday 11am to 7pm, Saturday 11am to 4pm. V. Múzeum körút 7. © 1/266-3080. www.manamana.hu. Metro: Astoria (Red line).

Fonó Budai Zeneház   The Fonó Budai Zeneház entertainment complex is your source for Hungarian folk music. The complex features a folk music store and an auditorium for live folk performances *(táncház).* It's open Monday and Tuesday 2 to 5pm, Wednesday through Friday 2 to 10pm, Saturday 7 to 10pm. Closed in July and August. I. Sztregova u. 3. © 1/206-5300. www.fono.hu. Tram: 47 or 49 from Deák tér (5 stops past Móricz Zsigmond körtér).

Hungaroton   The factory outlet of the Hungarian record company of the same name, this is definitely *the* place for classical-music buffs looking for Hungarian composers' recordings by contemporary Hungarian artists such as Zoltán Kocsis, Dezső Ránki, and András Schiff. Reasonable CD prices keep the Hungarian music alive. Open Monday through Friday 8am to 3:30pm. VII. Rottenbiller utca 47. © 1/322-8839. www.hungaroton.hu. Tram: 4 or 6 to Király utca.

Indie-Go   Developing independent artists, this head-twisting music shop featuring a wide selection of world music, alternative, break beat, hip-hop, jazz, and down tempo genres. The collections here provide a solid base for several alternative radio stations. Open Monday through Friday 11am to 8pm, Saturday 11am to 4pm. VIII. Krúdy Gyula u. 7. © 1/486-2927. www.indiego.com. Metro: Kálvin tér (Blue line) or tram 4 or 6 to Baross u.

Liszt Ferenc Zeneműbolt (Ferenc Liszt Music Shop)   Budapest's musical crowd frequents this shop, located near both the State Opera House and the Ferenc Liszt Academy of Music. Sheet music, scores, records, tapes, CDs, and books are available. The store carries an excellent selection of classical music, composed and performed by Hungarian artists. The store is open Monday through Friday 10am to 6pm, Saturday 10am to 1pm. VI. Andrássy út 45. © 1/322-4091. Metro: Oktogon (Yellow line).

Selekta   Located behind the impressive Opera House, this shop—with an enticing chill-out interior—presents a broad spectrum of rhythmic Jamaican music, current dance-hall, ska, hip-hop, and roots grooves. Open Monday through Friday noon to 8pm, Saturday noon to 4pm. VI. Lázár u. 7. No phone. Metro: Opera (Yellow line).

Trancewave Records   This store specializes in alternative and punk music, although the selection is scrimp. They also sell secondhand CDs, LPs, and vinyl. Party and concert information is available. Open Monday through Friday 11am to 8pm, Saturday noon to 4pm. VI. Révay köz 2. (© 1/302-2927. www.trancewave.hu. Metro: Arany János utca (Blue line).

Wave   On a small side street off Bajcsy-Zsilinszky út, directly across the street from the rear of St. Stephen's Basilica, Wave is a popular spot among young Hungarians looking for acid rock, rap, techno, and world music. Open Monday through Friday 11am to 7pm, Saturday 11am to 3pm. Révay utca 4. (© 1/331-0718. Metro: Arany János utca (Blue line).

PORCELAIN, POTTERY & CRYSTAL

Ajka Crystal   Hungary's renowned crystal producer from the Lake Balaton Region sells fine stemware and other crystal at great prices. Founded by Bernát Neumann in 1878, the company was privatized by FOTEX Rt. in 1990. Showcased are the company's brilliant yet simple crystal glasses, chalices, and crystal artwork. V. József Attila u. 7. (© 1/317-8133. Metro: Deák tér (All lines).

Herend Shop   Hand-painted Herend porcelain, first produced in 1826 in the town of Herend near Veszprém in western Hungary, is world-renowned (check it out at www.herend.com). This shop, the oldest and largest Herend shop in Budapest, has the widest selection in the capital. They can arrange shipping (visit www.touristpost.hu). Even if you don't intend to buy, come just to see some gorgeous examples of Hungary's most famous product. The store is located in Pest's Inner City, on quiet József nádor tér, just a few minutes' walk from Vörösmarty tér. Open Monday through Friday from 10am to 6pm, Saturday from 9am to 1pm. There is also a Herend shop at V. Kigyó u. 5 ((© 1/318-3439) that also offers shipping. If you're planning a trip to Veszprém or Lake Balaton, don't miss the Herend Museum in the town of Herend (see chapter 12, "The Lake Balaton Region"). V. József nádor tér 11. (© 1/318-9200. www.herend.hu. Metro: Vörösmarty tér (Yellow line) or Deák tér (all lines).

Herend Village Pottery   If the formal Herend porcelain isn't your style (or in your price range), this delightful, casual pottery might be just the thing. The majolika (village pottery) is a hand-painted folklore-inspired way of making pottery. Various patterns and solid colors are available; all are dishwasher and oven safe. Because everything is handcrafted, it's possible to order and reorder particular pieces at a later time. Prices are reasonable here. The owners are very knowledgeable and eager to assist, but not pushy. Open Tuesday through Friday 9am to 5pm, Saturday 9am to noon. II. Fő utca 61. (© 1/356-7899. Metro: Batthyány tér (Red line).

Zsolnay Márkabolt   Delightfully gaudy Zsolnay porcelain, from the southern city of Pécs, is Hungary's second-most-celebrated brand of porcelain, and this shop has Budapest's widest selection. They arrange shipping through Touristpost (p. 181). Even if you don't intend to buy, come just to see some fabulous examples of Hungary's other internationally known porcelain. (The Zsolnay Museum is in Pécs; see chapter 14, "Southern Hungary: The Great Plain & the Mecsek Hills.") Check out examples of the pottery at www.zsolnayusa.com. The store is open Monday through Friday 10am to 6pm, Saturday 10am to 1pm. V. Kígyó u. 4. (© 1/318-3712. Metro: Vörösmarty tér (Yellow line) or Deák tér (all lines).

TEA & COFFEE

1000 TEA   Set back in a courtyard of Váci u. 65 (a teapot-shaped sign points the way), this cozy little shop, with up to 50 different bulk teas available, is a haven for serious tea drinkers, mainly local students and intellectuals. A wall map indicates labels from the various teas and their places of origin. Information about the harvest of the different teas is also posted—in five languages. While the shop has recently changed management, the visionary founder, Zoltán Buzady, still shares ownership in the business and will hopefully continue to ensure the exceptional quality of its product. The shop continues to expand, and now features several unique tearooms. In summer, guests are seated in the courtyard, at makeshift tables made of the barrels in which the tea is shipped. Prices range from 600 Ft to 1,800 Ft ($2.90–$8.70) per pot for several infusions. Open Monday through Saturday noon to 9pm, Sunday 3 to 8pm. V. Váci u. 65. ⓒ 1/337-8217. www.ezertea.hu. Metro: Ferenciek tere (Blue line).

Sir Morik Kávé   Formerly known as Coquan's Kávé and originally opened in 1996 by an American, this coffee-selling shop was recently bought by a descendant of the Morik family, who owned the first company in Hungary that imported and roasted coffee in the 19th century. The shop is just as excellent as before under this new ownership. Morik sells high-quality Arabica coffee. Although several bulk coffee shops have opened up recently in Budapest, this is still the place to go when you want a nice cup for a decent price. About 20 different types of coffee are available. You can buy in bulk for 1,500 Ft to 2,500 Ft ($7.25–$12) per 250 grams (roughly half a lb.) or by the cup. Try an all-butter croissant, a slice of banana bread, or a wedge of carrot cake while you're at it. Morik's has two other shops as well, at IX. Ráday u. 15 (ⓒ 1/215-2444) and at II. Lövőház u. 12 (ⓒ 1/345-4275). Shops are open Monday through Friday 8am to 8pm, Saturday 9am to 7pm. The shop on Ráday utca is also open Sunday 9am to 7pm. V. Nádor u. 5. ⓒ 1/266-9936. Metro: Deák tér (all lines).

Teahouse to the Red Lion   Named after the masterpiece of Maria Szepesi, the Red Lion, the teahouse is a place to hide from hectic, vibrating Budapest. You can choose from various "atmospheres": business-talk-like chairs and tables, friendly bean-bags, or intimate private rooms with mattresses. Within the shop, a small yet fitting bookstore features a nice selection of exoteric, literary books in English as well. Tea-lovers will be amazed at the countless high-quality tea offerings from Indian green teas and Chinese black teas to Healing teas. Prices are moderate, 600 Ft to 1,500 Ft ($2.90—$7.25) per teapot. Open Monday through Saturday 11am to 11pm, Sunday 3 to 11pm.. Also located at IX. Ráday u. 9 (ⓒ 1/215-2101). VI. Jókai tér 8. ⓒ 1/269-0579. www.vorosoroszlanteahaz.hu.

TOYS

Rokiland *(Finds)*   This tiny upstairs shop, just off Blaha Lujza tér, is practically the only shop in town (with the exception of Toys Anno, reviewed below) that has been able to withstand the relentless onslaught of international chains. The products here are all sorts of handcrafted pipe-cleaner animals. Several display windows on the street give you an idea of what's available. In our opinion, the best animals here are clearly the monkeys, which one enthusiastic 42-year-old American collector that we know has been buying in great quantities since he first came to Hungary almost 15 years ago. The snakes are also great; watch the cashier give each one an expert twist before putting it into your bag. Incidentally, we have discovered that these pipe-cleaner animals make great cat toys, too.

There is a second Rokiland store just off Váci utca in central Pest, at V. Petőfi Sándor u. 3 (ⓒ 1/317-3131). Both shops are open Monday through Friday 10am to 6pm. VII. Erzsébet krt. 4. ⓒ 1/322-2495. Metro: Blaha Lujza tér (Red line).

Sárkányvár   This enchanting castle is staffed with playful teachers and offers state-of-the-art creative games to educate them and keep them occupied. It functions as a sort of child depository in the Campona mall, and the toys can be bought and borrowed, a unique idea that's worth visiting for. Check out the quality kids' program list. Open daily from 9:30am to 7:30pm. XXII. Nagytétényi út 35–47. ✆ **1/424-3140.**Bus: 3.

Toys Anno   Part museum, part specialty shop, Toys Anno might be of more interest to toy collectors than to kids. The shop sells exact replicas of antique toys from around the world. The tin toys are exceptional, especially the monkeys on bicycles, the Ferris wheels, and the Soviet rockets that prepare themselves for launch. There are also old-fashioned dolls and puzzles. Items are behind glass and tagged with serial numbers. Though you have to request prices and ask to see the toys that interest you, the clerk is more than happy to oblige. Open Monday through Friday 10am to 6pm, Saturday 9am to 1pm. VI. Teréz krt. 54. ✆ **1/302-6234.** Metro: Nyugati pu. (Blue line).

WINE & SPIRIT & CHEESE

Budapest Wine Society   Truly among the experts in wine, the Wine Society operates in four shops in Budapest. Founded by Tom Howells and Attila Tálos, the shop sells an immense amount of wines produced by over 50 local wine-growers. Drop in for free samples on Saturday. Open from Monday to Friday noon to 8pm, Saturday 10am to 3pm. XI. Ráday u. 7. ✆ **1/219-5647.** Metro: Kálvin tér (Blue line). www.bortarsasag.hu. Also: Batthyány u. 59. ✆ **1/212-2569.** Metro: Batthyány tér (Red line).

The House of Hungarian Pálinka   Locals say that good Pálinka (a traditional form of brandy) should warm the stomach, not burn the throat, a common side-effect of strong brandy. This shop offers the finest selection of Pálinka—distilled from everything from plums, pears, apples, and walnuts to honey-paprika—that will indeed delight both stomach and throat. Watch out for the head-spinning effect. Open Monday through Saturday 9am to 7pm. VIII. Rákóczi Street 17. ✆ **1/338-4219.** www.magyarpalinkahaza.hu. Metro: Blaha Lujza tér (Red line) or bus 7.

Le Boutique des Vins   Sophisticated, classy, and welcoming, this wine shop is a cut above the others. This is a great place to learn about and purchase Hungarian wines. The longtime manager of the shop, Ferenc Hering, speaks excellent English and is extremely well versed in his merchandise. Try the excellent Villány reds (some from the shop's own vineyard) or the fine whites from the Balaton region. You can pick up a fine bottle for as little as 1,500 Ft to 15,000 Ft ($7.50–$75). A wide range of Hungary's famous Tokaj dessert wines, in the general price range of 5,000 Ft to 25,000 Ft ($25–$125), is also available. Shipping can be arranged, but at a steep price. Open Monday through Friday 10am to 6pm, Saturday 10am to 3pm. V. József Attila u. 12 (behind the Jaguar dealership). ✆ **1/317-5919** or 1/266-4397. Metro: Deák tér (any line).

Présház   This tasteful wine store—named after the "press room," or the room where the grapes are rammed to extract the sweet nectar—is located in the Inner City area. They offer over 300 types of Hungarian wine and have a knowledgeable staff that is fluent in English. You can have your order delivered within Budapest if you purchase a crate. Open Monday through Friday 10am to 6pm, Saturday 10am to 4pm. The second shop is at V. Váci u. 10 (✆ **1/266-1100**). V. Párizsi utca 1–3. ✆ **1/266-0636.** www.preshaz.hu. Metro: Vörösmarty tér (Yellow line).

Szega Camembert   If you are a lover of cheeses, this vendor at the Fény utca market is worth knowing about. Located on the first floor of the recently renovated market hall

(p. 195), Szega Camembert offers a huge selection of domestic and imported cheeses. You can also buy delicious homemade butter and sour cream here, as well as wholesome breads. Open Monday through Friday 9am to 6pm, Saturday 8am to 1pm. II. Fény u. ✆ 1/345-4259. Metro: Moszkva tér (Red line).

T. Nagy Tamás Sajtkereskedése (Thomas T. Nagy's Cheese Shop)   Opened in 1994, this shop deals exclusively in cheese, selling more than 300 types of hard and soft cheeses, including Hungarian, as well as imported French, Italian, Dutch, and English varieties. Open Monday 10am to 5pm, Tuesday through Friday 9am to 6pm, Saturday 8am to 1pm. V. Gerlóczy u. 3. ✆ 1/317-4268. Metro: Deák tér (all lines).

Unicum   A beloved digestive bittersweet liqueur that is said to cure all ills—especially aching stomachs. Made with over 40 herbs and spices, Unicum is the trademark product of Zwack, the best-known spirit brand in Hungary. With its memorable bomb-shaped bottle, emergency-cross logo, and unforgettable taste—it's Uniqum. Try and buy at the Zwack Museum. Open Monday through Friday 1 to 5pm. Reservations are compulsory. IX. Dandár u. 1. ✆ 1/476-2383. www.zwack.hu. Tram: 2.

Wine & Arts Decanter Borszaküzlet   A club of wine-lovers, this shop features elegant wines from hidden provincial Hungarian wine-growers, top-notch award-wining wine-masters in addition to Italian and Spanish wines. Open Tuesday through Friday 6 to 8pm, Saturday 10am to 2pm. MOM Park, XII. Kléh István u. 3. ✆ 1/201-9029. www. grandvin.hu. Tram: 59 or 61.

10

Budapest After Dark

Budapest is blessed with a rich and varied cultural life. And there is no event that is unaffordable to the average tourist. In fact, you can still go to the Opera House, one of Europe's finest, for less than 800 Ft ($4). (The most expensive tickets in the house, for the fabulously ornate royal box once used by the Habsburgs, still go for less than 10,000 Ft, or $50.) Almost all of the city's theaters and concert halls, with the exception of those hosting internationally touring rock groups, offer tickets for 800 Ft to 4,000 Ft ($4–$20). (Of course, you can also get 5,000 Ft–8,000 Ft/$25–$40 tickets at the same venue if you wish.) It makes sense in Budapest (as elsewhere, of course) to select a performance based as much on the venue as on the program. If, for example, the Great Hall of the Academy of Music is presenting a program that you wouldn't ordinarily attend, it might be worth your while to reconsider due to the splendor of the venue.

The opera, ballet, and theater seasons run from September through May or June, but most theaters and halls also host performances during the summer festivals. A number of lovely churches and stunning halls offer concerts exclusively in the summer. While classical music has a long and proud tradition in Budapest, jazz, blues, rock, disco, and the world of DJs have exploded in the past couple of decades. Herds of stylish, unique new clubs and bars have opened up everywhere; the parties start late and last until morning. So put on your dancing shoes or slip your opera glasses into your pocket; whatever your entertainment preference, Budapest nights offer plenty to choose from.

PROGRAM LISTINGS The most complete schedule of mainstream performing arts is found in the free bimonthly **Koncert Kalendárium,** available at the Central Philharmonic Ticket Office on Madách utca. The **Budapest Sun** and the **Visitors' Guide** (see "Fast Facts: Budapest" in chapter 4, "Getting to Know Budapest") also have comprehensive events calendars; the weekly **Budapest Times** includes cultural listings. **Budapest Panorama,** a free monthly tourist booklet, offers only partial entertainment listings, featuring what the editors consider the monthly highlights. All of the publications mentioned above are in English.

TICKET OFFICES When purchasing opera, ballet, theater, or concert tickets in advance, you're better off going to one of the commission-free state-run ticket offices than to the individual box offices. There are always schedules posted, and you'll have a variety of choices. If none of the cashiers speaks English, find a helpful customer who can translate for you. On the day of the performance, though, you might have better luck at the box office. The **Cultur-Comfort Ticket Office (Cultur-Comfort Központi Jegyiroda),** VI. Paulay Ede u. 31 (© **1/322-0000;** www.cultur-comfort.hu), sells tickets to just about everything, from theater and operettas to sports events and rock concerts. The office is open Monday through

Friday 9am to 6pm. For **opera and ballet,** go to the **Hungarian State Opera Ticket Office (Magyar Állami Opera Jegyiroda),** VI. Andrássy út 22 (© **1/ 353-0170**), open Monday through Friday 11am to 5pm. Try **Concert & Media,** XI. Üllői út 11–13 (© **1/455-9000;** www. jegyelado.hu.), for classical performances as well as pop, jazz, and rock concerts. For just about everything from rock and jazz concert, opera, ballet performances, and theater tickets, try **Ticket Express,** VI. Jókai u. 40 (© **1/353-0692;** www. tex.hu), open Monday through Saturday from 10am to 7pm. Further Ticket

Express offices can be found at V. Deák Ferenc u. 19 (© **1/266-7070**), open Monday through Saturday from 10am to 9m; VI. Andrássy út 18 (© **1/312-0000**), open Monday through Friday 9:30am to 6:30pm; and VIII. József krt. 50 (© **1/ 344-0369**), open Monday through Friday 9:30am to 6:30pm.

Note: For cheaper tickets, try going to the actual box office of the venue, as the ticket agencies may not carry the entire price range of tickets. You may also find that agencies charge a commission (usually about 4%), especially for hit shows.

1 The Performing Arts

The major symphony orchestras in Budapest are the Budapest Festival Orchestra, the Philharmonic Society Orchestra, the Hungarian State Symphony Orchestra, the Budapest Symphony Orchestra, and the Hungarian Railway Workers' (MÁV) Symphony Orchestra. The major chamber orchestras include the Hungarian Chamber Orchestra, the Ferenc Liszt Chamber Orchestra, the Budapest String Players, and the newly established Hungarian Virtuosi. Major choirs include the Budapest Chorus, the Hungarian State Choir, the Hungarian Radio and Television Choir, the Budapest Madrigal Choir, and the University Choir.

Budapest is now on the touring route of dozens of major European ensembles and virtuosos. Keep your eyes open for well-known touring artists.

Note: Most Budapesters tend to dress more formally than casually when attending performances.

OPERA, OPERETTA & BALLET

Budapesti Operettszínház (Budapest Operetta Theater)   Referred to as the "palace of entertainment" in its incipient times, the building was designed by two acclaimed Viennese architects, Fellner and Helmer, in 1894. In the heart of Budapest's theater district, the recently renovated Budapest Operetta Theater is not only the site of operetta, but also of musicals and rock operas. Restored seating boxes, antique chandeliers, and period-style furnishings are paired with state-of-the-art stage equipment—an enchanting, quality experience is guaranteed. A highlight among Art Nouveau style buildings, the Theater hosts exquisite banquettes and balls—among which is opulent Operetta Ball. Performances of *Romeo and Juliette, Baroness Lili,* and *Ball in the Savoy* are the order of the day here. However, the greatest musical hits, like *Cats* and *The Phantom of the Opera,* whose European world premier outside England took place in Hungary in the spring of 2003, are shown in **Madách Theater** on the Outer Ring (reviewed later in this chapter). The off season is mid-July to mid-August. The box office is open Monday through Friday 10am to 7pm, and Saturday 1 to 7pm. VI. Nagymező u. 17. © 1/312-4866. www.operettszinhaz.hu. Tickets 2,000 Ft–5,000 Ft ($10–$25). Metro: Opera or Oktogon (Yellow line).

Tips **Bistros: For the Sophisticated Night Owl**

If you're looking for a late-night cocktail but want to avoid the typical bar and club scene, try a bistro. The **Café Incognito** (see page 123) is a popular, centrally-located bar/bistro that draws a mixed crowd until 2am. **Paris, Texas** (see page 124), on the popular walking street Ráday utca, is a pleasant place to sit down and talk or eat after a concert. See the "Cafés & Bistros" listings on p. 123 for more options.

Erkel Színház (Erkel Theater)   Named the "People's Opera," the Erkel Theater is the second home of the State Opera and Ballet. The largest theater in Hungary, it seats as many as 2,400 people. Though it was built in Art Nouveau style in 1911, little of its original character is apparent because of the various renovations it has undergone. If you have a choice, go to the Opera House instead (their seasons—mid-Sept to mid-June—are the same). Chamber orchestra concerts are also performed here. The box office is open Tuesday through Saturday from 11am till the beginning of the performance, or to 5pm, Sunday from 11am to 1pm and 4pm till the beginning of the performance. VIII. Köztársaság tér 30. *C* 1/333-0540. www.opera.hu. Tickets 800 Ft–4,000-Ft ($4–$20). Metro: Keleti pu. (Red line).

Magyar Állami Operaház (Hungarian State Opera House)   Completed in 1884, the Opera House is the crowning achievement of the famous Hungarian architect Miklós Ybl. It's easily Budapest's most famous performance hall, and an attraction in its own right. The lobby is adorned with Bertalan Székely's frescoes; the ceiling frescoes in the concert hall itself are by Károly Lotz. **Guided tours** of the Opera House leave daily at 3 and 4pm; the cost is 2,000 Ft ($9).

The splendid Opera House, home to both the State Opera and the State Ballet, possesses a rich history. A political scandal marked the opening performance in 1884: Ferenc Liszt had written a piece to be performed especially for the event, but when it was discovered that he had incorporated elements of the *Rákóczi March,* a patriotic Hungarian (and anti-Habsburg) melody, he was prevented from playing it. Gustav Mahler and Ferenc Erkel rank as the Opera House's most famous directors.

Hungarians adore opera, and a large percentage of seats are sold on a subscription basis; buy your tickets a few days ahead of time if you can. The season runs from mid-September to mid-June. Summer visitors, however, can take in the approximately 10 performances (both opera and ballet) during the Summer Operafest, in July or August. Seating capacity is 1,260. The box office is open Tuesday through Saturday from 11am till the beginning of the performance, or to 5pm. Sunday from 11am to 1pm and 4pm till the beginning of the performances. There are occasional weekend matinees selling for 300 Ft to 3,500 Ft ($1.50–$18). VI. Andrássy út 22. *C* 1/335-0170. www.opera.hu. Tickets 800 Ft–10,000 Ft ($4–$50). Metro: Opera (Yellow line).

CLASSICAL MUSIC

Bartók Béla Emlékház (Béla Bartók Memorial House)   This charming little hall is in Béla Bartók's last Budapest residence, and in addition to hosting concerts and exhibitions, it is the site of a Bartók museum (p. 147). Currently the house is undergoing a large-scale renovation project due to finish in March 2006. A regular concert series is given by the Bartók String Quartet, a prolific group founded in 1957 (they play a lot more than just Bartók). Concerts are performed from the end of September through December. For schedule information, check Budapest's free bimonthly *Koncert Kalendárium* or the museum's musical website at www.bartokmuseum.hu. Performances are on Friday at 6pm, and occasionally on Saturdays or other days, too, where tickets can be bought one hour prior to the performance or during opening hours of the museum. Open Tuesday through Sunday 10am to 5pm. II. Csalán út 29. ✆ 1/394-2100. Tickets cost 1,200 Ft, 1,500 Ft, and 2,000 Ft ($6, $7.50, and $10). Bus: 5 from Március 15 tér or Moszkva tér to Pasaréti tér (the last stop).

Budapesti Kongresszusi és Világkereskedelmi Központ (Budapest Congress & World Trade Center) A large modern hall that is a congress center and a concert site. The congress center has established itself in recent years as one of the more important venues in the city. With its newly renovated interior, the center features the main Pátria Hall—sitting some 1,800—as well as eighteen other well-equipped small and midsize rooms. The hall, the venue of many memorable events, concerts, and festivals—is spacious and comfortable, but lacks the character of the older venues. The center is part of the Novotel complex in central Buda. The performance schedule varies widely. The box office is open Wednesday through Friday from 4 to 6:30pm and Saturday from 2 to 4pm. XII. Jagelló út 1–3. ✆ 1/372-5400. www.bcc.hu. Tickets vary significantly according to performance, 3,000 Ft–20,000 Ft ($15–$100). Tram: 61 from Moszkva tér or Móricz Zsigmond körtér.

Károlyi Palace A renovated gem of the inner Budapest, the Palace is an intimate courtyard with a strong stay-a-while atmosphere while the Sándor Petőri Literary Museum occupies the bulk of the building. The Palace hosts the successful Summer Evenings in the Károlyi Gardens, a distinguished event featuring theater, dance, folk, and classical music—"culture-cool" performances throughout the summer heat. Open Tuesday to Sunday 10am to 6pm. V. Károlyi Mihály u. 16. ✆ 1/317-3450. Tickets 800 Ft–2,000 Ft ($4–$10). Metro: Ferenciek tere or Kálvin tér (Blue line).

Kiscelli Museum Located atop Remetehegy (Hermit's Hill) in Óbuda, this 18th-century baroque castle was initially a Trinitarian monastery. It is comprised of an impressive vast shell of a church hall, a bare courtyard, a baroque sculpture hall, and an enormous, mysterious crypt. During the summer months the built-in stage in the courtyard hosts intimate recitals and chamber music concerts. Open November 1 to March 31 and April 30 to mid-October, Tuesday to Sunday 10am to 6pm. III. Kiscelli út 108. ✆ 1/388-7817. www.btmfk.iif.hu. Tickets 1,000 Ft–3,000 Ft ($5–$15). Take tram 17 from Margit Bridge.

Matthias Church A Budapest icon in the center of the historic Castle district, this church is a neo-Gothic classic, named after Matthias Corvinus, the Renaissance king who was married here. The church is a key location for excellent organ recitals, sacred music concerts for a cappella choir, or orchestras. The box office is open Wednesday through Sunday 1 to 5:30pm. I. Szentháromság tér 2. ✆ 1/355-5657. Tickets 1,000 Ft–7,000 Ft ($5–$35). Take the Castle minibus from Moszkva tér (Red line).

Óbudai Társaskör (Óbuda Social Circle) Hidden by residential housing estates, this small, cozy building is a unique center of social and cultural life in Budapest. Temporary exhibitions, music workshops, and theatrical performances in the open-air stage during the summertime all elevate this tiny venue to compete with its larger rivals. Restored around the turn of the millennium, it is home to the Budapest Ragtime Band, a prominent venue of the Budapest Spring Festival, and also presents up-to-par chamber music concerts. The box office is open daily 10am to 6pm. III. Korona

u. 7. ⓒ **1/250-0288**. www.obudaitarsaskor.hu. Tickets 500 Ft–1,500 Ft ($2.50–$7.50). Take tram 1 from Árpád Híd (Blue line) over the bridge or the HÉV to Árpád-híd.

Palace of Art 🎭🎭   The Palace of Art's National Concert Hall and Festival Theater are the latest concert and performing arts venues: this is a must-see venue for visitors to Budapest. The theaters are situated in the Millennium City Center, which seems to grow every year. The main concert hall is the finest contemporary classical music venue in Budapest, and now hosts concerts from the most important orchestras from around the world. The concert schedule varies; check out their website which has excellent search features. IX. Komor Marcell u. 1. ⓒ **1/555-3000**. www.mupa.hu. Take tram 2 from downtown toward the Lágymányos bridge.

The Birth of the Palace of Art

Hungary welcomed the opening of the **Palace of Art** 🎭🎭 in early 2005, the latest cultural complex created in the Hungarian capital that includes a National Concert Hall, a new home for the Ludwig Museum of Contemporary Art, and the smaller Festival Theater.

The crown jewel in this gargantuan complex, situated on the Danube adjacent to Hungary's National Theater, is the **National Concert Hall**, the largest of its kind in Hungary, seating 1,699 with standing room for an additional 200. The room itself was sealed sonorously from the outside world and sits in a gargantuan box floating on steel and rubber springs. There are 66 resonant chambers around the walls, and a 40-ton canopy above the podium to make sure that listeners hear only the music. Previously unable to host larger symphonic orchestras in a world-class venue, Hungary now boasts a truly top-quality contemporary space able to welcome the most notable international orchestras—putting the country on the international classical music map.

The adjacent **Ludwig Museum** hosts temporary exhibitions on the first floor, while the two above will feature works from the Ludwig collection—largely American pop art and central European contemporary. The smaller **Festival Theater** hosts contemporary dance and other performing arts events. The 32-billion Ft ($160-million) project was created in a public-private-partnership agreement between the Hungarian government and developer TriGránit Development Corporation, spearheaded by central European real estate tycoon Sándor Demján. The developer is using the complex as a template for cultural and entertainment centers to be built in other central European cities.

The complex is housed in the **Millennium City Center**, a space that promises to be more than merely a cultural space. Plans dictate the creation of a conference and tourism-related hub here, of which the Palace of Art and Hungary's National Theater are the first two main attractions. The same developers have plans for a convention center, five hotels, office buildings, a casino and exhibition pavilion, and even a spa.

Pesti Vigadó (Pest Concert Hall)   Located smack in the middle of the famed riverside Danube Promenade (Dunakorzó), the Vigadó is one of the city's oldest concert halls, dating to 1864. All sorts of classical performances are held here. Although it's one of the city's best-known halls, Hungarian music lovers rate its acoustics and atmosphere second to the Academy of Music (see below). As part of a long-term reconstruction of the notorious Vörösmarty square and surroundings, the Hall will undergo a momentous renovation project—expectedly closing its gates until early 2006. The concert schedule varies; the box office is open Monday through Friday 10am to 6pm, while tickets can also be bought 1 hour prior to the start of the performance. V. Vigadó tér 2. ✆ 1/318-9903. www.vigado.hu. Metro: Vörösmarty tér (Yellow line).

Stefánia Palace   The eclectic-style 19th century palace formerly known as the Park Club—a beloved meeting point of the elite—promoted elite entertainment for local high society. Cultural hub of the Hungarian People's Army during communism— entertainment has always been the key. Today, working as the Cultural Center for the Ministry of Defense, the Palace presents numerous events with a wide selection of classical music events and quality ballet performances. XIV. Stefánia u. 34. ✆ 1/273-4128. Tickets 500 Ft–2,000 Ft ($2.50–$10). Tram: 3 from Mexikói út (Yellow line).

Zeneakadémia (Ferenc Liszt Academy of Music)   The Great Hall (Nagyterem) of the Academy of Music, with a seating capacity of 1,200 is—next to the recently opened National Concert Hall—Budapest's premier concert hall. Hungary's leading center of musical education, the Academy was built in the early years of the 20th century; the building's interior is decorated in lavish Art Nouveau style. If you go to only one performance in Budapest, it should be at the Opera House, the National Convert Hall, or here. Unfortunately, the Great Hall is not used in the summer months; the smaller Kisterem, also a fine hall, is used at that time. Home to the renowned Franz Liszt Academy of Music since 1907, student recitals can be attended sometimes even for free, although the main attractions are major Hungarian and international performances. A weekly schedule is posted outside the Király utca entrance to the academy. The box office is open Monday through Friday from 10am to 8pm, and weekends 2 to 8pm. Performances are frequent. VI. Liszt Ferenc tér 8. ✆ 1/462-4600. www.liszt.hu. Tickets 1,000 Ft–8,000 Ft ($5–$40). Metro: Oktogon (Yellow line) or Nyugati Pályaudvar (Blue line).

FOLK PERFORMANCES
Budai Vigadó (Buda Concert Hall)   The Budai Vigadó is the home stage of the Hungarian State Folk Ensemble (Állami Népi Együttes Székháza). The ensemble is the oldest in the country and includes 30 dancers, a 14-member Gypsy orchestra, and a folk orchestra. Under the direction of award-winning choreographers, the ensemble performs folk dances from all regions of historic Hungary. The *New York Times* commented: "a mix of high art and popular tradition . . . Every dance crackled with high speed." Tickets can be reserved by telephone. The box office is open 10am to 6pm daily. Performances usually start at 8pm on Tuesday, Thursday, and Sunday. I. Corvin tér 8. ✆ 1/317-2754. Tickets 4,600-5,600 Ft ($23–$28). Take bus 86 till Szilágyi Dezső tér or tram 19 till Halász utca stop.

Fonó Budai Music Hall   A sanctum for folk music lovers; folk and world music performances from all around the world keep visitors spinning. Besides performances of prominent local folk-old-boys like Félix Lajkó, Kálmán Balogh, and the Ghymes Ensemble, the Fonó makes way in presenting the current folk trends, hosting theaters, dance houses, and exhibitions. The box office opens an hour before the start of the performance. XI. Sztregova u. 3. ℰ **1/206-5300**. www.fono.hu. Tickets 500 Ft–2,000 Ft ($2.35–$9.50). Tram: 41 or 47 from Móricz Zsigmond körtér.

Hungarian Heritage House   Sharing a building with Budai Vigadó, the Heritage House was set up in 2001 to cultivate and keep alive the folk traditions of Hungary and countries around the region. Home to the largest folklore documentation center in central Europe, as well as a Folk Art Workshop and a new "Hungarian Dance House" club, visitors can learn traditional dances, most of which are rhythmical twirling, jumping, and thumping, with loud screams now and then to keep spirits high. I. Corvin tér 8. ℰ **1/201-5017**. www.heritagehouse.hu. Tickets 2,000 Ft–5,000 Ft ($10–$25). Take bus 86 till Szilágyi Dezső tér or tram 19 till Halász utca stop.

Petőfi Csarnok   Located in the tree-lined surroundings of the Városliget (City Park), this old-style no-frills hall has stages used for some of the best folk performances in the city. The venue hosts folk dance events, various national folk performances, and festivals. It also hosts jazz, blues, pop and rock concerts, exhibitions, workshops, and a weekend-only flee market. The main folk event is the annual Csángó Bál, which presents the colorful culture of this small, Moldavian-born community, and is a must-see event for folk dance and tradition seekers. The box office is open 2 to 7pm. XIV. Zichy Mihály út 14. ℰ **1/363-3730**. www.pecsa.hu. Tickets 1,500 Ft–4,000 Ft ($7.50–$20). Metro: Hősök tere (Yellow line).

THEATER & DANCE

Budapest has an extremely lively theater season from September through June. For productions in English, there are still some at the **Merlin Theater,** V. Gerlóczy u. 4 (ℰ **1/317-9338** or 1/318-9844; www.merlinszinhaz.hu), located on a quiet street in the heart of the Inner City. The Merlin now programs about 40% English-language shows, but somehow these efforts have never really resulted in a great following. In the productions, however, both Hungarian and foreign actors are featured. Tickets cost 600 Ft–2,000 Ft ($3–$20); box office open Monday through Friday noon to 7pm, Saturday and Sunday 2 to 7pm. Take the metro to Astoria (Red line) or Deák tér (all lines).

If you are looking for the best of international dance, music, or theater, head off to the **Trafó House of Contemporary Art,** IX. Liliom utca 41 (ℰ **1/215-1600** or 456-2040; www.trafo.hu), which has the aura of the Joyce Theatre in New York. This venue was once a building that housed a giant transformer (which connects it to the western European tradition of settling artistic centers and institutions in empty industrial buildings). Since it opened in 1998, this venue has introduced some bold programming (that occasionally upsets traditional-minded Hungarians). This is truly a place to go for intellectually adventurous and risky work. Prepare to gasp occasionally. We especially recommend the dance works debuted here by groups such as the French-Hungarian **Compagnie Pál Frenák** (www.ciefrenak.org); don't miss them if they're in town. Tickets cost 800 Ft–2,000 Ft ($4–$20); box office open Monday through Saturday from 5 until about 8pm. Reserve tickets in advance. Take tram no. 4 or 6, or go by metro to Ferenc Körut (Blue line).

For musical productions, especially those by Andrew Lloyd Webber, go to the **Madách Theater,** VII. Erzsébet krt. 29–33 (ℰ **1/478-2041;** www.madachszinhaz.hu), built in 1961 on the site of the famous Royal Orpheum Theater and beautifully restored in 1999. Their hit production—since spring 2003—is *The Phantom of the Opera;* Budapest is the only place in Europe outside of London where you can see the original production. Ticket prices are 800 Ft to 10,000 Ft ($4–$50). The box office is open daily from 3 to 7pm; performances are usually at 7pm. Take tram no. 4 or 6 to Wesselényi utca. Also staging musical performances, mostly by Hungarian authors, is the **Vígszínház (Comedy Theatre of Budapest),** XIII. Szent István krt. 14 (✆ 1/ 329-2340; www.vigszinhaz.hu), which was recently restored to its original, delightfully gaudy, neo-baroque splendor. In the 1950s the Vígszínház served as the venue for the Hungarian Communist Party's New Year's Eve balls, hosted by Stalinist-era dictator Mátyás Rákosi. With a show every night, the theater stages numerous audience-drawing plays by foreign and local writers. The box office is open daily 11am to 7pm. Ticket prices are 1,200 Ft to 3,000 Ft ($6–$15). Take the metro to Nyugati pu. (Blue line).

An intimate little theater, the **Kolibri Cellar,** VI. Andrássy út 77 (✆ 1/351-3348), is a family-entertainment-oriented theater featuring puppet, kids', and family productions. Also, the theater is home to the acclaimed expatriate theater company Scallabouche, a company that masters the art of improvisation. Acclaimed productions include the British style all-improvisational *Scabaret* and the one-man-show *John Donne—A Scream Within, Little Red Cinderella,* and *Puss in Boots.* Tickets cost 500 Ft to 1,500 Ft ($2.50–$7.50). Metro: Oktogon (Yellow line).

The International Buda Stage, II. Tárogató út 2–4 (✆ 1/391-2525; www.ibs-b. hu), hosts local and international theater performances. The box office is open Monday through Friday 10am to noon, 1 to 6pm, and on weekends 1 hour prior to the start of the performance. Tickets cost 1,200 Ft–2,500 Ft ($6–$13).

An important venue of the world of contemporary performing arts in Budapest is the **MU Theatre,** XI. Körösy József u. 17 (✆ 1/209-4014; www.mu.hu). This theater is becoming increasingly dynamic, with many young dancers and choreographers starting off their careers in this experimental, cozy environment. The box office is open Monday through Thursday 5pm till the beginning of the performance, and Friday through Sunday an hour before the start of the performance. Tickets cost 800 Ft to 1,500 Ft ($3.80–$7.20). Take bus no. 86, or tram no. 4 to Moricz Zsigmond körtér.

2 The Club Scene

Buzzing day and night, Budapest bars are present in cacophony of styles and music. Due to its constantly changing events, you'd be wise to check out *Pesti Est*—the largest free weekly program magazine listing all events from movies, theater offerings, and classical ballet performances to daily nightlife activities. Newcomers *Flyerz* and *Exit* also offer a less complete yet well-edited selection of events. English-language publications **Budapest Sun** (www.budapestsun.com) and **Budapest Times** (www.budapest times.hu) also list highlights. In order to help define the different categories of nightlife, we have tried to define an "average-age" guideline for the venues. Opening hours vary, but most clubs start dancing around 11pm and stay lively until closing time.

A38 Boat ✶✶ A former Ukrainian stone-carrying ship anchored at the Buda-side foot of the Petőfi Bridge. As soon as it appeared on the Danube, it struck a chord with the local youth, competing for the title of "hippest disco in town." Since its opening in 2003 it lost some of its allure, however. Taking place on the lower deck—feet-thumping crowds enjoy the city's best mainstream and alternative, underground live shows. The terrace is open only in the summer while the concert hall downstairs is open year-round. Open daily 11am to 4am, with crowds generally in their 20s and 30s. XI. Pázmány Péter sétány. ✆ 1/4643940. www.a38.hu. Cover: mostly free, concerts 1,000 Ft– 6,000 Ft ($5–$30). Tram: 4 or 6 to the Buda side of Petőfi bridge.

Alcatraz   A spicy prison-theme-ruled interior packs mixed crowds of daunting people-watchers, relaxed concertgoers, and dance-floor-devils alike. The casual, somewhat under-dressed but fizzy bar staff also lends to the insane party atmosphere. Open Monday through Wednesday 4pm to 2am, and Thursday through Saturday 4pm to 4am. Crowds: 30s. VII. Nyár u. 1. ✆ 1/478-6010. www.alcatraz.hu. No cover. Metro: Blaha Lujza tér (Red line).

Bahnhof Music Club   Located just around the corner from Nyugati railway station, Bahnhof is a sprawling party arena for travelers and locals alike. The train-station inte-rior setting—sitting areas designed as comfy leather train seats—is separated by the two dance floors, one playing mainstream pop and funky music while the inner room features thematic music nights from reggae to rock. People-watchers' paradise. Open Thursday through Sunday 9pm to 4am. Crowds: 20s and 30s. VI. Váci u. 1. ✆ 1/302-4751. Cover: 500 Ft–800 Ft ($2.50–$4). Metro: Nyugati pu. (Blue line).

Chachacha Underground café ✪   A retro-funky world beneath the ground, this cafe/club was built in the metro underpass of Kalvin Square; it's a glass-covered human boutique. The casino-bar lounge is decorated with zebra-striped couches and armchairs, with an oddly painted ceiling. Late night, this turns into an insane dance arena, with the drunken crowds overflowing into the underpass. The music typically brings back the hits of the '70s and '80s while also spinning some spaced-out tracks. Visit the bar's classy summer location on Margaret Island. Open daily 11am to 5am. Crowd: 30s. Metro under-pass, Kalvin Square. No phone. www.chachacha.hu. No cover. Metro: Kálvin tér (Blue line).

Citadella Club   A front-row view onto the prominent Citadella surroundings on the Gellért Hill. Citadella's infrequent parties feature mostly electronic music of high stan-dard to well-to-do crowds of underdressed women and men. Choose a decorative piece from their wide selection of cocktails. Open Friday and Saturday 10pm to 5am. Crowds: 30s. XI. Citadella sétány 2. ✆ 1/209-3271 or 1/365-6076. Cover: 1,000 Ft-6000 Ft ($5–$30).Bus: 27.

Club Seven   Hot women and hot parties attract a whale of foreigners and locals alike; Club Seven is ultra-funky. This action-packed basement cellar club has a well-equipped and crowded cocktail bar, excellent novel disco music—well known as a cheap place for women and expensive for men. Open daily 10am to 5am. Crowd: 30s. VII. Akácfa u. 7. ✆ 1/478-9030. Cover: 800 Ft–2,000 Ft ($4–$10). Metro: Blaha Lujza tér (Red line).

Fat Mo's Music Club ✪✪   This dive-y supper-club is always crowded. Live jazz concerts start at 9pm and dancing starts at 11pm. The best night is definitely Mon-day, with the Hot Jazz Band performing in the style of the '20s and '30s. Make sure to book a table if you wish to enjoy the club's superb food, including the best succu-lent American-style steaks in town. Open Monday through Wednesday noon to 2am, Thursday and Friday noon to 4am, Saturday 6pm to 4am, and Sunday 6pm to 2am. Crowd: 30s. V. Nyári Pál u. 11. ✆ 1/267-3199. No cover. Metro: Kálvin tér (Blue line).

Gödör Club   Smack dab in the middle of the city, Gödör ("Pothole") was built in/under a park—the previous location of the main bus station. This spacey, versatile art-music-lounge combo hosts abundant exhibitions, festivals, and must-see concerts. Open daily 4pm to 2am. Crowd: varied. V. Erzsébet tér. No phone. www.godorklub.hu. Cover: 600 Ft–6,000 Ft ($3–$30).

Home   Posh trance-dance fanatics line up at this massive 2,000-sq.-m (22,000-sq.-ft.) dance hall, located in the hills of Óbuda, for some of the city's best electronic music. The expensive bar, solarium-tanned go-go dancers, and renowned local and international DJs attract a wide clientele of platform-heeled, underdressed girls and

Mafiosa-type sporty tomcats—a lavish meat market. Bouncers have a reputation of being on the doggy side. Crowd: 20s and 30s. III. Harsány lejtő 6. No phone. www.homeclub.hu. Cover: 2,000 Ft–3,000 Ft ($10–$15).Bus: 18.

Jailhouse   Hidden underground, Jailhouse—with hotshot DJs rocking the floors—is the epicenter of new alternative-music lovers. Spinning is everything from break-beat, reggae, down-tempo, and drum 'n' bass to progressive. Open Wednesday through Sunday 10pm to 5am. Crowd: 20s and 30s. IX. Tűzoltó u. 22. No phone. Cover: 800 Ft ($4). Metro: Ferenc körút (Blue line).

Közgáz Cellar   Beneath the massive Budapest University of Economic Science lies this student-filled disco where dance floors are packed solid during weekends. Laid-back atmosphere, supreme happy hours, a cheerful karaoke and dance crowd, in addition to groovy disco tunes on the main dance floor offer bundles of fun. Open Tuesday through Saturday 9:30pm to 5am. Crowd: 20s and 30s. IX. Fővám tér 8. ℂ 1/215-4359. Cover: 500 Ft ($2.50) for men, free for women. Metro: Kálvin tér (Blue line) or tram 2, 47 or 49 to Fővám tér.

Kultiplex 🎭🎭   A bohemian two-story club, Kultiplex—an alternative cultural mul-tiplex—was converted from the Blue Box cinema, although a small art-movie house still operates within. Hosting the best local alternative beats, funky arty crowds rule the place. The summer cafe in the back is a pleasant, wallet-friendly place to unwind. Open daily 10am to 4:30am. Crowd: 20s and 30s. IX. Kinizsi u. 28. ℂ 1/219-0706. Cover: 500 Ft–6,000 Ft ($2.50–$30). Metro: Ferenc körút (Blue line).

Living Room 🎭   While to-be couples socialize in the loungelike atmosphere during daytime—this roomy classic disco-club becomes full with scores of dancers during weekends. Be careful of the all-you-can-drink university parties. Opening hours vary. Crowd: 20s and 30s. IV. Kossuth Lajos u. 17. No phone. Cover: 500 Ft–2,000 Ft ($2.50–$10). Metro: Astoria (Red line).

Macskafogó   This dynamic, jam-packed cellar club was named after the cult Hun-garian animation movie (roughly translated as *Cat City*). Mainstream disco tunes and pop classics draw a vast crowd of easygoing dance fanatics. Open Thursday 6pm to 3am, and Friday through Sunday 6pm to 4am. Crowds: 20s and 30s. V. Nádor u. 29. ℂ 1/473-0123. No cover. Metro: Kossuth tér (Red line).

Morrison's Music Pub 🎭   A 20-something crowd of mostly travelers and expats packs this busy club just around the corner from the Opera House. There's a busy dance floor, an eclectic variety of loud disco music, and a number of beers on tap. Open Wednesday through Saturday 9pm to 4am. Crowd: 20s. VI. Révay u. 25. ℂ 1/269-4060. www.morrisons.hu. Cover: 500 Ft ($2.40). Metro: Opera (Yellow line).

Old Man's Music Pub 🎭🎭   Old Man's offers the best jazz and blues in Hungary. The Pege Quartet plays here, as does Hobo and his blues band. Hobo was a friend of Alan Ginsberg and he broke new ground in Hungary by writing his master's thesis on rock 'n' roll in the 1960s, in addition to stunning Cotton Club Singers. A very hip spot. Open daily 3pm till the crowd leaves. Crowd: 30s and 40s. Akácfa u. 13. ℂ 1/322-7645. www.oldmans.hu. No cover. Metro: Blaha Lujza tér (Red line).

Piaf   Named after the remarkably soulful French singer, Piaf is renowned for its bohemian-like late-night, after-hours parties. Once inside the heavy iron door—guarded by a feisty woman—you'll find yourself among seductive red velvet furnish-ings in a distinct '80s Parisian style bar. In the downstairs dance floor the spinning of oldies can get pretty heated, and the crowds can be quite wild. Open daily 10pm to

6am. Crowd: varied. VI. Nagymező u. 25. ℰ **1/312-3823.** Cover: 800 Ft ($4). Metro: Oktogon or Opera (Yellow line).

Süss Fel Nap ★★ Fittingly titled "Sunrise," this newly expanded bar—a favorite among university students during the weekend—rocks the dancing crowd until dawn with punk and alternative music. Superb DJs and live bands provide the tunes. Open daily 5pm till dawn. Crowd: 20s and 30s. V. Szent István körút 11. ℰ **1/374-3329.** www.suss felnap.hu. Cover: 500 Ft–2,000 Ft ($2.50–$10). Metro: Nyugati pu. (Blue line).

Trafó Bar Tango A cultural center for young, alternative artists, this club is housed in an old electric power station that has been renovated. Trafó hosts the hippest selection of alternative artists, from reggae to classic Indian music. The small dance floor and scant bar area are supplemented by the relaxed, easygoing, loungelike chill-out area. Open daily 6pm to 4am. Crowd: varied. IX. Liliom u. 41. ℰ **1/215-1600.** www.trafo.hu. Cover: 500 Ft–2,000 Ft ($2.50–$10). Metro: Ferenc körút (Blue line) or tram 4 or 6 to Üllöi út.

Underground An oldie among clubs, Underground was initially built as an homage to Bosnian-born Emir Kusturica's film of the same name. Today, after a series of rebirths, the place has turned into a welcoming, red-dominant interior with a dance floor in the back where karaoke awaits visitors on Tuesday, Wednesday, and Sunday. A minimalist selection of homemade-style specialties is served during the day. Crowd: 20s and 30s. VI. Teréz körút 30. ℰ **1/269-5566.** www.underground-budapest.hu. No cover. Metro: Oktogon (Yellow line) or tram 4 or 6.

3 The Bar Scene

Aloe A sizzling bar filled with long-legged lovelies with warm-brown eyes, and powerful yet remarkably cheap drinks prepared by attentive bar staff. This place is known among locals as the temple of good, inexpensive cocktails. Open daily 5pm to 2am. VI. Zichy Jenő u. 34. ℰ **1/269-4536.** Metro: Nyugati pu. (Blue line).

Balettcipő A colorful, cheerful coffeehouse/bar in the heart of the theater district— behind the Opera house, "Ballet shoe" has a laid-back, open atmosphere—great for catching up with a longtime friend. A largely Hungarian client base and a simple yet refreshing cafe-style menu. Open Monday through Friday 8am to midnight, and Saturday and Sunday 10am to midnight. VI. Hajós u. 14. ℰ **1/269-3114.** Metro: Opera (Yellow line).

Becketts A lively authentic Irish pub, Becketts serves the best Guinness in the city to the crowd of expats and local high-class yuppies. The cheerful staff—some with a clear Irish accent—the spacious bar, a cozy restaurant, live music, and/or the lively sport telecasts pack the pub throughout the week. Open Monday through Friday noon to 1am, and Saturday and Sunday noon to 3am. V. Bajcsy-Zsilinszky út 72. ℰ **1/311-1033.** www.budapestsun.com/becketts. Metro: Nyugati pu. (Blue line).

Egri Borozó Packed with bodacious local 20-to-30-somethings, the Egri Wine Cellar is stuffed with heavy wooden chairs and tables. It's a cheap, simplistic pub featuring an extensive wine list from all around the country—wine is brought in large ceramic pitchers. Usually packed and smoky—reservations recommended. Open daily 4pm to midnight. V. Bajcsy-Zsilinszky út 72. No phone. Metro: Nyugati pu or Arany János u. (Blue line).

Extra A bizarre three-level cafe/bar playground for university students during the day. It is taken over by the local and outlandish crowds of hardcore, late-night boozers and dancers at night. It's difficult to find—but hard to leave. Open Monday

Best Hotel Bars

A hotel bar is a great place to grab a drink, mingle with a mixed crowd, and—sometimes, it's true—get a glimpse of a hotel that's nicer than yours. The **Art'Otel Budapest by Park Plaza** offers a great view, a crowd of professional-creative types, and drinks until 1am (see page 69). The cosmopolitan Zita Bar in the **Hilton Budapest WestEnd** is a good place for a drink after a movie (see page 74). The Corso Restaurant & Bar in the hotel **Inter-Continental Budapest** has a fantastic city view (see page 74). The **Four Seasons Hotel Gresham Palace** is simply stunning, and the The Bar & Lobby Lounge—with a piano player and an extensive martini list—is a good excuse to see the place (see p. 73). The Zebrano bar and restaurant at the **Hotel Andrássy** is swanky, stylish, and . . . orange (see p. 76).

through Friday 10am to 5am, and Saturday and Sunday 5pm to daybreak. V. Királyi Pál u. 14. No phone. www.extracafe.hu. Metro: Kálvin tér or Ferenciek tere (Blue line).

Fehér Gyűrű   The dark, sparse decor, smoky and busy ambience, and the dazed bar staff all add to the strange atmosphere of this place. Space at the bar is hard to come by, yet once you find a place among the semi-comfortable bench-chairs you're bound to stay a while. Open daily 1pm to midnight. V. Balassi Bálint u. 27. No phone. Tram: 4 or 6 to Jászai Mari tér.

Fregatt   This was the first English-style pub in Hungary, though now it's too crowded and noisy to really feel like one. Hungarians make up the better half of the clientele, but American and other English-speaking expats also frequent this place. Guinness stout is on draft. Live jazz is performed on Thursday and Sunday. Open Monday through Friday 3pm to 1am, and Saturday and Sunday 5pm to 1am. V. Molnár u. 26. ✆ 1/318-9997. Metro: Ferenciek tere (Blue line) or tram 2, 47, or 49.

Irish Cat Pub   This was the first Irish-style pub in Budapest; there's Guinness on tap and a well-equipped whiskey bar. It's a popular meeting place for expats and travelers. The pub features a full menu. Open daily 11am to 2am. V. Múzeum krt. 41. ✆ 1/266-4085. www.irishcat.hu. Metro: Kálvin tér (Blue line).

Janis Pub   Named and decorated after the illustrious wild-child Janis Joplin, this easily accessible pub features a fine selection of alcohols at moderate prices, '70s and '80s hits, and the occasional live concert. Open Monday through Thursday 4pm to 2am, Friday and Saturday 4pm to 3am, and Sunday 6pm to 2am. V. Királyi Pál u. 8. ✆ 1/266-7364. www.janispub.hu. Metro: Kálvin tér or Ferenciek tere (Blue line).

John Bull Pub   One in a chain of 28 popular English pubs in central and eastern Europe, the John Bull has a sporty décor (mostly focused on hunting and golf), with comfortable chairs and plush carpeting. The rooms are well ventilated and the service is impeccable. There's occasional live music (Irish, folk, country), with no cover charge. Look for other John Bull Pubs in Budapest, as well as in smaller cities elsewhere in the country. All are uniformly pleasant places to socialize. Open daily noon to midnight. V. Apáczai Csere János u. 17. ✆ 1/388-2168. www.johnbullpub.com. Metro: Vörösmarty tér (Yellow line).

Karma Point   With its strong speak-easy image, wallet-saving prices, and straightforward bar staff, this is an underground emporium for the easygoing, young, booze-loving crowd. You're bound to have a smashing time! Open daily 3pm to 5am. VI. Zichy Jenő u. 41. No phone. Metro: Nyugati pu. (Blue line).

Katapult   Recently opened bohemian-style bar in the vicinity of the Dohány Street Synagogue, this venue draws the slacker-looking-youth with loud music, outgoing bar staff, inexpensive beer, and shots in a soothing atmosphere. The weekly live Latino music is a rarity in Budapest. Great place to start a party night. Open daily 6pm to 2am. VII. Dohány u. 1. ℂ **1/266-7226.** Metro: Astória (Red line).

Kuplung   Located in a former warehouse, Kuplung ("Clutch") packs a lively, young crowd in its stony interior. In a squat-like atmosphere, table football (*csocsó*) fans spin away on one of the many tables, while loud groovy sounds fill this vast hangar. Cheap drinks might just make you "clutch" onto your chair. Open daily 6pm to 5am. VI. Király u. 46. No phone. Tram: 4 or 6 to Király u.

Picasso Point   This cafe-bar-restaurant joint is a popular hangout among the local youth, which is understandable knowing that Picasso Point has a downright warm, welcoming atmosphere which is only underlined by the ever-smiling staff. By day the restaurant offers a wide selection of local specialties, while adventure-seekers find pleasure in the basement party-arena during nights. Open Monday through Wednesday noon to midnight, Thursday noon to 3am, Friday noon to 4am, and Saturday 6pm to 4am. VI. Hajós u. 31. ℂ **1/312-1727.** www.picassopoint.hu. Metro: Nyugati pu. (Blue line).

Pótkulcs   A bohemian bar, Pótkulcs ("Spare Key") draws an artsy-looking crowd of travelers and locals alike. Beyond the rusty metal entrance, this large pub is filled with rickety chairs, couches, and tables—a great place to socialize. The friendly yet crazy-looking chef prepares tasty and ample meals. Presenting the local artists-to-be, the pub features an eclectic mix of temporary art exhibitions and unique concerts. Open daily 5pm to 2:30am. VI. Csengery u. 65/b. ℂ **1/269-1050.** www.potkulcs.hu. Metro: Nyugati pu. (Blue line).

Sark   Located on a corner—hence the name, Sark has three levels filled with utter coolness. On the gallery, powerful black-and-white prints of characteristic faces gaze at you from the walls, the bustling bar surroundings on the main floor are usually crammed, while the blank basement dance floor hosts occasional concerts and dance crazes. Open Monday through Wednesday noon to 3am, Thursday through Saturday noon to 5pm, and Sunday 5pm to 2am. VII. Klauzál tér 14. ℂ **1/328-0752.** www.sark.hu. Tram: 4 or 6 to Wesselényi u.

Szilvuplé   Lounge/cafe/restaurant/bar compacted into one, Szilvuplé's attractiveness lies in its steady, calm, welcoming atmosphere. The secession-style indoor design, colorful cocktail bar, attentive staff, moderate prices, and talented DJs create the buzz each night. Open Thursday through Saturday 6pm to 4am, and Sunday through Wednesday 6pm to 2am. VI. Ó u. 33. ℂ **1/302-2499.** www.szilvuple.hu. Metro: Opera (Yellow line).

Szimpla   A wholly unpretentious bohemian bar packed with ramshackle antique furniture, a favorite of the local arty and adventure-seeking traveler crowd. The dimly lit, couch-packed underground cellar is a relaxing, pleasant place to unwind. Open daily noon to 2am. VII. Kertész u. 48. ℂ **1/342-1034.** Metro: Oktogon (Yellow line) or tram 4 or 6 to Király u.

Szóda   The red-dominant retro-futuristic design with snug leather couches is coupled with fitting rows of empty soda bottles. The underground bar and dance floor is shelter for the whacky all-night dance-rats. Open Monday through Friday 9am to daybreak, and Saturday and Sunday 2pm to daybreak. VII. Wesselényi u. 18. ℂ **1/461-0007.** www.szoda.com. Tram: 4 or 6 to Wesselényi u.

Finds Budapest's Underground Courtyard Parties

One of Budapest's hippest nightlife scenes can be found deep inside dark **abandoned building courtyards** not visible from the street. While the unknowing passer-by sees merely a dilapidated facade or a battered door, inside the city's youth party until dawn.

How do these parties get started? Organizers are taking advantage of properties stuck in a sort of bureaucratic purgatory, buildings with no tenants but no immediate plans for renovation. Combine this scenario with city hipsters' love of the forbidden and the experimental—and the lack of cheap, available bar spaces—and voila: A courtyard party is born.

The only party-planners who can get their hands on these downtown gardens are those who diligently keep an eye on abandoned properties safe for a take-over. Then news about the existence of these almost-secret clubs is spread uniquely by word of mouth (so you'll need to ask a local about the latest parties).

But while these spaces seem perfectly constructed for hip revelry, their buildings often have tragic histories. The abandoned building at Király St. 25, at Szimpla-kert (Szimpla garden), for example, had been occupied by families of homeless squatters who were eventually evicted by authorities. The removal of the final family—which included two children—made front page headlines, and the dramatic eviction scene drew sympathetic politicians and liberal and Socialist MP protestors. But even the words of Budapest Mayor Gábor Demszky weren't enough to stop the ousting of the family, who had lived in the building for some 3 years.

The scene of this sad drama, of course, was soon transformed into the bustling bar known as **Szimpla-kert**. Colorful paintings hung on the walled-up doors, a bar and jukebox occupied the empty courtyard, and paper lanterns and strange sculptures were hung from above. The party was eventually shut down, but the "Szimpla-kert" party still operates at various venues—though its organizer, Ábel Zsendovics, predicts its days are numbered. "This is a transitory period: today there are only four remaining plots in the district that can be occupied. By next year there will only be two, and by the summer following that this nightclub-district will be gone and office buildings will take its place."

Another outdoor courtyard of sorts is **Pótkulcs,** along Csengery Street (ask a local for the exact location), though it is not part of the courtyard triangle as it belongs to a different district—and it has held out behind its unmarked gate for 4 years. The interior is constantly changing, with various modern art creations scattered throughout. (The most interesting piece, perhaps, is called "The memories of a lover," and consists of a red telephone with its insides removed, stuck on a piece of cardboard.) Pótkulcs was also close to being closed down but has managed to stay afloat.

Although Budapest's courtyards seem to disappear one after the other, there are always one or two open, and even when the dilapidated apartment blocks of Erzsébetváros are filled with offices, the party will move on to other districts (there are 23 in all). While local governments make no progress with their plans, the garden parties party on.

Vittula A hidden small and new-wave-intimate cellar bar for travelers, expatriates, and locals alike who squeeze in to listen to retro-funky vibes or live music by local youth talents. Consistently busy and almost always unbearably smoky. Open daily 6pm till dawn. VII. Kertész u. 4. No phone. Metro: Blaha Lujza tér (Red line).

4 Hungarian Dance Houses

Although Hungarian folk music is no longer a key characteristic of rural life (except, perhaps, in Transylvania, now part of Romania), recent years have seen the growth of an urban-centered folk revival movement known as the *tánchaz* (dance house). An interactive evening of folk music and folk dancing, in a neighborhood community center, might just rank as one of the best and most authentic cultural experiences you can have in Budapest. We've listed a few of the best-known dance houses below. The format usually consists of about an hour of dance-step instruction followed by several hours of dancing accompanied by a live band, which might include some of Hungary's best folk musicians, in an authentic, casual atmosphere. You can come just to watch and listen if you're nervous about dancing.

The leading Hungarian folk band, Muzsikás, whose lead singer is the incomparable Márta Sebestyén (they have toured the U.S., playing to great acclaim), hosts a tánchaz every Thursday (Sept–May only) from 8pm to midnight (500 Ft/$2.50) at the **Marczibányi Square Cultural House (Marczibányi tér Művelődési Ház),** II. Marczibányi tér 5/a (© 1/212-2820). Take the Red line metro to Moszkva tér. If you're in town during a Muzsikás performance, don't miss it. The **FMH Cultural House (Szakszervezetek Fővárosi Művelődési Ház),** XI. Fehérvári út 47 (© 1/203-3868), hosts activities from various yoga genres, creative dance, Irish tap dancing, dance therapy, and belly dancing to arts and craft clubs like painting, sewing, and basketwork. Folk bands that perform on traditional instruments play every Thursday or Friday evening, September through May, for 500 Ft ($2.50). The evening kicks off with a tánchaz hour at 7pm. Also at the FMH Cultural House, *csángó tánchaz,* the oldest and most authentic type of traditional Hungarian folk dance, is danced Friday or Saturday from 7 to 11pm, for 500 Ft ($2.50). On the first Saturday of each month, you can enjoy the best klezmer bands in town. Tram no. 47 from Deák tér gets you to FMH Cultural House.

The founder of the Dance House movement in the early 1970s, Béla Halmos leads the crazed Kalamajka (Ruckus) band and weekend dance houses in the **Downtown Cultural House (Belvárosi Ifjúsági Művelődési Ház),** V. Molnár u. 9 (© 1/371-5928). Take the Blue metro to Ferenciek tere.

An important heritage-preserving center, the **Almássy square Culture Center (Almássy téri Művelődési Központ),** VII. Almássy tér 6 (© 1/352-1572), stages some of the best folkdance dance houses in a relaxed, easygoing atmosphere on its multi-level complex. Traditional Hungarian dances, Transylvanian "moldova" dances, Sirtos—Greek dances and native Brazilian dances are taught throughout weekdays. For the specific monthly plan check out www.almassy.hu. Entrance fees vary, averaging around 500 Ft to 1,000 Ft ($2.50–$5). A short walk from Blaha Lujza tér (Blue line or tram no. 4 or 6) gets you to this folk center.

5 Gay & Lesbian Bars

As with the capricious dance club scene, gay "in" bars become "out," or even close down, at a moment's notice. The gay bar scene in Budapest is largely male-oriented at

The Budapest Klezmer Scene

Klezmer music was originally the traditional folk music of the Yiddish-speaking Jews in the ghettos of eastern Europe. Today there's no better place to listen to it than in Budapest. What exactly is Klezmer music? It was once used as a generic term referring broadly to Jewish music, was played by itinerant musicians at weddings, and is peppered with Jewish liturgy and catchy melodies.

Throughout the years, Klezmer has been influenced by other cultures that its musicians have been in contact with—like Slavic, Greek, Turkish, Arabic, Gypsy, and most recently, American jazz and blues—although it remains easily recognizable as Klezmer. The musical style was brought back to life in the 1970s by North American Jews in a revival fueled by jazz and folk musicians, and reached Europe later. The Budapest Klezmer Band was the band that brought the revival to Hungary, and was the first Klezmer band to be created here since World War II, says Ferenc Jávori, the band's founder and leader.

The band remains the country's most successful Klezmer band, basing its tunes on what Jávori learned in his childhood from the last surviving Jewish musicians from the once-flourishing Hungarian community (part of today's Ukraine) where he grew up. "In the '70s and '80s I didn't feel like there was strong ground here for this kind of music. But the change of the system in 1989 brought the possibility for it," he said. "Jewish music didn't exist as such before because there weren't roots and grounds for growth, so the musical life in Hungary could have been described as folk or Gypsy music." For the past 15 years, however, Jewish Klezmer music has also been a significant part of Hungarian musical and cultural life, he said.

The Budapest Klezmer Band is just one of the almost dozen Klezmer bands playing in Budapest. Klezmer no longer has a strictly Jewish fan base. "The Budapest Klezmer Band plays all around the world, and through this Jewish music, we represent Hungarian culture," said Javori. The fact that non-Jews became avid Klezmer fans as well "was an incredible breakthrough," he said, "and interest is still growing."

Where to find Klezmer Music in Budapest:

- The **Pannónia Klezmer Dance House** at the Fővárosi Művelődési Ház (District 11 Culture House) every second Saturday of every month at 7:30pm. XI. Fehérvári út 47. (℃) **1/203-3868.**
- The Chagall Klezmer Band plays at the **Vera Jazz Café** VII. Osvát utca 11, on the corner of Dohány utca every other Monday at 9pm. (℃) **1/322-3611.**
- The **Klezmer Táncház** at the Ferencvárosi Művelődési Központ (District 9 Cultural Center) (IX. Haller utca 27; (℃) **1/215-5741**) is every Monday at 7:30pm.
- The **Budapest Klezmer Band** plays often throughout the year in Budapest and in the rest of the country. For information on upcoming concerts, see www.budapestklezmer.hu.
- This isn't Klezmer, but there is also an Israeli dance house in Budapest at the **Bálint Ház,** VI. Révay utca 16 ((℃) **1/311-9214;** www.jcc.hu), which is scheduled to begin again in mid-October on Monday and Thursday evenings from 6 to 9pm. Check the website for more current details.

this point, though this is starting to change. For reliable and up-to-date information, visit **www.budapestgaycity.net** or **http://budapest.gayguide.net**.

Action Bar Hidden below a large yellow "A" sign, this dark, crowed basement bar draws a wide range of local and outlandish visitors. Highlights are the spicy strip-shows and go-go shows between 3 and 4am, busy dark video rooms, and the sizzling hot atmosphere. Open daily 9pm to 5am. V. Magyar u. 42. ℂ 1/266-9148. www.action.gay.hu. Metro: Kálvin tér (Blue line).

Angel A nondescript basement establishment with a bar, a restaurant, and a huge dance floor, Angel has been around for a while now and is here to stay. The clientele is not exclusively gay, especially on Friday and Saturday nights, when Angel hosts its now-famous transvestite show starting at 11:45pm. Saturday nights are men only. Sun is an "open day" (meaning straight folks are welcome). Open Thursday through Sunday 10am to dawn. VII. Szövetség u. 33. ℂ 1/351-6490. Cover 800 Ft ($4). Metro: Blaha Lujza tér (Red line).

Árkádia In the heart of downtown this small, intimate yet crammed bar is the per-fect place to meet, dance, or get cozy with an attractive stranger, with a popular back-room. Open daily 8pm to 5am. V. Türr István u. 5. No phone. www.arkadiagaybar.hu. No cover. Metro: Vörösmarty tér (Yellow line).

Capella This trendy and fashionable bar is one of the most popular homosexual clubs in the city, though we're not fans. The funky cabaret-style shows and extravagant drag shows and the house-centered music draw a rather hectic mixture of homo and heterosexuals. Open Wednesday through Sunday 9pm to 4am. V. Belgrád rkp. 23. ℂ 1/328-6231. Cover: 1,000 Ft ($5) Metro: Fereciek tere (Blue line)

Club Bohemian Alibi A sexually mixed club/restaurant combo; desire and lust fuel up during the evening hours as the Bohemian Transvestite team takes center stage per-forming a brilliant drag show. Shows start every day at midnight. Open daily 9pm until the last guest leaves. You charge drinks with a consumption-card that you pay on the way out. Beware, the penalty for losing the card is 10,000 Ft ($50). IX. Üllő út 45. No phone. www.clubbohemian.hu. Metro: Ferenc körút (Blue line).

CoXx Club A sizzling gay men-only bar in the underground shelter and an Internet cafe rolled into one, CoXx—formerly known as Chaos—has a large art gallery on the main level. Open daily 9pm to 4am. VII. Dohány u. 38. ℂ 1/344-4884. www.coxx.hu. Cover: minimum 1,000 Ft ($5) consumption. Metro: Astoria or Blaha Lujza tér (Red line).

Darling Bar This cozy, dark, men-only, two-level bar has a friendly and helpful staff, video areas, and darkrooms. Open daily 7pm to 4am. V. Szép u. 1. No phone. No cover. Metro: Astoria (Red line).

Eklektika Café This cafe is wonderfully decorated with 1950s Socialist Realist fur-nishings, and features live jazz on Thursday, mesmerizing DJ sessions on Tuesday, and cinema club on Sunday. A quiet, intimate place with cocktail and wine menus, Eklek-tika prides itself as a gay-friendly bar. Open daily noon till midnight. Semmelweis u. 21. ℂ 1/266-1226. No cover. Metro: Astoria (Red line).

Mystery Bar The first gay bar in the city—Mystery Bar is a very small but cozy place that draws a large foreign clientele and is perfect for conversation and meeting new people. Open Monday through Friday 4pm to 4am, and Saturday and Sunday 6pm to 4am. V. Nagysándor József u. 3. ℂ 1/312-1436. www.mysterybar.hu. No cover. Metro: Arany János utca (Blue line).

UpSide Down An elegant basement bar—formerly operated as a public bathroom—UpSide Down's clientele is mostly straight. Rather pricy, its laid-back lounge-like stylish decor is a suitable place to wind down at the end of the day. Monday and Wednesday night features gay and lesbian Karaoke. Open daily 8am to 5am. V. Podmaniczky tér 1. No phone. No cover. Metro: Arany János u. (Blue line).

6 More Entertainment

CASINOS Budapest has couple dozen casinos. Many are located in luxury hotels: **Casino Budapest Hilton,** I. Hess András tér 1–3 (© 1/375-1001); **Las Vegas Casino,** in the Atrium Hyatt Hotel, V. Roosevelt tér 2 (© 1/317-6022; www.lasvegas casino.hu); and **Orfeum Casino,** in the Hotel Béke Radisson, VI. Teréz krt. 43 (© 1/ 301-1600). Formal dress is required. Other popular casinos include: **Grand Casino Budapest,** V. Deák Ferenc u. 13 (© 1/483-0170), **Tropicana Casino,** V. Vigadó u. 2 (© 1/327-7250; www.tropicanacasino.hu), and the most elegant **Várkert Casino** on the Danube side, Ybl Miklós tér 9 (© 1/202-4244; www.varkert.com).

MOVIES A healthy number of English-language movies are always playing in Budapest. The best source of listings and addresses is either the *Budapest Sun,* or the free weekly, *Pesti Est,* which has an English-language section for movies. Movies labeled *szinkronizált, m.b.,* or *magyarul beszél* mean that the movie has been dubbed into Hungarian; *feliratos* means subtitled. Tickets cost around 600 Ft to 1,500 Ft ($3–$7.50). Most multiplexes provide the option of seeing movies in their original language (even if the movie itself was dubbed) while art movies are a bit more difficult. The two main art cinemas (www.artmozi.hu) that play daily English-language features are **Művész,** VI. Teréz krt. 30 (© 1/332-6726; tram no. 4 or 6), and **Puskin,** V. Kossuth L. u. 18 (© 1/429-6080; Red line metro to Astoria).

11

The Danube Bend

The Danube Bend (Dunakanyar), a string of small riverside towns just north of Budapest, is a popular excursion spot for both international travelers and Hungarians. The name "Danube Bend" is actually a misnomer, since the river doesn't actually change direction at this point. The Danube, which enters Hungary from the northwest, flows in a southeasterly direction for a while, forming the border with Hungary's northern neighbor, Slovakia. Just after Esztergom, about 40km (25 miles) north of Budapest, the river swings abruptly south. This is the start of the Danube Bend region. The river then swings sharply north again just before Visegrád, and then heads south again before reaching Vác. From Vác, it flows more or less directly south, through Budapest and down toward the country's Serbian and Croatian borders.

The delightful towns along the snaking Bend—in particular, Szentendre, Visegrád, and Esztergom—can easily be seen on day trips from Budapest since they're all within a couple of hours of the city. The great natural beauty of the area, where forested hills loom over the river, makes it a welcome haven for those weary of the city. Travelers with more time in Budapest can easily make a long weekend out of a visit to the Bend.

1 Exploring the Danube Bend

GETTING THERE

BY BOAT From April to September, boats run between Budapest and the towns of the Danube Bend. A leisurely boat ride through the countryside is one of the highlights of an excursion. All boats depart Budapest's Vigadó tér boat landing, which is located in Pest between Erzsébet Bridge and Szabadság Bridge, stopping to pick up passengers 5 minutes later at Buda's Batthyány tér landing, which is in Buda and is also a Red line metro stop, before continuing up the river.

Schedules and towns served are complicated, so contact **MAHART,** the state shipping company, at the Vigadó tér landing (*ⓒ* **1/318-1704;** www.mahartpassnave.hu, click on the British flag) for information. You can also get MAHART information from Tourinform.

Round-trip prices are 1,330 Ft ($6) to Szentendre, 1,390 Ft ($6.25) to Visegrád, and 1,460 Ft ($6.60) to Esztergom. Children up to age 14 receive a 50% discount, and children under 4 can travel free if they don't require their own seats.

The approximate travel time from Budapest is 2 hours to Szentendre, 3½ hours to Visegrád, and 5 hours to Esztergom. If time is tight, consider the train or bus (both of which are also considerably cheaper).

BY TRAIN For information and details on traveling by Budapest rail, see p. 32.

To Szentendre   The HÉV suburban railroad connects Budapest's Batthyány tér with Szentendre. Trains leave daily, year-round, every 20 minutes or so from 4am to 11:30pm. The one-way fare is 320 Ft ($1.45); subtract 125 Ft (55¢) if you have a valid Budapest public transportation pass. The trip takes 45 minutes.

To Visegrád   There's no direct train service to Visegrád. Instead, take the train departing from Nyugati Station to Nagymaros. The trip takes 1 hour, and there are 20 daily trains. From Nagymaros, take a **ferry (RÉV; ℂ 06/80/406-611)** across the river to Visegrád. The ferry dock is a 5-minute walk from the train station. A ferry leaves every hour throughout the day. The train ticket to Nagymaros costs 436 Ft ($1.95); the ferry ticket to Visegrád costs 200 Ft (90¢). The train-to-ferry trip is much more enjoyable than the long, slow bus ride.

To Esztergom   Seventeen trains daily make the run between Budapest's Nyugati Station and Esztergom. The trip takes about 1¼ hours. Train tickets cost 436 Ft ($1.95).

BY BUS   Approximately 30 daily buses travel the same route to Szentendre, Visegrád, and Esztergom, departing from **Budapest's Árpád híd bus station (ℂ 1/329-1450;** at the Blue line metro station of the same name). The one-way fare to Szentendre is 282 Ft ($1.25); the trip takes about 30 minutes. The fare to Visegrád is 451 Ft ($2), and the trip takes 1¼ hours. To Esztergom, take the bus that travels via a town called Dorog; it costs 563 Ft ($2.55) and takes 1¼ hours. The bus that goes to Esztergom via Visegrád takes 2 hours and costs 732 Ft ($3.30) (fare is determined by number of kilometers of travel, and this is a longer route). Keep in mind, of course, that all travel by bus is subject to occasional traffic delays, especially during rush hour.

BY CAR   From Budapest, Route 11 hugs the west bank of the Danube, taking you to Szentendre, Visegrád, and Esztergom. Alternatively, you could head "overland" to Esztergom by Route 10, switching to Route 111 at Dorog.

2 Szentendre ⭐⭐

21km (13 miles) N of Budapest

The center of Szentendre (pronounced *Sen*-ten-dreh) must rank with Pest's Váci utca and Buda's Castle District as one of the most heavily visited spots in all of Hungary. In the summer, it becomes one huge handicraft and souvenir marketplace. Despite the excess of vendors, Szentendre remains a gorgeous little town. In medieval times, Serbian settlers fleeing Turkish northward expansion populated Szentendre, which counts half a dozen Serbian churches among its rich collection of historical buildings. The town retains a distinctively Mediterranean flavor that's rare this far north in Europe.

Since the early 1900s, Szentendre has been home to an artists' colony. Today, about 100 artists live and work here. As a result, the town has a wealth of museums and galleries, the best of which are listed below. Surprisingly few people visit the museums, however, distracted perhaps by the shopping opportunities. We recommend that you explore more than the main drag, Fő tér. After the almost-suffocating hubbub of the center of the city, we're pretty sure you'll appreciate the peace and quiet of the many exhibition halls and the winding cobblestone streets that lead to a Roman Catholic churchyard at the top of the hill, with lovely views of the red-tile rooftops. Wander down side streets; Szentendre is too small for you to get lost in and too beautiful for a less-than-thorough exploration.

The Danube Bend

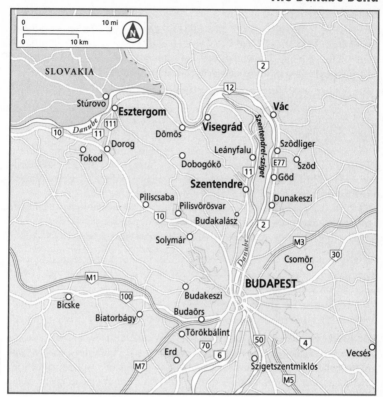

ESSENTIALS

For information on getting to Szentendre, see "Exploring the Danube Bend," above. One of Szentendre's information offices, **Tourinform,** is at Dumtsa Jenő u. 22 (✆ **26/ 317-965**), with maps of Szentendre (and the Danube Bend region), as well as concert and exhibition schedules. The office can also provide accommodations information. The office is open April through October Monday to Friday from 9am to 7pm, and weekends from 9am to 2pm; the office is closed on weekends in the off season but is open weekdays from 9am to 5pm. If you arrive in Szentendre by train or bus, you'll come upon this office as you follow the flow of pedestrian traffic into town on Kossuth Lajos utca. If you arrive by boat, you may find the **Ibusz** office sooner, located on the corner of Bogdányi út and Gőzhajó utca (✆ **26/310-181**). This office is open April to October Monday through Friday from 9am to 5pm and weekends 10am to 2pm. From November to March, it's open weekdays only, 9am to 4pm.

Another good source of information, particularly if you are planning to stay in the region more than a day, is **Jági Utazás,** at Kucsera F. u. 15 (✆/fax **26/310-030**). The staff here is extremely knowledgeable and dedicated. From planning hunting or horse-back-riding excursions to helping you find the right pension room to recommending the best *palacsinta* (crepe) place in town, they seem to know it all. The office is open weekdays 10am to 6pm in summer and 9am to 5pm in winter.

WHERE TO STAY

Róz Panzió, Pannónia utca 6/b (© **26/311-737;** fax 26/310-979; www.hotelroz szentendre.hu) has 10 units and a nice garden overlooking the Danube for breakfast when weather permits. Rooms are 40€ ($46) for a double during off season, 50€ ($63) in high season, breakfast included. Parking is available.

EXPLORING THE MUSEUMS & CHURCHES

Ámos and Anna Múzeum *✦* *(Finds*   This exceptional museum was the former home of artist couple Imre Ámos and Margit Anna, whose work represents the beginning of expressionist painting in Hungary. Opened after Anna's death in 1991, the collection is Szentendre's best-kept secret. Particularly engaging are the drawings Ámos did between periods of forced labor on the Russian front, where he eventually died of typhus. On a lighter note are Anna's wonderful puppets. Ámos' art seems influenced by Chagall, whereas Anna's work invokes Miró and Klee.

Outside the museum, in the courtyard, is Anna's gravesite, around which visitors have left wishing stones from the garden as tokens of respect.

Bogdányi u. 10. © **26/310-790.** Admission 500 Ft ($2.25). Summer daily 10am–6pm; winter daily 1–5pm.

Barcsay Museum   The conservative Socialist dictates of the day restricted the work of artist Jenő Barcsay (1900–88). Nevertheless, in his anatomical drawings, etchings, and charcoal and ink drawings, Barcsay's genius shines through. We particularly like his pastel drawings of Szentendre street scenes.

Dumtsa Jenő u. 10. © **26/310-244.** Admission 500 Ft ($2.25). Tues–Sun 10am–6pm.

Blagovestenska Church   The Blagovestenska church at Fő tér 4 is the only one of the town's several Serbian Orthodox churches that you can be fairly sure to find open. The tiny church, dating from 1752, was built on the site of a wooden church from the Serbian migration of 1690. A rococo iconostasis features paintings by Mihailo Zivkovic; notice that the eyes of all the icons are upon you.

Fő tér 4. Admission 200 Ft (90¢). Tues–Sun 10am–5pm.

Ferenczy Museum *✦✦*   Next door to the Blagovestenska in Main Square (Fő tér), the Ferenczy Museum is dedicated to the art of the extraordinary Ferenczy family. The featured artist is Károly Ferenczy, one of Hungary's leading Impressionists—you can see more of his work in Budapest's National Museum. Works by Ferenczy's lesser-known children, Noémi (tapestry maker), Valér (painter), and Beni (sculptor and medallion maker), are also on display.

Fő tér 6. © **26/310-244.** Admission 500 Ft ($2.25). Wed–Sun 10am–5pm.

Margit Kovács Museum *✦✦✦*   This expansive museum features the work of Hungary's best-known ceramic artist, Margit Kovács, who died in 1977. This museum displays the breadth of Kovács' talents. We were especially moved by her sculptures of elderly women and by her folk art–influenced friezes of village life. When the museum is full, people are required to wait outside before entering.

Vastagh György u. 1. © **26/310-244.** Admission 600 Ft ($2.70). Apr–Oct Tues–Sun 10am–6pm; Nov–Mar Tues–Sun 10am–4pm. Walk east from Fő tér on Görög utca.

Serbian Orthodox Museum   The Serbian Orthodox Museum is housed next door to a Serbian Orthodox church (services are at 10am Sun) in one of the buildings of the former episcopate, just north of Fő tér. The collection here—one of the most

Szentendre

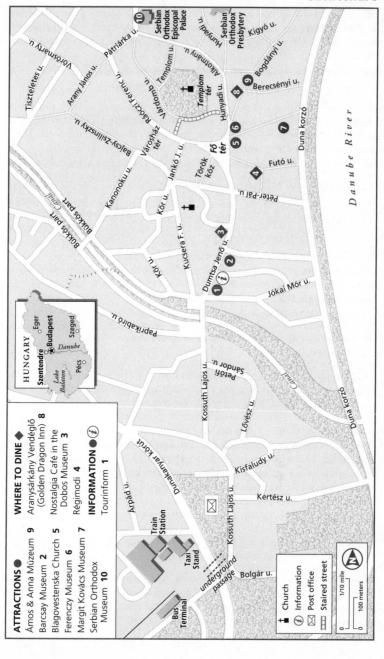

ATTRACTIONS ●
Ámos & Anna Múzeum **9**
Barcsay Museum **2**
Blagovestenska Church **5**
Ferenczy Museum **6**
Margit Kovács Museum **7**
Serbian Orthodox
Museum **10**

WHERE TO DINE ◆
Aranysárkány Vendéglő
(Golden Dragon Inn) **8**
Nostalgia Café in the
Dobos Museum **3**
Régimódi **4**

INFORMATION ● ⓘ
Tourinform **1**

■♦ Church
ⓘ Information
⊠ Post office
▨ Staired street

0   1/10 mile
0   100 meters

extensive of its kind in predominantly Catholic Hungary—features exceptional 16th-through 19th-century icons, liturgical vessels, scrolls in Arabic from the Ottoman period, and other types of ecclesiastical art. Informative labels are in Hungarian and English.

Pátriárka u. 5. ☎ 26/312-399. Admission 400 Ft ($1.80). Apr–Oct Tues–Sun 10am–5pm; Nov–Mar Fri–Sun 10am–4pm. Walk north from Fő tér on Alkotmány utca.

SIGHTS OUTSIDE TOWN

Pap-sziget (Priest's Island)   This island at the northern end of town provides a place to rest and relax, with thermal waters in the outdoor bathing pools. Bring a bathing suit and towel or rent towels there.

Facilities include basic locker rooms. No entrance fee. Buses for Leányfalu and Visegrád pass the bridge to Pap-sziget.

Skanzen (Open-Air Ethnographical Museum) *Kids*   About 3km (2 miles) north-west of Szentendre is one of Hungary's better *skanzens,* or reproduction peasant villages. This ambitious *skanzen,* the largest in the country, represents rural life from all regions of the country. There are several reconstructed 18th- and 19th-century villages, with thatch-roofed houses, blacksmith and weaving shops, working mills, and churches. A guidebook in English is available at the gate.

Buses that can get you to Skanzen depart from Platform 8 of Szentendre's bus station, adjacent to the HÉV station (get off at the Szabadság-forrás stop). If you're driving, follow Route 10 N. Turn left on Sztaravodai út.

Sztaravodai út. ☎ 26/312-304. www.skanzen.hu. Admission 700 Ft ($3.15). family ticket 1,750 Ft ($7.90). Apr–June and Sept–Oct daily 9am–5pm; July–Aug daily 9am–7pm (but the exhibitions are closed 5–7pm and you can purchase a so-called "walking ticket" only, for 250 Ft/$1.15). Closed Nov–Mar. See directions above.

WHERE TO DINE

Aranysárkány Vendéglő (Golden Dragon Inn) ✦ HUNGARIAN   Located just east of Fő tér on Hunyadi utca, which leads into Alkotmány utca, the Golden Dragon is always filled to capacity. The crowd includes a good percentage of Hungarians, definitely a good sign in a heavily visited town like Szentendre.

Long wooden tables set with sterling cutlery provide a relaxed but tasteful atmosphere in this air-conditioned restaurant. You can choose from such enticing offerings as alpine lamb, roast leg of goose, Székely-style stuffed cabbage (the Székely are a Hungarian ethnic group native to Transylvania), spinach cream, and venison steak. Vegetarians can order the vegetable plate, a respectable presentation of grilled and steamed vegetables in season. The cheese dumplings do a good job of rounding out the meal. Various traditional Hungarian beers are on draft, and the wine list features selections from 22 regions of the country.

Alkotmány u. 1/a. ☎ 26/301-479. www.aranysarkany.hu. Reservations recommended. Soup 700 Ft–800 Ft ($3.15–$3.60); main courses 1,900 Ft–2,600 Ft ($8.55–$12). AE, DC, MC, V. Daily noon–10pm.

Nosztalgia Café in the Dobos Museum *Kids* CAFE   Be sure to stop into the Nosztalgia coffee shop at this museum of desserts for a slice of authentic *Dobos torta,* a sumptuously rich layer cake named after pastry chef József Dobos, who experimented with butter frostings in the 19th century. The success of his recipe was immediate, and he was quickly appointed the official baker for the Habsburg emperor. Dobos's formerly secret recipe book and photographs of the man himself are on display upstairs in the cafe. This place tends to get crowded in the summer, but it's worth the wait.

Bogdányi u 2. ℭ **26/311-660.** Reservations not accepted. Pastries 250 Ft–800 Ft ($1.10–$3.60). No credit cards. Daily 10am–8pm; entrance to the museum upstairs is 300 Ft ($2.25).

Régimódi ⍟ HUNGARIAN   If you walk directly south from Fő tér, you'll find this excellent choice for dining. An elegant restaurant in a former private home, Régimódi is furnished with antique Hungarian carpets and chandeliers. Original artworks decorate the walls. Limited terrace dining is available, though you might not want to miss out on eating amid the rich interior decor. The menu offers a wide range of Hungarian specialties, with an emphasis on game dishes. The wild-deer stew in red wine is particularly sumptuous, while less adventurous diners might opt for the turkey breast stuffed with stewed fruit in cheese sauce. The menu also features numerous salad options. There's an extensive wine list.

Futó u. 3. ℭ **26/311-105.** Reservations recommended. Soup 400 Ft–500 Ft ($1.80–$2.25); main courses 1,200 Ft–3,000 Ft ($5.40–$14). DC, MC, V. Daily 9am–11pm.

3 Visegrád ⍟

45km (28 miles) NW of Budapest

Halfway between Szentendre and Esztergom, Visegrád (pronounced *Vee*-sheh-grod) is a sparsely populated, sleepy riverside village, which makes its history all the more fascinating and hard to believe: The Romans built a fort here, which was still standing when Slovak settlers gave the town its present name (meaning "High Castle") in the 9th or 10th century. After the Mongol invasion (1241–42), construction began on both the present ruined hilltop citadel and the former riverside palace. Eventually, Visegrád boasted one of the finest royal palaces ever built in Hungary. Only one king, Charles Robert (1307–42), actually used it as his primary residence, but monarchs from Béla IV, in the 13th century, through Matthias Corvinus, in the late 15th century, spent time in Visegrád and contributed to its development, the latter expanding the palace into a great Renaissance center known throughout Europe.

ESSENTIALS

For information on getting to **Visegrád,** see "Exploring the Danube Bend," earlier in this chapter. The information center, **Visegrád Tours,** RÉV u. 15 (ℭ **26/398-160**), is located across the road from the RÉV ferryboat landing (not to be confused with the MAHART boat landing, which is about .75km/½ mile down the road). It is open daily from April through October 9am to 6pm, from November through March weekdays 10am to 4pm.

⌜Kids⌝ An Annual Festival

Each summer on the second weekend in July, Visegrád hosts the **International Palace Tournament** ⍟⍟, an authentic medieval festival replete with dueling knights on horseback, and medieval music and dance. If you cannot make it to this fabulous event, you can enjoy a tournament on a smaller scale combined with a medieval dinner at 6pm on Thursdays in July and August. For more information, contact Visegrád Tours at ℭ **26/398-160.**

WHERE TO STAY

Good accommodations can be found at **Honti Panzió,** Fő utca 66 (© **26/398-120;** www.hotels.hu/honti), which has 7 units. Double rooms are 40€ ($46) year-round, breakfast included; parking is provided.

EXPLORING THE PALACE & THE CITADEL

The **Royal Palace** once covered much of the area where the MAHART boat landing and Fő utca (Main St.) are now found. Indeed, the entrance to the palace's open-air ruins, called the **King Matthias Museum,** is at Fő u. 29 (© **26/398-126**). Admission is 400 Ft ($1.80). The museum is open Tuesday through Sunday 9am to 4:30pm. The buried ruins of the palace, having achieved a near-mythical status, were discovered only recently. Almost all of what you see is the result of ongoing reconstruction, which has been vigorous in recent years. Aside from the general atmosphere of ruined grandeur, the main attractions are the red-marble base of the Hercules Fountain in the Ornamental Courtyard and the reconstructed Gothic arcaded hallway down below. Exhibit descriptions are in English. Because of the under-construction aspect of the place, you need to keep a close eye on the kids here.

The **Citadel** ✶✶ (© **26/398-101**), situated on the hilltop above Visegrád, affords one of the finest views you'll find over the Danube. Off to your left you can see the site of the controversial Nagymaros Dam, an abandoned Hungarian-Czechoslovak hydroelectric project (for more information on this dam dispute, see "Esztergom," below). Admission to the Citadel is 400 Ft ($1.80). It is open daily in summer 9am to 6pm, in winter on weekends only from 9:30am to 6pm. There are three buses a day to the Citadel, departing from the RÉV ferryboat terminal at 9:26am, 12:26pm, and 3:26pm, respectively. Otherwise, "City Bus," an inappropriately named van taxi that awaits passengers outside Visegrád Tours, takes people up the steep incline to the Citadel for the equally steep fare of 2,500 Ft ($11) apiece. If you decide to go on foot, keep in mind that it's more than a casual walk to the Citadel; the journey up the hill takes about 2 hours. There may be snack and ice-cream carts along the way, but there are no permanent establishments, so you many want to pack some snacks and drinks.

WHERE TO DINE

Don Vito Pizzeria & Ristorante ✶ *Kids* PIZZA   Don Vito Pizzeria serves very good pizza in a pleasant, relaxed atmosphere. It's a good option if you're traveling with kids. Try the "Don Vito," a delicious and very Hungarian mushroom, gooseliver, and apple pizza, or the beautiful "Albino," which is great for vegetarians with a ricotta, garlic, and herb topping. Beer and wine are served.

Fő u. 83. © **26/397-230.** Individual pizzas 600 Ft–1,400 Ft ($2.70–$6.30). No credit cards. Daily 11am–midnight.

Renaissance Restaurant ✶✶ *Kids* HUNGARIAN   This restaurant specializes in authentic medieval cuisine. Food is served in clay crockery without silverware (you only get a wooden spoon) and guests are offered Burger King–like paper crowns to wear. The decor and the lyre music enhance the fun, openly kitschy atmosphere. This is perhaps the only restaurant in the whole country where you won't find something on the menu spiced with paprika, since the spice wasn't around in medieval Hungary. If you're big on the medieval theme, come for dinner on a Thursday (July–Aug), when a six-course "Royal Feast" is served following a 45-minute duel between knights. No vegetarians, please! Tickets for this special evening are handled by Visegrád Tours (p. 18). The duel gets underway at 6pm sharp.

Fő u. 11 (across the street from the MAHART boat landing). ℂ **26/398-081.** Main courses range from 1,900 Ft–3,200 Ft ($8.55–$14). V. Daily noon–10pm.

4 Esztergom ⍟

46km (29 miles) NW of Budapest

Formerly a Roman settlement, Esztergom (pronounced *Ess*-tair-gome) was the seat of the Hungarian kingdom for 300 years. Prince Géza and his son Vajk, who was crowned by the pope in A.D. 1000 as Hungary's first king, István I (Stephen I), were the first rulers to call Esztergom home. István converted Hungary to Catholicism, and Esztergom became the country's center of the early church. Though its glory days are far behind it, this quiet town remains the seat of the archbishop-primate—it's the "Hungarian Rome." The first post-Communist regime in 1990 tried to enhance the city's political weight by bringing the Constitutional Court here.

From Esztergom west all the way to the Austrian border, the Danube marks the border between Hungary and Slovakia. There's an international ferry crossing at Esztergom.

ESSENTIALS

For information on getting to Esztergom, see "Exploring the Danube Bend," earlier in this chapter. **Gran Tours,** centrally located at Széchenyi tér 25 (ℂ **33/502-001**), is the best source of information in Esztergom. The office is open in summer Monday through Friday from 8am to 4pm and on Saturday from 9am to noon; in winter, Monday through Friday from 8am to 4pm. You can get city maps and concert information and book private rooms here.

EXPLORING THE TOWN

Castle Museum   This museum is next door to the cathedral, in the reconstructed Royal Palace. The palace, vacated by Hungarian royalty in the 13th century, was used thereafter by the archbishop. Though it was one of only two fortresses in Hungary that

---

Fun Fact   **Prímás-sziget: A Bridge Over Troubled Waters**

Across the Danube from Esztergom is the Slovak town of Sturovo. The Mária Valéria Bridge, a link that the Germans blew up in World War II, has recently reconnected the two towns. Until 2001 all that remained was a curious stump, along with four unconnected pylons in the river.

This was the last Danube bridge destroyed by the Germans in World War II to be rebuilt. A grassroots movement in Hungary favored reconstruction of the bridge, since travel between the two countries in this region was primarily dependent on boats. The reconstruction turned out to be a success: The personal friendship that is said to have developed between the Hungarian prime minister and the Slovakian president at the time seemed to ease the otherwise still-troubled relations between the two countries.

The site of the new bridge is halfway between the Hotel Esztergom and Szalma Csárda (see "Where to Dine," below). To get there, walk straight on Táncsics Mihály utca until you hit the river.

Moments **Braving the Tower**

Ascending the cramped tower of Esztergom Cathedral can be a somewhat creepy experience; but if you do venture up, you'll be rewarded with unparalleled views of Esztergom and the surrounding Hungarian and Slovak countryside.

---

was able to withstand the Mongol onslaught in 1241 and 1242, it fell into disrepair under the Turkish occupation. The museum has an extensive collection of weapons, coins, pottery, stove tiles, and fragments of old stone columns; unfortunately, the descriptions are in Hungarian only. Outside the palace, sections of the fortified walls have been reconstructed.

Szent István tér. ✆ **33/415-986.** Admission 350 Ft ($1.60); special exhibits 350 Ft–500 Ft ($1.60–$2.25). Summer Tues–Sun 10am–6pm; winter Tues–Sun 9am–5pm.

Esztergom Cathedral ✦ *Kids*   This massive, neoclassical cathedral on Castle Hill is Esztergom's most popular attraction and one of Hungary's most impressive buildings. It was built in the 19th century to replace the cathedral that was ruined during the Turkish occupation. The intricately carved red-marble, Renaissance-style **Bakócz Chapel** inside the cathedral (to the left) dates from the early 16th century. The chapel survived the Turkish destruction of the former cathedral; when the present structure was being built, the chapel was dismantled (into 1,600 numbered pieces) to be reincorporated into the new cathedral. The cathedral **Treasury (Kincstár)** contains a stunning array of ecclesiastical jewels and gold works. Since Cardinal Mindszenty's body was moved to the **crypt** in 1991 (he died in exile in 1975), this place has become a pilgrimage site for Hungarians, who come to see the final resting place of this uncompromisingly anti-Communist cleric who spent a good portion of the Cold War living inside the American embassy in Budapest. The **cupola** has, as far as church towers go, one of the scarier and more cramped ascents, but children seem to love the climb and the views from the top.

If you happen to be in town during the first week of August, don't miss out on one of the classical guitar concerts performed in the cathedral. The acoustics are sublime. The concerts are part of Esztergom's annual **International Guitar Festival** ✦✦.

Szent István tér. ✆ **33/411-895.** Treasury 350 Ft ($1.60); cupola 250 Ft ($1.10). Cathedral: summer daily 9am–5pm; winter daily 11am–4pm; closed Jan–Feb. Treasury, crypt, cupola: summer daily 9am–5pm; winter daily 11am–4pm.

Keresztény Múzeum (Christian Museum)   This museum, in the neoclassical former primate's palace, houses Hungary's largest collection of religious art and the largest collection of medieval art outside the National Gallery in Budapest. The Lord's Coffin of Garamszentbenedek is probably the museum's most famous piece; the ornately carved, gilded coffin on wheels was originally used in Easter celebrations.

To get to the museum, continue past the Watertown Parish Church on Berényi Zsigmond utca. Even if you don't plan on visiting this museum, it's definitely worth it to take a break from the crowds at the cathedral and take a stroll through the quiet, cobblestone streets of Esztergom's Víziváros (Watertown).

Mindszenty tér 2. ✆ **33/413-880.** Admission 350 Ft ($1.60) adults, free for children. Tues–Sun 10am–5pm. Closed Jan–Feb.

WHERE TO STAY

Alabárdos Panzió 🏵 This fine yellow building is located in the heart of Esztergom, just minutes from Castle Hill. Although it's situated on the town's main thoroughfare, the pension is set back off the road and is much quieter than you'd expect.
A restaurant of the same name is in the front of the building. Pension rooms are small
but clean and cheery. A cross hangs over every bed, and every room has a toilet and
shower. To find the reception, go up the steep cobblestone driveway to the left of the
building.

Bajcsy-Zsilinszky út 49, 2500 Esztergom. ✆ **33/312-640.** 21 units. High season 7,500 Ft ($34) single, 9,500 Ft ($43)
double; low season about 15% lower. Rates include breakfast. No credit cards. Free parking. Bus: 1, 5, or 6 from the
train station. **Amenities:** Restaurant. *In room:* TV, no phone.

WHERE TO DINE

Szalma Csárda 🏵🏵🏵 The food at this remodeled and enlarged restaurant is
absolutely first-rate, with everything made to order and served piping hot. The excellent house soups—fish soup *(halászlé),* goulash *(gulyásleves),* and bean soup *(babgulyás)*—are all large enough to constitute meals in themselves; they cost from 700 Ft to
900 Ft ($3.15–$4). For main courses, the stuffed cabbage *(töltött káposzta)* and the
stuffed pepper *(töltött paprika)* are both outstanding, though not always offered. Finish off your meal with a dish of sweet chestnut purée *(gesztenyepüré),* a Hungarian specialty prepared here to perfection. There are outdoor tables as well as seating in two
dining rooms.

Nagy-Duna sétány 2. ✆ **33/315-336.** Main courses 1,000 Ft–1,800 Ft ($4.50–$8.10). No credit cards. Summer daily
noon–midnight; winter Mon–Fri noon–8pm, weekends 10am–10pm.

12

The Lake Balaton Region

Lake Balaton may not be the Mediterranean, but don't tell that to Hungarians. Somehow, over the years, Hungarians have managed to create their own central European version of a Mediterranean culture along the shores of their long, shallow, milky-white lake. Throughout the long summer, swimmers, windsurfers, sailors, kayakers, and cruisers fill the warm and silky smooth lake, Europe's largest at 80km (50 miles) long and 15km (10 miles) wide at its broadest point. Around the lake's 197km (315 miles) of shoreline, vacationers cast their reels for pike; play tennis, soccer, and volleyball; ride horses; and hike in the hills.

First settled in the Iron Age, the Balaton region has been a recreation spot since at least Roman times. From the 18th century onward, the upper classes erected spas and villas along the shoreline. Not until the post–World War II Communist era did the lake open up to a wider tourist base. Many large hotels along the lake are former trade union resorts built under the previous regime.

Lake Balaton seems to have something for everyone. Teenagers, students, and young travelers tend to congregate in the hedonistic towns on the south shore, where the land is as flat as it is in Pest. Here, huge 1970s-style beachside hotels are filled to capacity all summer long, and disco music pulsates into the early morning hours. From these resorts, you can walk for 10 minutes and find yourself deep in farm country. The air here is still and quiet; in summer the sun hangs heavily in the sky.

Adult travelers and families tend to spend more time on the hillier, more graceful, north shore. There, little villages are neatly tucked away in the rolling countryside, where the grapes of the popular Balaton wines ripen in the strong southern sun. If you're coming from Budapest, the northern shore of the lake at first appears every bit as built up and crowded as the southern shore. Beyond Balatonfüred, however, this impression begins to fade. You'll discover the Tihany Peninsula, a protected area whose 12 sq. km (4¾ sq. miles) jut out into the lake like a knob. Moving westward along the coast, passing from one lakeside settlement to the next, you can make forays inland into the rolling hills of the Balaton wine country. Stop for a swim—or for the night—in a small town like Szigliget. The city of Keszthely, sitting at the lake's western edge, marks the end of the northern shore area. All towns on the lake are within 1½ to 4 hours from Budapest by an InterCity, a *gyors* (fast) train, or a much longer journey on a *személy* (local) train (p. 32).

Since the summer of 2000, a cultural event called "The Valley of Arts" has been held on the northern side of the lake, near **Kapolcs,** attracting thousands of local and international artists and travelers. It was started as a local project by a handful of Hungarian contemporary artists who settled down in Kapolcs, the center of six little adjacent villages in the gorgeous Káli valley. The 10-day-long arts event includes film, music, theater, visual art exhibits, and literature readings, and is held at the end of July, running through the beginning of August. Visit www. kapolcs.hu for information on exact dates. For general information on programs and services of just about any area of Balaton, see www.balaton-tourism.hu.

1 Exploring the Lake Balaton Region

GETTING THERE & GETTING AROUND

BY TRAIN   From Budapest, trains to the various towns along the lake depart from Déli Station. The local *(személy)* trains are interminably slow, stopping at each village along the lake. Unless you're going to a tiny village (sometimes a good idea), try to get on an express *(gyors)* train. To Keszthely, the trip takes about 3 hours and costs 2,030 Ft ($10). To reach Tihany, take a train to Balatonfüred for 1,420 Ft ($7.10; travel time 2 hr.), and then a local bus to Tihany.

BY CAR   From Budapest, take the M7 motorway south through Székesfehérvár until you hit the lake. Route 71 circles the lake.

If you're planning to visit Lake Balaton for more than a day or two, you should consider renting a car, which will give you much greater mobility. The various towns differ enough from one another that you may want to keep driving until you find a place that really speaks to you. Without a car, this is obviously more difficult. Also, wherever you go in the region, you'll find that private rooms are both cheaper and easier to get if you travel a few miles off the lake. Driving directly to the lake from Budapest will take about an hour and 15 minutes.

BY BOAT & FERRY   Passenger boats on Lake Balaton let you travel across the lake as well as between towns on the same shore. The boat routes are extensive, and the rates are cheap, but the boats are considerably slower than surface transportation. All major towns have docks with departures and arrivals. Children 3 and under travel free, and those 13 and under get half-price tickets. A single ferry *(komp)* running between Tihany and Szántód lets you transport a car across the width of the lake.

All boat and ferry information is available from the **BAHART** office in Siófok (© **84/310-050** or 84/312-144; www.balatonihajozas.hu). Local tourist offices all along the lake (several listed below) also have schedules and other information.

BY BUS   Once at the lake, you might find that buses are the best way of getting around locally. Buses will be indispensable, of course, if you take private-room lodging a few miles away from the lake.

WHERE TO STAY IN THE AREA

Because hotel prices are unusually high in the Balaton region, and since just about every local family rents out a room or two in summer, we especially recommend private rooms as the lodging of choice in this area. You can reserve a room through a local tourist office or you can just look for the ubiquitous SZOBA KIADÓ (or ZIMMER FREI) signs that decorate most front gates in the region. When you take a room without using a tourist agency as the intermediary, prices are generally negotiable. (Owners sometimes prefer hard currency.) In the height of the season, you shouldn't have to pay more than 6,000 Ft ($30) for a double room within reasonable proximity of the lake.

Many budget travelers pitch their tents in **lakeside campgrounds** all around the lake. Campgrounds are generally quite inexpensive, and their locations are well marked on maps.

Lake Balaton Region

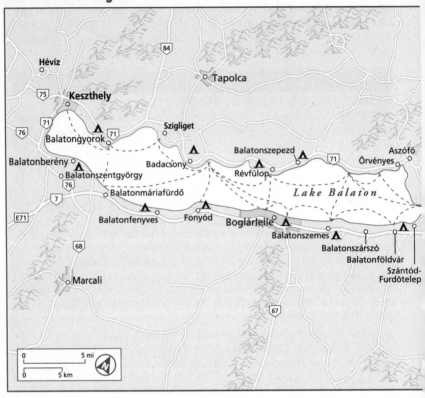

All the campgrounds have working facilities, but are probably not as clean as many people are accustomed to.

2 En Route to Lake Balaton: Veszprém ★★

116km (72 miles) SW of Budapest

Just 16km (10 miles) from Lake Balaton, Veszprém (pronounced *Vess*-praym) surely ranks as one of Hungary's most charming and vibrant small cities. It often serves as a starting point for trips to the Balaton resort area. You'll find a harmonious mix of old and new here: A delightfully self-contained and well-preserved, 18th-century baroque Castle District spills effortlessly into a typically modern city center, which is distinguished by its lively wide-open pedestrian-only plazas.

The history of Veszprém, like the scenic Bakony countryside that surrounds it, is full of peaks and valleys. The city was first established as an Episcopal seat in the time of King Stephen I, Hungary's first Christian king, but was completely destroyed during the course of the long Turkish occupation, the Habsburg-Turkish battles, and the subsequent Hungarian-Austrian independence skirmishes. The reconstruction of Veszprém commenced in the early 18th century, though the castle itself, blown up by

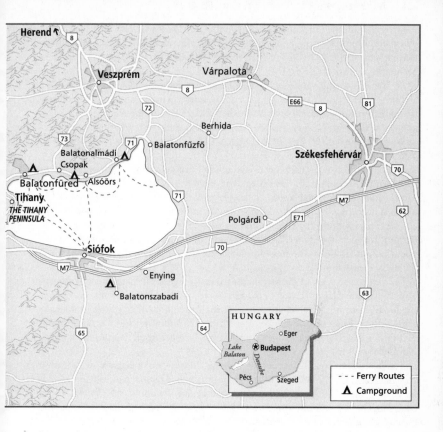

the Austrians in 1702, was never rebuilt. The baroque character of the city attracts thousands of visitors each year.

ESSENTIALS

GETTING THERE Nine daily **trains** depart Budapest's Déli Station for Veszprém, a 2-hour trip. Tickets cost 1,500 Ft ($7.50), or 2,400 ($12) if you take the faster Inter-City train.

If you're **driving** from Budapest, take the M7 motorway to Székesfehérvár, and then Route 8 to Veszprém.

VISITOR INFORMATION Tourinform, Vár u. 4 (© 88/404-548), is open Monday through Friday 9am to 6pm, Saturday and Sunday 10am to 4pm (only weekdays in winter); **Ibusz,** Rákoczi u. 6 (© 88/565-540), is open Monday through Friday from 8:30am to 4:30pm. Both offices provide information, sell city maps, and help with hotel and private-room bookings.

EXPLORING THE CITY

Most of Veszprém's main sights are clustered along Vár utca, the street that runs the length of the city's small but lovely Castle District. The Bakony Museum, though, is located in the new (low) part of town.

Housed inside an 18th-century canon's house, the **Queen Gizella Museum,** Vár u. 35 (℅ **88/426-088**), has a fine collection of religious (Roman Catholic) art. Admission is 300 Ft ($1.50). It's open May to October daily from 10am to 5pm; closed November to April.

At Vár u. 16, the vaulted **Gizella Chapel** (℅ **88/426-088**), named for King Stephen's wife, was unearthed during the construction of the adjoining Bishop's Palace in the 18th century. Today it houses a modest collection of ecclesiastical art, but is best known for the 13th-century frescoes that, in various states of restoration, decorate its walls. Admission is 100 Ft (50¢). It's open May to October daily from 9:30am to 5:30pm; closed November to April.

In addition to Roman relics uncovered in the surrounding area, the **Laczkó Dezső Museum** (℅ **88/564-310**), near Megyeház tér, features local folk exhibits (art, costumes, tools, utensils, and so on). There are also exhibits about the legendary highwaymen of the region, celebrated figures from 19th-century Bakony who share some characteristics with the legendary outlaws of the American West. Admission is 300 Ft ($1.50). It's open in summer Tuesday through Sunday from 10am to 6pm; in winter, noon to 4pm. To get to the museum, walk directly south from Szabadság tér, where the old and new towns converge.

For a wonderful view of the surrounding Bakony region, climb the steps to the narrow observation deck at the top of the **Fire Tower** ⚘, adjacent to Óváros tér. Though the foundations of the tower are medieval, the structure itself was built in the early 19th century. Enter via the courtyard of Vár u. 17, behind Óváros tér. Admission is 300 Ft ($1.50). The tower is open daily May to October from 10am to 6pm; closed November to April.

The **Veszprém Zoo (Kittenberger Kálmán Növény és Vadaspark)** is located at Kittenberger u. 15 (℅ **88/566-140**). It's open daily in summer 9am to 6pm, in winter daily from 9am to 3pm. Admission is 800 Ft ($4) for adults, 540 Ft ($2.70) for children. The zoo is set in a small wooded valley at the edge of the city center and boasts 550 animals from 130 species. It's rather sad and depressing by some zoo standards, but the kids will still learn something.

WHERE TO STAY

You'll pay some 2,500 Ft ($13) for a double room in a private home in Veszprém, and you can find a list of accommodations at www.veszpreminfo.hu. The room price usually does not include breakfast. You can book a private room through either of the tourist offices mentioned on p. 11.

Péter-Pál Panzió ⚘, Dózsa György u. 3 (℅ **88/328-091**), is a value option that's conveniently located a 5-minute walk from the city center. Currently, there are 16 tidy but very small rooms, all with twin beds, toilet, shower, and television. Insist on a room in the rear of the building, as the pension sits close to a busy road. Rates are 8,900 Ft ($45) double and 11,900 Ft ($60) triple. Breakfast is included and is served in the garden in summer. Call ahead for reservations.

Hotel Villa Medici ⚘⚘, Kittenberger u. 11 (℅/fax **88/590-070**), is a modern, full-service hotel set in a small gorge on the edge of the city, next to Veszprém's zoo-park. There are 24 double rooms and two suites; each has a telephone, a minibar, a TV, and a bathroom with a shower. The hotel also features a sauna and a small indoor swimming pool. Rates are 19,900 Ft to 21,000 Ft ($99–$105) for a double room; 27,500 Ft ($137) for a suite. Credit cards are accepted and breakfast is included. Bus

Herend: Home of Hungary's Finest Porcelain

About 16km (10 miles) west of Veszprém lies the sleepy village of Herend. What distinguishes this village from other villages in the area is the presence of the Herend Porcelain factory, where Hungary's finest porcelain has been made since 1826.

Herend Porcelain began to establish its international reputation as far back as 1851, when a dinner set was displayed at the Great Exhibition in London. Artists hand-paint every piece, from tableware to decorative accessories. Patterns include delicate flowers, butterflies, and birds.

The recently opened **Porcelanium Visitors Center,** at Kossuth Lajos utca 140 in Herend, features the newly expanded Herend Museum (© **88/261-801**), which displays a dazzling collection of Herend porcelain. A minitour of the factory and a porcelain-making demonstration film are also part of the visitor center offerings. The Porcelanium is open daily from May to October, 9am to 5:30pm; Tuesday to Saturday only, from November to April, 9am to 3:30pm. Admission is 400 Ft ($1.80). At the **factory store** (© **88/523-223**), which accepts credit cards, you might find patterns that are unavailable in Budapest's Herend Shop (p. 197). Prices will be comparable to those in Budapest, but much less than what Herend costs in the United States. The factory store is open in summer Monday through Saturday from 9:30am to 6pm, Sunday until 4pm; in winter Monday through Friday from 9:30am to 4pm, Saturday 9:30am to 2pm. The Porcelanium Visitors Center also has a coffeehouse and upscale restaurant. Food is served on Herend china, naturally. Herend is easily accessible via bus from Veszprém.

nos. 3, 5, and 10, leaving from the main bus station, and bus no. 1, leaving from the railway station, take you as far as the bridge overlooking the gorge. You can easily walk from there.

WHERE TO DINE

Veszprém does not have many dining options, but you should be able to find a satisfying meal at the following places:

Cserhát Étterem ⑅, also housed in the huge structure at Kossuth u. 6 (© **88/425-441**), is an authentic *önkiszólgáló* (self-service cafeteria). Cserhát serves up extremely cheap traditional fare. Hearty meals are available for less than 600 Ft ($3). The menu changes daily; it's posted on a bulletin board at the bottom of the stairs. This place is open Monday through Friday from 9am to 6pm and Saturday 9am to 3pm.

You can get lunch or dinner at **Óváros Vendéglő (Old City Guesthouse),** Szabadság tér 14 (© **88/326-790**), a traditional Hungarian restaurant with a large outdoor terrace and a number of smaller indoor dining rooms. The food is fine, and main courses run 850 Ft to 1,500 Ft ($4.25–$7.50). It's open daily 8am to 10pm.

For something more upscale, **Villa Medici Étterem** ⑅⑅ (owned by the same people who own the hotel), at Kittenberger u. 11 (© **88/590-072**), is the place. This restaurant is considered among the top restaurants in Hungary, with Hungarian/Continental dishes such as pikeperch stuffed with salmon, or the sirloin steak in a salt coating. Main courses here start around 3,000 Ft ($15), and the restaurant is open daily from noon to 11pm.

3 The Tihany Peninsula /★/★

The Tihany (pronounced *Tee*-hine) Peninsula, a national park since 1952, has several towns on it, the most notable of which is called, appropriately, **Tihany** (or Tihany Village). Because the peninsula is a protected area, building is heavily restricted; consequently, this area maintains a rustic charm that's unusual in the Balaton region.

The Tihany Peninsula also features a lush, protected interior, accessible by a trail from Tihany Village, with several little inland lakes—including the aptly named **Inner Lake** and **Outer Lake**—as well as a lookout tower offering views out over the Balaton. Give yourself at least an hour or two to explore the interior.

As you travel west from the Tihany Peninsula, the landscape begins to get hillier.

ESSENTIALS

GETTING THERE The rail line that circles Lake Balaton does not serve the Tihany Peninsula. The nearest railway station is in Aszófő, about 5km (3 miles) from Tihany Village. A local bus to Tihany, synchronized to the rail timetable, departs from just outside the railway station in Aszófő and from just outside the railway station in the larger nearby town of Balatonfüred. You can also go by ferry from Szántód or Balatonföldvár, or by boat from Balatonfüred.

VISITOR INFORMATION Visitor information and private-room bookings for the Tihany Peninsula are available in Tihany Village at **Tourinform,** Kossuth u. 20 (©/fax **87/448-804;** www.tourinform.hu). The office is open May through October only, Monday through Friday from 8:30am to 7pm and on weekends from 8:30am to 12:30pm.

EXPLORING TIHANY VILLAGE

The 18th-century baroque **Abbey Church** ⚑ is, undoubtedly, Tihany Village's main attraction. The church stands on the site of an earlier 11th-century Romanesque church (the charter for which contains the first words ever written in Hungarian), around whose remains the crypt of the current church was built. These remains include the marble gravestone of King Andrew, who died in 1060; this is the sole Hungarian royal tomb that remains in its original location. A resident Austrian-born monk carved the exquisite wooden altar and pulpit in the 18th century. The frescoes in the church are by three of Hungary's better-known 19th-century painters, whose work can be viewed throughout the country: Károly Lotz, Bertalan Székely, and Lajos Deák-Ébner.

Next door to the Abbey Church is the **Tihany Museum** (© **87/448-650**), housed in an 18th-century baroque structure, like the church. The museum features exhibitions on the surrounding region's history and culture. You pay a single entry fee of 500 Ft ($2.50) for both the church and museum. Both are open daily from 9am to 5:30pm.

Tihany Village is also the site of the legendary **Echo Hill,** a scenic spot overlooking the lake (near the Echo Restaurant), which is reached via a winding path that starts from the left side of the Abbey Church. Voices on Echo Hill reverberate back from the side of the church. See for yourself.

Some say the best ice cream on Lake Balaton is to be had at the shop on the road between the Abbey Church and Echo Hill.

4 Badacsony & Szigliget ★★

160km (100 miles) SW of Budapest

BADACSONY

Nestled in one of the most picturesque corners of Lake Balaton is Badacsony, an area which includes four villages noted for their beautiful vistas and some the best wines of Hungary. The Badacsony area is dotted with wine cellars, and the tradition of viticulture and winegrowing dates back to the Celtic and Roman times. Other than wine tasting, Badacsony boasts walking trails where you can study the diverse basalt forms and the former quarry walls. You'll also find a 4km-long (2.5-mile) circular trail, starting from the Kisfaludy House on the southern side of Badacsony Hill. Contact **Botanikai tanösvény Badacsony** (© 87/461-069; www.bfnpi.hu) for guided tours.

One of the better-known vintners in Hungary is Huba Szeremley, whose Badacsony wines have consistently been winners in Italy, France, and Hungary. The best way to find out about Szeremley's regular wine tastings is to visit his restaurant, **Szent Orbán Borház és Étterem,** Badacsonytomaj, Kisfaludy S. u. 5 (© 87/432-382; www.szeremley.com), open daily from noon to 10pm.

The **Borbarátok Panzió** ★★, Badacsonytomaj, Római út. 78 (© 87/471-000; www.borbaratok.hu), is a family-operated restaurant and hotel. They serve traditional Hungarian fare and also offer a wide variety of programs including wine tasting, harvest, fishing, and walking tours. Main courses at the restaurant run from 1,200 Ft to 2,700 Ft ($6–$14). The restaurant is open daily 11:30am to 11pm in high season, and in low season, daily 11:30am to 10pm.

SZIGLIGET

Halfway between Tihany and Keszthely is the lovely village of Szigliget (pronounced *Sig*-lee-get). If you are as taken as we were by the thatched-roof houses, the lush vineyards, and the sunny Mediterranean feel of Szigliget, you might consider spending the night. There are also the ubiquitous ZIMMER FREI signs indicating the presence of a private room, along the roads. **Szőlőskert Panzió** (© 87/461-264), on Vadrózsa utca, might be the best option, given its close proximity to the beach. Situated on the hillside amid lush terraces of grapes, the pension is open only in summer. A double is 9,000 Ft ($41).

Szigliget is home to the fantastic ruins of the 13th-century **Szigliget Castle,** Kossuth u. 54 (© 87/461-069; www.szigligetivar.hu), which stand above the town on **Várhegy (Castle Hill).** In the days of the Turkish invasions, the Hungarian Balaton fleet, protected by the high castle, called Szigliget home. You can hike up to the ruins for a splendid view of the lake and the surrounding countryside; look for the path behind the white 18th-century church, which stands on the highest spot in the village.

A good place to fortify yourself for the hike is the **Vár Vendéglő** ★, Kisfaludy u. 30 (© 87/461-040), on the road up to the castle. It's a casual restaurant with plenty of outdoor seating, serving traditional Hungarian fare. Main courses run from 1,000 Ft to 1,800 Ft ($5–$9). It's open daily 11am to 11pm in the high season.

The lively **beach** at Szigliget provides a striking contrast to the quiet village and is a good place to take kids. In summer, buses from neighboring towns drop off hordes of beachgoers. The beach area is crowded with fried-food and beer stands, ice-cream vendors, a swing set, and a volleyball net.

Szigliget is also home to the **Eszterházy Wine Cellar,** Kossuth u. 3 (© **87/461-044**), the largest wine cellar in the region. After a hike in the hills or a day in the sun, a little wine tasting just might be in order.

If you really enjoy hiking, you might want to take a local bus from Szigliget to the nondescript nearby village of **Hegymagas,** about 5km (3 miles) to the north along the Szigliget-Tapolca bus route. The town's name means "Tall Hill," and from here you can hike up **Szent György-hegy (St. George Hill).** This marvelous vineyard-covered hill has several hiking trails, the most strenuous of which goes up and over the rocky summit.

5 Keszthely ⟨★⟩

187km (117 miles) SW of Budapest

Keszthely (pronounced *Kest*-hay), which sits at the western edge of Lake Balaton, is one of the largest towns on the lake. Though Keszthely was largely destroyed during the Turkish wars, the Festetics family, an aristocratic family who made Keszthely their home through World War II, rebuilt the town in the 18th century. The town's main sites all date from the days of the wealthy Festetics clan. For more information on the city, or the surrounding region, see www.west-balaton.hu.

ESSENTIALS

For information on getting to Keszthely, see "Exploring the Lake Balaton Region," earlier in this chapter. For information about Keszthely, stop in at **Tourinform,** at Kossuth u. 28 (©/fax **83/314-144;** www.keszthely.hu). It's open daily Monday through Friday from 9am to 8pm, and on Saturday and Sunday in high season only, from 9am to 6pm. For hotels, pensions, and even private-room bookings, the Tourinform office can help you find and book your accommodations online.

EXPLORING THE TOWN

The highlight of a trip to Keszthely is a visit to the splendid **Festetics Mansion** ★, at Szabadság u. 1 (© **83/312-190**), the baroque 18th-century home (with 19th-c. additions) for generations of the Festetics family. Part of the mansion is now open as a museum. The main attraction is the ornate **Helikon library,** which features floor-to-ceiling oak bookcases—hand-carved by a local master, János Kerbl. The museum also features hunting gear and trophies of a bygone era. Recently added to the permanent collection: an exhibition of artifacts from Hungary's Christian history and another on the arts of the Islamic World. The museum is open July through August daily from 9am to 6pm, and in winter Tuesday through Sunday 10am to 5pm. Admission for non-Hungarians is 1,300 Ft ($6.50), 700 Ft ($3.50) for Hungarians. Adjacent to the castle is the **Carriage Museum,** which has the same opening hours as the castle and exhibits 18th- and 19th-century decorative horse carriages. Admission is 600 Ft ($3). Buy the combined ticket, and you'll get access to both museums for 1,600 Ft ($8).

The mansion's lovely concert hall is the site of **classical music concerts** almost every night throughout the summer. Student concerts usually start around 8pm; all tickets are 1,200 Ft ($6) and are available at the door or earlier in the day at the museum cashier. Every Thursday, year-round, well-known operettas are also performed at the castle, including *La Traviata, Turandot, Tosca* and sometimes Hungarian operettas, organized by the Budapest-based company **Music Classic International Concert Agency** (© **30/222-2111**). You can reserve tickets in advance over the phone for 5,500 Ft ($28).

The most recent addition to the Festetics Castle is a wine cellar, where you can taste wines from the regions of Balaton, Villány, Tokaj, Eger, and Etyek. If you believe their pamphlet—you can taste "50 of 1,500 bottles of wine" and, we assume, get completely inebriated. Tickets, which include a wine tasting, cost 2,500 Ft ($13), and the cellar is open daily from 10am to 6pm.

The two-story **Balaton Congress Center and Theater,** Fő tér 3 (© **83/515-231;** www.balatonszinhaz.hu), which opened in 2002, has reinvigorated the cultural life of

---

Kids An Excursion to the Thermal Lake in Hévíz

If you think the water of Lake Balaton is warm, just wait until you jump into the lake at **Hévíz** ✹✹ (pronounced *Hay*-veez), a resort town about 8km (5 miles) northwest of Keszthely. Here you'll find the largest thermal lake in Europe and the second largest in the world (the largest is in New Zealand), covering 50,000 sq. m (538,195 sq. ft.).

The lake's water temperature seldom dips below 85°F to 90°F (29°C–32°C)—even in the most bitter spell of winter. Consequently, people swim in the lake year-round. You are bound to notice the huge numbers of German travelers taking advantage of the waters. Hévíz has been one of Hungary's leading spa resorts for over 100 years, and it retains a distinct 19th-century atmosphere.

While the lakeside area is suitable for ambling, no visit to Hévíz would be complete without a swim. An enclosed causeway leads out into the center of the lake, where locker rooms and the requisite services, including massage, float rental, and a *palacsinta* (crepe) bar are housed (© **83/501-700**).

You can easily reach Hévíz by bus from Keszthely. Buses depart every half-hour or so from the bus station (conveniently stopping to pick up passengers in front of the church on Fő tér). The entrance to the lake is just opposite the bus station. You'll see a whimsical wooden facade and the words TÓ FÜRDŐ (Bathing Lake). Tickets cost 900 Ft ($4.50) for up to 3 hours or 1,600 Ft ($8) for a day pass; however, the latter is not available from November through March. The lake is open daily 8:30am to 5pm in the summer and 9am to 4:30pm in winter. Your ticket entitles you to a locker; insert the ticket into the slot in the locker and the key will come out of the lock. Keep the ticket until exiting, as the attendant needs to see it to determine whether you've stayed a half-day or a full day.

There is no shallow water in the lake, so use discretion when bringing children. However, there is a nice small playground on the grounds that they will enjoy.

If you want to stay in the town of Héviz at a wellness hotel, in walking distance of the lake, we recommend **Rogner Hotel and Spa Therme** ✹✹, Lótusvirág u. (© **83/501-700;** www.lotustherme.com). Open year-round, this 230-room hotel is located in what feels like a secluded wooded area and includes health cures, sports, medical treatments, and evening programs. A double room in high season is 81€ ($97).

Kesthely. With a 500-seat theater, this institution builds on a theatrical life in this city that goes back over a century and a half, with (occasionally tacky) jazz and dance shows. Every May, the venue organizes the Balaton Festival, which presents performances of Hungarian contemporary dance and music ensembles.

Not far from the Festetics Mansion is the **Georgikon Farm Museum,** Bercsényi u. 67 (© 83/311-563), on the site of Europe's first agricultural college (which is still active), built by György Festetics in 1797. The museum is devoted to an exhibit of the area's agricultural history. It's open May through October only, Monday to Friday from 10am to 5pm, weekends to 6pm. Admission is 300 Ft ($1.50).

In the pedestrian zone off Kossuth L. utca is the **Babamúzeum,** at Bakacs u. 11 (© 83/318-855), which includes an interesting selection of dolls dressed in various traditional Hungarian clothes. The museum is open daily from 10am to 6pm.

Another Keszthely museum worth a visit is the **Balaton Museum** ⊕, on the opposite side of the town center from the Festetics Mansion, at Múzeum u. 2 (© 83/312-351). This museum features exhibits on the geological, archaeological, and natural history of the Balaton region. It's open Tuesday through Sunday from 10am to 5pm in winter, 9am to 6pm daily in summer. Admission is 340 Ft ($1.70).

Located down the hill from Fő tér (Main Sq.), is Keszthely's **open-air market.** Vendors line the street here daily (the biggest days are Wed and Sat). While dawn to midafternoon is the busiest time, some vendors stay open into early afternoon. You'll find fruits and vegetables, spices, preserves, and honey, as well as household appliances, handmade baskets, and children's clothing. This is a great spot to pick up a good buy.

The center of Keszthely's summer scene, just like that of every other settlement on Lake Balaton, is down by the water on the "strand." Several large hotels dominate Keszthely's beachfront. Regardless of whether or not you're a guest, you can rent windsurfers, boats, and other water-related equipment from these hotels.

WHERE TO STAY

As elsewhere in the Lake Balaton region, private rooms are the recommended budget accommodations in Keszthely. Tourinform can help you book a private room. Rates are from 2,500 Ft to 5,000 Ft ($13–$25) per person.

You can also stay at one of the several large German-traveler–oriented hotels on the beach. Try the **Danubius Hotel Helikon,** Balaton-part 5 (© 83/889-633; www. danubiushotels.com/helikon). Rates are 116€ ($139) in summer and 60€ ($72) in winter for a double room with bathroom, and breakfast is included. The hotel has a good-size indoor swimming pool, a sauna, a massage parlor, and an outdoor sun deck.

WHERE TO DINE

John's Pub, at Kossuth utca 46 (© 30/993-1140), has been around a few years and serves simple steaks or pastas. **Oázis Reform Restaurant,** at Rákóczi tér 3 (© 83/311-023), is a self-service salad bar featuring adequate (if uninspired) vegetarian fare. There are cold and hot options. Go early, when the food is freshest. Oázis is open Monday to Saturday from 11am to 4pm. **Margaréta Étterem,** at Bercsényi út 60 (© 83/314-882), is a traditional Hungarian restaurant with popular *gulyás* soups. It's open daily from 11am to 11pm.

SIDE-EXCURSION TO SÜMEG

If staying in either Keszthely or Héviz, a fun excursion is a short trip to the small town of Sümeg, a half-hour drive North of Balaton. The main attraction here is the **Fortress of Sümeg** (© **87/352-598**; www.sumegvar.hu), originally constructed in the 13th century, it was subsequently rebuilt three hundred years later. The fortress fended away the Turks, but was set ablaze in the 18th century by the Habsburgs. Today, perched high on the hilltop, the fortress hosts performances that bring you back to the Middle-Ages, with horse shows, folk dances, and reenactments of knightly tournaments with period weaponry. At the foot of the hill is the **Hotel Kapitány** at Tóth Tivadar u. 19 (© **87/550-166**; www.hotelkapitany.hu), a recently constructed hotel and wellness center which includes saunas, fitness areas, and massage. The complex also includes a Turkish bath, restaurants, and a conference. Note that the town is also known for F.A. Maulbertsch's beautiful 18th-century frescos, located in the baroque **Church of the Ascension**, at Szent Imre tér.

GETTING THERE   Almost all local hotels and travel agencies offer day-trips to Sümeg, including a medieval dinner and show, for about 30€ ($36), plus transportation. For example, **Hotel Kristály** (© **83/318-999**; www.kristalyhotel.hu), in Keszthely, and **Hotel Europa Fit** (© **83/501-100**; www.europafit.hu) in Héviz offer this service.

6 Lake Balaton's Southern Shore

If you're looking for long days at the beach followed by long nights out on the town, the southern shore of Lake Balaton may be the place for you. After all, a million Hungarian students can't be wrong. Or could they?

Siófok, the largest resort town on Lake Balaton, is at the lake's southeastern end. Its growth dates back to the 1860s, when Budapest was first connected to the southern shore of the lake by rail. Thus, we suppose, nobody alive can remember a time (other than the war years) when Siófok was not overrun by summertime revelers. Many of the majestic old villas along the large platan tree-lined streets have been restored or renovated, and can even be rented in the summer months.

The bustling Siófok caters largely to a young, active crowd of students and teenagers who fill every inch of the town's beaches all day long and then pack their sunburned bodies into the town's discos until the early morning hours. Large, modern, expensive hotels line the shore in Siófok. You'll find no empty stretches of beach here, but you will find windsurfing, tennis, and boating.

While this city is no cultural capital, the architecture of some of the older buildings is impressive. Note the old railway station, and the many villas around the Gold Coast (Aranypart). You will also find some important contemporary buildings, notably the Evangelical Church, designed by one of Hungary's most appreciated architects, **Imre Makovecz**—who is known for his use of wood and light in his structures that dot the country. Most of the wood used for the building was imported from Finland.

Siófok is also trying to attract visitors to recently constructed wellness centers, open year-round, which offer an assortment of facilities plus the added benefit of Hungary's warm-water springs.

For more information on the southern shore, contact the **Tourinform** (©/fax **84/310-117;** www.siofokportal.com) office in Siófok, right below the immense water tower in the center of town.

WHERE TO STAY

Siófok is basically plastered with tourists during the summer months, and there are a wide variety of options from large hotels or resorts on the Gold Coast to the east of the center of town, or the Silver Coast (Ezüstpart), to the west. Additional accommodations can be found on the city's website at www.siofokportal.com.

We recommend pampering yourself at a "wellness center" for a few days. The **Hotel Azúr** 𝒢𝒢, Vitorlás u. 11 (© **84/501-400;** www.hotelazur.hu) is the most comfortable, plush and welcoming hotel and wellness center in town. The pools are large, it has a nice fitness room, and the whole complex is extremely tasteful. During the summer months, the hotel facilities look directly onto Lake Balaton. Rates are 135€ ($162) in summer and 85€ ($102) in winter for a double room, and breakfast is included. The hotel has a good-size indoor swimming pool, a sauna, a massage club, Finnish saunas, a beauty salon, and thermal pools.

The **Hotel Residence** 𝒢, Erkel Ferenc u. 49 (© **84/506-840;** www.hotel-residence.hu) also has an extensive list of services, including massages, gyms, baths, and aromatherapy. There is a private beach on the shores of Lake Balaton reserved for the hotel, but it is located several hundred meters away. Rates are 107€ ($128) in summer and 87€ ($105) in winter for a double room, and breakfast is included. The hotel has a good-size indoor swimming pool, a sauna, a massage club, Finnish saunas, a beauty salon and thermal pools.

WHERE TO DINE

Try the **Sándor Restaurant** (© **84/312-829;** www.sandorrestaurant.hu), on Erkel F. utca 30, popular with locals for large portions of contemporary Hungarian food. If you're looking for more traditional Hungarian fare, occasionally with live Gypsy music, try the **Csárdás Restaurant,** at Fő u. 105 (© **84/310-642**).

13

Northeastern Hungary: Traveling into the Hills

Northeast of the Danube Bend is Hungary's hilliest region, where the country's highest peak—Matra Hill, at 998m (3,327 ft.)—can be found. Here you can visit the preserved medieval village of Hollókő; see remnants of the country's Turkish heritage in Eger, also known for its regional wines; and explore the 23km (14-mile) cave system in Aggtelek.

1 Hollókő: A Preserved Palóc Village ⍟

102km (63 miles) NE of Budapest

The village of Hollókő (pronounced *Ho*-low-koo) is one of the most charming spots in Hungary. This UNESCO World Heritage Site is a perfectly preserved but still vibrant Palóc village. The rural Palóc people speak an unusual Hungarian dialect, and they have some of the more colorful folk customs and costumes in Hungary.

ESSENTIALS

GETTING THERE   The only direct **bus** to Hollókő departs from Budapest's central bus station, Stadionok Bus Station (© **1/382-0888**). It departs daily at 8:30am and takes about 2½ hours to reach the town. The fare is 1,400 Ft ($5.60). Alternatively, you can take a bus from Árpád híd bus station in Budapest (© **1/412-2597**) to Szécsény or Pásztó, where you switch to a local bus to Hollókő, of which there are four daily.

If you're **driving** from Budapest, take the M3 motorway to Hatvan, the M21 from Hatvan to Pásztó, and local roads from Pásztó to Hollókő.

VISITOR INFORMATION   The best information office is the **Foundation of Hollókő,** at Kossuth Lajos út. 68 (© **32/579-010;** www.holloko.hu). It's open in summer Monday to Friday 8am to 8pm and weekends 10am to 6pm; in winter, it's open Monday to Friday 8am to 5pm and weekends 10am to 4pm. You can also get information through **Nograd Tourist** in Salgótarján (© **32/310-660**) or through **Tourinform** in Szécsény, at Ady Endre u. 12 (© **32/370-777;** www.szecseny.hu).

SEASONAL EVENTS

At **Easter time** ⍟, villagers wear national costumes and participate in a folk festival. Traditional song, dance, and foods are featured. On the last weekend in July, the **Palóc Szőttes Festival** ⍟ is held in Hollókő. Folk dance troupes from Nógrád county as well as international folk dance troupes perform on an open-air stage. Folk art by local artisans is also on display. In the winter, groups visiting Hollókő can participate in a **wild-pig hunt** and subsequent roast.

EXPLORING THE VILLAGE

A one-street town, Hollókő is idyllically set in a quiet, green valley, with **hiking trails** all around. A restored 14th-century **castle** is perched on a hilltop over the village.

In the village itself you can admire the 14th-century wooden-towered church and the sturdy, traditional peasant architecture (normally seen only in stylized open-air museums, such as the one near Szentendre, that's reviewed on p. 224), and observe the elderly women at work on their embroidery (samples are for sale). You can also visit the **Village Museum** at Kossuth Lajos u. 82, where exhibits detail everyday Palóc life starting in the early 20th century. Official hours are Tuesday through Sunday from 10am to 4pm; closed in winter. Like everything else in town, though, the museum's opening times are flexible. Entry is 100 Ft (50¢).

WHERE TO STAY

In Hollókő, traditionally furnished thatch-roofed **peasant houses** are available for rent on a nightly or longer basis. You can rent a **room in a shared house** (with shared facilities), or rent an **entire house.** The prices vary depending on the size of the room or house and the number of people in your party, but 8,500 Ft ($43) for a double room is average. Standard **private rooms** are also available in Hollókő. All accommodations can be booked in advance through the tourist offices in Hollókő or Salgótarján (see "Essentials," above). If you arrive without reservations (which is not advised), the address and phone number of a room finder are posted on the door of the **Foundation of Hollókő** at Kossuth Lajos u. 68 (℗ **32/579-011**).

WHERE TO DINE

Dining options are limited in tiny Hollókő. The **Vár Étterem,** Kossuth Lajos u. 95 (℗ **32/379-029**), serves decent Hungarian food at very low prices. Try a dish prepared with the "treasure of the local forests," porcini mushrooms. There is indoor and outdoor seating. The menu is available in English, and the waiters are patient. The restaurant is open daily noon to 8pm, except Christmas Day.

2 Eger ★★

126km (78 miles) NE of Budapest

Eger (pronounced *Egg*-air), a small baroque city lying in a valley between the Matra and Bükk mountains, is best known for three things: its castle, its wine, and its women—the women of the 16th century, that is. In that dark era of Turkish invasions, the women of Eger claimed their place in the Hungarian national consciousness by bravely fighting alongside István Dobó's army in defense of Eger's castle in 1552. Greatly outnumbered by the invaders, the defenders of Eger fought off the Turks for 38 grueling days, achieving a momentous victory that would stall the Turkish advance into Hungary for nearly half a century. Forty-four years later, in 1596, the sultan's forces attacked Eger again, this time taking the castle without great difficulty. Dobó's initial victory, though, and particularly the role of the women defenders, is a much cherished and mythologized historical event, recalled in numerous paintings, poems, and monuments.

As for the wine, the area around Eger is known for producing some fine vintages. Most famous among the regional potions is undoubtedly the heavily marketed *Egri bikavér* (Eger Bull's Blood), a strong dark-red wine. There are many other wines that are worth sampling as well—and no shortage of places in Eger to sample them.

Eger

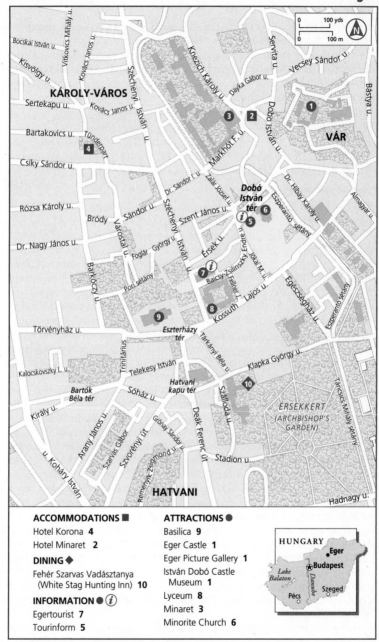

ACCOMMODATIONS ■
Hotel Korona **4**
Hotel Minaret **2**

DINING ◆
Fehér Szarvas Vadásztanya
(White Stag Hunting Inn) **10**

INFORMATION ● *ⓘ*
Egertourist **7**
Tourinform **5**

ATTRACTIONS ●
Basilica **9**
Eger Castle **1**
Eger Picture Gallery **1**
István Dobó Castle
 Museum **1**
Lyceum **8**
Minaret **3**
Minorite Church **6**

ESSENTIALS

GETTING THERE   Eger is a 2-hour direct **train** ride from Budapest. Sixteen daily trains depart Budapest's Keleti Station. Tickets cost 1,624 Ft ($8.10).

If you're **driving** from Budapest, take the M3 motorway east to Kerecsend, where you pick up Route 25 north to Eger. There is a 1,400 Ft ($7) toll; a toll ticket, valid for a week, is available at all MOL Petrol stations.

VISITOR INFORMATION   For information, visit or contact **Tourinform,** at Bajcsy-Zsilinszky u. 9 (© **36/517-715;** www.eger.hu). The office is open in summer Monday through Friday from 9am to 6pm and on weekends from 10am to 1pm; off season, the office closes an hour earlier and is closed on Sunday. For private-room booking, try **Egertourist,** at Bajcsy-Zsilinszky u. 9 (© **36/510-270;** www.egertourist.hu). This office is open Monday through Saturday from 10am to 6pm.

EXPLORING OLD EGER

All of Eger's main sites are within easy walking distance of **Dobó István tér** 🏵🏵, the lovely, dignified square that's the center of old Eger. Dobó István tér is home to the **Minorite Church,** a fine 18th-century baroque church. You'll also find a statue of town defender Dobó, flanked by a knight and a woman, by Alajos Strobl, one of the country's leading turn-of-the-20th-century sculptors. Strobl's other work includes the statue of King Stephen on Buda's Castle Hill and the statue of poet János Arany in front of the National Museum in Pest. The larger statue in the square, erected in the 1960s, is a more recent—and less subtle—rendition of the fight against the Turks.

The reconstructed ruins of **Eger Castle,** visible from just about anywhere in the city, can be reached by walking northeast out of the square; take the path out of Dózsa György tér. You can wander around the grounds free of charge daily from 8am to 8pm in summer and daily 8am to 6pm in winter, or you can explore the two museums on the premises. The **István Dobó Castle Museum** (© **36/312-744**) relates the history of the castle and displays some Turkish artifacts. The **Eger Picture Gallery** is particularly worth a visit for those who have not yet seen the Hungarian National Gallery in Buda; the same fine 19th-century Hungarian artists are featured in both museums. The museums are open Tuesday through Sunday from 10am to 5pm, until 4pm in winter. Admission to each museum is 800 Ft ($4); separate admission for each museum.

Just to the west of the castle, on Harangöntő utca, is Eger's most visible reminder of the Turkish period, its **Minaret** (© **36/410-233**). Though the mosque that held the minaret was destroyed in 1841, the 14-sided 33m-tall (110-ft.) minaret survives to this day in remarkably good condition. For 100 Ft (50¢), you can ascend its narrow height. It's a terrifying journey up a steep, cramped spiral staircase; because the space is so narrow, you can't turn back if anyone is behind you. Consequently, the ascent is not recommended for the weak-kneed or weak-hearted. Those who do make the climb, however, are justly rewarded with a spectacular view. Officially, the Minaret is open daily from 10am to 6pm, to 4pm in winter, but the ticket taker in the little booth at the Minaret's base is not always faithful to these hours; depending on the weather conditions, the hours may be longer or shorter. If no one is there, you should ask at the nearby Minaret Hotel.

Moving from the graceful to the overpowering, you'll find the massive **Basilica**—the second-largest church in Hungary (after Esztergom's Basilica)—a few blocks to the south on Eszterhazy tér. József Hild, who was one of the architects of St. Stephen's Basilica in Pest, built this church in the 1830s in the grandiose neoclassical style of the time. It's open daily from 6am to 7pm. Thirty-minute organ concerts are held in the church in summer, beginning at 11:30am Monday through Saturday and at 12:45pm on Sunday. These times are subject to change; check at Tourinform. Admission is free.

Opposite the cathedral is the **Lyceum** ☆☆ (© **36/520-400**), perhaps Eger's finest example of 18th-century architecture. The **library** *(kö nyvtár)* ☆ on the first floor is the highlight of a visit to the Lyceum; the ceiling fresco of the Council of Trent by Johann Lukas Kracker and József Zach ranks among the greatest pieces of Hungarian art. The baroque carved bookshelves are magnificent. The library has a letter written by Mozart, the only one of its kind in the country. The Lyceum is open to the public in summer Tuesday through Sunday from 9:30am to 3pm; in winter Saturday and Sunday from 9:30am to 1pm. Admission is 350 Ft ($1.75). In July and August, concerts are frequently performed in the yard of the Lyceum. Ask at Tourinform for the schedule and ticket information.

If you missed visiting a spa or bathhouse in Budapest, try Eger's own Turkish bath at Fürdó u. 1–3 (© **36/413-356**). The bath is mixed sex, open only on Saturday from 2 to 6pm and Sunday from 8am to 6pm. The rate is 700 Ft ($3.50) for an hour. Spa services are posted in English. Northeastern Hungary is rich in thermal waters; ask at Tourinform for a list of spas in the region.

WHERE TO STAY

Eger is blessed with several fine little hotels right in the center of town. Two stand out in particular: The **Hotel Korona** ☆, Tündérpart 5, 3300 Eger (© **36/310-287; fax 36**/310-261), is a clean, cozy establishment on an extremely quiet residential street just a few blocks west of Dobó István tér. The hotel has a shaded patio, where breakfast is served, and a wine cellar. There are 40 rooms, all with private bathrooms. A double room goes for 60€ ($72) to 90€ ($108) in summer, with prices about 15% lower off season. Rates include breakfast and sauna. Credit cards are accepted. Bus no. 11, 12, or 14 will get you there from the train station; get off at Csiky Sándor utca and you're practically at the doorstep.

Another guesthouse is right by the Beautiful Women's Valley and only a 15-minute walk from the historical center of the town, the **Bacchus Panzio** ☆, located at Szépasszony völgy utca 29 (© **36/428-950;** www.bacchuspanzio.hu). This hotel offers double rooms for 10,000 Ft to 14,000 Ft ($50–$70) in high season and 8,500 Ft to 12,000 Ft ($43–$60) in low season. Rates include breakfast.

For something peacefully removed from the downtown, try the **Garten Vendégház,** Legányi u. 6, 3300 Eger (© **36/320-371**). Operated by the Zsemlye family, this guesthouse is located on a quiet residential street in the hills overlooking the city. The view from the gorgeous garden is splendid. The price of a double room is 10,000 Ft ($50) in high season and 8,000 Ft ($40) in low season. Rates include breakfast.

Travelers on a tighter budget should consider renting a private room through **Egertourist** (see above) or **Tourinform.** Rates in Eger are as low as 2,500 Ft ($13) for a bed with a shared bathroom and as high as 6,500 Ft ($33) for an apartment with bathroom and kitchen.

WHERE TO DINE

The **Fehér Szarvas Vadásztanya (White Stag Hunting Inn)** ☆, located next door to the Park Hotel at Klapka u. 8 (© **36/411-129**), a few blocks south of Dobó István tér, is one of Eger's best-known and best-loved restaurants. The menu offers a full range of Hungarian wild-game specialties. The hearty, paprika-laced stews are especially good.

> **Tips   Cool Caves**
>
> Remember, no matter how hot it is outside, the Baradla caves are always damp and chilly (a constant 50° to 52°F/10° to 11° C), so dress appropriately.

Award-winning regional wines are featured. A piano and bass duet plays nightly amid the kitschy hunting lodge decor. The restaurant is open daily from noon to 11pm, and reservations are recommended. Credit cards are accepted.

WHERE TO SAMPLE LOCAL WINE

The best place to sample local wines is in the vineyard country just west of Eger, in the wine cellars of the **Szépasszony-völgy (Valley of the Beautiful Women).** More than 200 wine cellars are here, each offering its own vintage. Some cellars have live music. Although the wine cellars don't serve food, you can grab a meal at one of the local restaurants. Generally, the cellars open at 10am and close by 9 or 10pm.

The easiest way to get to the Szépasszony-völgy is by taxi, though you can also walk there from the center of town in 30 or 40 minutes. You could also take bus no. 13 to the Hatvani Temető (Hatvan Cemetery) and walk from there; it's a 10- to 15-minute walk.

3 Aggtelek: An Entrance to the Caves ★

224km (139 miles) NE of Budapest

Tucked away beneath the Slovak border in northernmost Hungary, about 80km (50 miles) north of Eger, **Aggtelek National Park (Aggteleki Nemzeti Park)** is home to the extensive **Baradla cave network,** one of Europe's most spectacular cave systems. Although the remote and sparsely populated Aggtelek region is also suitable for hiking, people tend to travel to Aggtelek primarily to explore the caves.

You can enter the Baradla cave system on guided tours from either of two villages: Aggtelek or Jósvafő, which is on the other side of the mountain. The tours are a lot of fun. The caves are open daily 8am to 6pm in summer, to 4pm in winter. Call Aggtelek National Park (© **48/350-006**) for tour information. If this is your first time in a cave, you'll be astounded by the magical subterranean world of stalactites, stalagmites, and other bizarre formations. Three different guided tours—appropriately called short *(rövid),* which is 1 or 2 hours long; medium *(közép),* which is 5 hours long; and long *(hosszú),* which is 7 hours long—depart at different times throughout the day.

The **Hotel Cseppkő** (© **48/343-075**), in the village of Aggtelek, is a popular place to crash after a day in the caves. Double rooms start at 8,400 Ft ($36), breakfast included. Though it's nothing to write home about, the Cseppkő is clean and conveniently located. Camping is also popular in the area.

Travelers without cars can get to Aggtelek by bus from Eger. The trip takes 3 hours. From Miskolc, the trip takes 2 hours. Ask about transportation at the local tourist office (such as Eger's Tourinform or Egertourist), where you can also ask for help booking a room in the Hotel Cseppkő. Off season there is no need to book in advance.

14

Southern Hungary:
The Great Plain & the Mecsek Hills

The mainly agricultural region of the Alföld (Great Plain), including the last remnants of the Puszta, Hungary's prairie, lies south and east of the Danube River. The main cities here are Kecskemét and Szeged. The Great Plain comprises approximately 51,800 sq. km (20,000 sq. miles). On the other side of the river, in southwestern Hungary, are the verdant Mecsek Hills. The city of Pécs is the focal point of this hilly region.

1 The 2,000-Year-Old City of Pécs ✴✴✴

197km (123 miles) SW of Budapest

Pécs (pronounced *Paych*) is a delightful, exuberant place, the largest and loveliest city in the Mecsek Hill region. Situated 32km (20 miles) or so from the Croatian border, the city enjoys a particularly warm and arid climate; in fact, the rolling hills around Pécs are the source of some of Hungary's finest fresh fruit. Few places in Hungary possess a more Mediterranean quality than Pécs, the city that was recently named to share the title of Cultural Capital of Europe in 2010.

Known as the "2,000-year-old city," Pécs was a major settlement in Roman times, when it was called Sopianae. It was later the site of Hungary's first university, founded in 1367. While that university no longer exists, Pécs remains one of the country's most important centers of learning. The city's present university, Janus Pannonius University (named for a local ecclesiastical poet of the 15th c.) was moved here from Bratislava after that city (known as Pozsony to Hungarians) was allocated to Czechoslovakia when Czechoslovakia was created after World War I.

Pécs thrived during the almost-150-year Turkish occupation, and reminders of this period fill the city. Although Pécs (like much of Hungary) was almost completely destroyed during the bloody liberation battles between the Ottoman and Christian armies, what did survive—particularly the Mosque of Pasha Gazi Kassim—may well be the best examples of Turkish architecture in the country.

The people of Pécs are proud of their city. If you travel just a block or two outside the historic core, you'll see that the city is booming: People throng the shops and streets, and buses thunder past in every direction. Pécs is a city on the move. It exhibits none of the torpor you might notice on a hot summer afternoon in Great Plain towns like Kecskemét or Szeged.

If you walk up Janus Pannonius utca toward Széchenyi tér, about a block up the street, you'll notice on your left a small metal fence covered with padlocks. Young lovers visiting Pécs have left these locks as a token of their desire to live in this beautiful city.

ESSENTIALS

GETTING THERE   Ten **trains** depart daily from Budapest's Déli Station; four of these are InterCity trains, which are quicker than the so-called "fast" trains. The fare is 4,060 Ft ($20). On an InterCity train the journey takes about 2½ hours and you are required to pay an additional fee for a seat reservation. On a "fast" train *(gyors)*, the trip is around 3 hours, but you don't need a reservation.

If you are **driving** from Budapest, take the M6 south for approximately 3 hours (the distance is 210km/130 miles).

VISITOR INFORMATION   The best source of information in Pécs is **Tourinform,** at Széchenyi tér 9 (*©* **72/213-315;** www.tourinform.hu). Tourinform is open April through October, Monday through Friday from 9am to 7pm and on weekends from 9am to 6pm; in winter Monday through Friday from 8am to 4pm. Tourinform can provide a list of local private-room accommodations, though you'll have to reserve the room yourself.

If you want to have a room reserved for you, visit **Mecsek Tourist,** at Széchenyi tér 1 (*©* **72/513-372;** www.mecsektours.hu). The office is open Monday through Friday from 9am to 5pm; and on Saturday from 9am to 1pm in summer.

A free weekly magazine called *Pécsi Est* contains lots of useful information; pick it up anywhere. You can also get city information online at **www.pecs.hu**.

EXPLORING OLD PÉCS

Today the old section of Pécs captivates visitors. One of Hungary's most pleasing central squares is here—**Széchenyi tér** *☺☺☺*, which is set on an incline with a mosque at the top and a powerful equestrian statue of János Hunyadi at the bottom. Hunyadi defeated the Turks in the 1456 Battle of Nándorfehérvár (present-day Belgrade), thus forestalling their northward advance by nearly a century. Grand pastel-colored buildings line the cobblestone streets that border the square.

Old Pécs is known for its many museums and galleries; after Budapest, Pécs is perhaps the biggest center of the arts in Hungary. The large student population contributes greatly to this creative state of affairs. We list several museums below, but there are many more, some containing works by contemporary and student artists. Pécs is also home to the Zsolnay ceramics factory. Zsolnay porcelain, though lesser known internationally than its rival Herend, may be more popular domestically. The Zsolnay Museum, also listed below, is a must-see in Pécs.

MUSEUMS

Jakawali Hassan Museum   This museum is housed inside a 16th-century mosque that has the distinction of being the only mosque in Hungary with a minaret still intact (though, unfortunately, you can't ascend the minaret as you can Eger's mosque-less minaret). Like the much larger mosque up in Széchenyi tér, this mosque was converted to a church after the Turks were driven from Pécs; however, in the 1950s the mosque was restored to its original form. The museum's main attraction is the building itself, although various Muslim religious artifacts are on display as well.

Rákóczi út 2. *©* **72/313-853**. Admission 150 Ft (70¢). Apr–Sept Thurs–Sun 10am–6pm (closed 1–2pm for lunch). Closed Oct–Mar.

Tivadar Csontváry Museum   *☺*   Tivadar Csontváry Kosztka (1853–1919), today one of Hungary's most beloved artists, remained unknown during his lifetime, scorned

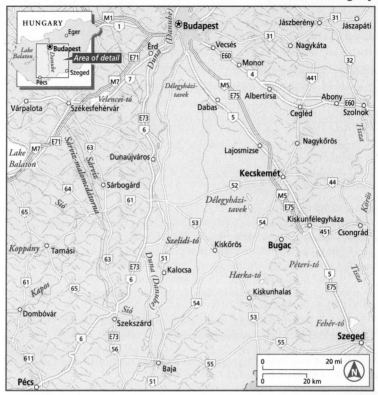

by the art establishment. His mystical post-Impressionist landscapes suggest a unique vision of the world—one that is both tormented and idyllic, an atmosphere attributed by some to the artist's schizophrenia. Hungarians like to point out that some time after Csontváry's death, Picasso saw an exhibition of his work and referred to him as the "other" artistic genius of the 20th century. This little museum houses an impressive collection of his work. Across the street from the museum, in the park beneath Pécs Cathedral, is a statue of Csontváry.

Janus Pannonius u. 11. ℂ **72/310-544.** Admission 600 Ft ($3). Summer Tues–Sun 10am–6pm; winter Tues–Sun 10am–4pm.

Victor Vasarely Museum ⚐ The late Victor Vasarely, internationally known father of "op art," was born in the house that this museum now occupies. This is one of two museums in the country devoted solely to Vasarely's work (the other is in Óbuda; see p. 139). While Vasarely's fame was achieved abroad, Pécs proudly considers him a native son.

Kaptalan u. 3. ℂ **72/324-822.** Admission 600 Ft ($3). Tues–Sat 10am–6pm; Sun 10am–4pm.

Zsolnay Museum ⚐⚐⚐ This is one of five museums on Kaptalan utca, Pécs's "street of museums," and you shouldn't miss it. The Zsolnay Museum displays some of the best examples of Zsolnay porcelain, produced locally since 1852. There are vases, plates, cups, figurines, and even ceramic paintings. Once you've seen the museum, check out the Zsolnay fountain at the lower end of Széchenyi tér.

Kaptalan u. 2. (℺ 72/324-822. Admission 700 Ft ($3.50). Tues–Sat 10am–6pm, to 4pm in winter; Sun 10am–4pm.

HOUSES OF WORSHIP

Mosque of Pasha Gazi Kassim   The largest Turkish structure still standing in Hungary, this former mosque now houses a Catholic church. It was built in the late 16th century, during the Turkish occupation, on the site of an earlier church. The mix of religious traditions is evident everywhere you look, and the effect is rather pleasing. An English-language description of the building's history is posted on a bulletin board on the left-hand wall.

At the top of Széchenyi tér. (℺ 72/227-166. Free admission. High season Mon–Sat 10am–3pm, Sun 11:30am–3pm; winter Mon–Sat 10am–2pm, Sun 11:30am–2pm.

Pécs Cathedral   Dating back to the 11th century, this four-towered cathedral has been destroyed and rebuilt on several occasions. During the Turkish occupation it was used as a mosque and sported a minaret. The neoclassical exterior is the work of the early-19th-century architect Mihály Pollack. The interior remains primarily Gothic, with some baroque additions and furnishings. Various paintings and murals by leading 19th-century artists Károly Lotz and Bertalan Székely are inside. Organ concerts are performed in the cathedral throughout the year; inquire at the cathedral or at Tourinform for the schedule.

   The square in front of the cathedral—as well as the little park beneath it—is a popular gathering place, and occasionally the site of folk concerts or dances.

On Dóm tér. (℺ 72/513-030. Cathedral admission (includes treasury and crypt) 800 Ft ($4). Apr–Oct Mon–Sat 9am–5pm, Sun 1–5pm; Nov–Mar Mon–Sat 10am–4pm, Sun 1–4pm. The church is not open to the public during weddings, which are often on Sat afternoons.

Pécs Synagogue ⍟   Pécs's grand old synagogue is incongruously situated in what is now one of the city's busiest shopping squares, Kossuth tér. Nevertheless, once inside you'll find it to be a quiet, cool place far removed from the bustle outside. The synagogue was built in 1869, and the original rich oak interior survives to this day. Next door is the former Jewish school of Pécs, now a Croatian school. Prior to World War II, the synagogue had over 4,000 members, of whom only 464 survived the Holocaust. Every year, Pécs's small Jewish community commemorates the 1944 deportations to Auschwitz on the first Sunday after July 4.

   Regular services are held in the smaller temple next door at Fürdő 1 (there isn't a sign; go through the building into the courtyard and cross diagonally to the right) on Friday at 6:30pm.

Kossuth tér. 1–3. (℺ 72/315-881. Admission 200 Ft ($1). May–Oct Sun–Fri 10am–5pm. Closed Nov–Feb.

SHOPPING

A short stroll through the center of town makes it clear that Pécs is prospering. Several pedestrian-only streets make shopping in Pécs a favorite activity. For a more exotic shopping experience, visit the **Pécsi Vásár (Pécs Flea Market)** ⍟⍟. At this crowded, bustling, open-air market you can find everything from antique china and silver to Turkish T-shirts and Chinese baby booties. Tables of homemade preserves and honey stand alongside boxes of used car parts. The main attraction, however, is the animal market, where people sell puppies and kittens out of the trunks of their cars. You

Pécs

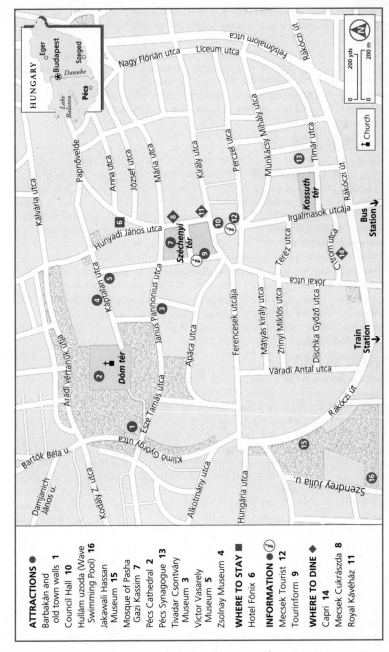

HUNGARY

Eger

Budapest

Szeged

Danube

Lake Balaton

Pécs

Nagy Flórián utca

Líceum utca

Felsőmalom utca

Rákóczi út

Papnövelde

Anna utca

József utca

Mária utca

Király utca

Perczel utca

Munkácsy Mihály utca

Timár utca

Rákóczi út

Kálvária utca

Hunyadi János utca

Kapalan utca

Janus Pannonius utca

Széchenyi tér

Kossuth tér

Irgalmasok utcája

Bus Station

Teréz utca

Citrom utca

Aradi vértanúk útja

Kodály Z. utca

Dóm tér

Apáca utca

Ferencesek utcája

Jókai utca

Mátyás király utca

Zrinyi Miklós utca

Dischka Győző utca

Train Station

Esze Tamás utca

Klimó György utca

Váradi Antal utca

Bartók Béla u.

Damjanich János u.

Alkotmány utca

Hungária utca

Rákóczi út

Szendrey Júlia u.

+ Church

200 yds

200 m

ATTRACTIONS ●

Barbakán and old town walls **1**
Council Hall **10**
Hullám uzoda (Wave Swimming Pool) **16**
Jakawali Hassan Museum **15**
Mosque of Pasha Gazi Kassim **7**
Pécs Cathedral **2**
Pécs Synagogue **13**
Tivadar Csontváry Museum **3**
Victor Vasarely Museum **5**
Zsolnay Museum **4**

WHERE TO STAY ■

Hotel Fönix **6**

INFORMATION ● ⓘ

Mecsek Tourist **12**
Tourinform **9**

WHERE TO DINE ◆

Capri **14**
Mecsek Cukrászda **8**
Royal Kávéház **11**

might also find chickens, rabbits, and even pigs and horses for sale. The market is open every day, though Sunday is the biggest and best day (particularly for the animal market).

To get to the flea market, take a special bus, marked VÁSÁR, which departs from the Konsum shopping center in the center of downtown Pécs regularly. You need two standard city bus tickets for this bus; these are available at newsstands and kiosks or ask the bus driver. You can also take the no. 3 bus from the Konsum (only one ticket required), but you'll have to walk some distance from the stop to the entrance of the flea market.

OUTDOOR ACTIVITIES

If you are visiting Pécs in the summer, you are bound to feel the heat. Cool off in the waves at **Hullám uszoda (Wave Swimming Pool)** on Szendrey Júlia utca (© 72/512-936). Admission is 600 Ft ($3). The pool is open daily from 6am to 10pm. Another swimming pool complex, which belongs to the university, is at Ifjúság útja 6 (© 72/501-519, ext. 4195). There is a wading pool for kids as well as a 25m (82-ft.) lap pool. Admission is 300 Ft ($1.50). After swimming, treat yourself to some of the best ice cream in town, right down the street at Egerszegi Cukrászda.

Pécs is home to perhaps one of the most appealing neighborhood playgrounds in all of Hungary. **Napsugár Játszókert (Sunshine Playground)** is on Vadász utca, a short bus ride from the city center. Built in 1997 by a foundation and with donations from the community, this small grassy playground has a quaint, friendly appeal. There are chunky wooden climbing structures, slides, seesaws, swings (including an infant swing), a sandbox, and picnic tables. To get there, take bus no. 27 from the Konsum to the "Ledina" stop.

WHERE TO STAY

You can book a private room through **Mecsek Tourist** (see "Essentials," above) or **Ibusz,** Király u. 11. (© 72/212-157; www.ibusz.hu).

If you're in the mood for a funky little hotel right in the center of town, try the popular **Hotel Fönix** ❀❀, at Hunyadi út 2 (© 72/311-682). This unique hotel, just off the top of Széchenyi tér, has 14 rooms and 3 apartments, each one with oddly angled walls and sloped ceilings. The rooms are a bit cramped, but all are clean and have refrigerators and TVs. Each room has a private shower, but only eight have their own toilets; the common facilities are well maintained. The three apartments have full facilities and their own entrance off the street. A double room costs 11,000 Ft ($55), a room without a private toilet is 9,500 Ft ($48), and apartments go for 19,000 Ft ($95). Rates include breakfast. Call several days ahead to reserve a room. Credit cards are accepted.

If the Hotel Fönix is full, the management can book a room for you at a pension that they operate called **Kertész Panzió,** at Sáfrány u. 42 (© 72/327-551).

WHERE TO DINE

Bagolyvár Étterem ❀ HUNGARIAN   Bagolyvár, a large, classy restaurant, serves delicious, hearty food in a fabulous setting, high in the hills overlooking the city. The view is excellent, the service is equally good, and there's a well-stocked wine cellar. *Note:* The same owner operates a second restaurant, **Dóm Vendéglő,** in the city center, at Király u. 3 (© 72/210-088 or 72/310-736). Dóm Vendéglő was recently expanded to include a fine pizzeria building (© 72/310-736).

Felsőhavi Dűlő 6/1. © 72/211-333. Reservations recommended in summer. Main courses 1,000 Ft–3,000 Ft ($5–$15). AE, DC, MC, V. Daily noon–midnight. Bus: 33 from in front of the Konsum shopping center to the last stop.

COFFEEHOUSES & ICE-CREAM PARLORS

Pécs offers numerous places to enjoy coffee and sweets. Try **Mecsek Cukrászda,** on Széchenyi tér 16 (© **72/315-444**), for a quick jolt of espresso and any number of sinfully good and inexpensive pastries. For a more leisurely coffeehouse experience, try the **Royal Kávéház,** at the corner of Király utca and Széchenyi tér (© **72/210-683**). There's outdoor seating, but the renovated Art Deco interior makes sitting inside worthwhile.

For ice cream, **Capri,** a very popular shop at Citrom u. 7 (© **72/333-658**), 3 blocks south of Széchenyi tér, serves up various sundaes as well as cones. Some locals, however, claim that the ice cream at Capri is inferior to that of the **Egerszegi Fagylaltozó,** on Rókusalja utca (© **72/256-660**), a 15-minute walk from the center. The owners of Egerszegi also own a second, easier-to-reach place at Bajcsy-Zsilinzsky u. 5 (© **72/327-540**). Our favorite for sweets and ice cream is **Magda Cukrászda** ✦✦, at Kandó Kálmán u. 4 (© **72/511-055**). This is a bright, bustling neighborhood *cukrászda,* where the selection and quality of cakes and ice creams is superb (though ice cream is not sold during the winter). Notable ice-cream flavors include poppy seed, chestnut, blueberry cream, cherry cream, and cinnamon. The slightly out-of-the-way location (near the train station) apparently hasn't deterred customers at all. The store is open daily from 10am to 8pm, in winter to 7pm.

2 Kecskemét ✦

85km (53 miles) SE of Budapest

Kecskemét (pronounced *Ketch*-keh-mate), a city of over 100,000 inhabitants in the western portion of the Great Hungarian Plain, has a decidedly small-town feel to it. A quiet, sun-baked city with wide, open squares and broad avenues, Kecskemét is blessed with some of the most interesting architecture in the Great Plain. The town's dizzyingly colorful Art Nouveau buildings may be the equal of any in the country outside Budapest.

Kecskemét was the birthplace of Zoltán Kodály, the early-20th-century musicologist, teacher, and composer who, along with his friend and colleague Béla Bartók, achieved worldwide renown for his studies of Hungarian folk songs and for his compositions. Today, a music school in town bears Kodály's name. Kecskemét is also famous throughout the country for its many varieties of apricot brandy *(barack Pálinka).*

ESSENTIALS

GETTING THERE   Twelve daily **trains** depart Budapest's Nyugati Station; four of them are InterCity trains. The fare on all trains is 1,212 Ft ($6.05). On an InterCity train the journey takes 1¼ hours, and you are required to pay an additional seat reservation fee. On a "fast" train *(gyors),* the trip is just over 1½ hours, but you don't need a reservation, so you don't have to pay the supplemental reservation fee.

If you're driving from Budapest, take the M5 motorway south. You will have to pay a highway toll each way.

VISITOR INFORMATION   The best source of information is **Tourinform,** at Kossuth tér 1 (©/fax **76/481-065;** www.kecskemet.hu). In summer the office is open Monday through Friday from 8am to 5pm and Saturday from 9am to 1pm; in July and August, it's open Sunday 9am to 1pm as well. In winter the office is open weekdays 8am to 5pm. **Pusztatourist,** at Szabadság tér 2 (© **76/483-493**), will be useful if you're planning a side trip to Bugac. It's open Monday through Friday from 9am to 5pm and Saturday from 9:30am to 12:30pm.

EXPLORING KECSKEMÉT

The museums mentioned here are in the immediate vicinity of Kossuth tér, Kecskemét's main square.

Photography lovers will not want to miss the excellent **Hungarian Photography Museum,** Katona József tér 12 (℃ **76/483-221;** www.fotomuzeum.hu), featuring the works of contemporary Hungarian photographers, including foreign photographers of Hungarian ethnicity. Admission is 200 Ft ($1). Open Wednesday through Sunday from 10am to 4pm.

Located inside the Cifra Palace, one of the city's Art Nouveau gems, the **Kecskemét Gallery (Kecskeméti Galéria),** Rákóczi u. 1 (℃ **76/480-776**), features Hungarian art of the 19th and 20th centuries. Even if you don't go inside, make sure you check out this incredible building. Admission is 260 Ft ($1.30). The museum is open Tuesday through Saturday from 10am to 5pm and Sunday from 1:30 to 5pm.

The **Museum of Hungarian Naive Artists (Naïv Múvészeti Galéria)** ⚘, Gáspár András u. 11 (℃ **76/324-767**), displays the works of local folk artists from the early 20th century to the present. In one gallery, artworks are available for purchase. Admission is 150 Ft (75¢). Open Tuesday through Sunday from 9am to 5pm.

Hungary's largest toy collection can be found at the **Toy Museum (Játék-műhely és Múzeum)** ⚘, at the corner of Gáspár András utca and Hosszú utca (℃ **76/481-469**). This quaint museum has exhibits on toy design and manufacturing, as well as exhibits featuring actual toys. Families with children should try to come on the weekend, when youngsters are allowed to play with some of the toys. Admission is 300 Ft ($1.50) for adults, 150 Ft (75¢) for children. Open Tuesday through Sunday from 10am to 5pm, with a lunch break from 12:30 to 1pm.

Town Hall ⚘   Built in 1893 by Ödön Lechner and Gyula Pártos, this delightful Art Nouveau structure is a must-see for aficionados of Lechner's later Budapest buildings: the former Post Office Savings Bank (p. 166) and the Applied Arts Museum (p. 135). Like the buildings in the capital, Lechner's Kecskemét masterpiece is generously decorated with colorful Zsolnay majolica tiles. The council chamber *(dísz terem)* contains ceiling frescoes by the artist Bertalan Székely, whose work is on exhibit in Buda's National Gallery. If the building is closed when you arrive, admire it from the outside while you listen to the bells playing music by Kodály and others throughout the day (usually on the hour).

Just in front of the Town Hall is an odd monument: a stone broken in two to symbolize the heart attack suffered on that spot by József Katona, the beloved early-18th-century playwright and native son, who is recognized as the father of modern Hungarian drama. Katona is best known for *Bánkbán,* a play that was later put to music by Ferenc Erkel, becoming the first Hungarian opera.

Kossuth tér 1. ℃ **76/483-683**. Admission 400 Ft ($2), by appointment only. Mon–Fri 8am–4pm.

WHERE TO STAY

Caissa Panzió ⚘   Centrally located and reasonably priced, the Caissa, named for the goddess of chess, is the hotel of choice for enthusiasts of the game. A family-owned and -operated pension, Caissa hosts official grandmaster tournaments every year. Recent guests have included the noted Hungarian chess masters, the Polgár family and Péter Lékó. The hotel's reception desk is on the fifth floor, where the kitchen and common room are also located. The small rooms are clean and bright; many overlook the quiet residential park in the front of the building. Four rooms have TVs, and two have private toilets and showers.

Gyenes tér 18, 6000 Kecskemét. ©/fax **76/481-685**. 10 units, 2 with private bathroom. 6,000 Ft–9,000 Ft ($30–$45) double, depending on the size of room. Breakfast extra (served 7–11am). No credit cards. **Amenities:** Common kitchen on the 1st floor. *In room:* TV (in 4 units).

WHERE TO DINE

We recommend the **Görög Udvar Étterem** ☞, a Greek restaurant housed inside the Greek Culture Museum at Hornyik János krt. 1 (© **76/492-513**). The authentic Greek fare here is delicious. Main courses cost 1,000 Ft to 2,500 Ft ($5–$12). Alcohol is served, including Greek specialty liquors and wine. Open daily from 11am to 11pm.

Another good dining option is **Liberté,** Szabadság tér 2 (© **76/328-636**). The restaurant serves Hungarian cuisine for 800 Ft to 2,200 Ft ($4–$11). There's outdoor terrace seating in summer. Open daily from 9am to 11pm.

3 Bugac & the Puszta

Much of the Great Hungarian Plain was once comprised of open, rugged *puszta* (prairie) country, home to a fondly remembered, much-mythologized culture of nomadic shepherds and fierce horsemen. The vast wilderness of grasslands and marshes has long since given way to the modern era of agricultural reclamation, but pieces of the native terrain—and the *puszta* way of life—are preserved in national parks in the Great Plain.

Kiskunság National Park (© **76/372-537**) and especially the village of **Bugac,** about 40km (25 miles) south of Kecskemét, are well worth a visit. If you're lucky enough to be in Hungary in late spring, you can see one of the region's finest sights: endless fields ablaze with wild red poppies.

You can book a tour to Bugac from Budapest through Ibusz (p. 147). The scheduled tour includes a traditional horse-riding show featuring Hungarian cowboys *(csikós),* horseback riding on the trails, and a traditional *puszta* dinner of *bogrács gulyás,* a hearty stew cooked over an open fire.

You can also travel to Bugac by train from Kecskemét; three trains depart and return daily. A local bus also departs Kecskemét for Bugac at 11am Monday through Friday, and at 2:35pm daily. The bus leaves from the main bus station (© **76/321-777;** next to the train station); the trip takes 30 minutes and costs 451 Ft ($2.25). You can also see the riding show with a combined ticket (1,100 Ft–2,200 Ft/$5.50–$11), which includes an hour-long horse-drawn carriage ride. Of course, you can always skip the show and hike out into the wilderness. There are no shows from November to March.

If you want to spend a night on the *puszta,* you can book a room through **Bugac Tours,** in Bugac at Szabadság u. 4/A (© **76/575-117;** www.bugactours.hu). Ask them for riding and trail information as well. One great place to stay is the **Gedeon Tanya Panzió (Gedeon Farm Boardinghouse)** (© **76/704-070;** fax 76/704-072), a traditional old farmhouse with three double rooms. An adjoining new building has five double rooms, a large dining room, and a wine cellar. A double room costs 36€ ($43), including breakfast. Gedeon Tanya has its own stables. Nonguests are welcome to visit for the horseback riding, which costs 2,100 Ft ($9.45) for an hour. Horse lovers looking for accommodations in Bugac should try **Táltos Lovaspanzió (Táltos Equestrian Pension)** (© **76/372-633;** fax 76/372-580). The pension operates a large stable.

There are double rooms with private shower costing 8,000 Ft ($40), and double rooms with shared facilities for 5,000 Ft ($23). Bungalows go for 15,000 Ft ($68). Each bungalow sleeps about six people.

No trip to Bugac would be complete without a meal at the **Bugaci Csárda** (℅ 76/ **372-522**), locally famous for "authentic" *puszta* meals: rich, hearty paprika stews. Meals cost between 750 Ft and 1,300 Ft ($3.35 and $5.85). Open only for organized groups from November to March.

4 Szeged: Hungary's Spice Capital ★★

168km (105 miles) SE of Budapest

Szeged (pronounced *Seh*-ged), the proud capital of the Great Plain, is a hot and dusty but hospitable town. World famous for its paprika and salami *(Pick Szalami)*, Szeged is also home to one of Hungary's major universities, named after Attila József, the brilliant but disturbed interwar poet who rose to artistic heights from a childhood of desperate poverty. As a young man, he was expelled from the university that would later change its name to honor him. Driven by private demons, Hungary's great "proletarian poet" committed suicide at the age of 32 by hurling himself under a train at Balatonszárszó, by Lake Balaton. József failed to achieve wide recognition during his lifetime; today, though, he is adored in Hungary, particularly by teenagers and students drawn to his rebellious, nonconformist, irreverent spirit. The national book fair is traditionally opened on his birthday, April 11, each year. A wonderfully unassuming statue of the poet stands in front of the university's main building on Dugonics tér. The only other statue of him that we know of is next to the Parliament Building in Budapest, sitting on the steps of the embankment, evoking thoughts of one of József's famous poems, about the multicultural Danube, written against the specter of nationalism in the 1930s.

In addition to its status as a center of learning and culture, Szeged is the industrial capital of the Great Plain (Alföld), though you wouldn't know it by spending a day or two in the city center. The Tisza River splits the city in two, with the historic center lying, Pest-style, within a series of concentric ring boulevards on the left bank. Indeed, the river looms large in Szeged's history: The city was almost completely destroyed when the Tisza flooded in 1879. With financial assistance from a number of European cities—Brussels, Berlin, Rome, London, and Paris—the city was rebuilt in the characteristic ring style of the time. The post-flood reconstruction explains why Szeged's finest architecture is of the *fin de siècle* Art Nouveau style. Don't miss the synagogue (see "Exploring the Historic Center," below) and the recently restored Reök Building (now a bank) on the corner of Kölcsey utca and Feketesas utca.

The people of Szegend, many of whom are students, love to stroll along the riverside, sit in cafes, and window-shop on the just reconstructed elegant **Karász utca** ★★, the town's main pedestrian-only street. Dóm tér, a beautiful, wide square, is home to the **Szeged Summer Festival** ★, a popular summer-long series of cultural events. At the end of July, Szeged also plays host to a theater festival known as **Thealter** for its focus on alternative performances. An international festival, Thealter was founded by drama students from the university and draws theater troupes from all over Europe. In 2003 Thealter celebrated its 13th season. Ask about both of these festivals at **Tourinform** or Szeged Tourist.

ESSENTIALS

GETTING THERE   Twelve daily **trains** depart Budapest's Nyugati Station, of which four are InterCity. The fare for all is 2,030 Ft ($10). On an InterCity train the

Szeged

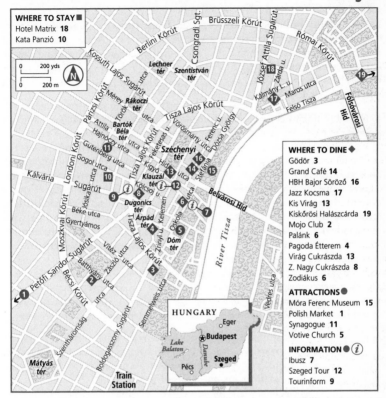

journey takes about 2¼ hours, and you are required to pay an additional fee for a seat reservation. On a fast train *(gyors)*, the trip is more like 3 hours, but you don't need a reservation. (Travel times by trains generally seem to have slowed down in the past several years due to the poor conditions of the tracks all over the country.)

If you're **driving** from Budapest, take the M5 motorway south through Kecskemét and Kiskunfélegyháza.

VISITOR INFORMATION   The best source of information, as usual, is **Tourinform,** at Dugonics tér 2 (*©* **62/488-690;** www.szeged.hu), located in the recently renovated 19th-century courtyard of the fine pastry shop Z. Nagy Cukrászda (reviewed below). The office is open Monday through Friday from 9am to 5pm. If you wish to book a private room, try **Szeged Tourist,** at Klauzál tér 7 (*©* **62/420-428**), open Monday through Friday from 9am to 5pm.

Pick up *Szegedi Est,* a free weekly magazine with lots of useful information.

MAHART, the Hungarian ferry line company, organizes boat tours up and down the Tisza River from the first of April through mid-October. For information, contact the MAHART boat station in Szeged at *©* **62/425-834.**

EXPLORING THE HISTORIC CENTER

Móra Ferenc Museum   Located near the river's edge, this imposing structure houses a varied collection of exhibits that relate local history. Of particular note is the display of local folk costumes and the exhibit that reconstructs the nomadic lifestyle of the early Hungarian settlers.

Roosevelt tér 1–3. (✆ **62/549-040**. www.mfm.u-szeged.hu. Admission 400 Ft ($2). Tues–Sun 10am–5pm.

Synagogue ✷   A relic of Szeged's once-thriving Jewish community, the synagogue was completed in 1903. Considered the masterpiece of architect Lipot Baumhorn, who was a disciple of Ödön Lechner and the most prolific and renowned synagogue architect in modern Europe, the great synagogue in Szeged exemplifies a confident eclecticism. The building mixes cupolas, turrets, tracery, and other ornamental effects. It occupies a full block in an otherwise sleepy, tree-lined residential neighborhood just west of the city center. The synagogue is fully functioning and holds services at 6pm every Friday.

Inside the vestibule is a series of marble plaques, listing by name the local victims of the Holocaust. Behind the synagogue, at Hajnóczy u. 12, stands the Old Synagogue, built in 1843 and badly damaged in the flood of 1879. Its reconstruction was completed in 1998. It serves as a cultural center and a venue for alternative theater groups and chamber-music concerts.

If you find the synagogue closed when it should be open, go to the address that's posted near the entrance and the caretaker will open the synagogue for you.

Jósika utca. (✆ **62/423-849**. Admission 300 Ft ($1.50). Summer Sun–Fri 9am–noon and 1–5pm; winter Sun–Fri 10am–2pm. Services at 6pm every Fri. From Dugonics tér, walk right on Tisza Lajos körút, and turn left on Gutenberg utca.

Votive Church   The symbol of Szeged's post-flood revitalization, this church, with its two tall, slender clock towers, was built in 1912. Its elaborately painted neo-Renaissance interior suggests a much older structure. Inside the church is one of Europe's largest organs, with over 9,000 pipes. Ask at Tourinform or Szeged Tourist (p. 260) about organ recitals.

In front of the church is the Broken Tower, a remnant of the 13th-century Romanesque church that stood on this spot. Across from the church, there is a wall clock from which wooden figures emerge on the hour to play a Kodály tune. Masses are held here at 6:30am, 7:30am, and 6pm every day.

On Dóm tér. Free admission. Mon–Sat 9am–6pm; Sun 9:30–10am, 11–11:30am, and 12:30–6pm. Masses take place at 6:30am, 7:30am, and 6pm daily.

OPEN-AIR MARKETS

Situated within 32km (20 miles) of two international borders (Romanian and Serbian), Szeged has long attracted shoppers and vendors from a variety of countries. If open-air markets interest you, check out the **Polish Market (Lengyel Piac)** ✷ at the southwestern edge of town. Once filled with Polish smugglers (the name has stuck), this dusty flea market is now home to Vietnamese, Chinese, Romanian, Serbian, Uzbeki, and other vendors. You never know what kind of junk you might find here—it all depends on what's "in season." Unfortunately, the Cold War souvenirs that once attracted Westerners to markets like this are seldom displayed any longer. The market is open Monday through Saturday from dawn to midafternoon. To get to the Polish Market, located in a dusty field at the corner of Petőfi Sándor sugárút and Rákóczi utca, walk straight out Petőfi Sándor sugárút from the center of town or take tram no. 4.

Szeged's **main fruit-and-vegetable market** ✷ is located behind the bus station on Mars tér (formerly Marx tér, and still known to many as such). The vendors are local

Hungarian farmers. If you haven't tried any Hungarian produce yet, you're missing out on something wonderful. You won't be disappointed with the peaches, apricots, watermelons, cherries, strawberries, plums, or pears. The market is open Monday through Saturday from dawn until midafternoon—arrive early for the best selection. Fresh flowers and dried paprika wreathes are also sold here.

You can buy Szeged's signature paprika and salami anywhere food is sold. See appendix B, "Hungarian Cuisine," for descriptions of types of paprika.

WHERE TO STAY

Private rooms can be booked through **Szeged Tourist** (see "Essentials," above) or **Ibusz** at Oroszlán u. 3 (© **62/471-177**).

Hotel Matrix   This fairly new choice is about 10 minutes from the central Dugonics tér by tram no. 4 or trolleybus no. 9. The tasteful, small hotel is clean and pleasant, with a friendly and professional management. Its pleasant rooms all have showers.

Zárda u. 8, 6720 Szeged. © **62/556-000.** Fax 62/420-827. 10 units. 9,600 Ft ($48) double. Breakfast 900 Ft ($4.50) extra. AE, V. **Amenities:** Laundry service. In room: TV.

Kata Panzió ☝   We highly recommend this lovely little pension, which opened in 1995 in a quiet residential neighborhood a 10-minute walk from central Klauzál tér. It features plenty of common space, sunny balconies on each floor, an enchanting terrace garden, and a friendly German shepherd named Ivan. Four double rooms, one triple, and one quad are available; all have private bathrooms.

Bolyai János u. 15 (between Gogol u. and Kálvária sgt.), 6720 Szeged. © **62/311-258.** 6 units. 9,600 Ft ($48) double, breakfast included; 600 Ft ($3) VAT extra. No credit cards. Free parking. In room: TV.

WHERE TO DINE

Gödör ☝ HUNGARIAN   Gödör is the local university's restaurant; faculty members pack it at lunchtime. The extensive menu of Hungarian specialties (including many vegetarian options) is very reasonably priced.

Tisza Lajos krt. 103 (next to the Hero's Gate). © **62/420-130.** Main courses 650 Ft–1,500 Ft ($3.25–$7.50). No credit cards. Daily 11am–10pm.

HBH Bajor Söröző ☝ HUNGARIAN/BAVARIAN   This is another good option for Hungarian and Bavarian fare. The HBH brews its own beer and is a popular nighttime gathering place. A half liter of beer will set you back 320 Ft ($1.45).

Deák Ferenc u. 4. © **62/420-934.** Soups 300 Ft–480 Ft ($1.50–$2.40); main courses 960 Ft–2,400 Ft ($4.80–$12). No credit cards. Mon–Thurs noon–11pm; Fri–Sat noon–midnight; Sun noon–4pm.

Kiskőrösi Halászcsárda ☝ HUNGARIAN   You'd do well to sample local fish at this authentic riverside restaurant. Paprika and onions are the spices of choice for hearty fish stews and bisques alike.

Felső Tisza-part 336. © **62/495-480.** Reservations recommended. Main courses 700 Ft–1,200 Ft ($3.50–$6). AE, DC, DISC, MC, V. Sun–Thurs 11am–midnight; Fri–Sat 11am–2am.

Pagoda Étterem ☝ CHINESE   This is our favorite Chinese restaurant in all of Hungary. The menu is extensive and the dishes are delicious. The Chinese lanterns and dragon-red tablecloths add to the appeal.

Zrinyi u. 5. © **62/312-490.** Main courses from 1,000 Ft ($5). AE, V. Tues–Sat noon–midnight; Sun–Mon noon–10pm.

Zodiákus HUNGARIAN/EUROPEAN   Zodiákus, formerly known as Alabárdos, is *the* choice for an elegant, upscale dining experience. It is more cheerful than its predecessor, with the previous cellarlike design replaced by a lighter and airier arrangement. Hungarian cuisine is served on Herend porcelain; the cutlery is sterling. Locals consider this the town's finest restaurant. We recommend all of the poultry dishes here, especially the chicken breast with zucchini in a creamy cheese sauce. There is a pub right next door, open 10am to 2am. The pub menu is small but wholesome: salads and cheese-based dishes. Draft beer is available. It's a popular place with Szeged's large foreign student population.

Oskola u. 13. ℂ **62/420-914.** Reservations recommended. Main courses 790 Ft–2,500 Ft ($3.95–$13). No credit cards. Mon–Thurs 11am–midnight, Fri–Sat 11am–1am.

COFFEEHOUSES & ICE-CREAM PARLORS

Szeged is famous for its **Virág Cukrászda,** an old-world coffeehouse on Klauzál tér. A local petition in the early 1990s prevented this Szeged institution from being turned into a car showroom. It is open daily from 8am to 10pm. The **Kis Virág (Little Flower)** ★★, across the square, is the Virág Cukrászda's takeout place, where you can pick up a wide variety of delicious pastries for a lower price and sample the best ice cream in town (in winter there is service inside the Kis Virág). Their specialty is *rakott rétes* (layered strudle), which is the divine local version of the traditional Jewish pastry *flodni*. In our opinion, it's the best we've tried anywhere in the country. Kis Virág is open daily from 8am to 8pm.

Rivaling (and some say surpassing in the realm of traditional pastries) the Kis Virág for takeout pastries and cakes is the tiny **Z. Nagy Cukrászda** ★, located on József Attila sgt. 24 (just off of Tisza Lajos krt. by the river). It's a good walk from the center of town but it's well worth it. If you're being lazy, there is a more spacious Z. Nagy shop, with a terrace in its courtyard, right in the center of town, on Dugonics tér, just off Karász utca (the pedestrian-only street). Z. Nagy dispenses a scrumptious *Erzsi kocka,* walnut paste sandwiched between two shortbread cookies, dipped in dark chocolate. On hot, dusty summer days, the line at the most popular ice-cream shop, **Palánk** (on the corner of Tömörkény utca and Oskola utca), snakes out the door and down the street. By all means, join the queue.

SZEGED AFTER DARK

Jazz Kocsma, at Kálmány L. u. 14 (℗ **62/326-680**), is the place for live jazz. Local bands play on Sunday. It's a groovy, smoky, student scene. The kitchen serves Mexican food. Open daily 11am to 2am; no cover. **Mojo Club,** Alföldi utca 1 (℗ **62/426-606**), next to the university building for the arts, is another jazz club. As the posters in the window proudly advertise (you will see the posters of OTPOR, the pioneering Serbian youth organization that successfully organized resistance to the Belgrade university collectives), the owners of this place have maintained their close links with their former country of residence, Serbia. The sunken rooms here have a distinctly bohemian appeal. There's a full bar and decent pizza and pasta on the menu. It's open Monday through Saturday from 11am to 2am, Sunday from 6pm to midnight; in summer open daily from 6pm only. There's no cover. Reservations are highly recommended at both these clubs.

Appendix A:
Help with a Tough Tongue

Part of Budapest's mystery stems from the complex and unusual language of the Hungarians, Magyar. Magyar originated on the eastern side of the Ural Mountains: Along with Finnish and Estonian, it's one of Europe's few representatives of the Finno-Ugric family of languages. The Hungarian language has long been one of the country's greatest obstacles; nevertheless, the Hungarian people are intensely proud of their language and its charms. Our transcription of Hungarian pronunciations is of necessity approximate. Stress is always on the first syllable, and all letters are pronounced. (There are no diphthongs in Hungarian.)

PRONUNCIATION GUIDE
Vowels

a	t*au*t	ó	same as above but held longer
á	b*ahh*	ö	s*u*b
e	*e*ver	ő	same as above but held longer
é	d*ay*	u	l*oo*k
i	m*i*tt	ú	b*oo*t
í	t*ee*n	ü	d*o*ve
o	b*o*ne	ű	same as above but held longer

Consonants

Most Hungarian consonants are pronounced approximately as they are in English, including the following: *b, d, f, h, k, l, m, n, p, t, v,* and *y.* There are some differences, however, particularly in the consonant combinations, as follows:

c	ge*ts*	r	slightly rolled
cs	*ch*ill	s	*sh*eet
g	*g*ill	sz	*s*ix
gy	he*dg*e	z	*z*ero
j	*y*outh	zs	a*z*ure, plea*s*ure
ny	as in Russian *ny*et		

1 Menu Terms

GENERAL TERMS

Bors black pepper
Fóételek main courses
Fózelék vegetable purée
Gyümölcs fruits
Halak fish
Húsételek meat dishes
Italok beverages
Kenyér bread

Levesek soups
Paprika red pepper/paprika
Sajt cheese
Saláták salads
Só salt
Tészták pasta/dessert
Tojás eggs
Vaj butter
Zöldság vegetables

COOKING TERMS

Csípős hot (peppery)
Forró hot (in temperature)
Fózött boiled
Friss fresh
Fuszerezve spiced

Hideg cold
Párolt steamed
Pirított toasted
Pörkölt stew
Sútve baked/fried
Töltött stuffed

MEAT & POULTRY *(HÚS ÉS BAROMFI)*

Agyonsütve well done
Bárány lamb
Bécsi szelet Wiener schnitzel
Borjú veal
Csirke chicken
Félig nyersen rare
Gulyás goulash

Kacsa duck
Kotlett cutlet
Közepesen kisütve medium
Liba goose
Marha beef
Pulyka turkey
Sertés pork
Tokány ragout

FISH *(HALAK)*

Csuka pike
Fogas Balaton pikeperch
Halászlé fish stew

Pisztráng trout
Ponty carp
Tonhal tuna

VEGETABLES *(ZÖLDSÁG)*

Bab beans
Burgonya potato
Fokhagyma garlic
Gomba mushrooms
Hagyma onion

Káposzta cabbage
Paradicsom tomato
Sóska sorrel
Spenót spinach
Tök squash
Zöldbab green beans

FRUITS (GYÜLMÖLCS)

Alma apple
Barack apricot
Cseresznye cherry
Dinnye watermelon
Körte pear

Meggy sour cherry
Narancs orange
Öszibarack peach
Sargadinnye cantaloupe
Szilva plum
Szóló grapes

DESSERTS

Almás rétes apple strudel
Dobos torta layer cake with caramel candied frosting
Fagylalt ice cream
Ischler chocolate-dipped shortbread cookie sandwich

Lekváros palacsinta crepe filled with preserves
Meggyes rétes sour-cherry strudel
Túrós rétes cheese strudel

BEVERAGES

Barna sör dark beer
Fehér bor white wine
Kávé coffee
Koktél cocktail
Narancslé orange juice

Sör beer
Tej milk
Víz water
Vörös bor red wine

2 Basic Phrases & Vocabulary

QUESTION WORDS (IN THE NOMINATIVE)

English	Hungarian	Pronunciation
Where	Hol	hole
When	Mikor	*mee*-kor
What	Mi	mee
Why	Miert	*mee*-ayrt
Who	Ki	kee
How	Hogy	hohdge

USEFUL PHRASES

English	Hungarian	Pronunciation
Good day/Hello	Jó napot	*yoh* napoht
Good morning	Jó reggelt	*yoh* reg-gelt
Good evening	Jó estét	*yoh* esh-tayt
Goodbye	Viszontlátásra	*vee*-sont-lah-tahsh-ra
My name is . . .	vagyok . . .	*vodge*-yohk
Thank you	Köszönöm	*kuh*-suh-nuhm
You're welcome	Kérem	*kay*-rem
Please	Legyen szíves	*ledge*-yen *see*-vesh

English	Hungarian	Pronunciation
Yes	**Igen**	*ee*-gen
No	**Nem**	*nem*
Good/Okay	**Jó**	*yo*
Excuse me	**Bocsánat**	*boh*-chahnat
How much does it cost?	**Mennyi bekerül?**	*men*-yee *beh*-keh-roohl?
I don't understand	**Nem értem**	*nem* ayr-tem
I don't know	**Nem tudom**	*nem too*-dum
Where is the . . . ?	**Hol van a . . . ?**	*hohl* von a . . . ?
bus station	**busz állomás**	*boos ahh*-loh-mahsh
train station	**vonatállomás**	*vah*-not-*ahh*-loh-mahsh
bank	**bank**	*bahnk*
museum	**múzeum**	*moo*-zeh-oom
pharmacy	**patiká**	*paw*-tee-kah
theater	**színház**	*seen*-hahz
tourist office	**turista iroda**	*too*-reesh-ta *eer*-ohda
embassy	**nagykövetség**	*nahdge koo*-vet-shayg
restaurant	**étterem**	*ayt*-teh-rehm
restroom	**wc**	*vayt*-say

RESTAURANT SERVICE

English	Hungarian	Pronunciation
Breakfast	**Reggeli**	*rehg*-geh-lee
Lunch	**Ebéd**	*eh*-bayd
Dinner	**Vacsora**	*vah*-choh-rah
I would like . . .	**Kérnék . . .**	*káyr*-nayk . . .
a table	**egy asztalot**	edge *ah*-stah-lot
a menu	**egy étlapot**	edge *ayt*-lah-poht
a glass (of water)	**egy pohár (vizet)**	edge poh-har (*vee*-zet)
to pay	**fizetni**	*ee*-zeht-nee
I have a reservation	**Foglaltam már**	*fohg*-lawl-tahm mahr

TRAIN TRAVEL

English	Hungarian	Pronunciation
A ticket, please	**Egy jegyet kérek**	*Edge ye*-dget *kay*-rek
Seat reservation	**helyjegy**	*heyh*-yedge
One-way only	**csak oda**	*chalk oh*-da
Round-trip	**oda-vissza**	*oh*-dah-*vees*-sah
First class	**elsó osztály**	*ell*-shooh *oh*-stahy
Arrive	**érkezik**	*ayr*-kez-eek
Depart	**indul**	*inn*-doohl
Track	**Vagány**	*vah*-ghine

POST OFFICE

English	Hungarian	Pronunciation
Airmail	**Légiposta**	*lay*-ghee-posh-ta
A stamp, please	**Egy bélyeget kérek**	Edge *bay*-yeh-get *kay*-rek
A postcard . . .	**Egy képeslapot . . .**	Edge *kay*-pesh-law-poht
An envelope . . .	**Egy borítéket . . .**	Edge *bohr*-ree-tay-ket

SIGNS

Bejárat Entrance		**Kijárat** Exit	
Érkezések Arrivals		**Tilos a dohányzás** No Smoking	
Indulások Departures		**Toalettek** Toilets	
Informácio Information		**Veszélyes** Danger	
		Vigyázat Beware	

NUMBERS

1	**egy**	(edge)	16	**tizenhat**	(*teez*-en-hawt)
2	**kettó**	(*ket*-tu[r])	17	**tizenhét**	(*teez*-en-hayt)
3	***három***	(*hahh*-rohm)	18	**tizennyolc**	(*teez*-en-nyohlts)
4	**négy**	(*naydge*)			
5	**öt**	(*u*[r]*t*)	19	**tizenkilenc**	(*teez*-en-kee-lents)
6	**hat**	(*hawt*)			
7	**hét**	(*hayt*)	20	**húsz**	(*hoos*)
8	**nyolc**	(*nyohlts*)	30	**harminc**	(*hahr*-mints)
9	**kilenc**	(*kee*-lents)	40	**negyven**	(*nedge*-vehn)
10	**tíz**	(*teez*)	50	**ötven**	(*u*[r]*t*-vehn)
11	**tizenegy**	(*teez*-en-edge)	60	**hatvan**	(*hawt*-vahn)
12	**tizenkettó**	(*teez*-en-ket-tu[r])	70	**hetven**	(*het*-vehn)
			80	**nyolcvan**	(*nyohlts*-vahn)
13	**tizenhárom**	(*teez*-en-hahh-rohm)	90	**kilencven**	(*kee*-lents-vehn)
			100	**száz**	(*sahhz*)
14	**tizennégy**	(*teez*-en-nay-dge)	500	**ötszáz**	(*u*[r]*t*-sahhz)
			1,000	**ezer**	(*eh*-zayr)
15	**tizenöt**	(*teez*-en-u[r]t)			

Appendix B:
Hungarian Cuisine

Hungary's cuisine reflects the rich and varied flavors of four major geographic regions. From Transdanubia, west of the River Danube, come rich mushroom sauces, sorrel soups, cottage cheese and onion dumplings, and high-quality gooseliver. A host of excellent wild-game dishes come from forested northern Hungary. Bucolic Erdély (Transylvania) introduces spices such as tarragon, summer savory, and fresh dill to the palate, and is also known for its lamb dishes and sheep's cheese. And, finally, from the Great Hungarian Plain, the home of Hungary's renowned paprika, come hearty fish, bean, and meat stews all spiced with the red powder ground from different varieties of peppers ranging from *édes* (sweet) to *csípős* (hot).

Lunch, the main meal of the day, begins with soup. *Gyümölcs leves,* a cold fruit soup, is excellent when in season. *Sóskakrém leves,* cream of sorrel soup, is another good seasonal choice. *Babgulyás,* a hearty bean soup, and *halaszle,* a fish soup popular at river- and lakeside spots, constitute meals in themselves.

The main course is generally a meat dish. Try the *paprikás csirke,* chicken cooked in a savory paprika sauce. It's especially good with *galuska,* a pasta dumpling. *Pulykamell,* turkey breast baked with plums and served in a mushroom gravy, is also delicious. Another great choice is *Pörkölt,* a stewed meat dish that comes in many varieties. *Töltött káposzta,* whole cabbage leaves stuffed with rice, meat, and spices, is another favorite.

Vegetarianism is gradually gaining acceptance in Hungarian restaurants; many establishments now offer a vegetable entree. Vegetarians might also request *lecsó tojással* (eggs scrambled in a thick tomato-onion-paprika sauce), *rántott sajt* (batter-fried cheese with tartar sauce), or *túrós csusza tepertő nélkul* (macaroni-and-cheese).

Snack foods include *lángos,* a slab of deep-fried bread served with your choice of toppings: sugar and whipped cream, or garlic sauce and cheese. *Palacsinta,* a paper-thin crepe stuffed with cheese or draped in hot chocolate sauce, is another excellent light bite. *Kürtős kalács,* a hollow, tubular honey-cake, is an old-fashioned treat sometimes available in metro stations and at outdoor markets and fairs. *Fagylalt,* ice cream, is the national street food. Scoops are small, so order more than one. Fruit flavors are produced seasonally: In the spring, try *eper* (strawberry) and *meggy* (sour cherry); in the fall, *szilva* (plum) and *körte* (pear). Summer regulars are delicious *fahéj* (cinnamon) and *mák* (poppy seed).

Hungarian pastries are scrumptious and cost a fraction of what they do in Vienna, so indulge. The light, flaky *rétes* are filled with fruit or cheese. *Csoki torta* is a decadent chocolate layer cake, and a *Dobos torta* is topped with a shiny caramel crust. *Mákos* pastry, made with poppy seeds, is a Hungarian specialty. *Gesztenye* (chestnuts) are another popular ingredient in desserts.

Picnickers should pick up a loaf of Hungarian bread and sample any of Hungary's world-famous salamis. A number of tasty cheeses are produced in Hungary as well: *Karaván füstölt* (a smoked cheese), *Edami* (Dutch cheese), *márvány* (similar to bleu cheese), and *juhtúró* (a soft, spreadable sheep's cheese similar in flavor to feta). In season, fresh produce is cheap and high quality. *Meggy* (sour cherries) in July are out of this world.

BEER, WINE & SPIRITS Hungary does not have a beer culture; as a result, its beer is unexceptional. A number of European beers are now produced under license in Hungary. These beers tend to be only marginally better than the best Hungarian beer—Dreher. Your best bet in Hungary is Czech beer, such as Budvar, Staropramen, or Pilsner Urquell, which are not produced in Hungary under license; they are the real thing.

Hungarian wines are excellent. The most renowned red wines come from the region around Villány, a town to the south of Pécs near the Croatian border. As a result of an aggressive marketing campaign mounted by the former Communist regime, many travelers are familiar with the red wines from Eger, especially *Egri Bikavér* (Eger Bull's Blood). However, Eger wines, though rich and fruity, are markedly inferior to Villányi reds. The country's best white wines are generally believed to be those from the Lake Balaton region, though some Hungarians insist that white wines from the Somló region (northeast of Lake Balaton) are better. *Tokaj* wines—*száraz* (dry) or *édes* (sweet)—are popular as aperitifs and dessert wines. For wine tips, visit Le Boutique des Vins (p. 199), a full-service wine store in Budapest. You can also pick up the free pamphlet *Wine Regions in Hungary* at Vista Visitor Center or Tourinform (see p. 46 in chapter 4, "Getting to Know Budapest").

Unikum, the richly aromatic bitter liquid that some call "Hungary's national drink," is a taste worth acquiring. It is still produced according to the original recipe owned by the Zwack family (the current company owner, a Zwack family member, was Hungary's first ambassador to the U.S. after the fall of Communism). The distilled fruit brandy *Pálinka* is another variety of Hungarian firewater. *Pálinka* is often brewed at home from apricots, plums, or pears; in folk wisdom, it's acclaimed for its medicinal value.

COFFEE & TEA Hungarians drink *kávé* (coffee) throughout the day, either at stand-up coffee bars or in elegant coffeehouses. Until recently, Hungarian coffee drinking borrowed from the Turkish tradition: Alarmingly strong, unfiltered espresso was served straight up, generally without cream or sugar. These days, coffee drinking has expanded to include milder and more refined tastes. In general, though, when ordering coffee in Hungary, you are still ordering espresso. Cappuccino (and its variant *cappuciner,* with chocolate shavings on top) is now available in most coffeehouses, as is *koffein mentes* (decaffeinated coffee). *Tejeskávé,* a Hungarian version of café au lait, is another option.

Tea drinkers will have a difficult time in restaurants; if tea is available at all, it's generally of the strong black variety. However, as a refreshing change, tea is now readily available in bars and cafes. For more variety and a peek at Hungary's burgeoning world of herbal medicine, look for teas in any of the numerous herbal shops: *gyógynövény, herbárium,* or *gyógytea.*

WATER While *csapvíz* (tap water) is safe to drink in Budapest, it isn't generally offered in restaurants, and few Hungarians request it. Instead they drink *Ásványvíz,* a carbonated mineral water, or *szóda víz,* carbonated tap water. *Szénsav mentes* (purified bottled water) is also widely available.

Index

See also Accommodations and Restaurant indexes, below.

COFFEEHOUSES & CAFES